JAMES USSHER AND JOHN BRAMHALL

*For Terry and Shirley Cunningham,
to whom I owe everything*

James Ussher and John Bramhall

The Theology and Politics of Two Irish Ecclesiastics
of the Seventeenth Century

JACK CUNNINGHAM
Bishop Grosseteste University College, UK

LONDON AND NEW YORK

First published 2007 by Ashgate Publishing

Reissued 2018 by Routledge
2 Park Square, Milton Park, Abingdon, Oxon OX14 4RN
605 Third Avenue, New York, NY 10017

First issued in paperback 2021

Routledge is an imprint of the Taylor & Francis Group, an informa business

© Jack Cunningham 2007

Jack Cunningham has asserted his moral right under the Copyright, Designs and Patents Act, 1988, to be identified as the author of this work.

All rights reserved. No part of this book may be reprinted or reproduced or utilised in any form or by any electronic, mechanical, or other means, now known or hereafter invented, including photocopying and recording, or in any information storage or retrieval system, without permission in writing from the publishers.

A Library of Congress record exists under LC control number: 2006003673

Notice:
Product or corporate names may be trademarks or registered trademarks, and are used only for identification and explanation without intent to infringe.

Publisher's Note
The publisher has gone to great lengths to ensure the quality of this reprint but points out that some imperfections in the original copies may be apparent.

Disclaimer
The publisher has made every effort to trace copyright holders and welcomes correspondence from those they have been unable to contact.

ISBN 13: 978-0-815-38991-0 (hbk)
ISBN 13: 978-1-351-12675-5 (ebk)
ISBN 13: 978-1-138-35622-1 (pbk)

Contents

Preface: The Levitical Candle	vii
Acknowledgements	xvii
List of Abbreviations	xix

1	James Ussher	1
2	John Bramhall	23
3	Dogmatic Theologies	41
	The nature of man	42
	Soteriology	46
	Predestination	51
	Perseverance	57
4	Sacramental Theologies	61
	Ussher and Bramhall on the sacraments	65
	Baptism	69
	The Eucharist	71
	Penance	80
5	Ecclesiastical Histories	85
	The biblical roots of denominational historical perspectives	86
	James Ussher's 'godly succession'	88
	John Bramhall's 'holy and apostolic succession'	93
	Ecclesiastical nationalism	99
	A religion anciently professed: the nationalism of Ussher	100
	A schism guarded against: the ecclesiastical nationalism of Bramhall	105
6	Secular Politics	111
	Ussher: the reluctant politician	111
	Bramhall: the resolute politician	115
	The Power of the Prince: James Ussher's theory of divine right and absolutism	119
	A royalist anti-venom: John Bramhall's theory of divine right and absolutism	128
	De jure divino aut non de jure divino: the question of absolutism	139

7	Ecclesiastical Politics	145
	Ussher on church government	145
	Bramhall on church government	149
	Ussher and Roman Catholicism	153
	Bramhall and Roman Catholicism	156
	Ussher and church unity	160
	Bramhall and church unity	164
8	Practical Policy	169
	Ussher's practical policy pre-Convocation	169
	Bramhall's practical policy pre-Convocation	175
	The Convocation of 1634	180
	Ussher and Bramhall, post-Convocation	191
	Conclusion	201
	Bibliography	205
	Index	229

Preface

The Levitical Candle

Writing from France in 1658, at the request of a friend, a discourse on the Sabbath controversy, John Bramhall closed his tract with a type of extended postscript in which he expressed some horror that during the course of the dispute, he had apparently become embroiled in a posthumous controversy with his late Lord Primate James Ussher, under whose 'pious and moderate government he had lived for sundry years.'[1] He assured his readers that this was far from his intentions, and as for there being any discord between them they had been, on the contrary, stalwarts of the Church in Ireland. Together they had pursued for it peace in the swiftest of manners, and there they would no doubt have continued had not the present religious upstarts and the naturally rebellious Irish conspired to make exiles of them. Bramhall adds, with retrospective confidence that if the 'pious prelate were now living, I verily believe he would allow all, or at least not disapprove anything, which I say in this treatise.'[2] Bramhall then provides a fairly detailed account of their relationship and in order to refute Ussher's biographer, Nicholas Bernard,[3] he recalls the spirit of deference and unanimity of purpose which prevailed between them during that most potentially incendiary of events, the Irish Church's Convocation in 1634. At some length Bramhall contests the claim that there had been an acrimonious rift resulting ultimately in Ussher's involvement in the trial and execution of Strafford. In attempting to salvage the legacy of their friendship, he is also attempting to maintain the compatibility of their theological outlooks. There may have been differences, he admits, but these were in *adiaphora*, things indifferent. In fundamentals, their foundation was common. Bramhall uses the analogy of the Jewish candelabra, whose branches are conjoined at the base. 'I praise God', he exclaimed, 'we were like the candles in the Levitical Temple, looking one toward another, and all towards the stem.'[4]

In the following chapters, this Levitical candelabrum will be examined against contemporary reports that suggest that dogmatically they were not only at opposite extremes, but the theology of one was actually antagonistic to the theology of the other. By examining the Christian theology contained within their respective works, sermons and letters, we will set out to demonstrate that twin illuminations they may

---

1   *BW*, vol. 5, p. 74.
2   Ibid.
3   N. Bernard, *The Judgement of the late Archbishop of Armagh and Primate of Ireland of Babylon, Revelations 18:4* (London 1658). Ussher's biographer published this treatise which sets out to show that Ussher's theology was Calvinistic and counter to the Laudian policy which afflicted the Irish and English Churches in the previous decades.
4   *BW*, vol. 5, p. 74.

have been, but just as the Jewish menorah spreads its lights, often the individual candles can find themselves with a wide gap separating them. It may have been Bramhall's proud boast that he and the great luminary of the established Church shared the same base, but a study of their understandings of the Christian dogma, liturgy, and history shows that in these areas they burned their candles each on the furthest branch.

Any discussion of early modern Christian theology must of course be viewed against the background of current historical controversy. There is at present a lively debate within the world of seventeenth-century English history over the importance of religion as a contributory factor to the conflict which erupted in these islands in the 1640s. On the one hand, writers such as Conrad Russell, Nicholas Tyacke, and Peter Lake stake a central claim for the rise of Arminianism within the English Church which was (at least theologically) Calvinist, as a major cause of the conflict, though it must be said that the term Arminian is not used without some qualification. Tyacke explained how it should be employed.

> Of the various terms which can be used to describe the thrust of religious change at this time, Arminian is the least misleading. It does not mean that the Dutch theologian Jacobus Arminius was normally the source of the ideas so labelled. Rather Arminian denotes a coherent body of anti-Calvinist religious thought, which was gaining ground in various regions of early seventeenth-century Europe.[5]

The slight incongruity of this leads Lake to use instead the word 'Laudianism,' again not to imply that it all originates from William Laud, but rather as a 'short hand' term for the movement as a whole.[6]

On the other hand, writers such as Peter White and Kevin Sharpe have attacked what has become by now a type of revisionist orthodoxy. They argue instead that nothing existed within the Laudian Church which could be identified as Arminian. It would, they say, be more accurate to see the Laudians as part of a long line of Church of England tradition which pursued a *via media*, steering a middle course on the calm waters of moderation, avoiding foundering on one side on the rock of Rome and on the other sinking into the confused whirlpools tossed up by Presbyterian anarchy. White and Sharpe suggest that those scholars who continue to employ such terms as 'Arminian' have allowed themselves to be misled by the propaganda of Laud's enemies and in so doing are guilty of perpetuating a puritan caricature.[7]

It is one of the purposes of this book to present an alternative method of categorising theological and consequently political approaches. Part of the problem has been with terminology and labelling. As we have seen above, when authors attempt to use precise labels they feel they can only do so with some qualification.

---

5   N. Tyacke, *Anti-Calvinists, the Rise of English Arminianism c.1590–1640* (Oxford, 1987), p. 245.

6   P. Lake, 'The Laudian Style, Uniformity and the Pursuit of the Beauty of Holiness in the 1630s', in K. Fincham (ed.), *Early Stuart Church*.

7   P. White, *Conflict and Consensus in the English Church from the Reformation to the Civil War* (Cambridge, 1992), passim; K. Sharpe, *The Personal Rule of Charles I* (New Haven, 1992), passim.

Besides, there is the added problem that once persons and movements have been forced into tight categorical boxes, it only needs someone like White to illustrate that a certain aspect of their theology runs contrary to such categorisation for the baby to be thrown out with the bath water.[8] It might be added that this problem does not only apply to the term Arminian. Other categories such as Calvinist, Anglican, Puritan, Presbyterian and even Protestant appear equally proficient at eluding a precise definition. It will be argued here that a more nuanced approach is needed in which individuals are not forced into sometimes artificially constructed boxes, but rather they are seen as more or less attracted to two distinct theological poles. It will be further argued that these poles existed not only throughout the history of the Christian religion, in all its forms, but can be traced back further into the religious womb of Christianity which is Judaism. These are the dual biblical concepts of the *yir'ath Yahweh* or the 'fear of the Lord.'

Scriptural theology is largely descriptive of the experiences both secular and religious of a primarily nomadic, vulnerable and justifiably anxious group of tribes known collectively as the Israelites. After their nomadic years they exchanged the hostile environment of the desert for another vulnerable position settled between three powerful and bellicose neighbours, Egypt, Babylon and Assyria. The proximity of danger was, not surprisingly, of formative importance in their religious understanding. More interesting, however, than this worldly apprehension was the attendant spiritual fear which was a more characteristic response and which proved to be an abiding feature in Judaeo-Christian traditions. Most importantly for the history of Christianity was the fact that this spiritual fear as experienced and expressed by the Jewish people must be understood in two quite distinct senses. In biblical literature these senses are interwoven and complementary, in Church history they were eventually to emerge as contradictory.

According to G.A. Butterick, the first sense of this fear is associated with man's apparent awareness of his own sinful condition and the expectation of divine wrath.[9] It is described in the shame and terror of Adam hiding in the garden after the first example of human disobedience, and the trembling of Moses as he beheld the golden calf. This is a theological interpretation based on the image of a jealous God and centred around the strictures of His laws and precepts as set out in the Mosaic covenant. The gist of this covenant was that God would protect Israel if the members of their tribes continued to observe His laws.[10] However, since the community bore responsibility (at least in the original form of the covenant) for each individual's actions, the prognosis for the future success of the relationship, as expressed in the prophetical writing, tended to be pessimistic. Anthony Philips described their general assessment.

> The Mosaic covenant was a straight arrangement between Israel and her God, so that no matter what individuals did within the community, the whole community was liable for

---

8   P. White, 'The Rise of Arminianism reconsidered', *Past and Present*, vol. CI (1983), passim.

9   G.A. Butterick, *The Interpreter's Dictionary of the Bible* (5 vols, Nashville, 1962), vol. 2, p. 624.

10   J. Bright, *A History of Israel* (London 1972), p. 144.

any breach of law. Jeremiah recognised that such an arrangement would inevitably bring doom upon Israel.[11]

This particular expression of the *yir'ath Yahweh* with its negative appraisal of the moral condition of Israel looked toward a divine intervention that is inevitably interpreted as destructive when Zion would become as 'ploughed as a field'; Jerusalem, 'a heap of ruins', (Micah 3:12). The fear in this instance describes the trepidation of a deserved judgment and punishment; it is the fear of the inevitable consequences of Yahweh's juctice. For the purpose of this work we might usefully term the experience the 'justice motif.'

Butterick identifies the second sense of this fear as being more closely associated with the sacred or the presence of God. In this religious experience there is dread but it is mixed with the contrary feelings of joy and fascination.

> But this kind of dread is not merely negative. It accompanies the perception of God's glory and may generate an emotion of exultation and joy at the discovery of God's intense concern and love for man. This kind of fear is the result not only of the knowledge that Yahweh is a holy God but also of the apprehension of his saving grace.[12]

This spiritual phenomenon has been described most fully in the twentieth century by the German theologian, Rudolf Otto, who labelled the contrasting aspects of this experience as the 'numinous.' According to Otto it involves 'blank wonder, and astonishment that strikes us dumb, an amazement absolute.'[13] These, he says, are the *mysterium tremendum*, or the feeling of nothingness against overpowering majesty which he summarises as 'absolute unapproachability.'[14] This is, however, only one aspect of the numinous experience, the other is fascination, it is compelling, alluring and enchanting. As in the book of Exodus when Moses sang that God had become his strength and salvation after he had witnessed His destruction of the Egyptians, it is most commonly associated with optimism and a positive self-appraisal for the human participants.

This feeling of divine presence led to ideas of sanctity, the sacred belonged to another realm and was by supernatural right to be regarded as separate. This word 'separate' in Hebrew is שודק [*hsodak*], which in turn is the real meaning of the word holy.[15] Throughout the Old Testament there is a divine injunction to appreciate this separateness.[16] This practice developed from the cultic sanctuary with its inner sanctum, the tabernacle, the altar, the surrounding court (holy to a lesser degree) surrounded in turn by the camp (not holy but clean) and finally by the unclean wilderness. In the settled period we only need to replace these terms with Temple

---

11   A. Philips, *God BC* (Oxford, 1977), p. 37.
12   Butterick, *Dictionary*, vol. 2, pp. 257–8.
13   R. Otto, *Mysticism, East and West* (London 1937), p. 26.
14   R. Otto, *The Idea of the Holy* (London, 1923), p. 19.
15   J.F.A. Sawyer, *A Modern Introduction to Biblical Hebrew* (London, 1976), p. 207.
16   R. de Vaux, *Ancient Israel, its Life and Institutions* (London, 1961), pp. 275–6.

and walled city.¹⁷ Added to this are particular incidents such as the one described in Exodus 3:5 after God has descended on Mount Sinai, if man touches its ground he will die.¹⁸ In order to distinguish this experience from the first throughout this work it will be called the 'numinous motif.'

It must be stressed that as contrasting as these biblical notions may appear to be, they must not be seen as conflicting. Nor indeed did the early Church have any problem incorporating them in tandem into their own religious system. However, in the late middle–ages, the reactions of Luther, Calvin and other Reformers to a Church which had so exploited this idea of the sacred as to make an industry out of it, appears to lead them to place much greater stress on the justice motif as a type of theological antidote. The further the Reformers moved away from ideas of the sacred numinous, the more they moved into the territory of the justice motif with its concomitant negative analysis of humanity. The medieval scholastics had characterised man as an amalgam of contradictory tendencies, the one to evil acts, the other drew him to good. This 'synteresis' theory, propounding an innate moral sense, was rejected outright by the early Protestants who stressed both the overwhelming power of original sin and the loss of righteousness.¹⁹ As a recent commentator put it, 'The Reformers stretched both these views of sin to the uttermost. They insisted that the "void", the absence of good, implied the presence of evil; they insisted that "concupiscence" tainted all human nature, not just the lower man.'²⁰

For the various protagonists involved, an element of antagonism developed between two previously complementary religious expressions. Whereas the medieval Catholic Church threw up cathedral monuments of its glory and majesty to inspire respect and fear, Protestant Reformers returned to the simplicity of God's commandments. This has been infamously characterised by Keith Thomas as the 'decline of magic' which accompanied the growth of Protestantism.²¹ However, Thomas's analysis is probably too sociological, stripping the experience of much of its genuine spiritual aspect. The real difference was not between magic and reason but between mystical religious experience and a covenant relationship; it is the difference between holiness (in the sense of the kadosh) and godliness (in the sense of being justified) and it is the difference between two religious expressions, the one based on awe and the other law.

If we accept these twin varieties of religious consciousness as defining the differences in post-Reformation theology we may observe that they have a centrifugal quality, other theological and political ideas spring outward from their central premise. Liturgy, the sacraments, the idea of a priesthood, church hierarchy and soteriology will all be determined by whichever concept they are derived from. If, for example, one is drawn to the justice motif, then they are more likely to stress the righteousness of God (as Luther did), then from this it is easy to conclude that man's

---

17   D.N. Freedman, 'The Pentateuch', in J.D.G. Dunn and J.W. Rogerson (eds), *Eerdman's Commentary on the Bible* (Cambridge, 2003), p.101.
18   18 de Vaux, *Ancient Israel*, pp. 275–6.
19   E. Cameron, *The European Reformation* (Oxford, 1991), pp. 84–5.
20   Ibid., p. 113.
21   K. Thomas, *Religion and the Decline of Magic* (London, 1971).

fallen state is part of the corruption of the whole of nature. If this is the case, then it follows that human institutions share in the malaise, including the institutions of the visible Church. Also affected is man's ability to save himself from this perdition, which is the core of the Christian experience. If a man is wholly bad then neither he nor his institutions can save him. This reaction was described by Charles and Katherine George.

> To Protestant critics, Roman Catholic errors in this category appeared to have a twofold origin: they arose first, from over-optimism regarding the ability of human nature to achieve its own salvation, and second, from over-confidence regarding the effectiveness of institutional devices in the stimulation of the process.[22]

Conversely, if the religious starting point is rooted in the numinous, then the means by which this is conveyed, the sacerdotal, the house of God, the consecrated priest as well as the participant himself, are all legitimate means or conduits through which salvation can be achieved. In what has been called 'incarnational logic', the boundaries of the sacred are permeable, the divine is experienced.[23] This is the theological irony of the numinous motif. The cultic experience by definition is communion with the separate.

One other important aspect of the justice motif has implications for the denominational development in Christianity. If any single concept can be used to characterize Luther's approach it is the term 'relational theology.'[24] As we have seen this theological phenomenon expressed itself in the Bible in terms of the covenant. As mentioned above the early Mosaic covenant contained a communal liability and this was certainly so up until 586 BC when judgement fell on Israel and their land was sacked by the Babylonians.[25] After this event, a new formula was worked out (by what biblical scholars call the priestly theologians) in which the individual could make a personal decision to opt in or out of the covenant. Two important consequences of this were that Jews were no longer seen to be punished for the sins of other people as before (Jeremiah 31:27–30) and now there would be an exclusive quality to the covenant relationship. Those who broke the law found themselves outside of the community and by default no longer part of the chosen people. Philips writes, 'It determined his membership of the elect community. If he did not obey the law, then he could not consider himself part of that community.'[26] Since this new covenant was more personal in emphasis than communal there was as a consequence a certain internalising of the old religious precepts. This process is summed up in one single passage in Jeremiah.

---

22 C.H. and K. George, *The Protestant Mind of the English Reformation* (New Jersey, 1961), p. 30.

23 F. Heal, *The Reformation in Britain and Ireland* (Oxford, 2003), p. 267.

24 M. Wriedt, 'Luther's theology' in D.K. McKim (ed.), *The Cambridge companion to Luther* (Cambridge, 2003), p. 103.

25 Philips, *God*, p. 33.

26 Ibid., p. 49.

> Behold, the days are coming, says the Lord, when I will make a new covenant with the house of Israel and the house of Judah, not like the covenant which I made with their fathers ... But this is the covenant which I will make with the house of Israel after those days, I will put my law within them, and I will write it upon their hearts;
>
> (Jeremiah 33: 31–3)

The biblical themes of this Israelite reformation are echoed in the European Reformation. The central message of the reform movement has been summed up as 'a call for a deepened spirituality for truly internal religion in contrast to mere external observance.'[27]

Other concepts and themes run through not only the justice motif but its numinous counterpart. Each motif has a momentum of its own that drove individuals and groups to often explore the most extreme of logical consequences. Patrick Collinson's definition of these opposing cultural expressions may be used as an outline of both motifs.

> On the far, late medieval side of the range, the landscape consists of images, concrete symbols, mime, the ritualized acting out of religious stories and lessons, a certain artlessness. Religion was 'intensely visual.' Seeing was believing, more than hearing and much more than the privatized mental discipline of absorbing information from a written text. On this side of the divide we confront the invisible, abstract and didactic word: primarily the word of the printed page, on which depended the spoken words of sermon and catechism. In crossing this range we are making a journey from a culture of orality and image to one of print: from one mental and imaginative 'set' to another.[28]

Diagrammatically, these conceptual devices might appear as below:

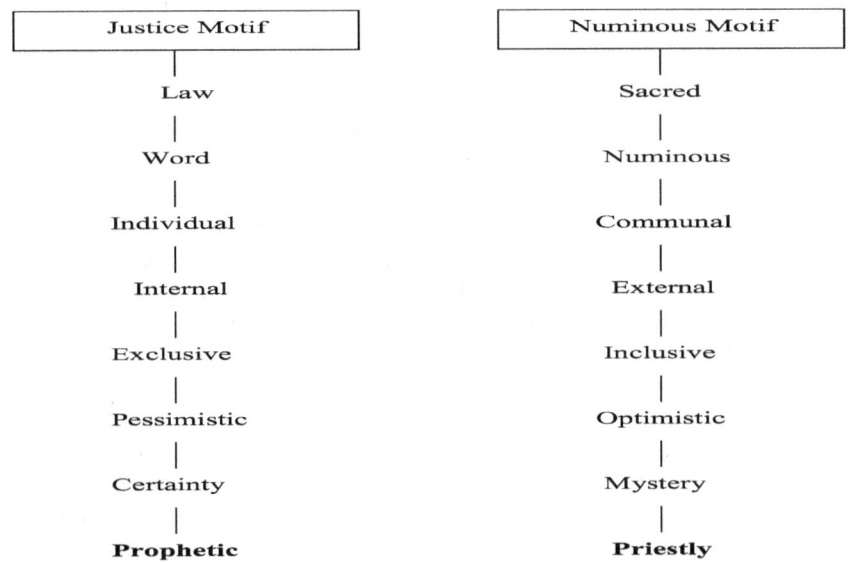

---

27 H.J. Hillerbrand, *The World of the Reformation* (London, 1975), p. 36.

28 P. Collinson, 'Protestant culture and the cultural revolution', in M. Todd (ed.), *Reformation to Revolution* (London, 1995), p. 37.

Before we look at the writings of Ussher and Bramhall, and attempt to place their respective theologies under the mantle of either of these motifs it is necessary to say that few but the most extreme characters of the Reformation belong exclusively to one camp or the other. Rather they tend toward one usually without denying totally the validity of the other. In theology, stress is all-important. Luther stressed God's justice to a very great extent, but this does not mean that he entirely relinquished the numinous. The Georges made an important point about this area of Christianity when they discovered the apparently contradictory themes of adulation and condemnation. They explained that the Church has always hovered, ' ... uncertainly between two antagonistic poles. In the historic succession of doctrines and sects, Christian philosophy may move nearer one pole or the other but it never succeeds in eliminating or in truly reconciling both.'[29] The failure to recognise this fact has at times dogged historical debate on early modern religion. The following study will avoid this by employing the motifs as poles in order to illustrate the manner in which the theological and political ideologies of James Ussher and John Bramhall are reflective of a tendency toward an understanding rather than a cleaving to inert dogma. Ussher's Calvinism originates from a prioritising of the law, or as he sees it, the word of God; this is how he interprets holiness. On the other hand Bramhall's broad Catholicism is a product of the centrality to his perspective of that which is separate unto God, or as he regards it, that which is holy; he interprets holiness to mean *kadosh*. In saying this it is important to recognise that neither cleric dismisses out of hand either the relevance or even the importance of God's word or the sacred. So long as we squeeze individuals into hermetically sealed ideological compartments we will never understand the subtleties of the strands of understanding thrown up by Christianity. Unless we place these intellectual and spiritual expressions into something more fluid, such as the biblical motifs, then we will not be able to comprehend how Calvinists might entertain notions of the sacred or how Arminians might have high esteem for the word of God. We might also never understand how Ussher and Bramhall could be regarded as candles of the same branch.

This volume sets out to examine the lives and writings of two prominent seventeenth-century ecclesiastics from the particular perspective of the above motifs. In the first instance we will discuss their theologies concerning doctrine, the sacraments and ecclesiastical history in order to illustrate that their central motivations derived not primarily from definable Christian schools of thought, but rather from well established Christian impulses. Ussher's belief system revolves around the word of God and relational theology. Conversely, Bramhall's Christianity rests on the numinous motif which means that his understanding of doctrine, sacrament and history of the Church have as their central theme the appreciation and preservation of buildings, people, institutions and traditions that he considers *separate unto God*. We will then turn our attention to their respective politics in order to demonstrate that once again, particularly in ecclesiastical politics and practical policy, Ussher and Bramhall are motivated by the justice and numinous motifs. In Ireland Ussher's primary concern was to create what might be seen as a type of confederacy of reformed Christians united around the basic principles of God's word. Bramhall

---

29   Georges, *Protestant Mind*, p. 24.

is more concerned to create a Church that will recreate, contain and convey the *Kadosh* ideal of holiness. In approaching our subjects in this way we aim to offer them here as exemplars of these motifs, not the most extreme examples perhaps, but there is distance enough between them to shed light on all forms of the theological bifurcation that was the Reformation.

Acknowledgements

The original of this script was a Ph.D thesis and I would like to express my thanks for the generous support, criticism and helpful comments which I received from my supervisor Prof Keith Lindley, while I was putting it together, it was above any expectations and deeply appreciated. Prof Alan Ford for his agreeing to be my external examiner and for his helpful comments, and Prof David Sturdy for his advice and support. I would like also to express my gratitude to Prof Alan Sharp and the School of History at the University of Ulster for awarding me the T.K. Daniels scholarship and therefore making this study possible. Donegal County Council for awarding me the Mac an tSaoir scholarship. Also to Dr Edwin Bacon, Head of Research at Bishop Grosseteste University College for his support during the later stages of my work and to Dr David Barber for all his technical assistance. I would also like to thank Prof Muriel Robinson, Principal of Bishop Grosseteste and Dr Ian Fisher for their help and support, in particular for allowing me to take a sabbatical leave to prepare this work for publication.

I would also like to thank the following people and institutions: Dr Mick Lemon for giving me a second chance at academic life, Dr John McCafferty at the University of Dublin for his help in the early stages, Elizabethanne Boran at Trinity College Dublin, Bob Hunter for lending me his ear on many occasions, the staff at the Huntington Library in San Marino, California for allowing me access to their important collection of manuscripts, and the staff at Bishop Marsh's Library in Dublin, Lambeth Palace Library and Dr Williams' Library.

On a personal level I would also like to thank my wife, Maureen, for the enormous amount of patience and fortitude she has shown through some difficult times. The following people have also been instrumental in helping me along the way: Cormac and Michelle Linehan for their incredible generosity, Michael and Fliss for all their help and generosity, and Mark Cunningham for accompanying me at the last stage; I may have been able to do it without him, but I don't know how. We'll have another night in the Harbour Lights very soon when there will be nothing more to worry about except how we will make it home along the beach. Chris, Catherine and Ann for making up the rest of a great family. I would also like to thank Liam McGinley who worked extremely hard on the script and without whom this work would not be possible. My family, Sorcha who we started with, and Caoimhe who was there when we finished.

Lastly I reserve a huge debt of gratitude to my parents who had every right to think their duties with regard to rescuing their off-spring were well and truly over. They continue to do so without question or complaint and that has meant everything to me; this book is therefore dedicated to the Rev Terry Cunningham and Shirley Cunningham.

Jack Cunningham, Subject Leader for Theology,
Bishop Grosseteste University College, Lincoln.

List of Abbreviations

All dates are given in the old style, except that the year is taken to begin on 1 January and not 25 March. The following abbreviations and short titles are used in the notes.

BW – John Bramhall, *The whole works*, ed. W.A. Hadden (5 vols, Oxford, 1842–45).

UW – James Ussher, *The whole Works*, eds C.R. Elrington and J.H. Todd (17 vols, Dublin, 1847–64).

Bernard, *Clavi* – N. Bernard, *Clavi Trabales* (London, 1661).

Bernard, *Life* – N. Bernard, *The Life and Death of the Most Reverend Father of our Church, Dr James Ussher* (London, 1656).

Carr, *Life* – J.A. Carr, *The Life and times of James Ussher* (London, 1895).

Collins, *Typical Churchmen* – W.E. Collins, 'John Bramhall', in W.E. Collins, *Typical Churchmen from Parker to Maurice* (London, 1902).

DNB – *Dictionary of National Biography*.

Elrington, *Life* – C.R. Elrington, *The Life of the Most Reverend James Ussher* (London, 1847).

Hadden, *Life* – A.W. Hadden, *The Life of Archbishop Bramhall* (Oxford, 1842).

R.B. Knox, *Ussher* – R.B. Knox, *James Ussher, Archbishop of Armagh* (Cardiff, 1967).

McAdoo, *Bramhall* – H.R. McAdoo, *John Bramhall and Anglicanism, 1663–1963* (Dublin, 1964).

Parr, *Life* – R. Parr, *The Life of the Most Reverend Father in God, James Ussher* (London, 1686).

Power of the Prince – James Ussher, *The Power Communicated By God to the Prince*, ed. C.R. Elrington (London, 1847–64).

Rawdon Papers – *The Rawdon Papers, Letters to and from John Bramhall*, ed. E. Berwick (London, 1819).

Serpent Salve – John Bramhall, *The Serpent Salve, a remedy for the biting of an Asp*, ed. A.W. Hadden (London, 1842–45).

Sparrow-Simpson, *Bramhall* – W.J. Sparrow-Simpson, *Archbishop Bramhall* (London, 1927).

Vesey, *Athanasius* – J. Vesey, J., *Athanasius Hibernicus or the Life of the Most Reverend Father in God John Lord Primate of Armagh* (London, 1676).

Wills, *Distinguished Irishmen* – J. Wills, *Lives of illustrious and Distinguished Irishmen* (Dublin, 1842).

Wright, *Yorkshire Divine* – W.B. Wright, *A great Yorkshire Divine of the Seventeenth Century* (York, 1899).

Chapter 1
James Ussher

James Ussher was born 4 January 1581, one of nine children (his entry in the most recent Dictionary of National Biography makes a claim for 10)[1] in the parish of St Nicholas in Dublin, in which church he was undoubtedly baptised, though no records remain.[2] This area was at the time a fashionable district and a literary centre boasting Ireland's first printing press for books and news sheets. One of his nineteenth-century biographers, however, alluded regretfully to a certain fall of this particular house of Ussher as 57, the High Street had by then become a grocer's shop.[3] The Usshers were Old English, but their lineage would appear to be less clear than his biographers have tended to assume. Most writers confidently trace James's line back as far as 1185 to a John Neville, who accompanied King John to Ireland, then subsequently settled in Dublin and changed his name to suit his profession. However W.B. Wright's genealogy of the Ussher family was more extensively researched and less conclusive. Wright claimed that the first to appear of that name on the Irish scene was an Arlantor or Arland Uscher in 1439, who was a merchant and bailiff of the city. Wright was unable to find any knightly or landed family of that name between 1185 and 1439 though he is not entirely dismissive of the Ussher pedigree; the coat of arms used by the Primate and his father, displaying a chevron ermine between three batons, is 'testimony of the tradition being founded on some such fact',[4] though of course arms can be fabricated.

Unusually amongst their social group, the Usshers were not recusants, but maintained a Protestantism which was as integral to their self-identity as their loyalty and service to the English crown. James' uncle, Henry, was the Archbishop of Armagh, his grandfather on his mother's side was three times speaker in the Irish parliament, and his father was one of six clerks of the Court of Chancery.[5] When James was later to choose a career in the Church he was to find himself alone amongst the Irish episcopate as the only native Irishman. Ussher showed no signs of discomfort, moving as he did in the Scottish and English society of the Irish Church hierarchy. Indeed the Usshers associated such Britannic civility not just with godliness, but with the antithesis of what they viewed as the wild and sensuous

---

1 *DNB*, (2004), vol. 56, p. 6.
2 The International Genealogical Index (http://www.familysearch.org) gives Ussher's parents as Arland Ussher and Margaret Stanihurst. They provide no information about his christening and curiously date his birth to 'about 1589.' This is very late and contrary to all other sources.
3 Carr, *Life*, p. 4.
4 W.B. Wright, *The Ussher Memoirs* (London, 1889), p. vii.
5 Bernard, *Life*, p. 15.

nature of the majority of their countrymen. Ussher's first biographer and one time chaplain wrote that though he lived in a barbarous nation, 'he savoured no more of that native barbarity, than the sea fish doth of the salt water.'[6]

If the Usshers were resolute Reformers, this was not the case for his mother's family. Her brother, Richard Stanihurst, was a Catholic émigré who wrote polemical works denouncing the new heresies. His mother also had only a lukewarm commitment to Protestantism. After her husband's death, and taking advantage of her son's absence in England, she reconverted to the Roman Church in which she remained to her death.[7] In this way James's own family reflected the religious divisions and conflict that rent their wider society. The split in his family and their position on the very edge of Protestant Europe appears to have affected Ussher profoundly so that even from an early age he determined to make Church controversy along with chronology, the chief foci of his intellectual endeavours.

The young Ussher received his pre-school education from two maiden aunts who, though blind from birth, possessed a remarkable capacity for learning, being able to recite from heart large sections of the Bible.[8] Nicholas Bernard paints a picture of a serious-minded and austere youth complete with all the prerequisites of puritan hagiography including the obligatory conversion experience which occurred when the ten-year-old Ussher heard a sermon on Romans 12:1, 'I beseech you brethren, by the mercies of God that ye present a living sacrifice acceptable unto God, which is your reasonable service.'[9] According to his one-time chaplain, Stanley Gower, it was at this point that Ussher was converted from the state of Nature to the state of Grace.[10] Early readings also had their effect. In particular, 'Master Perkins' on the sanctity of the sabbath 'took so with him, that he was ever after careful to keep it',[11] and a Latin copy of St Augustine's *Meditations* had so moved him that he often wept while reading it.[12]

Another obligatory element in the saintly career was provided, according to Bernard, when the Devil, recognising his potential sought to frighten him from his godly purpose with divers terrors including, 'sleeping as walking.' When somnambulance failed the old enemy tried a different tactic, inducing friends to

---

6   Ibid., p. vi.
7   Ussher's mother had been a Catholic prior to her marriage. Her return to the Roman faith caused the Reverend M.F. Day to lament in his lecture to the Dublin Young Men's Christian Association that with her 'lip-service' to Protestantism she was ill-fitted to act toward her eminent son, the part of Eunice to Timothy or Monica to Augustine. M.F. Day, *Archbishop Ussher, his Life and Character* (Dublin, 1862), p. 5.
8   Wright, *Memoirs*, p. 87.
9   Bernard, *Life*, p. 23. The nineteenth-century Anglican biographer of Ussher, C.R. Elrington, took great exception to this account as a puritan device, 'a mere attempt to support the doctrines of Calvin by a remarkable example'; C.R. Elrington, *The Life of the Most Reverend James Ussher* (London, 1847), p. 2.
10   S. Gower, *Eighteen Sermons preached in Oxford, 1640* (London, 1659). Thomason Collection, E1004, p. 3.
11   Bernard, *Life*, pp. 23–4. Carr says, this gave Ussher a 'life long Sabbatarian bias'; Carr, *Life*, p. 46.
12   P. Styles, 'James Ussher and his times', *Hermathena*, LXXXVIII (1956): 4.

teach him cards, ' ... which he found himself so delighted with, that it not only took the place of the love of his books, but began to be a rival with that spiritual part in him.'[13] Bernard tells us that on apprehending this he gave it over, never to play again. Writing later in the altogether different atmosphere of the restoration, Richard Parr's description of Ussher's childhood is less staid. Though he retains the theme of temptation it is made manifest in a more genteel form.

> He told me, that in this first scene of his life he was extremely addicted to Poetry, and was much delighted with it, but afterward growing to more maturity and consideration, he shook it off, as not suitable to the great end of his more resolved and profitable studies, and then set himself industriously to pursue learning of a higher nature.[14]

The formal education of Ussher began under unusual circumstances. In 1587, James Fullerton and James Hamilton, both agents of James VI, were sent to Dublin from Scotland in order to establish connections between the Scottish monarchy and such influential Irish Protestants as might prove useful. Parr tells us that 'these for a colour undertook the employment of school-masters, to instruct and discipline youth.'[15] They were, it turns out, very effective teachers. Ussher was later to count it a blessing 'That he had the opportunity and advantage of his Education from those men, who came thither by chance, and yet proved so happily to himself and others.'[16] They set up their school at the rear of the present Synod House in Christ Church Place[17] and the young Ussher soon excelled himself in Latin, poetry and rhetoric. When Trinity opened its doors in 1594, Ussher was elected one of the first scholars. E.W. Watson points out that the family decision to send James to a young and, as yet, unproven college was a sacrifice and a measure of their support when quite clearly they could have afforded to have sent him to one of the other institutions across the water. As it transpired it was a choice that was mutually beneficial.[18] The decision undoubtedly owed much to the family's involvement in the establishment of the Irish university. James's grandfather Stanihurst had first moved the motion in Parliament for an Irish University while his uncle, Henry, had twice visited London to negotiate the matter.[19] James came to the nascent college at the age of fourteen armed with a decent, though not remarkable education. He was proficient in Latin, though he had to wait for his university education to provide him with Greek as well as Hebrew.

An important aspect of Trinity was that in its early years it had a strongly Ramist ethos, something which Ussher was to carry with him throughout his life. The

---

13 Bernard, *Life*, pp. 23–4.
14 Parr, *Life*, p. 3.
15 Ibid.
16 Styles, 'Ussher and his times' :14.
17 Carr, *Life*, p. 17; For their efforts they were duly recognised. When James came to the throne in England, he raised Hamilton to the peerage and knighted Fullerton, though it is not clear whether this was for services to the crown or the field of education; J. Wills, *Lives of Illustrious and Distinguished Irishmen* (6 vols, Dublin, 1842), vol. 4, p. 68.
18 E.W. Watson, 'James Ussher', in W.E. Collins (ed.), *Typical English Churchmen* (London, 1902), p. 61.
19 Elrington, *Life*, p. 5.

philosophy of Pierre de la Ramée (1515–72) sought to throw off the Aristotelian divisions and metaphysics with a simplified, practical and logical alternative. In place of hierarchy it stressed calling, and thus ensured an inbuilt attraction for the godly.[20] The arch-protagonist of Ramism at Trinity was the provost William Temple who had brought forward an annotated edition of Ramée's *Dialecticae* in 1594,[21] but even before his arrival in 1609, the influence had been established not least by two newly appointed fellows, Ussher's old school masters, Fullerton and Hamilton. In Glasgow University, they had been pupils of Andrew Melville, a former student in Paris and enthusiastic disciple of Ramus.[22]

Added to all of this was Trinity's geographical position as an outpost on the Protestant frontier. This was always going to lend its reformed character a harder edge. The feeling common to missionaries, of vulnerability and superiority saw them cleave to anything identifiably Protestant whilst purging themselves of elements that smacked of popery. This resulted in a moderate puritan ethos demonstrated most clearly by its employment record and early friendship network.[23] According to one of Ussher's biographers, Trinity was called the 'Fanatics' College'[24] by its enemies and more recently it has been compared with English puritan seminaries such as Emmanuel College, Cambridge where the sole focus was theology with a view to evangelization.[25] Laurence Chaderton, whom Patrick Collinson called the pope of Cambridge puritanism, had turned Emmanuel College into a puritan seminary in all but name during the 1580s.[26] It seems Trinity was to be run along similar lines. Ussher the undergraduate proved to be remarkably industrious. After reading Sleidan's history of the four empires,[27] he drew up a chronology of exact times when each eminent person lived. Now, at the age of fifteen, he developed this into a chronology of the Bible as far as Kings which, 'excepting the enlargements in

---

20   W.J. Ong, 'Peter Ramus', in P. Edwards (ed.), *The Encyclopedia of Philosophy* (8 vols, New York, 1967), vol. 7, pp. 66–9.
21   H.L. Murphy, *The History of Trinity College* (London, 1951), p. 52.
22   'Melville' *DNB*, (1968), vol. 13, pp. 230–36.
23   See, E. Boran, 'An early friendship network of James Ussher, archbishop of Armagh 1626–1656,' in H. Robinson-Hammerstein (ed.), *European Universities in the Age of Reformation and Counter-Reformation* (Dublin, 1998).
24   Carr, *Life*, p. 79.
25   A. Ford, 'The Church of Ireland, 1558–1634, A Puritan Church?', in A. Ford, et al. (eds), *As by Law Established* (Dublin, 1995), p. 60; largely responsible for this early religious complexion was its puritan patron Lord Burghley, who ' ... in the exercise of his patronage, found the newly established College a convenient shelter for such of his friends as were debarred by the complexion of their religious convictions from promotion in England.' W.M. Dixon, *Trinity College Dublin* (Dublin, 1902), p. 27.
26   P. Collinson, *The Elizabethan Puritan Movement* (Oxford, 1967), p. 435.
27   *Sleidan de Quatuor Monarchiis* (London, 1556); according to the *Oxford Encyclopedia of the Reformation*, 'Sleidan's quest for inclusiveness may be daunting for the reader, but it achieves an unsurpassed immediacy with the complex interrelationships of religious, political, constitutional, and social issues in collision.' This may have been written about Ussher. *Oxford Encyclopedia of the Reformation*, ed. H.J. Hillerbrand, (4 vols, New York, 1996), vol. 4, pp. 68–9.

some exquisite observations, and the sycnronisms of heathen story ... '[28] provided the basis for his famous *Annales,* (1650). The previous year, Ussher had been called to receive communion, the sacramental importance of which he maintained for the rest of his life. Even whilst Nicholas Bernard was attempting to stress the puritan in his first biography, he described nevertheless the profound seriousness with which he undertook his preparation, in strict examination and penitential humiliation until, 'streams of tears ran from him.'[29] One sin was particularly lamented, ' ... his too much love of his book and humane learning, that he should be as glad of the Monday to go to that, as of the Lord's day for his service, it cost him many a tear.'[30]

As auspicious as Ussher's student career was proving, his life might never have taken an academic direction had not his father died in 1598. Arland Ussher's world was practical and political and he had ambitions to send his eldest son to the Inns of Court. Released from such filial obligations, James settled into the world of letters, outside which he was never to be entirely comfortable. Contemporary biographies inform us that Ussher drew up legal contracts on the death of his father which placed the family's not inconsiderable estate in the hands of his brothers and sisters, keeping only sufficient to purchase books and pursue his studies.[31] Bernard remarks that James was now chosen as a fellow of the College since previously he had been unable to take the fellows' requisite oath, 'That the present intent of their studies be for the profession of Divinity, unless God should afterwards otherwise dispose their minds.'[32] As usual, Parr's biography drifts into eulogy as he claims a very early fame for his subject stating that even from thirteen his reputation was spreading abroad, 'that which administered greatest cause of admiration was, that so much fruit should be found upon a plant newly set, and scarcely ripe for blossom ... '[33] This is undoubtedly a premature staking of an international claim to fame since the fruit had not as yet started falling from the tree; however at his college, the new fellow was clearly making quite an impression. In 1599, at the inauguration of the Earl of Essex, Robert Devereux, as the new Chancellor, Ussher was chosen as a respondent in a public disputation; his performance apparently excited general applause.[34] This rather theatrical dispute precursed a very real and important one the same year which saw

---

28   Bernard, *Life,* p. 28.
29   Ibid., p. 27.
30   Ibid.
31   Parr, *Life,* pp. 5–6. Parr is anxious to prove that this was not a 'rash act' but well calculated so that all seven sisters were well provided for and 'afterwards very well married.' Parr probably has the date wrong since Ussher was only seventeen years old at the time, and therefore not legally responsible.
32   Bernard, *Life,* p. 31. Trinity, in common with other theological establishments such as Emmanuel College, Cambridge limited their fellowships which were awarded for a set number of years instead of life. This was in order to ensure that students left the ivory tower and practised their preaching skills. See Ford, 'Church of Ireland – A Puritan Church?', p. 60.
33   Parr, *Life,* p. 6.
34   Elrington, *Life,* pp. 10–11; Wills was at pains to explain the popularity of these 'public acts' in which two scholars engaged each other over a philosophical point. In his usual flowery language he claims that at this period in history they were 'as attractive to the

Ussher take to the public stage for the first time. The opportunity came as the result of a challenge issued by a Jesuit philosophy teacher who was being held prisoner in Dublin Castle. Henry Fitzsimonds was a relative of Ussher[35] and a native of the city and after studying at Hart's Hall, Oxford, he had entered the Society of Jesus on the continent. His challenge stated that he was 'like a bear tied to a stake, and wanting some to bait him.'[36] Ussher's long career as a Christian controversialist had begun.

Returning to his study, James became convinced that central to the progress of truth and the victory of Protestantism over Catholicism, was thorough scholarship which, by trawling the early records, could establish the mendacity of Roman Catholicism. At the age of twenty, he read Thomas Stapleton's *A Fortress of Faith*, a Catholic apologetic very much in vogue at that time. The originality and strength of this work was the way it utilised patriarchal writing to illustrate the novelty of the reformed Churches.[37] Earlier in his life, the famous passage from Cicero had excited his interest in the historical, *Nescire quid antea quam natus sis acciderit est semper esse puerum* [To be ignorant of history is to be always a child].[38] After reading Stapleton he was much impressed that this was the way to pursue inquiry; thus began the formidable, eighteen year task of reading all the Church fathers setting his sights on the great heavy weight of Roman Catholic apologetics, Robert Bellarmine[39]. In addition, it has been pointed out that the polemical section of Ussher's library concentrated on the English Counter-Reformation writers such as Stapleton, Parsons and Wright.[40] It is clear that Ussher was priming himself for a domestic battle. The maturer student chose a new motto from the patriarch Tertullian, *Verum quodcunque primum, adulterum quodcunque posterius* [That which is primitive is true; whatever is later is corrupt].[41]

In 1601, Ussher was made M.A. and at the same time appointed catechist to the college.[42] Duties required that he lectured weekly on the pure principles of Christianity. As a result of the success he enjoyed he was pressed to take his learning to a wider and more necessitous audience and become a lay preacher.[43] Ussher held out on the principle that this was a sacred duty and a prerogative of the ordained until the scarcity of preachers led the Irish government to appoint three masters to preach at Christ Church on a weekly basis. One was to take as his subject Isaiah, the

---

cumbrous gaiety of that pedantic age as the rival strains of Pasta and Grisi are now to ears polite.' Wills, *Distinguished Irishmen*, vol. 4, p. 74.

35   *DNB*, (2004), vol. 56, p.7.

36   Ibid., p. 12.

37   *The Oxford Dictionary of the Christian Church*, eds F.L. Cross and E.A. Livingstone, (Oxford, 1983), pp. 1286–7.

38   Murphy, '*Ussher*' p. 146.

39   A. Ford, 'James Ussher and the creation of an Irish protestant identity,' in B. Bradshaw and P. Roberts (eds), *British Consciousness and Identity: the Making of Britain, 1533–1707* (Cambridge, 1998), p. 196.

40   E. Boran, 'The libraries of Luke Challoner and James Ussher, 1595–1608,' in Robinson-Hammerstein, *European Universities*, pp. 103–4.

41   Elrington, *Life*, p. 9.

42   *Alumni Dublinenses*, eds G.D. Burtchaeli and T.U. Sadleir, (Dublin, 1935), p. 833.

43   Parr, *Life*, p. 8.

second Christian roots in Scripture, and lastly Ussher was to take his usual theme of the controversy with Catholics. In spite of the urgency of the situation Ussher's regard for the sacred ministry (a principle at odds with the image of a low-Church Calvinist claimed by Bernard) was never going to sit easily with his new role. James was ordained deacon and priest in December 1601 by his uncle, the Archbishop of Armagh.[44] The newly legitimised preacher chose as his text Revelations 3:1 'I know thy works, thou hast a name that thou livest, and art dead.'[45] Bernard says this was on the same day as the battle of Kinsale when victory for the Spanish would have placed the Protestant community in a perilous position. Since their clergy would have been especially in danger, Ussher would have been well advised to delay proceedings; Bernard tells us that he demurred at such precautions.[46]

The new pastor's first appointment was at St Catherine's, Dublin where he preached to congregations made up mostly of Church Papists.[47] The post-Kinsale atmosphere in Ireland lead paradoxically to a softening of anti-Catholic policy, the more peaceable recusants petitioned and then received certain concessions. Previously, Catholics had been fined one shilling for non-attendance at services. In February, 1603, orders came via the Lord Lieutenant, Mountjoy, to relax this law, and Ussher's flock drifted away.[48] The spirit of the Protestant controversialist was strongly stirred and, fearing that anything short of a firm enforcement of the act of uniformity would lead to a general disturbance, he preached against government policy in Christ Church Cathedral. The text he chose was Ezekiel 4:6 'and thou shalt bear the iniquity of the house of Judah forty days; I have appointed thee each day for a year.' This sermon was to become possibly Ussher's most famous since it was later interpreted as a prophetic vision of the 1641 rebellion and was therefore ensured a place in the mass of Protestant apocrypha that surrounded that event.[49] Such an outburst against official government policy of course earned a ticking off.

---

44   Buick Knox says this was 2 December while P. Styles claims it was 20 December. Knox, *Ussher*, p. 28; Styles, ' Ussher and his time' p. 16.

45   Elrington, *Life*, p. 19.

46   Bernard, *Life*, p. 36. Since the battle of Kinsale was on 24 December, this provides another date.

47   Ian Green has recently pointed out that with Ussher we have one of the only examples of genuine Protestant efforts to catechise in Ireland in the early decades of the seventeenth century. Besides preaching he produced his own catechism with two summaries pitched at different levels of learning. I. Green, '"The necessary knowledge of the principles of religion" – catechisms and catechising in Ireland, c.1560–1800', *As by Law*, Ford, McGuire, Milne, pp. 72–3; Ussher is, for this reason, one of the heroes of Killen's ecclesiastical history of Ireland. He portrays a singular figure forced to plough a lonely furrow. Mournfully, he concludes, 'Had ministers of the Established Church, as a body, followed the example of Ussher, Protestantism would have soon made great progress all over Ireland. But the pious Primate had few imitators'; W.D. Killen, *The Ecclesiastical History of Ireland* (2 vols, London, 1875), vol. 2, p. 7.

48   Bernard, *Life*, p. 33.

49   Biographers such as Parr and Bernard, anxious to align this prediction more exactly to the 1641 rebellion placed the sermon in 1601; Elrington is not convinced; he calls the prophecy a 'judicious conjecture', and claims for it this later date since Ussher was not ordained until December 1601. Elrington, *Life*, p. 23; Carr revives the prophetical tone, and

Christopher Hampton, the Archbishop of Armagh, immediately wrote to Ussher, and whilst he offered some sympathy, his message was clear, 'I am sensible of that which my brethren suffer ... I should have counselled your Lordship to give lenitives of your own accord, for all which was conceived over harsh or sharp.'[50]

After Kinsale, the English army, wanting to leave in Ireland a 'lasting memorial of the gallantry of military men', bequeathed £1,800 to furnish the new university with a library.[51] Ussher and Luke Challoner set off for London on the first of his book buying expeditions which were to ultimately provide such a valuable resource. It was on this particular visit that Ussher was supposed to have taken some pains to visit the renowned puritan, Christopher Goodman, on his death bed.[52] On his return, Ussher was presented by Archbishop Loftus to the Chancellorship of St Patrick's Cathedral with a living at Finglas to be held in commendam.[53] For this reason in 1606 he resigned his fellowship. The academic link was not entirely severed however and the next year he graduated B.D. and was made Professor of Divinity, a chair that was known at the time as Professor of Theological Controversies.[54] This was an important position not only because it provided the function of proselytising Roman Catholics, but perhaps more importantly it would provide Irish Protestants with a grasp of the fundamentals of their faith. Declan Gaffney explained how controversy functioned as a consolidating agent, 'public controversy was ... intended to go some way towards providing the educated members of the faithful with a surer grasp of the principles of their religion, and of the unassailability of those principles.'[55] The post carried with it a stipend of £8 per annum.

Two more book buying visits to London in 1609 brought Ussher into the acquaintance of a number of scholarly luminaries. Firstly, Camden and Robert Cotton in 1606,[56] then in 1609 he began a friendship with Selden which was to

---

rightly states that Ussher preached before his ordination, forgetting however that he himself dates Mountjoy's measures to 1603. Carr, *Life*, p. 83.

50   *UW*, vol. 15, p. 183.

51   Parr, *Life*, p. 8.

52   Christopher Goodman had been professor of Divinity during the reign of Edward VI. A virulent non-conformist, he wrote a book against the government of women while Mary was on the throne; he was silenced during the reign of her sister. Depending on how much his biographers want to stress Ussher's godliness, they tend to play up or down the association. Bernard presses it, writing that Ussher 'would be often repeating some grave wise speeches he heard from him.' Bernard, *Life*, p. 42; Elrington distances Ussher, stating that he would not have approved of Goodman's opinions. Elrington, *Life*, p. 24.

53   Carr, *Life*, p. 96. According to Carr, he preached here each Sunday, 'with great assiduity.'

54   *Alumni Dublinenses*, p. 833.

55   D. Gaffney, 'The practice of Religious Controversy in Dublin, 1600–1641', in W.J. Sheils and D. Wood (eds), *The Churches, Ireland and the Irish* (London, 1989), p. 145.

56   Wills, *Distinguished Irishmen*, vol. 4, p. 78. Camden paid a visit to Dublin the same year to collect material for his edition of *Britannia* in which Ussher assisted him. For his services, Camden acknowledged, 'the diligence and labour of James Ussher, Chancellor of St Patrick's, who in various learning and judgment, far exceeds his years.'

last the latter's lifetime.[57] It is clear, however, from contemporary evidence that, in spite of making such influential associations, Ussher's image as a supporter of Irish Calvinism was already a handicap to progress in London. On one such journey in 1612, James Hamilton furnished him with a letter to Sir James Semphill asking him to 'Clear them [Ussher and Challoner] to his majesty, that they are not puritans, but they have dignitarieships, and prebends in the Cathedral ... '[58] The following year Ussher made his publishing debut. The work was his *Gravissimae Quaestionis de Christianarum Eccleiarum* and it was dedicated to James I.[59] Ussher's first book represented a gargantuan effort in which he gathered a mountain of Church writing to illustrate the veracity of the Protestant cause. Ussher hoards sources into a montage of quotations. It is a style which was to become characteristic of his later writing in which he seldom uses his own words, but prefers to employ the authority of others. In this way he makes his points by proxy and resembles an editor more than a writer. Unfortunately, considering the enormity of the task, it is a method which prematurely dated Ussher. Later ages with greater proficiency in printing and easier access to libraries failed to appreciate the effort. Fortunately however for the young scholar, his contemporaries were more impressed. Isaac Casaubon 'highly eulogised' Ussher in Greek verse,[60] and James I apparently rated it very highly 'on account of its apocalyptic discussions, in which branch of theology that learned monarch had deeply speculated.'[61]

Ussher was careful that its dedication to James might solicit a favourable political response. Alan Ford points out,

> The dedication went out of its way to link the King's theological interest in apocalyptic with his practical responsibilities as supreme governor of the Church of Ireland. His achievements in Ireland were so comprehensive that only one task remained for him: to 'hurry and help our dying people, and cure them from the miserable disease of the popish plague.'[62]

The approval for the monarch for such a comprehensive defence of Anglicanism notwithstanding, a programme of sectarian cleansing was not forthcoming. However, the two volumes established their author's reputation as one of the most learned theologians of his day, both with the crown and with continental Reformers.[63] A third volume was intended by Ussher that would bring the history up to the present.

---

57 Carr, *Life*, p. 350. Carr mentions that Ussher visited Selden on his death bed and absolved him, though Selden had refused to see any clergymen. He has this from *Macray's Annals*, Bod. Lib., p. 77, fn.

58 *Montgomery Manuscripts (1603–1706)*, ed. G. Hill, (3 vols, Belfast, 1869), vol. 1, p. 104.

59 Carr, *Life*, p. 99. It was presented to the King by Archbishop Abbot who proudly described it as 'the eminent first fruits of the University of Dublin.'

60 J. Stuart, *Historical Memoirs of the City of Armagh* (Newry, 1819), p. 315.

61 J. Aikin, *The lives of John Selden, esq. and Archbishop Ussher* (London, 1812), p. 218.

62 A. Ford, 'James Ussher and the Godly Prince in early Seventeenth-Century Ireland', in H. Morgan (ed.), *Political Ideology in Ireland, 1541–1641* (London, 1999), p. 212.

63 Carr, *Life*, p. 99.

However, he awaited the response of his uncle, Stanihurst, and in actual fact the work was never completed.[64]

In 1613, Ussher was made Doctor of Divinity in a ceremony which included a stately procession through the city wearing scarlet robes and hood.[65] To attain the doctorate, the student had read two papers on prophetic texts of scripture, the first on Daniel 9:24 on the 'seventy weeks' and the second on Revelations 20:40 on the 'Reign of the Saints for a Thousand years.'[66] The purpose of his thesis was to demonstrate how these passages had been 'misapplied by the Millenaries, both in elder and later times.'[67] In spite of a reputation developed posthumously, but acquired even during his life, as a contemporary prophet, it was an exercise that Ussher often felt uncomfortable with. He was saddled with a renown in this field which he did little to encourage. It rested largely on the 1603 sermon and was to become something of an industry after his death with the publication of a number of catch-pennies purporting to be the testimonies of Ussher to people close to him.[68] Such speculation in fact went against the Ramist training of Ussher, with its reasoned and mathematical approach, its precision scholarship and its firm maintenance of logical enquiry. As E.W. Watson pointed out, on the puzzles of Daniel and Revelations, the 'New and admirable logarithms' of Napier provided a more learned key to unravelling the mystery than the dangerous arena of prophecy.[69]

The next year, Ussher was elected Vice-Chancellor of Trinity by the Provost and fellows; he was now thirty-three, but he had already established a strong position within the Irish Church in what appeared at the time at least, to be a crucial period in its formative history.[70] During 1613–15, a Church Convocation was held in Dublin in tandem with a meeting of the Irish Parliament; they were about to commit themselves to a greater definition on a national basis. This self-definition would be

---

64 Richard Stanihurst published a volume in response entitled, *Brevis praemunito pro futura concertatione cum Jacobo Usserio*, in which he attempted to purge his nephew of the 'disease of Calvinism.' The opening lines declare, 'I take my stand in the defence of the Catholic faith in this spiritual duel which sees an Irishman contending with an Irishman, a Dubliner with a Dubliner, and saddest of all, an uncle with his nephew.' C. Lennon, *Richard Stanihurst, the Dubliner* (Dublin, 1981), pp. 3–4; Stanihurst was unsuccessful of course, and Wood made the assertion, 'Tis thought and verily believed by some that Ussher was too hard for his uncle in controversial points relating to divinity.' A.A. Wood, *Athenae Oxonienses*, ed. P. Bliss (2 vols, London, 1820), vol. 2, p. 254.

65 *Alumni Dublinenses*, p. 833; Carr, *Life*, p. 57. Carr wrongly dates this event at 1601.

66 66 A. Barry, 'Ussher', *New Ireland Review*, Apr. 1896, vol. V: 75.

67 R.B. Hone, *Lives of Eminent Christians* (London, 1839), pp. 20–21.

68 *The prophecy of Bishop Ussher*, 1687; *Bishop Ussher's second prophesies which he delivered to his daughter on his sick bed*, 1681; *The Life of the Most Learned and pious divine, Bishop Ussher, with his wonderful prophesies* (London, 1712). These publications are largely similar in format and content. They vaguely claim a foreknowledge of the civil wars and the King's death, but mostly they concern Ussher's apparent prediction of a forthcoming Protestant massacre in Europe at the hands of Catholics. They no doubt served as a popular form of anti-Catholic propaganda.

69 Watson, *Typical Churchmen*, pp. 64–5.

70 *Alumni Dublinenses*, p. 833.

expressed in a series of distinctive articles[71] and Ussher, in his capacity as Professor of Divinity was chosen to draw them up.[72] Not only were these articles designed to annunciate a certain measure of autonomy (which might be characterised as a type of ecclesiastical home rule) but they also served to articulate the general Irish trend to a more strident form of Calvinism than was current in England. The Irish ecclesiastical historian, John T. Ball stated,

> That a motive to this course was a desire to act independently: to show that the Reformed Irish Church had for itself considered the doctrines respecting which it pronounced judgement, and had arrived in respect of them at its own conclusions, is certain; but there is reason also to think that with this was united a desire to speak upon the question of predestination more exclusively in favour of the views of the German Reformers than the English Articles did.[73]

The Irish Articles, which were published in 1615, consisted of one hundred and four statements, twenty of which can be regarded as original.[74] Included among these is Article LIX which denounces the papal claim to depose the King, whilst in Article LXXX the Pope is explicitly referred to as the 'man of sin.' Article LVI is strongly sabbatarian, against the express wishes of King James, and XCI prohibits the use of oil, salt or exorcism at baptism. Other Articles simply extend their English counterparts, CI and CIII–CIV tackle the final judgement and are elaborated to comprise not just the election of saints, but the damnation of sinners.[75]

In 1619, Ussher went to England in an official capacity for the first time; he was to be presented at Court.[76] Writers from Richard Parr to Charles R. Elrington have made much of the cloud under which he arrived[77] and R.B. Knox commented that the King received him 'somewhat frigidly' at odds with the usual warm welcome he afforded to scholars.[78] Apparently, aspersions had been cast by enemies to the effect

---

71   Previously the Church of Ireland had not articulated a confession, relying instead on a terse statement of belief as well as the twelve 1566 Articles.

72   Debate has always surrounded Ussher's role in drawing up the articles. Contemporary critic, Peter Heylin, claimed that they were part of Ussher's design to undermine the moderate tradition of English Calvinism. P. Heylin, *History of Presbyterianism* (London, 1670), XI, ch.33; a century later; Carte agreed that Ussher had not only inserted the precisian Lambeth articles into the Irish ones, but also 'several particular fancies and notions of his own.' T. Carte, *Life of Ormonde* (London, 1736), vol. 2, p. 77. Most modern scholars agree that he was too junior to be given such an onerous task and that he acted only as editor; recently, however, A. Capern makes a spirited defence of the 1615 Articles' Ussherian authorship. A. Capern, 'The Caroline Church, James Ussher, and the Irish Dimension', *Historical Journal*, XXXIX (1996): 57–85.

73   J.T. Ball, *The Reformed Church of Ireland* (London, 1886), pp. 99–100.

74   Knox, *Ussher*, p. 16.

75   *UW*, vol. 1, Appendix IV.

76   Sykes wrongly states that Ussher was introduced to James I for the first time in 1609, and was offered the Provostship which he declined. N. Sykes, 'Ussher as Churchman', *Theology*, (February, 1957): 62.

77   Parr, *Life*, p. 15. Elrington, *Life*, p. 51.

78   Knox, *Ussher*, p. 98.

that Ussher's low-Church Calvinism made him an enemy of authority. The royal visitor was, however, prepared once more, bearing with him a recommendation this time from the Lords of Council exonerating him from charges of puritanism and recommending him for appointment to the Privy Council.[79] Most commentators account for the King's aversion by pointing out that Ussher's close association with the 1615 Articles would have made him unpopular in some English quarters. In his history of Ireland, Thomas Leland typically remarked, 'Some attempts were made to prejudice the King against the compiler of those articles, which in so many instances were repugnant to his principles, but Ussher had the address to guard against the insinuations of his enemies.'[80] This version of events usually ends with their first conference after which King James was pleasantly surprised, declaring, 'That the knave Puritan was a bad, but the knave's Puritan an honest man.'[81] However, this narrative has all the hallmarks of biographical device in which the young aspirant overcomes the initial odds to eventually win over against the unfair hostility manufactured by his enemies. Besides, it rests on a shaky premise, that is that the king would have been averse to articles of faith that he himself had endorsed via his Lord Deputy, Chichester.[82] Whilst it was undoubtedly true that Ussher went to England that year with a letter discounting any rumours that discredited him, contemporary sources would suggest that this was more of a precaution than a concerted campaign to reinvent a public image. Biographers have all tended to overlook the patronage of Bishop Montgomery who met Ussher in London and appears to have done a good deal of work in his favour at Court even before his arrival.[83] Montgomery sought to introduce his charge to the Archbishops of London and Canterbury and by the time he brought him to kiss the royal hand, the king declared, 'I long grieved to see you, of whom I have heard a great deal of praise.'[84] A monarch with such an affection for theological discourse was predictably going to be impressed with such a learned practitioner and the Bishop of Meath clearly knew what he was doing in presenting

---

79 The letter reads, 'May it please your Lordships, The extraordinary merit of Mr Doctor Ussher prevaileth with us to offer him that favour (which we deny to many that move us) to be recommended to your Lordships; and we do it the rather, because we are desirous to set him right in his Majesties opinion, who it seemeth hath been informed, that he is somewhat transported with singularities, and unaptness to be conformable to the rules and orders of the church. We are so far from suspecting him in that kind, that we may boldly recommend him to your Lordships, as a man orthodox, and his majesty may be pleased to advance him.' Elrington, *Life*, p. 51.

80 T. Leland, *The History of Ireland from the Invasion of Henry II* (2 vols, Dublin, 1814), vol. 2, p. 459.

81 Elrington, *Life*, p. 51. In other words, Puritans are knaves, and therefore bad. Ussher is only a Puritan according to some knaves, in actual fact he is honest.

82 R. Mant, *History of the Church of Ireland from Reformation to Revolution* (2 vols, London, 1841), vol. 1, p. 388.

83 *Montgomery Mss* vol. 1, p. 106–8. Bishop William Montgomery was Ussher's predecessor at Meath. He was, according to the manuscripts, a particular favourite of James Stuart who referred to him as his 'black Ireland bishop.' There was much curiosity at court to observe the 'countenance and deference which the bishop afforded his young protégé.

84 Ibid., p. 107.

him. Montgomery describes the success of their first acquaintance, 'The King bade him rise and discoursed him on divers obtruse points of religion, and received learned pertinent answers, the King saying, "Doctor, I find you are sufficiently able, and therefore you must soon preach before me, as my chaplain, for I can advance you."'[85] Montgomery adds that the King would not allow excuses of youth, or the envy it might excite, and Ussher was admitted as personal chaplain. Ussher remained in this position at court until 1621 when, on Montgomery's death, he was nominated for the bishopric of Meath. On 2 December 1622, Ussher became a bishop.[86] He spent most of his episcopal years in England until 1626. That year, Primate Hampton died, and James was elevated to the see of Armagh. In the same year, that of his consecration, the new Lord Deputy arrived in Ireland, and was greeted with a sermon on the text, 'He beareth not the sword in vain.' The Catholic population naturally took umbrage and the mellée that ensued threatened the peace. Ussher was forced to preach an explanatory sermon.[87]

The fruits of these years before the primacy were two major works. The first, *A Discourse of the Religion anciently professed by the Irish and British* (written in the 1620s but not published until 1631) once more appealed to history, this time to prove the independence from Rome of the Irish and British Churches. The second was Ussher's most theological work, *An Answer to a Challenge made by a Jesuit in Ireland* (1625) which provides us with the clearest example of the author's position on the fundamentals of Christian faith. The Irish Jesuit, William Malone, had issued a manuscript challenge around 1617 or 1618, posing two questions. Firstly, if Protestants upheld the purity of doctrine and discipline for four or five hundred years after Christ, which Pope changed it? Secondly, how may the Protestant faith be true and yet deny chief articles of faith held by the patriarchs, such as prayers for the dead, free will, and purgatory? The dispute was much celebrated at the time and Malone published his own lengthy reply to Ussher in 1627 which Parr was to describe as 'stuffed with scurrilous, and virulent expressions against the Lord Primate.'[88]

Barely had the new Primate settled in Ireland than his first major pronouncement once more contravened official policy. In an effort to garner support from the Catholic population, Charles had dangled before them the tantalising prospect of the Graces. Feeling was high amongst them that full toleration would soon follow. Ussher called a meeting of twelve prelates in order to issue a protestation. Their protest fell on deaf ears and the Primate was quickly brought into line with English policy.

---

85   Ibid.
86   Elrington dates this at June 1621, he does however admit that this is only probable and that he has no evidence. Elrington, *Life*, p. 56; Buick Knox gives it the correct dating, showing that June 1621 was when he was nominated. Knox, *Ussher*, p. 28.
87   Elrington, *Life*, pp. 59–60.
88   Parr, *Life*, pp. 25–6. In spite of the somewhat barbed nature of much of this polemic in these works, relations between Ussher and Malone were much more affable than they cared to be let known. This is witnessed in the surviving correspondence in which they exchange valuable manuscript sources as well as pleasantries; See O'Sullivan, *Correspondence of Rothe and Ussher*, pp. 12–13.

During the early 1630s Ussher contributed to the contemporary debate which was increasingly dividing the Protestant world with the publication of his *History of Gotteschalk* (1631) in which he specifically dealt with the thorny theological issue of predestination which was proving such a current bug-bear. In this work, Ussher revives an account of the medieval monk whose insistence on double predestination had led to charges of heresy and eventual burning. This of course flew in the face of the 1628 royal moratorium on public discussion of the subject but Ussher took the double precautions of having it published in Latin and dedicating it to Laud to whom he claimed, rather disingenuously, that his volume was not intended to establish orthodoxy, but was rather a cautionary tale with the moral that such religious minutiae should not be pressed.[89]

It is not true, however, that Ussher was completely malleable in the hands of authority. He was a loyal servant rather than a blind slave, and if the servant would not countenance disobedience, there were occasions when he was not above a little foot dragging. William Brereton in his travels observed the less than full co-operation he gave to the royal obligations to read the *Book of Sports*. Though careful not to break the law, he was very far from active in his implementation.[90] The Primate was also not averse to the occasional moan. In a letter to secretary Coke, he is surprisingly forthright in his objection to what he sees as the increasingly autocratic nature of Charles's government, 'I see ... sometimes there is so much made of his majesty's letters that there must be no dispute made of them; simple obedience, they say, is required, and no inquiry into the legalness of the command.'[91] Such an outburst may not have been characteristic but it does prove Ussher was capable of thinking and acting independently. Nor was Ussher pusillanimous in the face of English authority; when the occasion provided, he was capable of being less than timorous. Even the daunting figure of Thomas Wentworth had cause to complain to Laud when Ussher angrily closed a theatre in Dublin that the Lord Deputy had himself sanctioned.[92]

In 1633, Wentworth had arrived in Ireland as not only the King's representative but also plenipotentiary of Archbishop Laud. Travelling as his chaplain was a Yorkshire cleric by the name of John Bramhall. High on their agenda was the replacement of the troublesome Irish Articles. The English party lost no time and a

---

89   *Cal.S.P.Ire., 1625–32*, p. 618. Ussher added, 'It [the publication] shows that the questions now afoot touching predestination, faith, and goodwill have of old been discussed by the Church and indifferently maintained by its doctors. If the moderation used by Remigius and others were now observed things would not have gone so far as they have done.' In a second letter to Laud dated 22 September, 1631, Ussher went so far as to declare that the history, 'does not differ much from that of Vossius ... ' Ibid., p. 631; he was perhaps hoping that Laud had not had time to read it. For his part, the Archbishop of Canterbury commented later that whilst he was flattered by the dedication, he did not agree, adding that whilst the monk may have been 'repressed ... with undue severity', this did not make him a moderate. *Cal.S.P.Ire., 1647–1660*, p. 227.

90   W. Brereton, *Travels in Holland, the United provinces, England, Scotland and Ireland* (London, 1634), p. 139.

91   Historic Manuscripts Commission, Cowper archive, ed. W.D. Fane (London, 1888), vol. 1, 10 August 1631, p. 438.

92   V.C. Wedgewood, *Strafford 1593–1641* (London, 1935), p. 179.

Church Convocation was called in 1634. What resulted will be dealt with in more detail in Chapter 8, suffice to say neither party was either completely victorious or entirely defeated. The resultant compromise did in fact characterise the established Church in Ireland for the rest of its history.

After the rigours of the 1634 Convocation Ussher acquiesced to a quieter life out of the capital, and out of the eye of the political storm, at his house and palace in Drogheda. We are afforded an insight into his existence here from Brereton who describes the episcopal palace near the east gate of the town as 'a neat handsome, and convenient house'[93], and his country residence at Termonfechon as,

> ... four square of wood, rough cast and not high; a handsome, plain, though long and narrow hall; two dining-rooms; a little neat gallery leads into the chapel ... there is a little pair of organs therein, in the garden cut into the grass bank are the words 'O man, remember the last great day.'[94]

In his church, Brereton mentions that the communion table was placed lengthways in the aisle and the chancel was 'in bad repair, not being used.' This clearly left Brereton with the impression that Ussher's worship was not particularly altar centred. As for his routine, he kept to his study seeing nobody from five in the morning to six in the evening. There were chapel services at 6 a.m. and 8 p.m. and his chief recreations were walking, riding, telling stories and the relation of wise and witty sayings.[95]

In 1640 Ussher entered the increasingly critical debate on the episcopacy that was escalating into war with Scotland. Ussher travelled to London for the purpose of submitting his work on the subject of bishops to press; he was never to return to Ireland. While he had been about the business of settling the Scottish question, the Gaelic Irish and Old English had set aside the differences that Ussher had always asserted and were laying siege to the country. In his absence, Ussher had become something of a refugee.[96] Just as Ussher's theological standpoint has been the subject of varying interpretations, so too has his role in the civil wars. On the one hand Conrad Russell portrays him as heading a moderate episcopal party which pushed for, but was unable to obtain, a compromise.[97] On the other, Ussher offered only a muddled alternative as he was increasingly unable to reconcile his anti-Catholic godliness with his extreme royalism.[98] Potentially, of course, Ussher provided the possibility of a mediator. His Calvinist background, as well as his association with

---

93 Brereton, *Travels*, pp. 134–40.
94 Ibid.
95 Ibid.
96 T. Johnston, J.L. Robinson and R.W. Jackson claimed that during the 1641 rebellion, unsuccessful plans had been laid for Ussher, 'to burn him, using his own books for fuel.' T. Johnston et al., *A History of the Church of Ireland* (Dublin, 1953), pp. 17–18; not that Ussher escaped completely, in October, his house was seized, his flocks were killed or driven away, and he was left all but destitute. Only his library remained and as a consequence he was obliged to sell or pawn all his plate and jewels. Wright, *Ussher Memoirs*, pp. 97–8.
97 C. Russell, *Fall of the British Monarchies, 1637–1642* (Oxford, 1991), pp. 249–51.
98 Knox, *Ussher*, chapter 4.

the 1615 Articles, ensured him the parliamentary ear, whilst his unquestionable loyalty to the throne ensured his high regard at court. This potential seems to have been recognised even at the outset, coinciding with his publishing mission. Ware reports that Ussher arrived in England at the invitation of 'some eminent persons on account of the then differences between the King and Parliament.'[99] Since the place of invitation was Warwick House, it is not difficult to conjecture who these eminent persons were. Indeed in a letter from George Wentworth to Bramhall, he wrote, 'Mr Prynne is very much with his Lordship, who lives at Warwick House whose company we have sometimes.'[100]

Ussher was employed by Parliament at a very early stage in the 1640s. The House of Lords appointed him to a committee to review the doctrine and discipline of the Church and reduce the current tension.[101] The committee produced a report which was published in 1641. It condemned not only such theological innovations as turning the communion table altarwise and calling it an altar as the 'grosse substance of Armianisme' and the '*electio est ex fide praevisa*' [election is on the basis of foreseen faith], but also the political notion that subjects pay any tax imposed on them 'though without law.'[102] It is perhaps surprising to see Ussher's name on the list of signatures to this pamphlet but these were the early stages of the conflict and an indication that Ussher was putting his years of experience of tight-rope walking in Ireland to use, and taking his role as mediator seriously. Yet even at this juncture, Ussher was gravitating naturally to the emerging royal and formal Church groups. Soon after his arrival he began to preach at Cheam in the Church of Dr Hacket,[103] who, though no Laudian, was a royalist and maintained the Book of Common Prayer throughout the parliamentary proscription. Elrington indicated their common position was one of 'loyalty to the monarchy' whilst 'refraining from emphasising details of doctrine and canonical obedience likely to alienate ...'[104] It was a position that Ussher was more or less consistent to throughout the various conflicts.

Parliament was naturally reluctant to recognise that they were losing such a prize and on 21 September 1643, they voted Ussher £400 per annum.[105] Buick Knox

---

99   J. Ware, *Whole Works concerning Ireland* (2 vols, London, 1739), vol. 1, pp. 108–9.

100   Elrington, *Life*, pp. 207–8; H. Trevor-Roper points out that the Earl of Warwick was 'the greatest patron of puritans and a close friend of Cromwell and Pym.' He adds, 'To all those men ... Ussher though absent in Ireland, though so discrete, so outwardly deferential to present power, had been a hero, perhaps the only hero of the Church hierarchy.' Trevor-Roper, *Catholics*, p. 148.

101   *Journal of the House of Lords* (London, 1879), vol. 4, pp. 177 and 180.

102   Lambeth Palace Library, Ms., 1603.25.13, *Touching Innovations in the Doctrine and Discipline of the Church of England* (London, 1641).

103   *Tanner Letters*, ed. C. McNeill (London, 1943), p. 142.

104   Elrington, *Life*, p. 57.

105   Knox, *Ussher*, p. 64; In November the previous year, Ussher had been awarded £200 out of the contribution monies for Ireland; *Cal.S.P.Ire., 1633–47*, p. 371. This vote by the Commons formalised and regularised his allowance. It was usually voted by both Houses at six monthly intervals; as late as October 1648 he was continuing to receive a favourable vote in the Commons for 'support, subsistence and encouragement of his studies.' Commons Journal,

has stated that parliament 'consistently failed to grasp Ussher's basic royalism, as also did Cromwell.'[106] Nonetheless, in 1643, when the Primate not only refused an invitation to join the Assembly of Divines but preached against it[107] the scales began to fall from the Parliamentary eyes. Whilst it is clear from Clarendon that in the Assembly's early days he did at least act as a go-between with Charles,[108] it is a measure of his growing disfavour that Dr Featley, who was the lone episcopal voice at the Assembly was sequestered, his books seized, and he was charged with spying after a letter from him to Ussher was intercepted.[109]

Ussher was by now resident at Oxford, lodging with Dr Prideaux, the Bishop of Worcester. Here he had previously acted as a middle man between the two sides.[110] However, disillusionment was steadily growing; certain quarters in Parliament were beginning to conclude that Ussher had let more worldly considerations cloud his better judgment. Edward Ludlow had been arrested in 1644 and brought to Oxford that he might speak with Ussher on the assumption that 'if he cannot work on you, I know not who can.'[111] The prisoner was less than impressed, ' those arguments which could not prevail with me, when used by others, were not likely to be of more efficacy from his, who in a business of such concernment had been diverted from the discharge of his duty by such low and sordid consideration.'[112] It is clear on the other hand that others in Parliament had not entirely given up on their presupposed ally. In an appeal in July 1645, the anonymous author recalls the prelate to his natural inclinations and the 'evident demonstrations you have formerly given to the truly godly ... that you are one of them.' According to the letter writer, if Ussher once considered his religion he would see that the King's party was made up of 'professed papists, superstitious, ignorant, and profane persons', whilst the members of the two Houses were for the most part 'regenerate men.'[113] Amongst the parliamentarian leaders, Ussher's role in the suppression of George Downham's work on predestination had not gone unnoticed during the trial of Laud. Prynne

---

VI, 260; in 1649, it was maintained at the same level. *The Diary of Bulstrode Whitelocke, 1605–1675*, ed. R. Spalding (Oxford, 1990), p. 24.

106   R.B. Knox, 'A Caroline Trio, Ussher, Laud, and Williams', *Church Quarterly Review*, (October–December, 1960): 453.

107   Knox, *Ussher*, p. 67; Commenting on this nomination, John Selden remarked 'they had as good inquire, whether they had best admit Inigo Jones ... to the company of mouse-trap-makers.' D. Neal, *The History of the Puritans* (5 vols, London, 1822), vol. 4, p. 131.

108   *Clarendon's History of the Rebellion*, ed. W.D. Macray (6 vols, Oxford, 1988 edition), vol. 3, p. 204.

109   *Cal.S.P.Dom., 1641–43*, p. 489; It is not quite true as Carr stated that Featley was imprisoned for the charge. Carr, *Life*, p. 338.

110   *Cal.S.P.Dom., 1640*, p. 722. Secretary Windebanke wrote to Charles I in September 1640 that the Earl of Warwick (the moderate Robert Rich) had arrived at Oxford and held a long conference with the Primate of Armagh.

111   *The Memoirs of Edward Ludlow, 1625–1672*, ed. C.H. Firth (2 vols, Oxford, 1894), vol. 1, p. 84.

112   Ibid.

113   Dr Williams Library, Ms.12.58.12(c), *A most pithy and Pious letter*, 10 July, 1645.

called the Primate 'Canterbury's tool'[114] and noted that his actions were all the more reprehensible since he ought to have known better, 'his commands in this kind were punctually executed by those Archbishops in both kingdoms, who should have most stoutly opposed his Arminian Innovations.'[115]

In spite of his steadfast loyalty to the Stuart household, Ussher left Oxford in 1645 in an attempt to get to his son-in-law's residence at Cardiff. It appears from a contemporary source that his departure was not on the best of terms. Sir Edward Langdale described in two letters how an army of around 1500 or 2000 unarmed men had arrived at Oxford, who knew no English and were conceived to be Irish. Ussher was clearly disconcerted that such negotiations between his Prince and such godless barbarians were taking place. Langdale states that the Archbishop was 'so much discontented that he will not come there again but is gone to live with his son who has a government in Wales. His excuse was to wait on the Prince, who, I hear, he has already left.'[116] The previous April, a petition had been presented to Charles by agents for the Protestants of Ireland. Its twenty-four points called for, amongst other things, the suppression of the confederate, together with 'exemplary punishment according to the law ... for the act of treason', as well as the establishment and maintenance of a Protestant army in Ireland.[117] On 5 November 1645, the Archbishop had preached before the King on the text Nehemiah 4:11, 'And our adversaries said, they shall not know, neither see, till we come in the midst among them, and slay them, and cause their work to cease.'[118] He pressed the King not to repose any trust in the Irish party 'that on the first opportunity they will serve us here, as they did the poor Protestants in Ireland.'[119] When Charles began his negotiations with these adversaries, Ussher's political world collapsed. He had placed complete trust in a monarch as the bulwark and unifying force around which Protestants must rally in order to face the real enemy which was Catholicism. Throughout the conflicts, Ussher had remained confident that the pervading 'factious spirit' was the work of priests, friars, and Jesuits. He added that 'if not timely weeded out by a severe suppressing them; we would either

---

114 W. Prynne, *History of the Tryall of Laud* (London, 1644), p. 13.

115 W. Prynne, *Canterburies Doome* (London, 1646), p. 172; Lamont argues that previous parliamentary faith in moderate bishops by people such as Prynne was based on a misconception of the extent of their disagreement with Laud, it was a faith that once dissipated resulted in an angry backlash. 'Prynne's attitude to Ussher faithfully charts his changing moods about moderate bishops: enthusiastic praise in 1630; pained criticism in 1660.' W.M. Lamont, *Marginal Prynne, 1600–1669*, 1963, pp. 23 and 77; In spite of this loss of faith, Prynne was still using the name of Ussher in 1648 as a means of defending himself against the standing committee for Somerset, causing the committee to comment, with a touch of irony, 'Sir, you may do well, having so many friends as you boast of ... ' *Cal.S.P.Dom., 1648–49*, p. 12.

116 *The Letter Books, 1644–45 of Sir Samuel Luke*, ed. H.G. Tibbutt (London, 1963), p. 199.

117 *The Humble proposition of the Agents for the Protestants in Ireland*, 18 April 1644. Thomason, E49(15).

118 Bernard, *Life*, p. 100.

119 Ibid.

tend to popery, or massacres or both ... '[120] In spite of the obvious disillusion he suffered after Charles' Irish negotiations, his fundamental loyalty remained.[121]

In the years that followed his departure from Oxford, Ussher's peregrinations took him to Cardiff and then back to the capital. In 1646, he had attempted but failed to get to the continent. He had managed to procure a passport but at the coast, Admiral Melton threatened to hand him over to Parliament.[122] On 21 September a petition of Ussher's reached the House of Lords describing his low condition and maintaining that there was nothing left in his estate towards his subsistence.[123] The next time he met his monarch was at Newport on the Isle of Wight whence Charles had called him, along with Joseph Hall, in order to consult with them before responding to propositions made by the Houses concerning Church government.[124] Parliament appears to have lost what little faith it had in the Archbishop by this time. John Crewe, one of the commissioners for the treaty indicated in a letter that he was pessimistic about his influence, 'The Primate of Armagh ... hath been with the King. The rest are not yet come. What will be the conclusion I am doubtful.'[125] Others in that camp were more scathing; a popular pamphlet produced in 1648 reported that Ussher's influence had now become nefarious, ' ... we had thoughts that the Primate of Ireland would have been moderate here, and done some offices, but since he came, none hath been so mischievous amongst all the King's Chaplains, insomuch that he hath prejudiced the Treaty.'[126] Contrary to this parliamentary conception of Ussher's influence on Charles there is evidence that he was once more working for a compromise solution. In a conversation with Richard Baxter he later relayed a discussion with the King at Newport. Asked if there was any validity in Presbyterian ordination, Ussher assured him, 'I can show your Majesty more, even where presbyters alone successively ordained bishops, as instanced in Hierom's [St

---

120 Ibid., pp. 90–91.

121 Characteristically he interpreted Charles's execution as a disaster for Protestants, 'from thence-forward the priest would with greater success advance their designs against the Church of England and Protestant Religion in general.' Parr, *Life*, p. 47.

122 Stuart, *Historical Memoirs*, p. 329.

123 *A perfect summary of chief passages in Parliament*, 20–27 September 1647, Thomason Tracts, E518/37.

124 The King had requested they be admitted, 'with all convenient speed, that so His Majesty may receive all possible information for the clearing of his judgment in a matter meerly touching him, as is that of his conscience', *His Majesties last message to the Parliament*, Thomason, E470(11), p. 688.

125 *Cal.S.P.Dom., 1643–48*, p. 300.

126 *A message from the Isle of Wight brought by Major Cromwell*, Nov 27, 1648, Thomason, E473(32), p. 1. The 'message' describes a sermon Ussher preached before the King on his birthday which caused the author of the tract to blush because of its fawning; in a published response, the charge was refuted and the pertinent question posed, 'whether the King was in a position to be flattered or whether Ussher could have expected any preferment from him if he was?' *A Detection of the falsehood in a pamphlet entitled – A message from the Isle of Wight brought by Major Cromwell*, Thomason, E475(15), pp. 3 and 5. A copy of the sermon on primogeniture is contained in the Huntington Library, California, Printed Collection, Ms. 243349.

Jerome] words ... of the presbyters of Alexandria choosing and making their own bishops.'[127] The royalist bishop had not cast off all his godly garments.

Whilst in London, Ussher lodged with Lady Peterborough in Covent Garden and preached regularly at Lincoln's Inn. In January 1648 it was reported that there had been ten coaches to hear Ussher's sermon. An impressive score, but one that was put into some perspective as the report added, 'there were above six-score on the last Thursday in Golden Lane to hear the players at the Fortune.'[128] From Lady Peterborough's residence he witnessed the death of Charles I.[129] He ever afterward kept the day as one of mourning.[130] Here, his earlier reputation amongst the godly, as tarnished as it had become, was enough to ensure his safety. Apart from some minor skirmishing, the most devastating resulting in the temporary loss of his library, he was left largely unmolested.[131] In spite of this much has been made by Ussher's biographers, from Parr to Carr, of the great man's harsh treatment under the Commonwealth. M.F. Day's portrait is typically pathetic.

> He was driven from his native land, withdrawn from the duties of his high station, deprived of his income, having no certain dwelling place, sharing for a time the torture of his unhappy sovereign, and dependent in the end on the Christian kindness of friends for shelter and support.[132]

Bernard claims that Ussher was silenced for a time during the interregnum, unless he preached in private houses. However the cloud did not remain long over his head, when 'with much a doe' he was permitted to preach at Lincoln's Inn. The Honourable Society gave him 'a competent maintenance' until failing eyesight meant he had to give it up.[133]

Regardless of this almost Dickensian image of the destitute scholar and statesman, there is evidence that his relationship with the Commonwealth authorities, especially Cromwell was a good deal more commodious. Parr reported that Ussher had been promised the lease of lands in Armagh, 'which my Lord Primate thought it no harm

---

127 *The Autobiography of Richard Baxter*, ed. N.H. Keeble (London, 1974), p. 141.

128 *The Kingdom's Weekly Intelligences*, 18–25 January 1648, Thomason Tracts, E423(23).

129 R.B. Knox, 'The English Civil War, Archbishop Ussher, and his Circle', *The London Quarterly and Holborn Review*, Jan. 1962: 64.

130 Elrington, *Life*, p. 261.

131 Parr, *Life*, p. 50.

132 Day, *Archbishop Ussher*, p. 38.

133 Bernard, *Clavi*, p. 50; No date is given for this but Rushworth mentions 'A great debate was in the House, whether Dr Ussher should continue preaching at Lincoln's Inn, he having formerly adhered to the enemy against Parliament; and the House was divided; and it was carried in the affirmative, he taking the Negative Oath.' J. Rushworth, *Historical Collections of Private Passages of State, Weighty Matters of law*, ed. Necomb (8 vols, London, 1701), vol. 7, p. 937; It would seem that Ussher had been given leave to preach in January 1647 but it appears to have been granted in conjunction with a position in the Assembly of Divines; since he refused the latter he could not take up the former. *Lord's Journals*, IX, p. 646.

to accept considering it was but his own.[134] Then, in 1655, the Primate received a fulsome response to a request for a lease of land in County Louth for his son-in-law, Sir Timothy Tyrrell. Cromwell granted the petition concluding, 'We have thought fit to recommend him and his business to your care and consideration, and desire that you will favour him in that or any other desire he hath to make to you ... '[135] This, in spite of the fact that in September the previous year, Ussher had been asked to attend a Grand Committee for the drawing up of fundamentals of faith. The offer was once more rejected.[136] There is even evidence that the divine-right monarchist and episcopal champion made some concessions to the republican ideal. Carr mentioned that during these years he dropped 'the empty title' of Archbishop and Primate, under the circumstance a pragmatic gesture.[137] Though it is hard to take at face value Bulstrode Whitelocke's account of an anti-clerical sermon from Ussher,[138] it would seem that earlier accounts of clashes between Cromwell and Ussher require some qualification.[139] In January 1656, Ussher represented the episcopal clergy to the Lord Protector when an edict had been issued banning them from exercising

---

134   Parr, *Life*, p. 74. Parr does however maintain that this was received only posthumously.

135   *The Writings and Speeches of Oliver Cromwell*, ed. W. Abbot (4 vols, Oxford, 1947), vol. 3, pp. 713–14.

136   The historian and royalist, Robert Waring left an account of Ussher's attitude to the offer. 'There is a committee for moulding and establishing religion, ten of the House with ten other Assistants that they should choose to themselves among the divines, amongst whom Lord Broghill having chosen for his assistant Angel (as he termed him) the Bishop of Armagh, he was not without a grave check rejected; as if he should countenance a Lay Synod that thought the Assembly not fit company for him, and set up a New Religion with them who had destroyed the old Religion and Episcopacy.' *Tanner Letters*, p. 388; Lord Broghill, 3rd Earl of Cork, made the acquaintance of Ussher in 1654; he was highly regarded by Cromwell. According to Knox, 'his relationship with the Primate was based on the misconception that Ussher shared his views on religious toleration. Knox, 'Ussher Circle': 65. However, they appear to be close enough for the Archbishop to earn the sobriquet 'Angel.'

137   Carr, *Life*, p. 351; One of Ussher's correspondents was clearly distressed by the omission. 'What, I said within myself, has become of the Archbishop and Primate of all Ireland? Alas! And can you suffer your honours to be thus taken from you with so much patience and without resistance' *UW*, vol. 16, pp. 124–5.

138   At the funeral of John Selden, according to Whitelocke, Ussher described the great man approvingly not only as a 'prodigy of learning and hospitality', but also 'no lover of the clergy and their pride and greatness.' *The Diary*, p. 403. It is hard to imagine the intermittent years had seen quite such a political conversion; besides, such a turnabout would almost certainly have been greeted with a high profile promotion, not to mention an upturn in fortune.

139   Parr was anxious to deliver his subject from the hands of the puritans where he had been placed by his first biographer, Bernard. He reports that Ussher described Cromwell as 'This false man, ... he will have little cause to glory in his wickedness, for the King will return; though I shall not live to see it, ... The Government both in Church and State is in confusion, the Papists are advancing their Projects, and making such advantage as will hardly be prevented.' Parr, *Life*, p. 76; Smith gives an equally damning account of Ussher's opinion. 'He often expressed the opinion that the usurpation was like that of the Grecian Tyrants, and would obtain a similar fate; just as it began with an army, so it usually ended with the

their ministerial function. Though he was unsuccessful, he was at least dismissed with 'professions of civility and kindness.'[140] Cromwell was, at some stage during his protectorate, to think highly enough of Ussher as to consult him on a proposed Protestant mission to Ireland.[141] Indeed it is clear from Bernard, who was almoner to Cromwell, that this relationship caused some resentment in the episcopal camp. The questioning of his loyalty caused the Primate much pain at the end of his life. Bernard wrote, 'I think he never resented any thing more deeply, not living many months after unto which the ungrateful censures and rash extravagant language of such, whom he thus endeavoured to serve, added the more to it.'[142]

Ussher was never a trusted member of the Cromwellian regime, nor was he a late convert to the cause of English republicanism. Yet it is a measure of his repute as a godly scholar that given his extreme royalism and unwavering defence of the episcopacy he was yet indulged at some length by the arch-iconoclast of these very ideologies. Perhaps the greatest measure of this indulgence is the elaborate efforts the republican government went to in honouring the great archiepiscopal monarchist at this death in 1656. *Mercurius Politicus* reported that, at the request of Cromwell, on the 9 April;

> ... the funeral of that reverend, pious and learned man, Dr Ussher ... will be upon Thursday. The Body to be brought that morning from Ryegate to George's Church ... such friends as intend to honour the funerall may be pleased to meet the corps and from thence to Somerset House in the Strand, where at one of the Clock those of the ministry and others conveniently meet to accompany the corps to Westminster Abbey, there to be interred in the chapel. And Dr Bernard of Grays-Inn is to preach the funeral sermon.[143]

On the same day the poet laureate Payne Fisher went to Oxford to deliver a funeral oration in Christ Church Hall.[144] The Epitaph inscribed on his grave at Westminster was written by the poet John Quarles, it reads, 'Reader, these narrow confines doe contain, Rome's envy, Ireland's loss and England's gain.'[145]

---

usurper's death.' T. Smith, *Vitae quorundam eruditissimorum et illustrium Virorum* (London, 1707), p. 109.

140 Elrington, *Life*, pp. 273–4; It seems that on his first visit Ussher even managed to solicit a favourable response, procuring a promise that clergy would be unmolested provided they did not interfere with government. However, at their second meeting Ussher was told that on the advice of his council he had decided not to grant indulgences to men 'who were restless and implacable enemies to his person and government.' Collier, *Ecclesiastical History*, p. 868.

141 Neal, *Ecclesiastical History*, vol. 4, p. 132.

142 Bernard, *Clavi*, p. 53.

143 *The English Revolution*, III, no. 304, 3 April –10 April 1656, Newsbooks 5, vol. 13, p. 84.

144 Elrington, *Life*, p. 279.

145 J. Quarles, *An elegie on the Most Reverend and Learned James Ussher* (London, 1656), p. 7.

Chapter 2

John Bramhall

Some obscurity surrounds the early life of John Bramhall; indeed even the date of his birth initiates some argument.[1] The information we have at our disposal is once more largely thanks to the research of W. Ball Wright who has provided us with so much valuable research into the Usshers. From the register of St Giles Church he discovered that John had been baptised in that chapel on November 18, 1594.[2] His mother's name was not recorded, but his father was Peter.[3] The Bramhalls were originally a Cheshire family who, according to one biographer, Arthur West Hadden, were 'ancient and genteel'[4], and according to Alexander Gordon, were of Bramhall Hall in that county.[5] Wright tells us they settled in Yorkshire sometime in the sixteenth century, though precisely why is not recorded.[6] Bramhall attended the King Edward VI Grammar School at Pontefract, of which little is known, except that despite its location in the white rose county, it was a Tudor bastion. Wright wrote of Bramhall's early years 'being brought up under the shadow of that mighty fortress of the House of Lancaster.' It appears that the young student was to later share a common enemy with his *alma mater* since Wright adds that it 'afterwards was besieged and dismantled by the Cromwellians.'[7]

On 21 February, 1608, the youthful scholar went up to Sidney Sussex College, Cambridge, which owned property in Pontefract and drew many of its students from that town.[8] It was the same college attended, eight years later by Oliver Cromwell, and it was complained of by Laud in 1628 as 'a nursery of Puritanism.'[9] Sidney Sussex had been founded in 1596 by the Countess of Sussex and, like Trinity in Dublin, it was with the express purpose of training a preaching ministry. Also, like

---

1   There is a dispute over the year of Bramhall's birth. R. Mant claims that it must have been 1593, because a rule enacted by Laud in 1633 said no one under the age of forty was to be elected bishop, yet he apologises for violating this in the case of Bramhall. Bramhall was recommended for the bishopric on 14 May, 1634. See Mant, *Church History*, vol. 1, p. 471; According to the International Genealogical Index, John Bramhall was baptised on 18 November, 1594 in Pontefract, Yorkshire, (http://www.familysearch.org).

2   Wright, *Yorkshire Divine*, p. 4.

3   Ibid., Though his mother's maiden name is unknown, it appears that George Walker (the famous mayor of Derry) was Bramhall's cousin on his mother's side. Vesey, *Athanasius*, p. 5.

4   Hadden, *Life*, p.iv.
5   *DNB*, (1968), vol. 2, p. 111.
6   Wright, *Yorkshire Divine*, p. 3.
7   Ibid., p. 5.
8   Ibid.
9   J. Morley, *Oliver Cromwell* (London, 1900), p. 9.

Trinity, it seems that its ethos was distinctly low-Church and it quickly developed a reputation as a puritan establishment. This reputation caused some concern for Queen Elizabeth who questioned Sir Philip Sidney on the erection of this 'puritan foundation.' He replied, 'No, madam, far be it for me to countenance any thing contrary to your established laws, but I have set an acorn, which when it becomes an oak, God alone knows what will be the fruit thereof.'[10]

At Sidney Sussex, Bramhall came under the tutelage of a Mr Howlett[11] who Jeremy Taylor described as an important influence and 'a grave and worthy man.' Bramhall was not only able to repay his tutor as a 'fruitful plant by his great progress in his studies', but later as his career advanced in Ireland he 'made him another return of gratitude, taking care to provide a good employment for him ... '[12] Little is known of Howlett except that Bramhall was able to describe him to Laud as a man who 'has no enemies, and moderate tenets.'[13] In spite of his background as a tutor in such an apparently Calvinistic establishment, Howlett was clearly well able to make his way on the *via media* and flourish in the Laudian Church. The other mentor of Bramhall at Cambridge was the equally moderate Samuel Ward who was master of the College, and later Lady Margaret Professor of Divinity.[14] Even more of a formative influence than Howlett, Ward was, according to the biographer the 'single influence of his life.'[15] Patrick Collinson regarded Ward as the type of puritan prone to train the organ of conscience on his daily life.[16] Another of Bramhall's biographers rather anachronistically described Ward as an Anglo–Catholic, but the truth is that he is much more difficult to label than this.[17] He had attended the Synod of Dort as a representative of England.[18] This synod had of course condemned Arminianism, and he was never to lose his antipathy to this form of Protestantism. We know most about his theology from his correspondence with Ussher to whom he wrote with concern about the growing influence of Laud and the steady progress of Arminianism.[19] On the other hand, he disputed with William Bedell on the efficacy of infant baptism,[20] and

---

10 W. Haller, *The Rise of Puritanism* (London, 1957), p. 20.

11 *DNB*, (1968), vol. 3, p. 203.

12 J. Taylor, *A Sermon preached in Christ's Church, Dublin, July 16, 1663, at the Funeral of the Most Reverend Father in God, John late Lord Archbishop of Armagh. BW*, vol 1, p. lvii; Bramhall was able to secure for him the Deanery of Cashel. *Original letters of The Church of Ireland*, ed. E.P. Shirley, 'Bramhall to Laud, July 12 1638', (London, 1851), p. 58.

13 *Cal.S.P.Ire.*, Ibid.

14 *DNB*, (1968), vol. 20, p. 792.

15 McAdoo, *Bramhall*, p. 2. This biography was written in 1963 as a celebration of Bramhall's life and influence on the tercentenary of his death.

16 P. Collinson, *The Elizabethan Puritan Movement* (Oxford, 1967), p. 435.

17 Sparrow-Simpson, *Bramhall*, pp. 1–2.

18 He was according to Episcopus the most learned member of the whole body. *DNB*, (1968), vol. 59, p. 335.

19 *UW*, vol. 15, pp. 508–9.

20 Ward argued that baptism involved the absolution of sin, this was obviously unpalatable to Calvinists who looked to a personal, adult commitment to God. *U.W.* vol. 15, pp. 512–20.

when later conflict arose he was imprisoned by the Presbyterian majority for refusing to take the Covenant.[21] Ward was clearly of the moderate puritan mould, Calvinistic, yet strongly attached to the establishment, low-Church, yet largely appreciative of all genuine reflections of broad Protestantism, and in this he resembles in more ways than one his long-term correspondent, James Ussher.

Whatever Ward's theological leanings, he left on his charge a clear stamp of his educational philosophy; like the young Ussher, Bramhall was imbued with a strong appreciation of the early Church scholars. Just as Ussher had learnt from Sleidan, Bramhall learned from Ward that patristics provided the key to their present interfaith disputations. Bramhall later wrote,

> When I was a young student in theology, Dr Ward declared his mind unto me to this purpose, that it was impossible that the present controversies of the Church should be rightly determined or reconciled without a deep insight in the doctrine of the primitive Fathers, and a competent skill in school theology. The former affordeth us a right patter, and the second smootheth it over and planeth away the knots.[22]

In spite of the seemingly moderate complexion of his educators, Laud's 'puritan nursery' clearly had some effect on Bramhall's intellectual development. This found expression in that most conspicuous of puritan hallmarks, virulent anti-Catholicism. Bramhall had graduated B.A. in 1612 and M.A. in 1616. In 1630 Bramhall was made Doctor of Divinity.[23] John Vesey tells us that one of the examiners was his uncle George Walker. He later provided his biographer with information on the thesis: it was summed up by John Vesey as the Pope far from being 'an infallible pilot, in the seas of controversy, that he looked on him as either a mother of the Nurse that gives life or nourishment to all or most of those doctrines, that have so long disquieted the Christian world ... .'[24] Neither was this anti-papal stance a purely academic one. Once more, his early career reflects aspects of Ussher's as he was drawn into the world of controversy. In 1623, Bramhall had accepted a challenge to a public debate with two Catholic priests at Northallerton. The topic of discussion was transubstantiation and Bramhall apparently won the day by getting the priest to say that eating was drinking and drinking was eating. Vesey rather alarmingly, if not implausibly, tells us that this fatal error caused the death of one of the priests when he tried to quench his thirst with a loaf.[25] What is certain from the incident is that in the 1620s, Bramhall was just as eager to enter the confessional fray as Ussher, even in times when it went against the prevailing mood of the country. He was quick to remind Richard Baxter that this episode took place in 1623 when the King was in Spain negotiating a possible marriage, 'I adventured, with more zeal than discretion when the religion of England seemed to be placed *in aequilibrio*.[26] It proved, claimed Bramhall, that

---

21   *DNB*, (1968), vol. 20, p. 792.
22   *BW*, vol. 3, p. 568.
23   *Alumni Cantabrigienses*, eds J. Venn and J. A. Venn, (Cambridge, 1992), p. 204.
24   Vesey, *Athanasius*, p. 5.
25   Ibid., pp. 3–4.
26   *BW*, vol. 3, p. 540; the renowned Presbyterian writer Richard Baxter had written an attack on Arminianism entitled, *The Grotian Religion Discovered*, in 1658. In this work,

he was neither a crypto-Catholic nor an opportunist but rather that he had ever been a stout defender of their common faith. Three years after the Northallerton incident he took up the cudgel once more when called upon to preach before the Northern Synod. Bramhall chose as his subject 'the pope's unlawful usurpation of jurisdiction over the Britannic Churches.'[27]

On 24 December 1615, Bramhall had been ordained deacon. Then on 22 December the following year, priest, by Archbishop Tobias Matthew.[28] Vesey maintained that the new curate's first appointment was in the city of York, then later in the country at a good living called Elvington or Etevington, he was presented by Christopher Wandesforde who was afterwards Lord Deputy of Ireland.[29] However, Wright had evidence that casts doubts on Vesey as an authority. From the parish register of St Martin's-cum-Gregory, in Micklegate, York, he found that 'John Bramhall was inducted by Mr Hoache and took possession of this parish church (as rector) the 2nd day of August, 1617.'[30] Another document unearthed by Wright was Bramhall's marriage license dated 10 November, 1618.[31] The license gives his wife's name as Helen Collingwood, though previous biographers had named her Halley. This may indicate that she had married before. In any event, she was well established enough to provide Bramhall with a good library though she may have regretted it since she apparently became a very early widow to scholarship. John Vesey tells us, 'he was so wedded to his studies, that all the temptations of a new-married life could not divorce him from them.'[32]

After the Micklegate rector had caused such a stir at Northallerton in 1623, he was summoned before Archbishop Matthew, who after ticking him off for accepting so public a challenge without authority, made him his personal chaplain. Wright tells us that in this capacity, and due to his patron's ill health, the lion's share of the administration fell to Bramhall.[33] In the same year he was appointed one of the York High Commissioners.[34] During these years, according to A.W. Hadden, 'he was frequently chosen arbitrator between contending parties, and by that and his good behaviour in all other respects, he obtained so much honour and interest, that there was scarcely any public transaction over which he had not a considerable influence.'[35] As testimony to this high standing in his locality there was a high degree of loyalty to the established authority engendered by Bramhall's good administration. It was, claims Collins, to pay dividends in the ensuing conflict, 'Some sign of this influence

---

Baxter accused the Laudian wing of the Church in general, and Bramhall in particular, of attempting to bring the Church of England into the Roman fold.

27 Wright, *Yorkshire Divine*, p. 9.
28 Wright, *Yorkshire Divine*, p. 6.
29 Vesey, *Athanasius*, p. 3.
30 Wright, *Yorkshire Divine*, p. 6.
31 Ibid., pp. 6–7.
32 Vesey, *Athanasius*, p. 3.
33 Wright, *Yorkshire Divine*, p. 9.
34 Hadden, *Life*, p.v.
35 Ibid., pp.iv–v. This influence extended to the choosing of a member for Parliament.

of Bramhall's may be seen in the fact that no less than fifty-two land owners within the liberties of Ripon rose on behalf of the King in 1645.'[36]

Whilst acting as chaplain to Archbishop Matthew, he was made prebendary of York after Ripon and a master of the hospital of St John the Baptist.[37] Here he earned the respect not just of the land owners but also of the ordinary people, due to heroic actions during a particularly bad bout of plague. Not only did Bramhall remain amongst them but he visited infected houses in order to baptise their children.[38] Such saintly acts of courage enhanced a growing reputation as a churchman and scholar. Under these circumstances it was only a matter of time before a prebend in the diocese of York would be considered too lowly to contain such a jewel. As events transpired his value was recognised by a fellow Yorkshire man who had just been given charge of an important mission. Jeremy Taylor tells us in his requiem oration, 'While he lived there, he was like a diamond in dust, or Lucius Quinctius at the plough, his low fortune covered a most valuable person, till he became observed by Sir Thomas Wentworth.'[39]

Wentworth had of course been made Lord Deputy of Ireland and Taylor claimed that in Bramhall he saw a 'fit instrument' to serve his designs, that was 'the reformation of religion, and the reparation of the broken fortunes of the Church.'[40] It had been usual among biographers to follow Taylor on this point that Wentworth was the early patron of Bramhall; one example described the choice occurring as the new Lord Deputy sought to furnish his mission with industrious and like-minded men, 'Before he faced his tremendous task, Wentworth looked round for congenial supporters; able men who shared his convictions, and would render his undertaking less impossible. Bramhall was already known to him in his work in the North.'[41] It would seem that Bramhall was brought to his attention by his assistant, Sir Christopher Wandesforde,[42] however, whilst Wandesforde may have been responsible for bringing Bramhall into the Wentworth fold, it is also certain that Archbishop Laud played an important role in his promotion. The Presbyterian historian James Seaton Reid included this point in a list of 'animadversions' he held against Elrington's biography of Ussher. It was Laud he claimed, not Wentworth who was Bramhall's patron. The point is an important one for a Presbyterian like Reid to make against Elrington's Anglican version of events because it proves to Reid that Bramhall was part of the English establishment's scheme to Laudianize the Irish Church. As proof, Reid cites a letter from Laud to Wentworth as early as 1631 prompting his patronage. He asks, 'Now my Lord, what do you, or have you done about Dr Bramhall for the prebend; for my Lord of Durham is actually translated and

---

36   Collins, *Typical Churchmen*, fn. p. 84.
37   Vesey, *Athanasius*, p. 4; *DNB*, (2004), vol. 7, p. 313.
38   W.E. Collins, 'John Bramhall', in W.E. Collins (ed.), *Typical English Churchmen* (London, 1902), fn. p. 84.
39   *BW*, vol. 1, p. lviii.
40   Ibid., p. lix.
41   Sparrow-Simpson, *Bramhall*, p. 6.
42   McAdoo, *Bramhall*, p. 1.

so out of it?' Reid asks, 'Was not this the act of a vigilant and zealous patron?'[43] A further letter written in 1633 seems to confirm the impression that Laud was, if not instrumental in appointing Bramhall to Strafford's team, he was at the very least his strong advocate. The letter to Wentworth vindicates the appointment, 'And for Dr Bramhall, I think, with your Lordship's direction and countenance, he will be able to do any service that can be put upon him. And as there is enough to do, so I presume you will set him on work.'[44] Hugh Trevor-Roper also argued that Laud was the key figure in choosing Bramhall as he cast around him for a suitable agent in Ireland 'one who would be not a scholar only, like Ussher, nor a saint like Bedell, but an administrator.' He found this man in the curate of Ripon. Trevor-Roper claimed that Strafford and Bramhall represented perfectly the sort needed by Laud to execute his designs, 'Two more valuable confederates Laud could not have wished to discover. Indeed, they were more than confederates. They took the work out of Laud's hands, and merely left him to applaud the fait accompli.'[45]

It may not now be certain how Bramhall came to the attention of Laud[46] but it is certain that by the early 1630s he had made quite an impression on the bishop of London who was Primate in everything but name. Whatever the circumstance of his initial employment with Strafford, they complemented each other well, and it is testimony indeed that at the end of his life, even as the fruits of his endeavours proved so disastrous, Wentworth was able to claim, 'If I were to begin the world again ... I would use him still.'[47] Bramhall was invited to accompany Wentworth to Ireland as his chaplain in 1633, and he accepted the invitation in spite of an impending English promotion and in spite of the advice of his friends.[48] The same year he left England after apparently resigning all his prebends[49] and shortly after his arrival in Ireland he

---

43 J.S. Reid, *Seven Letters to the Reverend C.R. Elrington occasioned by animadversions in his life of Ussher* (Glasgow, 1849), pp. 32–3.

44 W. Laud, *The Works of the Most Reverend Father in God, sometime Lord Archbishop of Canterbury*, ed. J. Bliss (7 vols, London, 1847–60), vol. 6, p. 321.

45 H. Trevor-Roper, *Archbishop Laud* (London, 1962), pp. 239–41. Trevor-Roper goes on to credit the workman-like efforts of Bramhall in an otherwise unflattering assessment. 'He was a hard and bigoted character not unlike Laud, of mean presence and sharp tongue; but he was a tireless administrator of relentless efficiency, far better qualified to carry out Laud's policy in a backward country than Ussher or Bedell.'

46 John McCafferty conjectured that it was Archbishop Neile who was the link since Vesey mentioned that he and Bramhall were 'in good esteem', and Neile had at the beginning of 1632 been removed from Winton to York. However, McCafferty seems to have wrongly dated the letter of 30 July from Laud to Wentworth, which was actually written in 1631 and not in 1632, as stated. J. McCafferty, 'John Bramhall and the reconstruction of the Church of Ireland', unpublished Ph.D. Thesis, 1997, p. 11.

47 J. Rushworth, *The Trial of Strafford* (London, 1680), p. 123.

48 Vesey, *Athanasius*, p. 7. Vesey enigmatically remarks that he was offered to be made King's chaplain in ordinary by 'some noblemen.'

49 Reid pointed out that though resigning his prebends in England was a stipulation of his appointment and though it has been much eulogised as an example of his disinterest, it is clear that he did not do so. The evidence for this is contained in a letter from Laud to Wentworth on Bramhall's elevation to the episcopacy that he must leave what he has in England, 'that bishopric being good needs no commendams.' And, so concluded Reid, 'Thus

was assigned to be treasurer of Christ Church Dublin.[50] He was further graced some months later with the Archdeaconry of Meath which was claimed to be 'the best in that kingdom.'[51]

Wentworth's mission in regard to the Irish Church, in which Bramhall was being positioned to maximise his role, had a clear agenda. They were to restore it to a position in which it could evangelise the Catholic population. In order to pursue this they conceived that two things were principally necessary. Firstly, the physical and financial rejuvenation that might elevate it into being a credible alternative to the majority faith, and secondly the Church in Ireland would be given the surer foundation of complete union within the Anglican fold. This meant essentially the scrapping of the Irish Articles and canons in favour of the English.[52] Strictly speaking, Wentworth did not embrace Laud's theological views, something of which the Archbishop of Canterbury was only too aware, chaffing him in his correspondence for his unwillingness to genuflect.[53] As John McCafferty illustrated, Wentworth's enthusiasm for restoration of the Church to a position of power and respect was founded on his belief that the Church and crown 'mutually prosper and decrease together.'[54] Besides, it has been demonstrated that Wentworth associated religious independence as an affront to lawful authority.[55]

One of Bramhall's first duties in Ireland was a regal visitation in his capacity as one of the King's Commissioners.[56] Laud received graphic reports on these occasions which set out the extent of the spiritual and structural decay of the Irish Church in salacious language. Churches lay in ruin while ministers were the 'very ebullition of Scotland'[57]. Bramhall set about an immediate economic campaign with an impressive energy and not a little success. Laudian policy clearly had the material infrastructure of the Church high on its agenda. On 26 May 1634, Bramhall received a more public recognition for his industry when he was consecrated bishop of Derry in the chapel of Dublin Castle. The ceremony was presided over by Ussher and

---

vanishes the dream of Bramhall's disinterestedness in coming to Ireland, a voluntary and disbeneficed man.' Reid, *Seven Letters*, pp. 34–5.

50 Wright, *Yorkshire Divine*, p. 9. Hadden points out that Wentworth immediately recognised Bramhall's business acumen and employed him not just in a public capacity, but in his own family affairs. Hadden, *Life,* p.v.

51 *BW*, vol. 1, p.v.

52 A. Ford, 'Dependent or Independent: the Church of Ireland and its colonial context, 1536–1649', *The Seventeenth Century*, vol. X, no.2, (August 1995): 174.

53 Laud, *Works*, 'Laud to Wentworth, 12 May 1635', vol. 7, p. 132, 'As for the name of Jesus, since they will have no joint in their knees to honour Him, they may get the gout in the knees not to serve themselves. I doubt, if the truth were known, you to humour the place and time have forborne your duty in public in that behalf. And if you have I shall wish the gout may continue in your knee till you be better minded to honour Jesus with it.'

54 J. McCafferty, 'John Bramhall and the Church of Ireland in the 1630s', in, A. Ford et al. (eds), *As by Law Established* (Dublin, 1995), p. 100.

55 H.F. Kearney, *Strafford in Ireland, 1533–1641* (Manchester, 1959), p. 113.

56 Vesey, *Athanasius*, p. 7.

57 Trinity College Dublin Ms. 1697, 'Letter of Bramhall to Laud, 1631–39, relating to the Church', paper vi.

Archbishop Dopping.[58] Some months earlier Laud had instigated an act whereby forty years of age was to be the minimum age requirement for episcopal preferment and it therefore caused a little inconvenience that he was flouting his own requirement so soon after it had been passed. Some three–hundred years later, Richard Mant was still expressing surprise, 'It is not a little remarkable, that the first vacancy which occurred amongst the Irish bishops, caused a deviation from the rule thus formally announced.'[59] In a letter to the Lord Deputy, Laud showed that he was willing to go to not inconsiderable trouble in order to get his man nominated.

> Now, my Lord, to your great business: since the Bishop of Derry is dead, I have [though against the rule which I have lodged with his Majesty] moved earnestly for Dr Bramhall to succeed him, and given him the reasons why, for his own service, and the good of the Church in that kingdom, he should dispense in this particular for the Doctor's being a little too young.[60]

Laud goes on to say that the effort he has made on his behalf has all been a service to Wentworth and he adds that the new prelate 'must not leave, till that Church be better settled ... .'[61] Mant need not have been so surprised; the pattern of replacing Calvinists such as George Downham in Derry, with candidates who were cut from a Laudian cloth was to be much repeated. Besides there was a rush to elevate Bramhall since the forthcoming convocation of that year was set to settle the issue of divergent articles, the Archbishop of Canterbury was very anxious to get his man into the Upper House.

Bramhall's elevation only hastened the transformation of the Irish Church and when he had received the purple cloak he then became the key figure behind all future preferments, according to Vesey recommending 'stout and prudent' persons to carry out their work.[62] In 1634, George Webb, the bishop of Limerick died, he was replaced by the Laudian chaplain to the King.[63] When Robert Echlin died the following year, Bramhall wrote to Laud, 'The united bishopric of Down and Connor is vacant ... . If a Disciplinarian should succeed him, farewell hopes of better order and revenue.'[64] Henry Leslie was found to be a very suitable replacement. John Atherton became bishop of Waterford, William Chappel received the better part of Cork and after the bishop of Elphin proved tolerant of Puritans he was replaced by the high Anglican John Maxwell. By 1640 the Irish episcopacy had been transformed.[65] J.S. Reid voiced a general low-Church complaint that was still evident even in the nineteenth century.

---

58 M. Perceval-Maxwell, *The Outbreak of the Irish Rebellion of 1641* (London, 1994), p. 24; Wills, *Distinguished Irishmen*, vol. 4, p. 168.
59 Mant, *Church History*, vol. 1, p. 472.
60 Laud, *Works*, 'Laud to Wentworth, 14 May 1634', vol. 6, pp. 375–6.
61 Ibid.
62 Vesey, *Athanasius*, p. 13.
63 Kearney, *Strafford in Ireland*, p. 113.
64 *Hastings Manuscripts*, ed. J. Harley (London, 1928), vol. 4, p. 69.
65 Kearney, *Strafford in Ireland*, pp. 112–13.

None but men of Arminian and intolerant principles were promoted, while, at the same time, every means was employed to discountenance and harass, not merely the professed non-conformists, but even all moderate Episcopalians, who did not fully coincide in the views of doctrine and modes of worship now obtaining the ascendancy in England.[66]

It is indicative of the general situation that Bramhall now possessed a more influential voice in Ireland than his own Primate whose nominations were either ignored or denied. In 1634, Ussher had recommended Dean Andrews to the see of Limerick. Writing to Strafford, Laud explained his reaction to such an unsuitable nomination.

'Tis true, the Primate hath recommended Dean Andrews to me, but 'tis upon the old stock, and very fairly, and I have returned him an answer, fit for me, and true from the King. I came to know that man's zeal before these last letters of yours described him, I doubt it is not much according to knowledge.[67]

Ussher made one last effort to tip the scales in favour of the low Church. This occurred in 1634 at the Convocation of established clergymen. Here the apparently unstoppable force of 'thorough' was set to meet the unmovable object of Irish Calvinism. The Laudians, using Bramhall as their main agent set themselves the task of building a new doctrinal framework in order to provide a foundation for not only raising the established theology but also facilitating a more general Anglicization by erasing the kind of independence that they saw as fertilising disloyalty. The Irish party were determined if not to halt any Canterburian impositions then at least to salvage some of their distinction and independence in a type of damage limitation exercise. The outcome was something of a compromise with Bramhall successfully imposing the English Articles whilst not rescinding the Irish. Whilst this was a slight fudge Bramhall was left in no doubt that his Church's tenets of faith would be first among equals.

In the ensuing years after convocation, John Bramhall proved as stern and unyielding an imposer of Laudian policy as could have been wished for by the Archbishop himself. Acting as Primate in all but name, he purged the Irish Church of those he perceived as enemies, in particular those of Presbyterian leaning. In one instance he caused two Scottish ministers along with one hundred and forty followers to set sail for New England.[68] Comparison is often made with Ussher whose tolerance and forbearing is used as a contrast to the bullying comportment of Bramhall. Such images can verge on caricature but they are nevertheless largely true. Ussher and Bramhall both sought unity but the former did so by attempting to have the Protestant fold as inclusive as possible, the latter by making it as uniform as possible. Their respective approaches made Ussher as many friends as it made Bramhall enemies.

---

66   J.S. Reid, *The history of the Presbyterian Church in Ireland* (3 vols, Belfast, 1867), vol. 1, p. 168.

67   Laud *Works*, 'Laud to Wentworth, 20 October 1634', vol. 6, p. 402. Laud had previously called Andrews a 'reverend ignoramus' and an 'Ananias.' Ibid., vol. 7, pp. 98–9. His opposition during convocation had not been appreciated.

68   M. Perceval-Maxwell, 'Strafford, the Ulster-Scots and the covenanters', *Irish Historical Studies*, 1973, vol. 18: 527.

In the words of Jeremy Taylor, wonder at Bramhall's achievements 'quickly passed into the natural daughters of envy, suspicion, and detraction, the spirit of obloquy and slander.[69] Perhaps the gravest of offences was Bramhall's perceived involvement with the Black Oath. The Oath had been formulated by Wentworth at the beginning of 1639 in an attempt to get Scottish settlers to forswear the Solemn League and Covenant. Though Bramhall had no part in its composition he was implicated by his active role in its imposition[70]. If the Scottish Calvinists needed any more reasons for despising Bramhall they were well provided by this incident.[71] In a letter to Laud in 1638, Bramhall had been in typical ebullient form, citing the patronage of Laud as sufficient protection.

> ... for my employment, though I know it to be troublesome, expensive, subjected to the envy of some and the hatred of others, yet upon your encouragement, and under your Grace's protection, I will gird myself seriously to it ... and defy all those that dare charge me with a sinister end.[72]

The tide, however, was turning against the Laudian triumvirate; in November 1640, the Commons had resolved to impeach Strafford and the following year, articles of High Treason were exhibited against the bishop of Derry by the Irish Commons to the Irish House of Lords.[73] More recently it has emerged that Bramhall was apparently in even more trouble. John Allerton, the bishop of Killala was at this time executed on the charges of incest, infanticide, fornication, adultery, rape, sodomy and simony (though there was probably little more to the charges than homosexual activity). According to Bedell's chaplain 'another of the same order' was to be arraigned and due to be condemned for similar crimes when the 'rebellion gave him the benefit of absolution', and the Restoration promotion. The only member of the bishops' bench of 1640 to be promoted in 1660 was John Bramhall.[74] At the same time, the Commons in England appointed a committee to draw up charges in support of their impeachment.[75] Against the advice of his friend, Bramhall travelled to Dublin to answer his accusers whereupon he was imprisoned and held in the castle under black rod.[76] Underlying the move there may well have been various political motivations, the charges relating to various forms of liberticide were so

---

69   *BW*, vol. 1, p. lxiii.
70   *Strafford's Letters and Dispatches*, ed. W. Knowler (2 vols, Dublin, 1740), vol. 2, pp. 344–6.
71   D. Bowen, *The History and Shaping of Irish Protestantism* (New York, 1995), p. 87.
72   Trinity College Dublin Ms. 1697, paper XIII, 'Bramhall to Laud, 13 September 1638'.
73   C. Nye, 'John Bramhall', *The Church Quarterly Review*, CXVII, (1934): 11.
74   A. Clarke, 'A woeful sinner: John Atherton,' in V.P. Carey and U. Lotz-Heumann (eds), *Taking Sides, Colonial and confessional mentalities in Early Modern Ireland* (Dublin, 2003), p. 149.
75   *Cal.S.P.Dom., 1641–43*, p. 20.
76   Bramhall wrote to his wife, 12 March 1641, 'I have been near a fortnight at the black rod, charged with a treason.' *BW*, vol. 1, p. xxxviii.

vague[77] and even false that it is difficult to avoid the conclusion that they had been manufactured with another purpose in mind. According to Cicely Wedgewood, the impeachment was served for no other reason than to stop Bramhall giving evidence in the trial of Strafford.[78] Certainly, the Irish Parliament seems to have had an eye on their English counterpart when they made their move. Perceval-Maxwell argued that the proceedings against Bramhall were part of a larger attempt to reverse Poynings law, and achieve greater legislative independence. 'In making this move, the Irish Commons was asserting rights over the executive similar to those exercised by the English Commons.'[79]

From prison, Bramhall wrote to Ussher in England asking for his assistance. Ussher obliged representing Bramhall's case to the King along with Strafford's dying testament that Bramhall ought not to be forsaken. Ussher's letter reads,

> My Lord Strafford, the night before his suffering, [which was most Christian and magnanimous, *ad stuporem usque*] sent me to the King, giving me in charge, among other particulars, to put him in mind of you and of the other two Lords that are in the same pressure, who thereupon declared to me that he had already given order that the Parliament was not to proceed in their judgment, until they could show some precedent of such legal process ... .[80]

Bramhall was released after Charles I halted proceedings against him in 1642, but without any acquittal. The charges against him stood as Arthur Hadden wrote 'to be awakened when his enemies pleased.'[81] In the meantime, whilst at liberty, Bramhall returned to Derry which was by now crowded with Scottish planters who sought refuge from the rebellion that was taking place. They were not inclined to give him the welcome he had perhaps dreamed of during his incarceration. One night a cannon

---

77   In presenting the charges to the Irish Commons, Captain Audley Mervin made a beautifully eloquent speech in which he claimed to the house that he was presenting 'the Grey-headed Common law's funeral.' It had been, claimed Mervin, like Caesar murdered in the senate by his friend Brutus. Beyond such poetic imagery, he made three general allegations. Firstly, that Bramhall intended the destruction of the realm by subverting the fundamental laws, secondly, that he had traitorously assumed regal power, and lastly that he had laboured to subvert the rights of Parliament. Huntington Library, Printed Collection, Ms. 43286, *A speech made before the Lords in the Upper House of Parliament in Ireland*.
78   Wedgewood, *Strafford*, p. 279.
79   Perceval-Maxwell, *Outbreak*, p. 122.
80   *The Rawdon Papers*, p. 75.
81   *BW*, vol. 1, p. ix; In July 1641, the Lords Justices wrote to secretary Vane saying that they had drawn up a bill of general pardon, but feeling was so high against Bramhall that they were unable to include him in the amnesty. 'Without that it would be very hard to pass it.' *Cal.S.P.Ire., 1633–47*, p. 310; The following year in a reply to a question from the House of Lords the Irish Commons declared that the charges were retained against Bramhall. *Commons Journal Ireland*, vol. 1, p. 181; Indeed in the ensuing conflict the bishop was to become so much a part of the diabolization of Wentworth that as late as 1648, when parliament sent a list of propositions to the King at Newport, Bramhall was listed among those who could expect no pardon. *Cal.S.P.Dom., 1648–49*, p. 304.

was turned on his house[82] and Bramhall was persuaded that under the circumstance he would be of better service to his King in his home country.

During the early 1640s, Bramhall took up residence once more in Yorkshire, largely at the estate of William Cavendish, the Marquess of Newcastle.[83] Newcastle was an ardent royalist and during the hostilities of the 1640s he was the king's commander in the North. No longer with a real office Bramhall returned to the world of scholarship, like Ussher he became part of a scholarly body of royal apologists. In 1643 he published a reply to Henry Parker's anti-royalist *Observations upon some of his Majesties late answers and expresses* (1640). Bramhall entitled his work *The Serpent Salve*, and it represents a robust defence of divine-right monarchical government.[84] Bramhall backed up such scholarly outpourings with morale boosting homilies. One, before Newcastle as he prepared to meet the Scottish in January 1643, compared the plight of Charles with that of King David. The chosen text was 2 Samuel 10:12 in which the Israelite King had treated the heretic Hanun kindly only to be repaid with hostility. The lesson was clear; like the Ammonites who tore the garments of David's servants, the Scots had lately 'abused those holy garments and books.' Their conflict was clearly identified by Bramhall as one in defence of the sacred, and he exhorted the congregation, 'the sword is never more justly drawn than to defend religion.'[85] Five months later in the Cathedral Church at York, Bramhall gave public thanks for Newcastle's victory. The sermon he preached was published by special command. In it Bramhall identified an enemy closer to home, 'Our very own Anabaptists' and in a language other Protestants usually reserved for papists, he professed that they were like Nero, 'made up of charity and meekness', but afterwards they proved a monster. Bramhall asked 'what shall a man think of such a religion, but as a school of rebellion, a nursery of traitors, a mother of all abominations.'[86] Thus Bramhall may have been playing a role very much similar to that of Ussher's at this time. However, his career had not been sufficiently ambivalent to gain him any friends on the parliamentarian side, and unlike the Archbishop of Armagh, he could expect to find nobody on that side favourably disposed toward him. When events started to turn against the King in the north of England after the battle of Marston Moor in July 1644, Bramhall ascertained that it was no longer safe for men of his persuasion to remain; along with Newcastle, he embarked for the Continent.[87]

---

82   *BW*, vol. 1, p. ix.
83   *DNB*, (1968), vol. 3, p. 1273–8.
84   *BW*, vol. 1, p. x.
85   *BW*, vol. 4, pp. 941–2.
86   J. Bramhall, *A sermon preached in the Cathedral Church of York, June 30, 1643* (York, 1643), p. 10.
87   There appears to have been some sort of breach between the Marquess and Charles. Apparently, he had urged the King to await the arrival of reinforcements at Marston Moor. He did so in vain and the following day he left England saying, 'I will not endure the laughter at court.' *DNB*, (1968), vol. 3, p. 1275; Lady Margaret, the wife of Newcastle, wrote in her diary that her husband foresaw that defeat 'would produce, by which not only those of his Majesty's party in the northern parts of the kingdom, but in all other parts of his Majesty's dominions ... were lost and undone ... .' With only £90 left, Newcastle went to Scarborough where a barque

During his exile, Bramhall changed his residence a good deal, but mainly he lived in Brussels at the residence of Sir Henry de Vic[88] from where he preached at the English embassy.[89] Here he immersed himself in polemical scholarship, though impecunity forced him to use the Jesuit library. As Vesey explained, 'having none of his own, he was forced to whet his sword among the Philistines with whom he was to fight.'[90] In Paris in 1646, Bramhall met with Thomas Hobbes and debated with him before the Marquess of Newcastle on liberty and necessity.[91] The original discussion was intended to be private but a prolonged literary dispute ensued in which Bramhall wrote three volumes, all of which defended man's ability to choose between right and wrong against the Hobbesian idea that humans were compelled to act by a series of imperatives.[92] Hobbes was not the only celebrity who chose to cross swords with the exiled bishop. In common with Ussher he excited the republican spirit in John Milton, though this was only after the poet had misidentified him as the author of a book entitled, *Pro Rege et Populo Anglicana apologia contra Johannis Polypragmatic* (i.e., Milton) *defensionem destructivam regis et populi Anglicani*. Bramhall disclaimed 'That silly book which he ascribed to me'; it was in fact written by a John Rowland. The bishop added that if Milton's friends knew him, 'they would make him go near to hang himself.'[93]

These years of forced leisure were Bramhall's most scholarly; they were, however, not completely confined to the world of letters, and they did include some rather Dumasesque adventures. In 1648, Bramhall returned to Ireland 'on the King's business.'[94] During his stay in Cork, the city declared for Parliament and he left hurriedly in a bark which was promptly set upon by two Parliamentary ships.[95] Only a fortuitous wind saved him, inducing Cromwell in some state of vexation to

---

was prepared for himself, his brother, and Bramhall. Margaret, Duchess of Newcastle, *The Life of William Cavendish, Duke of Newcastle* (London, 1667), p. 43.

88   *BW*, vol. 1, p. x. Henry de Vic was the king's agent in Brussels. G.E. Aylmer, *The King's Servants: The Civil Service of Charles I, 1625–42* (London, 1974), p. 103.

89   *DNB*, (1968), vol. 2, p. 1111; throughout his exile it is significant that Bramhall kept exclusively to his national church. Sykes points out that he was one of many expatriots who declined to join with the French reformed Church in communion. As Sykes indicates, this is in stark contrast to Ussher's attitude which was much more universal. N. Sykes, *Old Priest and New Presbyter* (Cambridge, 1956), p. 152.

90   Vesey, *Athanasius*, p. 27.

91   Collins, *Typical Churchmen*, p. 106.

92   The three volumes are entitled: *A defence of true liberty from Antecedent and extrinsecal necessity* (London, 1655); *The Castigation of Mr. Hobbes his animadversions* (London, 1658); and *The catching of the Leviathan* (London, 1658).

93   *Rawdon Papers*, p. 109.

94   Wright, *Yorkshire Divine*, p. 13.

95   Interestingly, in his own version of events, written as a riposte to Baxter, it is the Roman Catholics who drove him out of Ireland. They had he claims at the time wrested some power of the sword in that country, and they 'never left until they had thrust me out of the kingdom, as conceiving me to be a great impediment to them in their making of proselytes.' Bramhall is doing his best to portray himself as a stout defender of the Reformation and he changes the religion of his pursuers to suit his need. *BW*, vol. 3, p. 540.

exclaim that he would have given a large sum of money for 'that Irish Canterbury.'[96] A second threat to his life, this time apparently at the hands of Catholics, came when he journeyed into Spain on a mission to compare liturgies around the year 1650.[97] The authorities of the inquisition according to Vesey had circulated a print of his portrait with a reward on his head. He escaped only when the sympathetic landlady of a tavern tipped him off.[98] However, the story has all the hallmarks of a biographical device, especially when one considers that Vesey would have been anxious to claim some Catholic persecution to add to his subject's Protestant credentials. Even the otherwise credulous Wills was sceptical of this passage and though he did not doubt that Parliament would have done anything to rid themselves of Bramhall, even to the point of co-operating with the Spanish inquisition, he urged caution, writing 'We should doubt that the sagacious intelligence of Bramhall would have walked heedless into so formidable a trap.'[99] The tale is thrown into further doubt by the bishop's own remark that it was 'a tedious and chargeable voyage in Spain.'[100]

During these earlier years of exile, Bramhall was forced not only to defend the Anglican faith from a Catholic critic but to enter what developed into a written duel over the soul of Charles II. A French Catholic by the name of Theophile de la Milletière[101] had written an open letter to Charles, entitled *The Victory of Truth*, in which he urged him to end the schism of his national Church and embrace the mother faith.[102] In reply, Bramhall published *The Answer to Milletière*, and counter–claimed that the King had embraced the Catholic faith, but it was not of the Roman variety.[103] The tract more or less sums up Bramhall's position regarding the argument with Rome. That is, that all national Catholic Churches are equal; the schism came when Rome usurped a greater share of power.[104] Apparently Milletière became so heated with the prospect of a royal conversion that he spoke as if from the 'infallible chair.' According to Vesey, Bramhall's service was that he saved the King for the Church of England.[105] Not that Rome claimed all the attention of his polemic in his exiled years. In 1659, he published his *Vindication of himself and the Episcopal clergy from*

---

96   Wills, *Distinguished Irishmen*, vol. 4, p. 179.

97   *Rawdon Papers*, p. 85.

98   Vesey, *Athanasius*, p. 33; Vesey is supposed to have got the story off George Walker, the uncle of Bramhall. Collins, *Typical Churchmen*, fn. p. 102.

99   Wills, *Distinguished Irishmen*, p. 179.

100   *BW*, vol. 1, p. xciii.

101   De la Milletière had been raised as a Huguenot and by the time he was thirty he was a zealous Protestant and secretary to the Huguenot assembly of La Rochelle. However subsequent to writing a conciliatory address to Richelieu, he was cast out of his own faith, and after some hesitation he became a Catholic. Sparrow-Simpson, *Bramhall*, p. 118.

102   Ibid.

103   *BW*, vol. 1; *DNB*, (2004), vol. 7, p. 315.

104   See also, *A schism disarmed* (London, 1654) which was written in reply to the Jesuit polemicist Edward Knott (1582–1656) who wrote *Infidelity unmasked* (London, 1652).

105   Vesey, *Athanasius*, p. 30. He claims in superlative language that Bramhall stood 'like Aaron between the living and the dead, and stayed the plague ... for the success whereof then, and the value of it at all times, he merits the thanks of all the Reformed Churches, which some of them were so ingenious as to pay him.'

the Presbyterian charge of Popery. It was written against Richard Baxter and has been described as exciting a great deal of controversy on account of its violence.[106] In spite of his renewed interest in anti-Catholicism, he had not lost any of his anti-separatist invective.

Bramhall was also involved in assisting the royal cause in more practical ways. There had been in 1651 a discussion between Hyde and Secretary Nicholas in which they hatched a scheme to maintain the line of episcopal succession so that it might survive in exile.[107] Arrangements were to be made in 1655 to bring over to France the remaining bishops who would be united with Bramhall and then set about consecrating banished clergy. The plan however came to nothing after, it seems, Bramhall became seriously ill.[108] Lady Burghclere wrote of a later incident involving Hyde in which Bramhall seemingly allowed himself to become embroiled in an unsavoury plot to drive him from public life. Sir Richard Grenville attempted to represent Hyde to Charles II as a traitor, in the pay of Cromwell, quoting the bishop as one of his sources. She described a situation in which she claims that Bramhall's tongue was once more the source of much trouble.

> It is clear that the exciting possibility of detecting the impeccable chancellor in treason had led the Bishop to speak inadvisedly with his lips, but he had no more positive knowledge of the matter than Wyndham. The prelate was indeed, somewhat scared by the great fire his idle chatter had kindled.[109]

Lady Burghclere tells us that Bramhall's alarm was not ungrounded, 'as the easy-going sovereign was now thoroughly incensed.'[110] A letter from Sir Richard Grenville tells us that the king investigated the matter himself. Grenville adds that the allegations were 'weak and deficient.'[111] In spite of the incident, Bramhall seems to have extricated himself from the hot water once more, and Clarendon remained on good terms with him. In 1659, he was writing to the bishop at Utrech, praising his excellent book, *A Schism Guarded Against and beaten back upon the right owners*. He went so far as to entreat Bramhall to enlarge sections of it, adding, 'tis an excellent piece and hath entered upon the most important point which can give peace to the Christian Church.'[112] Bramhall wrote back thanking him not only for the character he had given his poor labours but for his New Year's gift. As for the proposal to enlarge the treatise, 'although his books ... have been the cause of all his sufferings, he may

---

106 *BW*, 1, p. xxxi.
107 Sparrow-Simpson, *Bramhall*, p. 221.
108 According to Barwick, the programme was halted when sickness threatened the bishop's life. 'The Bishop of Derry (upon whom the canonical dispatch of it, as to that Election, wholly depends) is infirm, and cannot live long.' P. Barwick, *The Life of Dr J. Barwick* (London, 1724), p. 427.
109 Lady Burghclere, *The Life of James, First Duke of Ormonde* (2 vols, London, 1912), vol. 1, p. 452.
110 Ibid.
111 *Calendar of Clarendon State Papers*, ed. J. Routledge, (Oxford, 1932), vol. 2, p. 279.
112 *Hastings Manuscripts*, vol. 4, p. 98.

be induced to complete it .... The chief remora will be want of books, since he dare cite no man upon trust.'[113]

These years on the Continent were indeed difficult ones for Bramhall, without money, books or family he did not even have a proper function into which he might plunge himself. In 1653, he had been reduced to act as a 'prize master' for Charles II, even selling the prizes personally.[114] As if recognising these dire circumstances, efforts were made by some Anglican Protestants who had managed to work out an accommodation with the Commonwealth to win him over. Ussher's biographer, Bernard made one such effort. In his reply, Bramhall acknowledges the advantages of such a proposal for he missed his native country, as well as 'the comfortable society of his wife and children.' He was not however tempted, explaining to Bernard that he was 'bred in the communion of the Church of England and in that Communion I propose to die.' He adds that he was unable to sacrifice his conscience 'either publicly or privately.'[115] The reward for such steadfast loyalty came in 1660 when Bramhall returned to England. He was generally considered to be the prime candidate for the see at York but when he was instead proposed for the primacy of Ireland, it was felt to be a natural choice.[116] On 18 January 1661, he was translated to the metropolitan see of Armagh which had been vacant since the death of Ussher.[117] The man who had for so many years acted as the Archbishop was now legitimately installed.[118] One of his first public duties as Primate was to preach in Dublin on the day of the coronation of King Charles II. The lesson was Psalms 126:7, and he used as a metaphor for the interregnum and the exile of King and bishops, the destruction of the holy of holies, the temple at Jerusalem which was destroyed by the heathen.

> First the Temple, which was the glory of Sion, was demolished. Then, the ceremonies and sacrifices, and ordinance of Sion were abolished. Thirdly, the holy vessels and garments and other utensils and sacred ornaments were exported. Lastly, the priests, and Levites and people of God were all carried away captive. These were the living Sion, without these Sion was but a dead carcase of itself.[119]

---

113 *Clarendon State Papers*, vol. 4, p. 126.

114 Wright, *York Divine*, p. 13.

115 Huntington Library, Hastings Collection, Ms. H.A. 14067, 'Bramhall to Bernard March 11, 1658.'

116 Wills, *Distinguished Irishmen*, vol. 4, p. 180. Wills wrote 'as he had been tried and found faithful in the seasons of a fiery trial, so he was to be rewarded by the station for which he had been thus severely approved;' there had been some very initial debate about what sort of an ecclesiastical settlement England would return to. J.I. McGuire points out that the Irish had been already set as episcopal. The name of the Irish prelate was known some time before his English counterparts. J.I. McGuire, 'The Dublin Convention, the Protestant community, and the emergence of an ecclesiastical settlement.' in A. Cosgrove and J.I. McGuire (eds), *Historical Studies Series,* XIV (Belfast, 1983),p. 121.

117 *Cal.S.P.Ire., 1660–62*, p. 20.

118 William Sancroft wrote to him on 9 October 1660, declaring that justice had finally been done '... having for many years been really the universal father of that Church in your care of it and provision for it.' *Hastings Manuscripts*, vol. 4, p. 98.

119 *BW*, vol. 5, p. 14.

What is striking about this homily is not the association of England with the chosen nation of Israel, which was common enough, but the strong language employed to depict the violation of every aspect of God's holiness. The real crime of the Commonwealth according to the new archbishop had been to lay profane hands on God's sacred vessels.

Bramhall appeared not to have lost his old energy and sense of purpose despite his advancing years. In one stroke not a week after his own blessing, he presided over the consecration of no less than two archbishops and ten bishops, the nomination of whom he had carefully secured in London before his departure.[120] During the proceedings a victorious hymn composed especially for the occasion rang out triumphantly, 'Now that the Lord the Mitre hath restored, Which with the crown lay in the dust abhorred.'[121] The consecrations had very important political overtones. Bramhall had proceeded with such haste in order to move the Anglican Church more quickly along an episcopal road whilst talks were taking place with the Presbyterians. The previous year he had urged Hyde to accept the Irish way of appointing bishops not by election but by the Crown. Presumably this would have the two-fold advantage of being quicker and involving the King in a process they hoped he would adopt. In Hyde's letter to Barwick he advised them to move quickly in order to steal a march on the opposition.[122] In Ireland the effect was immediate. Not only did it fill a void in the established Church hierarchy it also sent a clarion message to those who had hoped the lacuna would remain. Bramhall's mass consecration, which was almost certainly the largest of its kind in Western Christendom,[123] was a statement that the Restoration not only involved the return of a King to his throne but the return of his bishops to their sees. In making such a statement, he was dashing any hope of compromise. As James Wills wrote,

> The appointment of so many new bishops as such a state of things demanded was for a time the rallying point of party and sectarian excitement: the desolate condition of the Irish Church had raised the strong hopes of its enemies of every persuasion, that it could hardly be restored: and above all at the present moment the expectation was, that the sees would not be filled.[124]

Bramhall remained as Primate until 25 June 1663, when he died from the effects of a stroke. Jeremy Taylor's funeral sermon proclaimed his skill as a man both practical and scholarly. He closed with the words, 'he wrote many things fit to be read, and did very many things worthy to be written.'[125] His own last will and testament thanked God that he had been spared to see the Restoration with his own eyes and declared of the Church which he had served all his life,

---

120 Sparrow-Simpson, *Bramhall*, pp. 225–6.
121 McGuire, 'Dublin Convention', p. 121. The author William Fuller had apparently suffered also for his loyalties, which goes some way to excusing such woeful verse.
122 *Clarendon State Papers*, vol. IV, p. 253.
123 See, McCafferty, 'Reconstruction of the Irish Church', p. 12.
124 Wills, *Distinguished Irishmen*, vol. 4, p. 180.
125 *BW*, vol. 1, p. lxxvi.

I doe not believe that the whole world hath any Church that cometh nearer to Apostical truth, both in doctrine and discipline. And I doe heartily praise God that ordained me to be born and bred up in it, and pray that I may end my days in the communion of it.[126]

---

[126] Ibid., p. cviii.

Chapter 3

Dogmatic Theologies

Heiko Oberman has written forcefully of a modern trend that squeezes theology out of the study of the Reformation. Cities, social crises, empire and princes occupy our attention before any consideration of matters religious.[1] In his book *The personal rule of Charles I* Kevin Sharpe seems to be following this fashion as closely as anyone as he plays down religion and Laudianism in particular as contributory factors in the crises of the Civil Wars. In his review of Sharpe's book, Derek Hirst is not convinced of the diminution of Laud's Arminianism. Finally, he writes that the author would have done better to look more closely at the Irish dimension to Charles' rule, 'More generally, a thorough discussion of Ireland and Scotland in the 1630s might have recast his characterization of the personal rule as a whole. If, as he insists, Charles did not seek to innovate, Wentworth seems to have been out of step in Ireland.'[2]

Though Hirst does not develop his advice, it is not difficult to see why he would urge such a direction. When William Laud sent his emissary, Bramhall to Ireland in 1634, he was faced with something of a blank canvas. Ussher's Church was at best moribund and at worst destitute. For this reason, the Laudians had something of a free hand to enact the sort of programme in their own back yard that they might one day implement in their own home. Put bluntly, their 'thorough' could be almost as thorough as they wished. Because of this the theologies of Ussher and Bramhall, their relationship and the relationship of their respective Church bodies is of immense value to historians of the period. Ussher, Bramhall and the Church in Ireland in general have been given all too little attention as this most important of historical debates has remained too Anglo-centric. The following chapter seeks to illustrate the point that in the most fundamental area of the Christian intellectual experience which is dogmatic theology there is sufficient evidence in the works of Ussher and Bramhall to support the historical view that there was a substantial difference between the pre-Laudian religious understanding as represented by Ussher and those of the Laudian regime as represented by Bramhall. The Irish Church in this period offers with Ussher and Bramhall two clear examples of not just theological differences but the potential for conflict based on these principles. We are now finally getting a more inclusive approach to the causes of the wars in these islands in the 1640s and it is hoped that the following chapters will be a contribution to this redressing of the balance.

---

1   1 H.A. Oberman, *The Reformation, Roots and Ramification* (Edinburgh, 1994), p. 8.
2   D. Hirst, 'The King Redeemed', *Times Literary Supplement* (15 January 1993): 3.

The nature of man

The surest way to categorise a Christian controversialist of the post-Reformation is to determine their understanding of the nature of man, and in this James Ussher and John Bramhall are no exceptions, and it is perhaps in this area of dogmatics that their theological lights burn furthest from each other. Ussher's position on the nature of man sets him out as belonging to the left-wing of Calvinist Protestantism employing as he does the justice motif in its most radical form. In true Augustinian fashion Ussher argued that the stain of Adam's sin had so polluted the generations which followed him that they were incapable of achieving anything that could be described as even approaching moral goodness. The 'natural man' is guided by these three pilots, the world, the Devil and the flesh. The first guide means that man is not only disposed to be 'singular', but rather he conforms to the evil around him and 'swims along in the stream of the world.' In the second, the Devil leads him in place of the Spirit with a lust he cannot resist. Finally the flesh drives him to fulfil the desires of the flesh and mind. Therefore it is not merely a case that the natural man can do no good, he is compelled also to do much that is bad.[3]

> Here he is wholly set upon the commission of sins and trespasses. He not only 'brings not forth meet fruit' or good fruit, or no fruit, but he brings forth thorns and briars; and is therefore rejected, and nigh unto cursing, whose end is to be burnt.[4]

Earlier in his twenties, Ussher had summed up man's condition in a type of short catechism that he called *The Principles of the Christian Religion* (1654).[5] In a style which betrays his Ramist predilection for listing, he provides an itinerary of the consequences of the fall. Firstly, there was a blindness of understanding from which we are not able to conceive of the things of God. There was a forgetfulness by which we are unable to recall the good that once belonged to our first father. Our will is now turned against God, making us naturally rebellious, our affections are now disordered so that we love what is bad, and likewise our human conscience is thrown into fear and confusion and every member of our body is made an instrument whereby we sin.[6] Elsewhere Ussher puts it more succinctly, 'we are utterly indisposed, aliens to all good, and bent to all evil.'[7] Nor indeed is our own repentance capable of saving us. In a sermon delivered in 1640, he informed the congregation that even this faculty, traditionally man's last refuge, was tainted beyond use. Unless given the true repentance, which is a gift of God, man's efforts were useless, 'No, no, repentance is a grace out of reach, it is not in man's powers. The opening of the eyes of the blind is in God's hands.'[8] Following on logically from his denigration of human nature even man's penance and atonement were part of the general corruption. Ussher looked instead to the freely given grace of God in a process in which man's role

---

3 *UW*, vol. 13, pp. 48–9.
4 Ibid., p. 55.
5 This early work was not published until late in Ussher's life.
6 *UW*, vol 11, p. 13.
7 *UW*, vol 13, p. 59.
8 Ibid., p. 11.

was not merely negligible but non-existent. In his *Antiquities of the British and Irish Churches*, (1639), he warned his readers to 'firmly hold and doubt not that none here can perform the repentance of men, but he whom God shall illuminate and by his free mercy convert.'[9]

Commenting on a statement from Ussher that all men are 'by nature dead in sin as a loathsome carrion', the Georges declared, 'We doubt that stronger statements of this concept could be found anywhere in Christian argumentation.'[10] Here Ussher maintains the justice motif in its most undiluted form, though he may be chosen by God, such election if it occurred would be totally unwarranted. Man is to Ussher as Israel is to the prophets, not only unworthy but morally disabled. Both have spurned the generosity of God and have fallen into a profoundly dissolute state, their only hope is miraculous intervention. This is the message of the prophet Ezekiel who declared, 'You will know that I am the Lord, when I have dealt with you. O men of Israel not as your wicked ways and your vicious deeds deserve but for the honour of my name.' (Ezekiel 36:22); in other words, God saves the unworthy Israel because He chooses to do so and for no other reason.[11] This is essentially the soteriological message of the justice motif.

According to Conrad Russell the Laudian assertion of 'the free will of all men to obtain salvation' was, in a society steeped in Calvinism, considered to be their worst offence.[12] In the writings of one member of that regime, John Bramhall, the defence of free will and human nature in general present a stark contrast to Ussher's gloomy dictums. Here the numinous motif presents an entirely different image of creation in general, and man in particular. The Israelites, by virtue of their chosen status reflected within themselves some of Yahweh's greatness within the cult, whose main purpose was the continual sanctification of the people, making the good better.[13] Now through Christ, the gentile Christians inherit this blessing. The members of Christ's Church draw on her sources of grace via the sacraments, but they are also heirs to a certain amount of grace which provides them with the faculty to choose and do good. This is why exponents of the numinous motif, of which Bramhall is an eloquent representative, may talk of man being 'naturally' motivated toward God. For Bramhall nature dictates the existence of religion and the worship of God, they are 'rays of heavenly light which God Himself hath imprinted in the heart of man.'[14]

---

9 Trinity College Dublin Ms. 1185, *Antiquities of the British and Irish Churches* (London, 1639), p. 292.

10 Georges, *Protestant Mind*, p. 43. Notwithstanding Ussher's denial that he wrote the book here quoted, *A Body of Divinitie or the Summe and Substance of Christian Religion* was published in 1647 under Ussher's name. Ussher objected to the attribution but only on the grounds that it was altered in places, numerous similar incidents occurred in 1654. There is however nothing in the 1647 publication that is not in keeping with the accepted canon of his writings.

11 H.D. Preuss, *Old Testament Theology* (2 vols, Edinburgh, 1996), vol. 2, p. 81.

12 C. Russell, *The Origins of the English Civil War* (London, 1973), p. 20.

13 Preuss, *Old Testament Theology*, pp. 251–2.

14 *BW*, vol. 4, p. 521.

Hence it is, that there never was any nation so barbarous or savage throughout the whole world which had not their God. They who did never wear clothes upon their backs, who did never know magistrate but their father, yet have their God, and their religious rites and devotions to him.[15]

In this passage, Bramhall comes as close as any seventeenth-century Christian could to valuing the non-Christian religious experience and it is worth comparing to a passage in Ussher which described similar 'Pelagian' sentiments emanating from Rome as one 'for which the Christian Church doth most of all detest you.'[16]

Bramhall's positive appraisal of the human condition is nowhere stated more clearly than in his renowned controversy with Hobbes. Following a verbal discussion in the presence of the Marquis of Newcastle there commenced a written exchange which Keith Thomas politely described as going 'beyond sober philosophizing.'[17] Hobbes in the course of their debate nailed his colours firmly to the determinist mast. In a type of philosophical predestination, man is determined in his actions, not by the divine hand, but rather by a range of contributory factors which together impel a certain response. Hobbesian man does not enjoy an elective capacity. This is not to say that he denied any freedom, but he does interpret it in a way which means it is not contrary to necessity. Freedom is subordinate to necessity, his philosophy recognises a freedom to act but as the last part of the process by which we are determined. Hobbes writes, 'I acknowledge this liberty, that I can do if I will, but to say I can will if I will, I take it to be an absurd speech.'[18] This position is what modern philosophers call 'compatibilism', in that freedom is made compatible with necessity. In his opposition, Bramhall is an 'incompatibilist' of a distinct type. The meaning of the term has been elucidated in the introduction to the new edition of this debate, 'An incompatibilist has two alternatives: accept necessity and forgo freedom, or keep freedom and reject necessity. Since it is the latter Bramhall opts for, his position is called libertarianism.'[19]

Bramhall has two main objections to Hobbesian philosophy. Principally, as may be expected of a senior clergyman, he dislikes Hobbes' denial of incorporeal bodies, his dismissal of theology as a useful discipline, and the thorough materialism, all of which he characterizes as 'atheistic.' But Bramhall also sees in it a subversive element, for if we are compelled to act a certain way then reproach and praise, punishment and reward are rendered superfluous. Men will become blameless, Hobbes has expunged their responsibility along with their liberty. Not only is such a method dangerous, but it is contrary to reason, 'No man blameth fire for burning whole cities, no man taxeth poison for destroying men, but those persons who apply them to such wicked ends.'[20] Throughout their protracted exchange, Bramhall claims to be a champion of liberty, pointing out as he does its vital role in the functioning of our society and the understanding of our religion as well as its importance in

---

15   bid., p. 518.
16   *UW*, vol. 3, p. 519.
17   Thomas, *Magic*, p. 32.
18   *BW*, vol. 4, p. 25.
19   V. Chappell, *Hobbes and Bramhall* (Cambridge, 1999), p. xi.
20   *BW*, vol. 4, p. 32.

scripture which has according to Bramhall an underlying moral logic based on real choices. He illustrates his point with passages where choice is offered by God to David, by Herod to his daughter and Pilate to the Jews.[21] The underlying assumption is always that there is a sufficient portion of natural human goodness to merit such liberty, man must have some good if he is to choose it. Nor is he happy with the meagre portion of liberty that the Hobbesian system serves up precisely because this reflects a low estimate of man's ability to do good. Bramhall complains that whilst the limited freedom envisaged by Hobbes may be sufficient for children or animals, it would not suffice men. In other words, mature man has acquired with age and experience a natural capacity which has raised him above these levels, 'And such a liberty as is in brute beasts, as bees and spiders, which do not learn their faculties as we do our trades, by experience and consideration. This is a brutish liberty. Such a liberty as a bird hath to fly when her wings are clipped.'[22]

Bramhall's man is reflective of the synteresis understanding of the scholastic writers, and is of course capable of sin, but he is, crucially, also inclined to good; this understanding allies Bramhall to the Catholic thinkers of his day such as Suarez and Molina,[23] and it is certainly a long way off Ussher's 'carrion' statement. Ussher would rob post-Eden man of any redeeming qualities in the literal sense. His description of the fall of man makes for an interesting comparison with Bramhall's which reads, 'But by the fall of Adam, the image of God became defaced in man, the rays of heavenly light eclipsed, the sparkles of Divine grace cooled, the understanding infatuated, the will confounded, the affections disordered.'[24] Such a description implies that with the fall man has stumbled some way from his elevated condition, but he has not plummeted to his spiritual death. God's image is 'defaced' not erased, the divine spark is 'cooled' not extinguished and the once pure affections 'disordered' but not lost. Elsewhere Bramhall gave a similarly moderate assessment.

> ... this death in sin is not a natural, but a spiritual death; and therefore no utter extinction of the natural powers and faculties of a man. Such are the understanding and the will; which, though they were much weakened by the fall of Adam, yet they were not, they are not, utterly extinct.[25]

The twin principles of man's goodness and man's liberty are mutually complementary precepts that derive from the numinous motif. Just as Ussher's man stands condemned before the law of the justice motif, Bramhall's man has been infused with something of God's goodness by experiencing the numinous. The cornerstone of Ussher's theological understanding is that man, *Coram Deo*, is all bad and therefore needs salvation; the cornerstone for Bramhall is that he is both good and bad and he requires liberty. In the history of Anglican theology these conflicting approaches were highly significant. It has been argued that this insistence on free will that marked the controversy of the 1620s amounted to nothing less than

---

21 Ibid., p. 224.
22 Ibid., p. 29.
23 Vere, *Hobbes and Bramhall*, p. xi.
24 Ibid., p. 148.
25 bid., pp. 233–4.

a revolution.[26] Not counting the upheavals of the 1640s and 1650s it was a road that Anglicanism continued to move down. According to Jonathan Spurr when Bramhall enquired of Hobbes where his rigid system of determinism left prayer and resistance it was a question pregnant with historical significance.

> The implications of this enquiry suggest how fast the churchmen were travelling away from their theological inheritance in the 1650s – such a question would not have troubled the Reformers of the sixteenth century or the Calvinists of the early seventeenth.[27]

Soteriology

The above question certainly does not seem to have given James Ussher much concern. This is not to say that Ussher was not aware of the theological problem of antinomianism. Christians of Ussher's persuasion all had to defend themselves against the accusation that their system gave people license to behave in any way they wished. In order to avoid slipping into such heretical waters, Ussher's riposte is pure Calvinism.[28] A person is unable to assist in his own salvation, but this is true only of a man in his natural state; regenerate man internalises something of the divine and via this is capable of good. This theological system allows regenerate humans to do good whilst protecting the notion that 'goodness' is exclusive to God. Actions are *opus Dei* [works of God], not *opus hominis* [works of man]. This process transforms a believer, as if a seed of divine goodness were placed within his wretched nature, 'so that if there be no change in thee by new birth, it is a sure sign, as yet mercy belongeth not unto thee.'[29] Ussher gave a graphic practical instruction as to how this spiritual rejuvenation may be initiated by way of a prayer, 'Lord I am an emptie caske, no goodness in me, but thou art the fountain of wisdom, and giveth to all men liberally, and reproachest no man, thou will not hit me in the teeth ... .'[30] Through these means one may be blessed with a small, smouldering flame of the 'smoking flax.' Christ will never, Ussher assures his reader, 'leave blowing this spark till he have got the victory.'[31] Not that this now makes the individual worthy. Ussher is careful to avoid such a theological presumption, but rather αχιον [*achion*] which is translated 'meet.' Ussher makes the distinction, for whilst man may never be worthy, he is able to attain what is required in order to face the perfection of God.[32]

In an earlier sermon, Ussher described the way in which this metamorphosis transforms God's relationship with man. There is with God a double love, one of 'commiseration', the other of 'complacency.' Ussher explained that before we accept grace, God can only love us in the former sense, out of pity. After 'vivification',

---

26 N. Tyacke, 'Puritanism, Arminianism and Counter Revolution', in M. Todd (ed.) *Reformation to Revolution* (London, 1995), p. 54.
27 J. Spurr, *The Restoration Church of England, 1646–1689* (Yale, 1999), p. 258.
28 A.E. McGrath, *The Life of Calvin* (Oxford, 1990), p. 165.
29 *UW*, vol. 13, p. 427.
30 J. Ussher, *A Method for Meditation* (1656), Thomason, E1665, p. 35.
31 Ibid., p. 100.
32 *UW*, vol. 13, p. 195.

God's love is out of complacency, though not in the modern understanding, rather as like is inclined to like, ' ... this love God never hath but to his saints after conversion, when they have his image enstamped in them, and are reformed in their understanding and wills, resembling them both, then and not till then bears he this love toward them.'[33]

Ussher is on a doctrinal tightrope here and he is careful to add a further qualification lest he may appear to be falling into Romanism. In his discourse with a William Malone S.J., he acknowledges that good works may be the fruit of a soul restored to God, but he takes fierce issue with another theologian in Malone's order who had implied that these worked for man a μισθος [*misthos*] or stipend of the workman. This equated salvation with some kind of just desert. The very idea of this caused Ussher to exclaim, 'This is the doctrine of merits, which from our very hearts we detest and abhor, as utterly repugnant to the truth of God, and the common sense of all true hearted Christians.'[34] In the same work Ussher offers another qualification of his stance which works less well as a systematic theological solution. It does, however, illustrate that he was anxious to preserve some sense of free will. After making the bold statement that 'man hath free will, is not by us gainsaid', Ussher explains that man is not made as an angel παντεξουσιους [*pantexousious*] but rather he is αυτεξουσιους [*autexousious*].[35] That is, man has the freedom to do all things, but no longer the ability, which critics may argue is rather like saying that a blind man is still at liberty to see. Ussher defends the free will of mankind but he is unwilling to give it to them.

Bramhall too offers his own qualifications to the dogma of free will that he professes, though in the opposite direction. As if recognising the extremities their theories are likely to lead them to, both theologians take a qualifying step back toward the middle ground of orthodoxy. In the case of Bramhall he is possibly more in danger than Ussher of stepping out into the *terra non firma* of heresies. Bramhall is aware that as attractive as the equation of 'humanity equals goodness' is to him, he must as a Christian, exercise some caution. Free will had long been a thorny issue within the Church, but since the fourth century when Augustine had engaged in a similar combat with Pelagius, the determinists had all but won out. Pelagius, by allowing man such a large part in the drama of his own salvation had seemed to have written God out of the script. If, after all, man earned salvation with good works, where did God come into it ? St Augustine of Hippo restored God to the leading part with sole responsibility for salvation. With this framework as the established orthodoxy, writers such as Bramhall struggled to glean for mankind something more than a bit part in the final soteriological script. Care had to be taken not to encroach on the established role of the main player.

Hobbes made much of this Achilles' heel. He informed Bramhall that not only did the early fathers write nothing on free will, but it was an error brought in by the doctors of Rome. In a lesson on Church history, Hobbes plays to the Protestant gallery, citing Luther and Calvin as defenders of the truth who threw out liberty only

---

33   Ibid., p. 178.
34   *UW*, vol. 3, p. 550.
35   Ibid., p. 516.

to see Arminius attempt its restoration.[36] Here Hobbes is sounding a contemporary note. The Church he and Bramhall had left behind in England had been riven by an internal feud which was roughly divided along the lines of what today might be described as low-Church Calvinist and high-Church Anglican. Those of the former party blamed much of the dispute on the theology that had emanated from Hermandszoon (1560–1609), otherwise known as Arminius. They branded their opponents Arminians who were at best semi-Pelagians or at worst closet Roman Catholics. Hobbes clearly touched a nerve with Bramhall. Fortunately for the bishop in this area of the discourse he was the philosopher's superior. The bishop was able to lecture his opponent on ecclesiastical antiquity. The early fathers had written on free will, indeed according to Bramhall, 'there is scarcely one Father that doth not mention it', and possibly more importantly the great Reformer, Luther, had changed his opinion on the subject as he grew in age and wisdom.[37] Bramhall adds for good measure that this was ever the opinion of the Church of England and, 'It was such deep "controvertists" as himself [Hobbes] that accused the Church of England of Arminianism, for holding those truths which they ever professed before Arminius was born.'[38] Then, as an example of someone who knows that theologians who elevate free will may be accused of heterodoxy, he defends the 'semi-Pelagians', claiming that they had always subordinated free will to the grace of God. Quoting Arminius to show that he maintained that unregenerate man was incapable of good, he surmises that Hobbes had not read a word of his writing (something he would have had in common with many who used his name as a derogatory term) adding that if the Dutch theologian were not dead, Hobbes would owe him an apology.[39]

This line of defence is curiously similar to the argument of Peter White, that is the theology of Arminius is not, strictly speaking, akin to what has become known as 'Arminian' since it espouses a predestinarianism not unakin to Calvinism.[40] Here we have a good example of why it is safer to talk of poles or motifs towards which people are drawn rather than restrictive labels. So long as somebody is called a Laudian, Arminian or even Calvinist, it will always be possible to prove the contrary. The question is not whether theologians maintained certain tenets; they are compelled to, since they were fundamental to Christian belief, but rather, how much they stressed them. Arminius, no less than Bramhall, cannot be dismissed as theologically indistinct simply on the strength of a remark or a certain piece of writing, their work must be looked at as a whole in order to determine what attracted them. Therefore, when we read Bramhall's numerous qualifications to his free will theory, it must be viewed in this context. His overall adductor is the numinous motif and if he tempers his statements it is because he knows he has to. Bramhall manages this by declaring categorically that man, as capable as he is, may achieve nothing without divine assistance, 'No man can have the actual will to believe and to be converted, but by the preventing grace of God. Our endeavours are in vain, except

---

36   *BW*, vol. 4, pp. 216–18.
37   Ibid., p. 218.
38   Ibid.
39   Ibid., p. 219.
40   White, *Conflict and Consensus*, p. 37.

He help them, and none at all, except He excite them.'[41] All this is very necessary. In a neat, clear statement Bramhall restores to the creator what Christian orthodoxy has already designated His by right, but the operative word here is 'help.' Man needs the assistance of God in a world which is, since the fall, full of pitfalls and dangers. He is not the same as Ussher's man, he does not need to be plucked out of perdition. God's role is instrumental but because he aids man, by definition the recipient has a part to play. When Hobbes had contended that God is the giver of graces and also the provider of the will to receive such grace, Bramhall insisted that such will belonged squarely to man, claiming, 'It is most true, that all grace is from God, but it is most false, that God hath not given man a will to receive it freely.'[42]

Ussher, on the other hand, displays the classical Protestant desire to direct the soteriological focus back from man to God. Historically this was partly as a response to what the Reformers saw as abuses of the numinous motif. By the middle-ages the Catholic Church had learnt to exploit their status as a repository of not only the things sacred but also the grace of God. To use an economic analogy, theirs was a spiritual bank, a bank into which members invested and sought loans on interest. Its assets the indulgences, sacred relics and the confessional were all dependent on the Church's ability to maintain a sense of the numinous. The instigators of protest were naturally horrified at the more exploitative aspects of this system, but their reaction was also theological. The soteriology of the Roman Church was too anthropocentric, a theory of salvation in which man could earn or even buy his reward involved an elevation of human nature that they were not prepared to accept. Their fundamental challenge to this notion was to replace it with a soteriological system in which God was at least central and sometimes exclusive. They sought confirmation for this in the primitive Church. Here Ussher uses a quotation from one of the early fathers, the 'golden mouth' John Chrysostom.

> No man sheweth such a conversion of life that he may be worthy of the kingdom, but this is wholly the gift of God. Therefore, he saith: when ye have done all, say we are unprofitable servants, for what we ought to do we have done. Although we did die a thousand deaths, although we did perform all virtuous actions, yet should we come short by far of rendering any thing worthy of those honours which are conferred upon us by God.[43]

The theory of sin and salvation was of great moment to Reformers and conservatives alike. It was summed up in the term 'justification', and justification by faith is the kernel of Lutheran teaching. It is worth comparing Ussher's theory set out above with Martin Luther's early theory of 'forensic justification.' This idea developed out of the deeply held conviction of man's *iustitia aliena*, that is, the inability of man to live up to the exacting demands of God's righteousness. Luther agreed with Augustine that God imputed His own righteousness to man, however, whereas Augustine located this righteousness within men, complementing their goodness, Luther claimed it was external. The Augustinian location of God within man was too close an association of divine and human for the founder of Protestantism. He therefore developed the

---

41 *BW*, vol. 4, p. 232.
42 Ibid., p. 233.
43 UW, vol. 3, pp. 556–7.

theory of forensic justification which placed it without, believers are righteous by virtue of the alien righteousness of Christ which is imputed to them, as if it were their own through faith.[44]

Later Reformers may have been more radical than Luther on many issues, but they often appear to dilute this striking theocentric element of his soteriology. Martin Bucer attempted to circumvent the problem of *iustitia aliena* with his theory of double justification. Bucer maintained that in the first stage (*iustificatio impii*), the ungodly were justified by God's forgiveness of sin. In the second, because of their response to the moral demands of the Gospel the sinner experiences regeneration (*iustificatio pii*).[45] Bucer is as much drawn to the justice motif as Luther, and he sets out to defend the primacy of God yet also restoring some capacity for good to man, or at least to regenerate man. Ussher clearly has both feet in the Bucer camp. Throughout his writing, he made great claims for the effects of a faith which has been internalised, sufficiently so that he earns the ironic praise of the William Malone. In his lengthy reply to Ussher's treatise he congratulates his young assailant who unlike the other pillars of Protestantism (Luther, Melanchthon and Calvin) does not reject totally the idea that man may do good, 'The main reasons we do rejoyce and congratulate with you, our learned countryman, that you have so sincerely renounced the beastly error which spoileth man of so noble a power.'[46] Ussher was never going to go as far as many Anglican divines during the earlier part of the seventeenth century, who treated justification as both an event and a process. For them the teachings of Paul and James were harmonised so that faith and works provided man's justification.[47] For Ussher, the imputation of Christ's righteousness is a single event, distinguishable from the subsequent sanctification. The debate could be characterised as largely centring on where one places good works: either pre- or post-justification. For someone as attracted to the justice motif as Ussher they can only be regarded as a consequence of God's saving grace.

Bramhall's treatment of nature, apart from the necessary qualifications mentioned above betray none of the usual Protestant discomfiture with positive appraisal. The Laudians demonstrated a theological affection for God's created order. God and creation were in union as part of this divine order.[48] Bramhall's shibboleths associate what is human with what is good, and what is good with God. God is even portrayed as the ideals of human qualities: He is wisdom and justice. Bramhall's work, *Of Persons dying without Baptism* is underpinned by man's inherent goodness. Primarily there is a certain amount of circumspection (he is aware of the dogmatical traps he may set himself) wherein he denies that the Christian children derive any sanctity via propagation, 'as is by some imputed to us amis.'[49] However, having

---

44 A.E. McGrath, *Reformation Thought* (Oxford, 1988), pp. 106–7.
45 Ibid., p. 112.
46 W. Malone, *A Reply to Mr. Ussher's Answere* (London, 1627), pp. 670–71.
47 A.E. McGrath, *Iustitia Dei: A History of the Christian Doctrine of Justification* (Cambridge, 1998), p. 296. McGrath mentions William Forbes and Henry Hammond.
48 I.M. Mackenzie, *God's Order and Natural Law: The Works of the Laudian Divines* (Aldershot, 2002), p. 9.
49 *BW*, vol. 4, p. 980.

taken care of such potential accusation, he is able to state boldly that a child who dies before the commission of sin, is undoubtedly saved. 'Even an infant dying in the womb, contrary to doctrine of the Roman Church, we ought to leave ... also to be the extraordinary providence of God.'[50] It would be impossible for Bramhall to make such statements without believing in an intrinsic human worth. In this work Bramhall may be observed wrestling with a theological dilemma. His natural inclination leads him to conclude that a child dying before the commission of sin is undoubtedly saved, however he does not want to devalue Christian baptism which he holds in very high esteem. Bramhall resolves this problem by employing a theological clause which is usually associated with the justice motif, he claims a divine exemption. It is usual for Calvinists to counter objections to the lack of justice in predestination by arguing that God is not bound by man's law. In this treatise, Bramhall uses the same argument to opposite ends when he asks rhetorically if God is tied to his own law.[51] This is not to show that God is not bound to man's justice (as the Calvinist would argue) rather it releases God to do more good. The former argument is employed to show God's power, the latter to indicate his goodness, and this is indicative of the driving concerns of both motifs.

Predestination

Such dogmatical musing on the salvific process of man's role and the part of God lead inevitably to that most distinguishing feature of Protestant theology which is predestination. It must be stated of course that predestination is not an invention of the Reformation, in some form it has always been a part of Christian orthodoxy. St Paul as much as Thomas Aquinas believed that God had preordained some to salvation and others not. However in recognition of the fatalistic element of such a notion it tended not to be stressed or elaborated. During the Reformation, the Protestant tendency toward the justice motif inevitably meant that sensibilities about the harshness of this apparently arbitrary system were largely dissipated. Predestined salvation emerged from its state as a concept clouded in a miasma of mystery, until in some cases it became a life-influencing maxim.[52] This was largely due to Calvin who seemed to be congenitally unable to obfuscate. Though Calvin certainly could not be accused of making it central to his doctrine (he devoted only four chapters of his *Institutes* to it)[53] nevertheless, as Owen Chadwick indicates, it had an important effect on religious life as he perceived it.

> Therefore it [predestination] possessed for him an importance for religious devotion and practice which it had not possessed for Aquinas nor even for Luther ... . The Christian's

---

50 Ibid., p. 981.
51 *BW*, vol. 5, p. 172.
52 D.L. Edwards, *Christianity, The First Two Thousand Years* (London, 1997), p. 315.
53 McGrath, *Calvin*, p. 166.

assurance of his election to eternal life was the deepest source of his confidence, his fearlessness, his humility, and his moral power.[54]

For centuries predestination had been something of an embarrassing relation of the Christian doctrinal family. The justice motif effects its rehabilitation, and if Calvin brought it out of the back bedroom, then the Calvinists sat it at the head of the table.

The Anglican position on this issue was (along with its conservative hierarchical system) one of the features which distinguished it from the continental Reformation. The seventeenth article of the Thirty-nine Articles sets out its stall somewhere between moderation and extremity. As Ian Green has written, it 'straddled rather than exactly mirrored the views of Lutherans and Calvinists.'[55] This is not to indicate that there was something vague or wishy-washy about the Anglican approach. The Thirty-nine Articles make a clear and anti-Pelagian statement, and predestination was one issue on which even the most moderate and career-minded traditionalist found it hard to compromise.[56] However, by the 1630s a new theological wave was purposefully eroding the old conservatism. On the eve of Laud's promotion to Canterbury a new edition of the English/Latin dictionary dedicated to the archbishop defined 'praedestinatiani' as 'a kind of heretiques.'[57] Not that either Laud or his followers ever openly declared the old creed as heresy, they could not, but a newer stress on the numinous meant that the natural inclination to it had vanished. In this area of predestination there were marked differences between the old Anglican school and the Laudian cortege. These differences are indicated starkly in the writings of Ussher and Bramhall.

Ussher's reputation as a Calvinist probably rests more on this issue than on any other. As a concept, it permeates his writings and it forms one of the most controversial aspects of the 1615 Irish Articles with which he was closely associated. Article twelve spelled out in clear terms that some were predestined to life, some reprobated to death, the number was known only to God.[58] There is much debate at present as to whether Ussher was responsible for these articles, but even if we discard direct authorship, their sentiments on ordained salvation are replicated throughout his writing. Indeed in his *Discourse of Religion Anciently Professed* he argues that predestination was not only part of an original tenet of an uncorrupted Church but also that it was one of its distinguishing features from the Roman Church. In other words, it formed a crucial part of his Church's self-identity as an independent body. When Pelagius and Celestius had begun to spread their poison, Ussher maintained

---

54 O. Chadwick, *The Reformation* (London, 1964), p. 94.

55 I. Green, 'Anglicanism in Stuart and Hanoverian England', in S. Gilley and W.J. Sheils (eds), *A History of Religion in Britain* (Oxford, 1994), p. 170.

56 P.G. Lake, 'Calvinism and the English Church, 1570–1635', *Past and Present*, 114, (1987): 45.

57 N. Tyacke, *Anti-Calvinists: the rise of English Arminianism, c.1590–1640* (Oxford, 1990), p. 183.

58 The Irish Articles are printed in W.D. Killen, *The Ecclesiastical History of Ireland* (2 vols, London, 1875), App. III; C. Hardwick, *A History of the Articles of Religion* (London, 1895), App. VI.

that Palladius and Patrick were the 'great depressers' of this grace.[59] Accordingly, Ussher identifies this as a fundamental feature of the Irish confession of faith,

> The doctrine which our learned men observed out of the Scriptures and the writings of the most approved fathers, was this, that God 'by his immoveable counsel ... ordained some of his creatures to praise him, and to live blessedly for him and in him, and by him:' namely, 'by his eternal predestination ... .'[60]

That Ussher continued to hold fast to this as a fundamental of faith is sometimes questioned. According to E.W. Watson, the elder Ussher 'emancipated himself from the narrow Calvinism of his education and approached the Anglican type of thought',[61] though it must be said that such statements are often more reflective of their authors' sympathies than their subject's. Richard Hone presents the most thorough case for Ussher's change of mind. Hone uses contemporary evidence from writers such as Henry Hammond, Peter Gunning and Herbert Thorndike to show that 'on the deep subjects of election and predestination', the archbishop's views underwent serious revision.[62] John Ball quotes another contemporary, Dr Brian Walton to similar effect. However, these nineteenth-century churchmen are anxious to reclaim Ussher to their established branch of Protestantism and dilute his somewhat Presbyterian theology.[63] Much of their evidence is characteristically typical of a theological grappling with a difficult aspect of doctrine rather than a relinquishing of it. The evidence suggests the contrary, that an extreme form of predestination remained a key part of Ussher's Christian understanding. A short piece of work written in his early twenties, and published as late as 1654 (as a true catechism to counter many others in circulation that were falsely attributed to him) indicates that just such a belief spanned his lifetime. *The Principles of Christian Religion* defines his belief on the matter in uncompromising terms. Here he states that God decreed 'from all eternity' what should come to pass in every small circumstance. To the question, did God determine some for salvation, others to rejection? he gives the following answer, 'Yes surely before they had done either good or evil, God in his eternal counsel set some apart upon whom he would in time shew the riches of his mercy and determine to withhold the same from others, upon whom he would shew the severity of his justice.'[64] This statement contains the two hallmarks of classic Calvinism, that is, supralapsarian determinism and double predestination. The former declared that before God created the world he decreed who should be elect. This was in contrast to the rival school of infralapsarians who claimed that the divine decree takes sin for granted, therefore it existed before the decree. God did not ordain this fall, rather he gave his permission.[65]

---

59   *UW*, vol. 4, pp. 259–60.
60   Ibid.
61   Watson, *Typical Churchmen*, p. 59.
62   R.B. Hone, *Lives of Eminent Christians* (London, 1839), pp. 51–3.
63   J.T. Ball, *The Reformed Church of Ireland, 1537–1886* (London, 1886), pp. 133–4.
64   *UW*, vol. 11, p. 203.
65   *Encyclopedia of Religion and Ethics*, ed. J. Hastings, (24 vols, Edinburgh, 1909), vol. 1, p. 808.

The latter is what Calvin termed the *decretum horribile*[66] which the second generation of Reformists developed from the medieval movement of *Schola Augustiniana*. This went further than declaring that God elected a minority, by stating uncategorically that he damned a majority.[67]

However much this hard-line stance of Ussher's is acknowledged, once again it does deserve slight qualification. Firstly, there is at times in his work a certain coyness that is unexpected in such an apparently unreconstructed Calvinist. In a preface he wrote to a sermon published in 1634 he recognises the delicate nature of the issue, ' ... reverent and modest fear how we pry too far into God's secret counsels seeing the best and ablest Divine on both sides acknowledge, that in many Questions about this Mystery we must be sane to take up St Paul's exclamation, O the depth.'[68]

There are two reasons for this, one implied, the other explicit. The first being that ordinary people ought not to be troubled with such weighty and potentially confusing issues. Here it is noteworthy that Ussher's book, *The History of Gotteschalk* (1631), which constitutes his most thorough statement on the controversy, was subject to elaborate arrangements to ensure that it was printed in Latin, thus limiting its audience to the educated few. The Second reason is probably even closer to Ussher's heart, and this has to do with Church unity. Both religiously and politically, an undivided Church is a motivating ideal as central to Ussher as it is underestimated. As this has important political implications, it will be explored more fully in Chapter 7 of this volume. Suffice to say his awareness that this particular issue was capable of generating more strife than any other meant that sometimes he was inclined to underplay it.

There is a further sign that Ussher was struggling somewhat, as others had done, with the apparent injustice of an elective process which excludes. In a sermon addressing this issue he berates those who cry '*Fatis agimur, credite fatis*' [Fate drives us, give in to fate] imputing their fate to destiny.[69] According to this sermon, God has foreordained salvation yet man is damned for his own wickedness. Ussher's obvious discomfort at this seemingly harsh image of God moves him to apportion the real blame to men in a way that leads him to self-contradiction and it is something which he never successfully resolves. It is just the uneasiness with antecedent judgement that forces him into this theological impasse. He is trying to place man back into a process he has already reserved exclusively for God. In the same sermon he claims that salvation is offered universally to every 'child of perdition.' He adds, for good measure, 'If any therefore be not delivered it is because they have said in their hearts, *Nolumus hunc* [we do not want this], our present pleasure shall be still our God.'[70] This is at total variance with other statements of Ussher which limit the number of elect. Elsewhere he attempts to square this circle in a number of ways. In his *Body*

---

66 Calvin, *Institutes*, III, xxi,5.
67 McGrath, *Calvin*, p. 166.
68 J. Ussher, *The Opinions of the Most Reverend Father in God, James Ussher* (London, 1634), p. 4.
69 *UW*, vol. 17, p. xxxii.
70 Ibid.

of Divinity (1647), to answer the rhetorical question, 'Does God mock reprobates' he uses a parable in which a king invites guests to a banquet. When they refuse, he does not compel them, instead he invites a second group, though this time the invitation is a command. ' ... in calling the latter forth, his will was absolute that they should come indeed, and so caused, that they did come, but to the first he only signified what he liked if they had done it.'[71] In the parable, Ussher only succeeds in watering down the divine injustice claiming that the initial invitation of the master was inclusive, yet the reader might reasonably object that the second guests still have an unfair advantage. Another, more purely theological attempt to resolve the problem is somewhat more successful. In his tract on the mystery of the incarnation, *Immanuel* (1633), he deals with the fullness of Christ's sacrificial act, which he maintains paid the ransom for all sinners. However, it is the third person of the Trinity which imparts faith and his actions are not comprehensive but 'wrought in those who are capable of understanding by that same spirit.'[72] Put more succinctly, Christ's redemptive gift may have been for all, but it was distributed by the Holy Spirit to the few.

All this theological speculation proves that although Ussher had pitched his predestination tent on very solid justice motif ground (since he maintains all its fundamentals) yet his attempts to explain and justify show that he is not always, to use a modern expression, a 'happy camper.' This was something he shared with many of the fellow residents on this particular site and should not be used as evidence of any doctrinal wavering. Patrick Collinson wrote that just such struggling was definitive of Protestantism which according to him was 'the religion which in principle rested upon but in reality wrestled with the mystery of predestination.'[73] In a recent article Crawford Gribben has taken Ussher to task for his use of this 'hypothetical effiency', that is Christ's death was sufficient for all, but efficient only for the elect. In this way Christ's death does not generate forgiveness; it only makes the sins of mankind forgivable. For Gribben this reduces Christ's death to a sign or 'trope.' The very theological method that Ussher previously castigated, 'The irony of Ussher's position was that his search for "proper speech" to describe Christ's passion – a speech devoid of tropes or figures – had turned the passion itself into a sign.'[74] To the present writer this seems a little harsh and it is argued here that in Ussher's explanation of atonement Christ's death represents more than a mere trope, it achieved something real, it is just that this reality still needed to be purchased in the life of the individual sinner by his conversion. Not being immediately effective does not render something unreal or symbolic.

Just as Ussher struggles with predestination so does Bramhall, but once more his struggle is taking place at the opposite end of the spectrum. Peter Lake argues that it was the very irreconcilability of radical theological pronouncements on universality

---

71   J. Ussher, *A Body of Divinitie* (London, 1647), p. 56.
72   *UW*, vol. 4, p. 607.
73   P. Collinson, *The Religion of Protestants* (Oxford, 1982), p.x.
74   C. Gribben, 'Rhetoric, fiction and theology: James Ussher and the death of Jesus Christ', *Seventeenth Century*, XX (2005): 67.

and election which led the new movement in English theology to challenge received opinion.

> ... the internal contradictions within Calvinist conformity were prompting a new style of divinity which was not based on Calvinist views of predestination, and indeed was capable of generating a critique of tenets central to contemporary Calvinist orthodoxy.[75]

Bramhall was very much a part of this 'new style of divinity', and characteristically his main objection to the method of the old school is that it would make God the author of sin. In a sermon in St Patrick's Cathedral, Dublin, he castigated those Protestant divines who fell into this trap because they so pressed the notion of election and reprobation.

> Some make God Himself the cover of their sins. Of all covers this is the worst ... Such are they, which make all things in the world, even sin itself, to come to pass fatally, inevitably, by virtue of a necessitating decree of God. Such are they, which make their Redeemer their packhorse ... to bear their presumptuous sins.[76]

Elsewhere, he branded such Christian distortions as not only heretical but worse. 'It was no 'passion' but a sad truth to call the opinion of fatal destiny 'blasphemous;' which maketh God to be directly the author of sin, which is a degree worse than atheism.'[77]

Bramhall's own internal struggle with predestination does not come, like Ussher's, from attempts to integrate it but rather how to limit its implications. He is well aware that he may not deny it without appearing heterodox, but he goes as far as he can to maintain a substantial amount of freedom in its schema. Also, like Ussher, his attempts to reconcile contrary statements almost lead him to self-contradiction. He manages to avoid this in two ways.

Firstly, he uses the infralapsarian argument that God does not cause sin. He may allow sin as He allows the sun to set but His part is not proactive. God may also be too patient, which hardens the heart, as He did with Pharaoh. The sin however was still Pharaoh's. The onus is placed squarely back onto man, even the Devil's role is somewhat pedestrian.

> No man is extrinsically, antecedently, and irresistably 'necessitated by temptation to steal.' The Devil may solicit us, but he cannot necessitate us. He hath a faculty of persuading, but not a power of compelling. '*Nos ignem habemus, spiritus flammam ciet ...* ' he blows the coals, but the fire is ours.[78]

Secondly, Bramhall uses a theological device that is often employed by those who want to rescue liberty from the constraints of God's prescience. It would appear from Christian dogma that God's knowing how we will act in future implies that we are not free to act how we will. Bramhall sets out to release prescience from

---

75 Lake, 'Calvinism': 45.
76 *BW*, vol. 5, p. 153.
77 *BW*, vol. 4, p. 250.
78 Ibid., p. 91.

this determinist straitjacket. God has foreknowledge because he is eternal, existing outside time. In this position, He is able to view all things, past, present, and to come simultaneously.

> ... because the infinite knowledge of God, encircling all times in the point of eternity doth attain to their future being ... The main impediment which keeps men from subscribing to this, because they conceive eternity to be everlasting succession, and not one indivisible point.[79]

Bramhall argues that it is in a sense wrong to talk of prescience or foreknowledge, or even before or after since these words are descriptive of time, 'For in God's knowledge there is neither before nor after, past nor to come.'[80] Therefore they have sense only in the chronological sphere. Outside of this, God may see and know all things without determining them. In this way, justice and goodness, both divine and human, survive and the omniscience of God is left intact. By employing this method, Bramhall resolves the contradiction in a manner which is altogether more satisfactory than Ussher, because not only does it have logic, but it preserves the integrity of God and man.

Perseverance

It is hardly surprising, given Ussher's hard-line defence of predestination doctrine that he declared also for the concomitant belief in perseverance. The idea that the elect, once justified, may not afterwards fall became something of a hallmark of the British-Protestantism of Ussher's generation. This was, according to the Georges, in part to antagonise the opposition, emphasising certainty of knowledge against Roman Catholic claims that limited such insights to miraculous events in the lives of saints.[81] However this was not merely an English phenomenon; it was crucial to the dogmatical systems of the Continental Reformers. For Luther, belief in personal salvation was requisite to good Christianity. To fail to have confidence in one's own salvation was tantamount to doubting the trustworthiness of God.[82] It is an paradox of the justice motif that the theological product of the initially pessimistic self-appraisal is in fact certainty. Such certainty does not work well with those who seek to promote the numinous, reliant as it is on precisely the opposite, uncertainty in the face of overwhelming mystery. It is hardly surprising then to find the Council of Trent's reaction to such a development is uncompromisingly dismissive. 'The just man cannot be certain of his predestination to eternal salvation. He remains liable to sin and is bound to work out his salvation in fear and trembling.'[83]

Writing in his *Antiquities of the British and Irish Churches*, Ussher argued that it was as impossible for the elect to fall as it was for the reprobate to achieve salvation.

---

79   Ibid., p. 153.
80   Ibid., p. 247.
81   Georges, *Protestant Mind*, pp. 58–9.
82   McGrath, *Reformation*, p. 115.
83   H. Jedin, *A History of the Council of Trent* (4 vols, London, 1961), vol. 2, p. 308.

The specific number of saved was known to God and this was unalterable, ' ... for if that number is not certain with God, either the Divine knowledge is deceived or the Divine will changed or the Divine power over swayed, but none but the impious and possibly not they themselves, will dare to affirm any of these.'[84]

For Ussher, justification was an actual event in the life of an individual when he accepted the word of God and he was sealed to salvation in a type of early modern version of being 'born again.' The word 'seal' is important denoting the once and for all nature of the event. In his sermons at Oxford in 1640, Ussher refers to this specifically as 'a day.' As if God had allotted to an individual a moment of Divine invitation. 'This day God holds out the golden sceptre, and my life for yours, if you accept it you shall be saved.'[85] This is what Ussher calls the 'effectual calling' and it is vital if being elect was to mean anything. Ussher argued that election is only the severing of one from the corrupt mass of Adam's posterity. The effectual calling was when one was translated from the death of sin to a life of grace.[86] After this event the nature of man remains sinful, but the power of sin has lost its effect. Ussher compared it to a fallen star which remains though its light does not shine, 'So it is with us, when sin doth lose its light, that it cannot work and shine as formerly to bind, imprison and condemn us, then it is said to be done away, when it cannot murder us, and hath lost its wanted force.'[87] Ussher took pride in the fact that this distinguished Protestants from their Catholic counterparts who lived their religious lives in a state of spiritual insecurity.

> ... they shall not serve God like unto the Papists [whose fearful and trembling consciences can have no assurance of their life, no comfort nor assurance of God's love], but they shall serve him joyfully without fear in full assurance of his love, wearing upon their heads the helmet of salvation, looking up boldly when their salvation appeareth.[88]

As mentioned above, it is an paradox of Reformed theology that the Christian eventually fares very well in spite of its underlying pessimism. Such a paradox had practical implications which could be exploited for evangelical purposes. The traditional Protestant line of approach involved two parts: 'mortification', in which the law 'terrified the conscience', followed by 'vivification', as one accepted Christ's salvation.[89] If one follows Ussher's 1640 Oxford sermons[90], it is not difficult to see that they were designed with exactly this purpose in mind.

Taken to its logical conclusion this dogma would ultimately imply separation since discernable salvation would allow restricted membership of the visible Church. This issue engendered a good deal of debate within Calvinism from which two wings emerged, one maintaining that a visible Church of Saints was feasible, the other

---

84 Trinity College Dublin Ms. 1185, *Antiquities of the British and Irish Churches*, p. 293.
85 *UW*, vol. 13, p. 12.
86 Ibid.
87 Ibid., p. 39.
88 Ibid., p. 475.
89 Cameron, *Reformation*, p. 127.
90 *UW*, vol. 13.

that it was not. These groups have been distinguished by the terms 'experimental' and 'credal' Calvinism.[91] Ussher's opinion was that the visible Church was made up of saints and sinners, but as William Sheils makes clear this does not indicate that he was not an experimental predestinarian. According to Sheils, Ussher's work demonstrates the more moderate tendency of the experimentalist, that is, a greater stress on the individual's salvation as opposed to a more congregational experience. In this he was not unusual. The logical consequences of such a position may have been separatism, but few followed that route and, in the seventeenth century, experimental predestinarianism focused on individual piety rather than on the congregation.[92]

The contrary notion of the single event salvation experience was the idea of the continuum, or a lifetime process of sanctification. This has been characterised as a continual search for forgiveness. Just as the Reformed expressions of fall and redemption had a practical value, the uncertainty of Catholic dogma on personal salvation stimulated a spiritual anxiety which would result in greater reliance on the Church, its sacraments and institutions.[93] Carter Lindberg describes how this process functions, 'In order to encourage more effort, pastoral practice consciously stimulated anxiety and introspection. The Church's pastoral theology suspended people between hope and fear – a sort of spiritual carrot-and-stick incentive system.'[94]

On the subject of perseverance, Bramhall is silent, which is significant in itself since stress in an important theological tool. One way to deal with an element of doctrine which one is not in agreement with is not to mention it at all. An advantage of this technique is that it does not leave the theologian open to direct attack, especially if he is (like Bramhall) susceptible to the charge of Popery. The second theological device open to Bramhall is to enforce his deafening silence on this issue by stressing the contrary approach, that is, a life of devotion which is reliant on the sacraments and the search for forgiveness. This wing of the Anglican Church had no need to respond in a purely theological way; their reaction was much more practical.[95] Since Bramhall's sacramental theology will be discussed in the next chapter an in-depth analysis here will not be necessary. Suffice to say his writings place considerable emphasis on their importance as a means of conferring grace; this was especially so of the sacrament of communion. 'The blessed sacrament is a means ordained by Christ to render us capable, and to apply unto us the virtue of that all-sufficient sacrifice of infinite value, which Christ made upon the cross.'[96]

Aside from the high evaluation of the Eucharist, Bramhall also pressed another characteristically Catholic response which was the pursuit of atonement. Whilst he is critical of the Roman Catholic versions of this sacrament (he could hardly get away with not being) he is also scathing of the Protestant's typical attitude, which confesses that we are sinners, and that is all. For Bramhall this signified nothing

---

91   R.T. Kendal, *Calvin and English Calvinism to 1649* (Oxford, 1979), passim.
92   W.J. Sheils, 'Reformed Religion in England, 1520–1640', in Gilley and Sheils, *History of Religion in Britain*, p. 163.
93   Green, 'Anglicanism', p. 172.
94   C. Lindberg, *The European Reformations* (Oxford, 1996), p. 63.
95   Tyacke, *Anti-Calvinists*, pp. xii–xiii.
96   *BW*, vol. 4, p. 221.

and was a 'little too presumptuous', elsewhere he adds, 'Those who would not trust their own judgement about their estate without advice of lawyer or bodies without physician, are wise enough of their own souls with any other direction. This is plain mocking of God.'[97] According to Bramhall, confession is as ancient as our first parents. With its requirements of contrition and atonement it makes a complete repentance, or as he claimed, some of the fathers of the Church would have it a 'second table after shipwreck' and that it 'extinguish[ed] the fire of Hell.' Compared to Ussher's statement that even repentance was irretrievably corrupted, this is very far-reaching. Bramhall's version of the Christian response is reflective of the whole numinous experience; it is a spiritual infusion the purpose of which is to exhilarate. Not only does it not encourage confidence but it relies on the opposite. Rudolf Otto's *mysterium tremendum* involves, as the term implies, an experience of something that is mystery.

It would appear then from the evidence of their dogmatic theologies that there was much which divided Ussher and Bramhall. Ussher's man is lost and inclined to damnation just as Bramhall's is lost but inclined to salvation. Ussher looked to the single salvific event that would salvage man from perdition. Bramhall looked to the ongoing religious experience of God in the numinous. At first sight it might appear that these approaches are straightforward representations of Calvinism and Laudianism. However, such labels present difficulties. Firstly, as will be seen in the following chapters on liturgy and Church government, Ussher was far from being a strict Calvinist. Secondly, with regard to Bramhall, it is doubtful that anything theological existed which could be usefully termed Laudian. Instead, the twin poles of the Justice and Numinous motifs more usefully describe that which captured the religious imaginations of Ussher and Bramhall respectively. As mentioned above, these poles are much more theologically nebulous than the rigid confines of previous categorisation. If we accept this, then not only does it explain how even fervent exponents of one might not entirely eliminate the other, but also how theologians as diverse as Bramhall and Ussher could, when circumstances demanded, maintain a working relationship.

---

97   *BW*, vol. 5 p. 160.

Chapter 4

Sacramental Theologies

The previous chapter described the respective approaches of Ussher and Bramhall in terms of the justice and numinous motifs. This is not to suggest that any conscious decision was made by either to opt for these particular strands of theology; Ussher did not decide in his early life that this particular element was the core of orthodoxy any more than Bramhall plumped deliberately for expressions of mysticism. Nevertheless, what Christians of the seventeenth century inherited from the Reformation was an almost subliminal attraction to separate expressions of the Judaeo-Christian religious experience, separate expressions which had been distinctive, even antagonistic yet never, in biblical or early Christian history, exclusive the one from the other. Nowhere is this cleavage more easily observed than in the areas of sacramental understanding and liturgical practice. The following chapter will explore the sacraments in terms of these biblical motifs and explore the implications of this theory for Ussher's and Bramhall's conceptions of the sacramental.

Before we explore these post-Reformation divergences, it is worth examining the biblical treatment of the law and holiness as well as the harmony and tension provided by such an unlikely symbiosis of theological understandings. As mentioned previously, the meaning in Hebrew of holiness is *Kadosh*, that is, separation[1]. In the book of Leviticus, there is a holiness code in which sacred places, objects, people are treated as if they belonged to another realm, where it is treated without the necessary fear or awe it is, as a consequence, profaned. Concomitant with this idea of separation is the רזן [rzn] or dedication and consecration. According to G.A. Butterick this is a conscious recognition of holiness and all that this entailed, 'man is forbidden to appropriate what belongs to God, ... The holy is unapproachable; man must not come near to it.'[2] In terms of physical reality this understanding of what is holy and separate is to be encountered in the various shrines, places of worship especially chosen, according to Roland de Vaux 'because the mysterious and fearful presence of a divinity in his sanctuary radiated around the place of worship.'[3] These places were of obvious importance amongst the various tribal groups especially because of their local significance and it is not difficult to see in them the roots of Christian practice. As Butterick indicates it is in the devotion of the Jewish sanctuary that we must look to find the precursor of Christian sacraments and liturgy.

> The ancient accounts of the establishment of sanctuaries through the holy presence and the *hieros logos*; the remembering, celebrating, teaching, sacrificing, and confessing activities

---

1 G.A. Butterick, *Dictionary of the Bible* (5 vols, Nashville, 1964), vol. 2, p. 617.
2 Ibid., p. 618.
3 R. de Vaux, *Ancient Israel* (London, 1961), p. 276.

of the ongoing life of the cult, the sacred objects ... with its elaborate paraphernalia and imagery; the cultic personnel, the life and worship of the synagogue, the liturgical development in hymns and prayers – to all these the Church was heir.[4]

However, such religious appreciation of the innate holiness of places, objects or buildings are problematic for two different reasons. The first of these problems is concerned with the image of Yahweh; the God of Israel was an aniconic deity, that is, He could not be represented in a visible or manageable way.[5] This is in contrast to other ancient religions of the Near-East whose gods could be used in totemic form for magic purposes or to pronounce curses. Yet there is at least a potential for the religious observances at sanctuaries with its use of sacred objects to infringe on the aniconic character of God. Walter Brueggemann described this tension between the aniconic and iconic in terms of the accessibility of Yahweh and his freedom.[6] There was a need to encounter God which counteracted the theological assumption that He was above manipulation.' Roland de Vaux sees this tension as most pronounced in that most sacred of Israelite objects, the Ark of the Covenant. The Ark was the vessel created according to biblical stipulations to house the ten commandments. In detailed passages of 1 Samuel 4–6 and 1 Kings 8 the Ark is described as the visible sign of God; it is to be considered as His 'footstool.' In contrast to this, Isaiah 6 expresses an idea which is almost a polemic against such notions of containment, 'Heaven is my throne, and the earth my foot-stool. What kind of a house could you build for me' As de Vaux points out the protest is certainly directed against the Temple of Jerusalem, but it refers also directly to the sacred furniture of the Temple.[7] Nor is the protest confined to Isaiah. According to Deuteronomy 10:1–5, the Ark is nothing more than a chest containing the tablets of the commandments.[8] Here, we may observe the way in which the justice and numinous motifs worked together in a theological version of a bad marriage, in spite of the friction, in spite of the apparent incompatibility and in spite of their obvious differences, they function together and even manage to complement each other. One can imagine that the importance of the decalogue received an added imperative being housed as it was in such a powerfully totemic object. Brueggemann insists that it is just such contradictions which give the Bible its vibrancy, 'No doubt the text contains a deep incongruity, but the God of the Bible does not flinch from this incongruity. It is this incongruity that makes human life possible and makes biblical theology endlessly problematic and promising.'[9]

The second problem raised by continual use of sanctuary worship is more practical. Such local usage, whilst initially only semi-autonomous has a tendency toward not only greater autonomy but lack of uniformity. This is a congenital problem of the numinous motif; greater local devotion is a threat to the general religious corpus, this is ultimately only dealt with by a greater centrality of worship along with a more asserted religious authority and this is precisely what happened

---

4   Butterick, *Dictionary of the Bible*, vol. 2, p. 624.
5   W. Brueggemann, *Old Testament Theology* (Minneapolis, 1992), p. 119.
6   Ibid., p. 137.
7   de Vaux, *Ancient Israel*, p. 299.
8   Ibid., p. 301.
9   Brueggemann, *Old Testament*, p. 43.

in Israel. As the previously nomadic tribes settled into a sedentary life, the Temple at Jerusalem emerged as the only place where sacrificial worship could legally be performed.[10] Where initially there had been no official priesthood in the time of the Patriarchs (acts of public worship were performed by the head of the family) later priests were 'sanctified for Yahweh.'[11] Jerusalem thus evolved as the holy city and the Temple that Solomon built was 'the holy of holies.' In this way not only was uniformity imposed but religion was to come under a much more official control. This considered, a further characteristic of the numinous motif may be added to those charted in the introduction, it has within it a propensity toward centralisation. Whereas the justice motif's concern with orthodoxy allows for certain flexibility of practice, the numinous motif's must by its very nature concern itself with orthopraxy, or else, as W.B. Yeats wrote, 'Things fall apart, the centre cannot hold.'[12]

If the saddling of the justice and numinous motifs that is biblical theology can be described as a bad marriage that survived in spite of the hidden grumblings, then divorce came in the sixteenth century of Christianity and the estranged parents dragged their children off in opposite directions. On the one hand the Reformers clung to the justice motif as an antidote to general corruption, and on the other the Church of Rome clung more closely to their repositories of the numinous. Nicholas Tyacke quoted Max Weber's famous summary of developments in this period, 'that every consistent doctrine of predestined grace inevitably implied a radical and ultimate devaluation of all magical, sacramental and institutional distributions of grace.'[13] The consequences of such elevations and devaluations are manifold. The Word of God was elevated over the sacramental, the church body becomes pulpit centred rather than altar centred, and the invisible grace of God is favoured over those visible representations of His power which are the Church, its sacraments and sacred objects. The theology of Luther was primarily a theology of the word of God. Protestants groups described themselves a *nach Gottes wort reformiert,* reformed according to the word of God.[14] On a liturgical and sacramental level what became crucial for those who favoured the numinous motif was the divine presence of God in the world. There is a strand running through the Reformation from Zwingli to later Reformers for whom such an approximation of divine and human was anathema.

The English Church at the time of Bramhall and Ussher provides something of an ecclesiastical conundrum in the history of the European Reformations. Here we have an example of a regime under Laud which, though ostensibly Protestant, seemed to be drawn to the numinous motif. Perhaps one of the clearest expressions of this attraction is to be found in the attitude to the church building. As Peter Lake points out, for a 'whole chorus of writers from the 1630s the church [was] conceived

---

10   de Vaux, *Ancient Israel,* p. 330.
11   Ibid., p. 345.
12   W.B. Yeats, *Selected Poetry* (London, 1991), p. 124.
13   N. Tyacke, *'Anti-Calvinists', The Rise of English Arminianism c.1590–1640* (Oxford, 1987), p. 10.
14   J. Pelikan, *The Christian Tradition: A History of the Development of Doctrine* (Chicago, 1984), p. 183.

as a physical structure, a specific place or site of worship; it was the house of God.'[15] When Laud blessed St Catherine Cree Church, Leadenhall Street, London, he did so with the words 'We consecrate this Church and separate it to Thee as holy ground not to be profaned any more to common use.'[16] According to James Wylie, admittedly no fan of Laud's, he afterwards pronounced curses on those who should profane it.[17]

Such deliberations were of course extremely controversial. In 1625, John Prideaux had urged that there was no inherent sanctity in church buildings. They were not holy in the objective sense except through Christ. For Laud they were *extra usum* the greatest residence of God.[18] Just how such a concept rankled is indicated by the London Root and Branch petition of December 1640 which condemned bishops for 'the Christening [sic] and consecrating of churches and chapels, the consecrating of fonts, tables, pulpits, chalices, churchyards and many other things, and putting holiness in them;'[19] This liturgical tug-of-war has obvious biblical parallels. The church building represents, for those of Laud's inclination, the sanctuary, the holy site of God in which one encounters the spirit in the numinous experience. The more reformed objectors are the theological inheritors of Isaiah, they are repeating in their own words his original question, that is, 'What kind of a house could you build for me?' They echo the deuteronomists who claimed that the Ark of the Covenant was nothing more than a chest containing the tablets of law.[20]

Aside from this disinclination toward the numinous there was a second problem for the Reformers with the prevailing attitude towards the sacraments. The previously held ideal that sacraments conferred grace was inconsistent with the notion that salvation was a once in a lifetime and wholly unwarranted experience. There was a real practical problem posed by Reformed dogma because the sinner who had achieved salvation had to ask himself what further need he had of added blessing. Euan Cameron explained the difficulty, 'The Reformers insisted that salvation came as an unmerited free gift direct from God, apprehended through the preaching of the Word; therefore, *any* rituals which claimed to "confer grace", let alone to "win merit", should have been drastically curtailed or entirely abolished.'[21] However, two of the sacraments were based on scripture which was so central to the Reformers' cause, in short, as Cameron says they were 'saddled with the sacraments.'[22] The solution for the first generation of Reformers came straight from their justice motif understanding of human corruption. The sacraments were God's response to man's weakness. This general attitude has been usefully summarised, 'Knowing our difficulty in receiving and responding to his promise, God has supplemented his Word

---

15   P. Lake, 'The Laudian Style, Uniformity and the Pursuit of the Beauty of Holiness in the 1630s', in K. Fincham (ed.), *The Early Stuart Church* (London, 1993), p. 164.

16   J.A. Wylie, *The History of Protestantism* (3 vols, London, 1879), vol. 3, p. 538.

17   Ibid.

18   J. Davies, *The Caroline Captivity of the Church* (Oxford, 1992), p. 53.

19   *Documents Illustrative of English Church History*, eds H. Gee and W.J. Hardy (London, 1896), p. 541.

20   De Vaux, *Ancient Israel*, p.299.

21   E. Cameron, *The European Reformation* (Oxford, 1991), p. 156.

22   Ibid.

with visible and tangible signs of His gracious favour. They are an accommodation to our limitations.'[23]

The English Church of the 1630s displayed no such difficulty with the idea of sacraments as a means to grace. The spirit of Laudianism has been defined as 'the divine presence in the world and the appropriate ritual response to that presence.'[24] One of Laud's priorities had been the conversion of the communion table into an altar. An Elizabethan injunction of 1559 had stipulated that it should be moved into the chancel for convenience. The very etymology of these words conveys a fundamental theological difference. The altar is the raised platform on which sacrifice is offered, the table is the place of nourishment. Laud's liturgical and sacramental theology is largely informed by his preference for the former at the expense of the latter. Kevin Sharpe objected recently that Laudian policy was less about theology and more about uniformity. Sharpe claims that while there was room in the Church for differences of belief and doctrine, the hedge of ceremony had to be uniform in all parts, 'unity cannot long continue in the Church where uniformity is shut out at the door.' There was nothing unusual in this since it had been a driving concern of Archbishops Parker, Whitgift and Bancroft.[25] In order to refute this claim, this chapter will set out to examine in Ussher's and Bramhall's work the fundamental liturgical and sacramental theological differences in two authors who are representative of the pre- and post-Laudian phases of the Anglican Church. It will also, as indicated at the start, set out to root these differences in the two strands of Old Testament theology which we have described.

Ussher and Bramhall on the sacraments

Given Ussher's doctrinal background it is hardly surprising that he delivers a very robust defence of the general Reformed position on sacraments. They are for him an addition, a complement and a confirmation of the Word. The main salvific event in the life of a sinner is the reception of the Word, what comes after this is a type of nourishment, an assistance on the journey of salvation. In his eighteen sermons at Oxford which set out the course recommended for the true conversion of a soul, it is only by sermon thirteen that Ussher gets to the sacraments, their function is clearly secondary.

> Now it hath pleased Almighty God, not only to teach us this by his Word; but because we are slow of heart to believe and conceive the things we hear, it pleases his glorious wisdom, to add to his word his sacraments, that so what we have heard with our ears we may see with our eyes, being represented by signs.[26]

For Ussher even the institutions of the Church are tainted since they are part of the general fallen world that is humanity. In his dialogue with Malone, he specifically

---

23 A. McGrath, *Reformation Thought* (Oxford, 1988), p. 162.
24 Lake, 'Laudian Style', p. 162.
25 K. Sharpe, 'Archbishop Laud', in Todd, *Reformation to Revolution*, p. 95.
26 *UW*, vol. 8, p. 192.

makes a distinction between the purity of God's Word which is 'the points of religion revealed unto the prophets, for the perpetual information of God's people', and the rites, ceremony and ordinances, 'which are left to the disposition of the Church, and consequently be not of divine but of positive and human rite.'[27]

This does not mean to imply that ceremony and sacraments are regarded by Ussher with the same disdain he had for the rest of man's work, they alone of human activity seem to escape outright condemnation. Indeed, elsewhere, Ussher displays a somewhat surprisingly high regard for things liturgical and sacramental (of which more will be discussed later). However they function as a distinctly secondary mode of encountering God. In his definition of a sacrament, Ussher makes the point that they are 'A ... visible sign ordained by God to be a seal for confirmation of the promises of the Gospel unto the due receivers thereof.'[28] There is a sense in this that the 'visible' sign is necessary since we may not, in our present state, rely on more spiritual capacity to see otherwise. There is also a sense that this is merely a 'seal' to the main soteriological event which has already taken place. In the same way Calvin saw the sacraments as dependent on the Word, aside from which they were devoid of function.[29]

The fundamentals of Bramhall's sacramental theology are based on an entirely different premise, though members of the congregation in Dublin Cathedral in 1661 would have been forgiven for thinking otherwise. Preaching as their new Primate, Bramhall sounded a very Protestant note with his definition of good religion.

> ... it preferreth grace before nature, the written Word before uncertain traditions, and the all sufficient Blood of Jesus Christ before the stained works of mortal men. A religion, which is neither garish with superfluous ceremonies, nor yet sluttish and void of all order, decency, and majesty in the service of God.[30]

However, regarded in its context, these sentiments lose some of their zeal, and must be seen as an attempt to convince his listeners that the restored regime was *bona fide* Protestant. The Dublin establishment prided themselves on maintaining a wide gulf of clear Protestant water between themselves and the rest of the Catholic population, such a strong identification with Reformed sentiments would no doubt have been appreciated. Yet a wider examination of Bramhall's work on liturgy and the sacraments reveals a greater enthusiasm than the above sermon might suggest. In his *Answer to S.N.*, after some slight words of caution that rites and ceremonies ought not stray into 'excessive superfluity' and become burdensome, Bramhall waxes lyrical on their meaning and purpose.

> Used as adjuments of decency, order, gravity, modesty, in the service of God, as expressions of these holy and heavenly desires and dispositions, which we ought to bring along with us to the House of God ... [they are] furtherances of edification, visible instructors, the

---

27   Ibid., p. 41.
28   Ibid., vol. 11, p. 193.
29   Pelikan, *Christian Tradition*, p. 188.
30   *BW*, vol. 5, p. 123.

books of ignorant men, helps of memory, exercises of faith, the leaves which preserve the tender fruit, and the shell which defends the kernel of religion from contempt.[31]

In his reply to Richard Baxter written in 1659, the leading Presbyterian who had charged Bramhall with popery, he defends the policy of himself and the 'episcopal clergy' in terms which reflect what the numinous motif interprets as man's inherent goodness. In the 1630s they had recognised in raising the sacramental and ornamental aspects of liturgy and worship the natural preference of man for reverence before profaneness. Men loved monuments of piety;

> ... they are for memorials of ancient truth, for an outward splendour of religion, for helps of mortification, for adjuments of devotion; all which our late innovators have taken away. Nature itself doth teach us that God is to be adored with our bodies as well as with our spirits. What comfort can men have to go to the Church where they shall scarcely see one act of corporeal devotion done to God in their whole lives These are the true reasons why the Roman emissaries do gain ground daily upon them, why so many apostate from them.[32]

Once more the positive appraisal of nature is a theological linchpin for Bramhall. In order to create memorials of ancient truth or to express the splendour of religion man must be in possession of some of the divine spirit; it is this divine spirit which also informs us of the will of God and it is this spirit which communes with God by acts of corporeal worship.

It would have been impossible for Ussher to defend the use of ceremony and sacrament on the same basis as Bramhall, and yet he manages from his own perspective an equally spirited defence. Ussher would not have gone as far as Bramhall in his use of such high liturgy but in his private practice and in his works he displays a regard which is initially surprising. Ussher defended formal liturgy to the House of Commons in 1642 when freer spirits would not be similarly restrained and he confirmed young adults. He wrote of the benefits imparted by both Protestant sacraments and he went so far as to defend auricular confession. In his own private worship, Ussher stuck to a highly formalized version of daily prayer which his chaplain used as proof of his sympathy with the established Church.[33] It would be wrong to interpret all of this as a deeper or unrevealed appreciation of the numinous. It is not possible to find a single utterance which reflects any kind of move in this direction. In order to understand where this emerges from one must look in a different direction and it is argued here that their source is twofold, that is, concern about order, and historical appreciation.

In his *Directions concerning the Liturgy and Episcopal Government* (1640), Ussher defends the Book of Common Prayer for the first of these reasons. In typical Ussherian fashion he turns immediately to the Bible for endorsement claiming, 'that God himself appointed in the law a set form of Benediction as Numbers 6, verses 23, 24, 25, 26.' Christ also had commanded his followers to pray by formula, and

---

31   Ibid., vol. 4, p.215.
32   Ibid., vol 3, p. 529.
33   Bernard, *Clavi*, pp. 58–60.

the entire act is intrinsic to uniformity and order. 'Of all prayers, premeditated are the best, ... and of premeditated prayers those which are allowed by public authority are to be preferred before those which are to be uttered by any private spirit.'[34] The practice and policy of Ussher with respect to liturgy will be discussed elsewhere in this work though it needs to be mentioned here that he was not so rigorous in pressing uniformity as the above would suggest. However, this passage is an important indication that a primary function of liturgy and ceremony for Ussher was not an encounter with the numinous but rather as a spiritual glue that held the body of the Church together, and as a mode of impressing authority. As suggested, in Ireland Ussher allowed for a certain amount of latitude in this area, but conversely the bonds of sound practice and the displays of service and authority were also of great importance. Orthopraxy for Ussher represented the fortress walls offering protection, identity and power; if Ussher extended those walls he did so in order to strengthen and not weaken his Protestant citadel.

The second source of Ussher's high regard for liturgy comes from historical appreciation. As an historian and antiquarian he knows too much of ancient Church custom to dismiss it, the question for him is how to interpret it in a way which is compatible with his theology. This is especially so with his work on the Irish and British Churches which he holds up as repositories of an independent and non-heretical faith. After such claims, Ussher struggles with lengthy explanations for such practice as the prayer to saints or invocation of the dead.[35] It is perhaps to his credit as an historian that he does nothing to avoid the task.

Bramhall was also concerned with the historical significance of sacraments, or rather their significance in history, and he was even more concerned with uniformity. However, their primary importance, their *raison d'etre* was spiritual. They represent the modus of acquiring the grace which would redeem the sinner. Yet just as Ussher's theology appears to move higher when he deals with sacraments, Bramhall's theology can appear lower on the same subject. Also, like Ussher, this appearance is largely misleading. When Bramhall attacks the Roman Church for its seven sacraments, image worship, or prayers in a 'tongue unknown,'[36] he can be as barbed as any of the Protestant polemicists, but beneath the rhetoric his objections are largely semantic. On the subject of sacramental ordination he even allows that it is a question of terminology and he concedes that the Roman Church ought to be allowed to describe the conferring of priesthood as a sacrament. Bramhall correctly indicates that such a usage is a recent development devised by the medieval theologian Peter Lombard and confirmed at Trent.[37] The word taken largely, argues Bramhall, would cover all manner of religious activities such as the washing of the disciples' feet. Sacrament in the real sense should only be used to describe the two that are scripturally based. Bramhall wrote, 'But strictly taken as a visible sign, instituted by Christ, to convey or confirm grace to all partakers, in this sense there are only two, these alone are

---

34 J. Ussher, *Directions concerning Liturgy*, Thomason Tracts, E1004, pp. 1–2.
35 *UW*, vol. 3, pp. 256–70.
36 *BW*, vol. 1, p. 54.
37 Ibid., p. 55.

necessary to salvation. Their sacramental virtue we acknowledge.'[38] This sacramental pruning may appear very Reformed, but as far as it was rejecting Catholic doctrine it was only rejecting recent Catholic doctrine. Besides, any description that contains the statement 'necessary to salvation' when discussing the sacraments most certainly can never be seen as orthodox Protestantism. It must also be added with regard to confirmation, ordination, matrimony, penitence and prayers for the sick, that they were not in practice rejected but kept, though not as sacraments. They were precisely for this reason, according to Bramhall, retained all the more purely.[39]

Baptism

On the first of these sacraments, that is baptism, Ussher's pronouncements give us a general indication of his overall approach to this area of dogma. In his *A Body of Divinitie*, he declares that baptism, is a high ordinance of God ... and not to be neglected ... yet where God denieth it ... there come no danger from the want of the sacraments, but only from the contempt of them.'[40] This is a particularly thorny issue for divines of Ussher's persuasion owing to the fact that it was a sacrament instituted by Christ and yet if its importance is allowed it would impinge on perseverance, which as a doctrine rests on inner conversion. Perhaps for this reason, Ussher shows some reluctance to enter the controversy. In a letter to his theological confidant Samuel Ward, Ussher is uncharacteristically reticent.

> You have done me a great pleasure in communicating unto me my Lord of Salisbury and your own determination touching the efficacy of baptism in infants; for it is an obscure point, and such as I desire to be taught in by such as you are, rather than deliver mine own opinion thereof.[41]

Ward was engaged in a dispute with William Bedell[42] at this time, and he kept his friend informed of the issues, and we can learn much about Ussher's position from his comments to Ward. The Cambridge professor had argued that baptism was not 'obsignatory' nor is the ablution of sins conditional or expectative. Bedell on the other hand maintained that it simply anticipated the salvation event of later life.[43] There is more at stake in this debate than perseverance since the efficacy of infant baptism taken to its logical conclusion would question the whole dogma of election, reprobation and predestination. Ward had been part of the English delegation at Dort where he had argued that baptism and predestination ought not to be connected. In his correspondence with Bedell he asked what need there would be of baptism during

---

38   Ibid.
39   Ibid., p. 56.
40   J. Ussher, *A Body of Divinitie or the summe and substance of Christian Religion* (London, 1647), p. 419.
41   *UW*, vol. 15, p. 482.
42   William Bedell (bap. 1572–d. 1642) a graduate of Emmanuel College, Cambridge was made provost of Trinity College, Dublin at the instigation of Ussher in 1627. In this role he was most famous for championing the use of the Irish language as a proselytizing tool.
43   Ibid., p. 543.

infancy if it produced no effect until the years of discretion. What is significant for us is Ussher's approval of these sentiments and his disapproval of the contrary position which he calls 'the opinion more vulgarly received.'[44] and the 'rigid part.'[45] In a letter to Ward in 1630, he pressed him to publish his opinions in 'answer to animadversions' of Bedell.[46] This said, Ussher's esteem for the efficacious nature of the first sacrament never infringed on his first principle of single event salvation. In terms of imparting grace sufficient to salvation baptism was always going to come a poor second to the reception of the word. Ussher spelled this out in his series of sermons at Oxford. ' ... it is twice set down in the Galations, 'neither circumcision nor uncircumcision' but faith which worketh by love; and again 'neither circumcision nor uncircumcision' but 'a new creature.'[47]

For the main body of Reformers, baptism as a sacrament had grown and not diminished in importance. This may be seen as simply a result of their paring away of others that had lost their value. In some sense baptism now took on some of the functions of other sacraments. This was especially so of confession. Euan Cameron quotes Luther, Melanchthon and Calvin to describe this development.

> The importance of baptism, then, increased as the 'sacrament' of penance was abolished. Baptism *was* the 'sacrament of penance'; penance was 'nothing but a return to baptism'; baptism was 'a sufficient substitute for all the sacraments which we might need as long as we live.'[48]

However, these same Reformers were too attached to the justice motif to accept any notion that the rite represented some kind of spiritual cleansing. To the Lutherans, baptism still effected a change, imbibing a newness of life, without which salvation was not possible. For Calvinists it was the outward sign of a previous election.[49] The prevailing Reformed theology suggested instead that baptism, though not an elimination of sin, was a sign that this sin had lost its effect, it was no longer imputed. Calvin described it as a promise that sin would not dominate the baptised.[50]

If this was the prevailing Reformed definition then we must conclude that Bramhall is well outside of the broad tradition. His own definition is a plain statement that succinctly states the contrary position that the sacramental rite of baptism involves a spiritual ablution. 'We acknowledge that sins are remitted by Baptism; that thereby we are made the children of God, the members of Christ, and inheritors of the Kingdom of Heaven.'[51] As stated above, Bramhall also regarded baptism as *necessary* for salvation, an opinion which could never be described as Protestant orthodoxy no matter how much the Reformers regarded its sacramental role. These

---

44 Ibid., p. 482.
45 Ibid., p. 584.
46 Ibid., p. 540.
47 Ibid. vol. 8, p. 247.
48 Cameron, *European Reformation*, p. 159.
49 S.C. Karant-Nunn, *The Reformation of ritual: an interpretation of early modern Germany* (London, 1997), p. 61.
50 Calvin, *Institutes*, IV, xix, 17.
51 *BW*, vol. 5, p. 190.

features of Bramhall's sacramental theology are indicative of the numinous experience with its roots in the cultic practice and the high importance it placed on ceremonial worship. Membership of the tribe of Israel determined who participated in the cult of Yahweh, who approached the sanctuary, and it was marked with the outward sign of circumcision (Genesis 17:11–12). It also determines who may be considered part of the salvation experience which is the covenant of God.[52] As part of the Christian numinous experience this initiation into the salvation experience involved instead of the visible sign, the invisible cleansing of sin. It is, however, important to point out that saying that baptism is necessary for salvation is not the same as saying that it is essential for salvation. The difference lies in those cases of emergency when baptism is not otherwise available. As mentioned in the previous chapter, Bramhall castigates the Roman Catholics who will not allow salvation for the unbaptised.[53] Bramhall regards the necessity as part of God's law; however, he asks the question, 'Is God bound by His own law?' The resounding answer to this rhetorical question is of course 'no.' God alone is able to forgo this necessity to allow for good. This position is almost a replica of Laud's as expressed in his *Conference with Fisher* where he stated, ' ... it may be concluded directly out of scripture, both that infants ought to be baptized, and that baptism is necessary to salvation ... [in the ordinary way of the Church, without binding God to the use and means of that sacrament, to which He hath bound us].'[54] There is in the theology of Laud and his cohorts a thoroughly modern tinge which means that their enthusiasm for the numinous is never allowed to get in the way of their basic humanism. Just as the Roman Church was entering into one of the most harsh and pedantic phases of its history, the precursors of Anglo-Catholicism were refusing to follow a similar route. It is perhaps ironic that one of the most draconian of English Church governments was also the natural father of its version of liberal theology. In the nave they may have been dictators but in the pulpit and on the page they were progressives. A feature which sits curiously with their general bombast; perhaps, in the eyes of history, this might mitigate some of the worst extremes of their behaviour.

The Eucharist

Baptism, as already stated, emerged from the Reformation as both a winner and a loser. It won greater kudos from its position as a genuine sacrament at the expense of others, yet for Reformers such as Ussher who had already placed all their soteriological eggs in the basket of the single salvific event it was difficult to find any more room for a rite of Christian initiation. Perhaps even more significant was the Reformed assessment of that other remaining sacrament which was the Eucharist. The re-evaluation of the nature and efficacy of this key sacrament was according to the Georges the most important feature in the Protestant break from the Roman Catholic system.[55] Here too the new emphasis on the soteriological was bound to

---

52   D. Cohn-Sherbok, *The Blackwell Dictionary of Judaica* (Oxford, 1992), p. 90.
53   *BW*, vol. 4, p. 981.
54   Laud, *Works*, vol. 4, p. 560.
55   Georges, *Protestant Mind*, p. 348.

result in a shift in focus from the sacramental. The difficulty was what to do with the thing that had been not only the most important of the sacraments, but also the centre of Christian worship. The earlier Reformers had been too steeped in Catholic tradition to ditch the central liturgical importance of the Eucharist. Their followers were not so deferential. For this reason there was a Protestant theological evolution which saw a general demotion of the sacred and a promotion of the symbolic. This development reflected also the movement toward the word and the law of the justice motif as opposed to the mystical imagery of the numinous motif. The great liturgical historian Gregory Dix described this historical process,

> The Reformers themselves therefore tried hard to retain a central importance and meaning for the Eucharist in Christian worship. But in every case they failed to carry their followers with them. Throughout the Churches of the Reformation, the Eucharist rapidly assumed the position of an occasional addition to a worship which ordinarily consisted only of praises, prayer, exhortation and reading. [56]

Such liturgical marginalising had two main theological effects which may be seen as counterblasts not only to Roman Catholic orthodoxy but also to the developments of the medieval period. During this time the host had become the greatest of all relics, as a sacred object it was worshipped and adored by people who brought to it their petitions.[57] It was the central presence of Christ in the churches. Secondly, it was also seen as the sacrificial victim, which is the literal translation of the Latin word *hostia*. Such notions are so firmly rooted in the numinous motif that it is difficult to see how they would have survived any move toward the justice motif. As the Reformation progressed, such metaphysical leftovers from a more mystical age dropped off like leaves from a tree leaving only the branches of the law and the word of God.

One of the main features of Laudian reforms in the English Church was an attempt to retrieve some of these leaves which had fallen during what they saw as the Puritan winter, or at least to provide some blooms of their own. Chief of all their concerns was to reverse the trend that had divested the Eucharist of all its metaphysical qualities. For Laud the sacred bread, and not election was the remedy for sin.[58] New emphasis on the Eucharist in the 1630s worship attempted to revive the feelings of awe which characterise the numinous experience. The communion table became an altar; it was placed in the east and was immovable, and it was railed to indicate its sacredness. In this way the congregation's heads were turned from the pulpit to the altar. The church was the house of God, this status was conferred by the presence of the divine, but that presence was not evenly spread throughout the building. The intensity of the divine presence in the Eucharist lent a glow of holiness to the altar upon which the sacrament was administered.[59]

Such a development must have tested the loyalty of James Ussher. It had been his proud boast in his work on the religion of the early Church in Ireland and Britain that such divisions, barriers or inaccessibility was not a feature of their forefathers'

---

56   G. Dix, *The Shape of Liturgy* (London, 1942), p. 600.
57   C. Lindberg, *The European Reformations* (Oxford, 1996), p. 186.
58   N. Tyacke, 'Archbishop Laud', in Fincham (ed.), *Early Stuart Church*, p. 62.
59   Lake, 'Laudian Style', p. 171.

early practice. Categorically the altar was not cut off from the people as the place of sacrifice as it had been in the later corruption of liturgy.⁶⁰ One of the consequences of the devotional stress on 'fear' and 'awe' (which he argued had emanated out of the East in deference to Syrian devotional liturgy) was that there had been a general cessation of lay communion.⁶¹ In response to this it had been an important feature of the Reformation that access to the sacraments would be freer; this was especially important as they had come to be regarded as an auxiliary means of proclaiming the gospel message. E. Cameron explained that such an idea emerged from the new importance of faith. 'Since they worked through faith, sacraments had to be publicly proclaimed, they were in effect simply a different way of setting forth the Word.'⁶² This new emphasis on faith meant of course that the efficacy of the Eucharist was dependent on the faith of the communicant. This was a new theological way of thinking and it is one which finds considerable favour with Ussher. Arguing that in real terms the bread and wine of communion underwent no change he maintained that its transformation was purely spiritual and that furthermore it was totally reliant on the faith of the recipient, 'So that in the use of this holy ordinance, as verily as a man with his body, hand and mouth receiveth the earthly creatures; so verily doth he with his spiritual hand and mouth, if any such he have, receive the body and blood of Christ.'⁶³ Ussher went on to state plainly that you cannot receive the benefits unless you have communion with Christ first. We must 'have the son' before we 'have life.'⁶⁴ As with baptism the conversion event is of primary importance. What happens after this is a seal or confirmation. In short, it is the reception of God's word that is decisive; Ussher agrees with William Perkins that the sacraments act as 'appendantes.'⁶⁵ Arnold Hunt has done much to dispel the notion that English Calvinists had little regard for the Eucharist; nevertheless the word was always going to be primary. The sacrament was a spiritual food to sustain and nourish the saved Christian. Hunt points out that it was seen as a 'visible word.'⁶⁶ For this reason any high estimation of the sacramental in Ussher, Perkins, or others of their leaning, must be seen as an expression of the justice motif. This idea that the individual's faith had a defining effect on the nature of a sacrament was contrary to a concept universal since Aquinas had described the *opus operatum*. This set out that the effectiveness of the sacrament was independent of the piety of the recipient.⁶⁷ As early as 1519, Luther was expounding the contrary *opus operantis* and pinning all sacramental significance on 'the faith on which everything depends.'⁶⁸

---

60   *UW*, vol. 4, p. 278–9.
61   Dix, *Shape of Liturgy*, p. 594.
62   Cameron, *European Reformation*, p. 255.
63   *UW*, vol. 2, p. 429.
64   Ibid.
65   A. Hunt, 'The Lord's Supper in Early Modern England', *Past & Present*, 161 (1998): 55.
66   Ibid.
67   Lindberg, *Reformation*, p. 187.
68   M. Luther, *Luther's Works*, ed. T. Lehmann (55 vols, Philadelphia, 1960), vol. 35, p. 66.

Accessibility is somewhat surprisingly of importance to Bramhall who uses it in his *Answer to S.N.* as a stick with which to beat the Roman Church. In his general defence of the English approach to the sacrament he declares that far from devaluing its importance they have retained it more purely since they do not debar the congregation from participation.

> For all the essentials of their sacrifice are contained in our celebration of the Holy Eucharist, that is, according to their schools the consecrations, and consumption of the whole or part. Both these we have as well as they: the former more purely than they, the latter more eminently than they, inasmuch as with us both Priest and people do receive, with them the Priest only.[69]

This said, Bramhall's reverence for the Eucharist which he described to his Dublin congregation as 'the very conduit pipe of grace to all worthy communicants, the manna of life and immortality',[70] means that he maintained a great sense of its awe and fear-inspiring properties. In the same sermon, he urged his flock to prepare themselves as the wedding guest approaching the nuptial feast for it was, he grimly warned, death for the uncircumcised to eat the paschal lamb.[71] It is also interesting to note that Bramhall does not balk at the term sacrifice when describing the Eucharistic rites. This is not to say the he did not express some strongly held objections to contemporary Roman interpretations of the term. Of course Bramhall was not alone in this respect (Bucer was happy to use the word), nevertheless it is significant when someone could speak from inside the Protestant fold and uses the term with impunity. As far as Bramhall was concerned the whole issue was once again a question of semantics. In his argument with the Roman Catholics he tussled over its exact meaning defining it in a more limited sense.

> ... that is, a commemorating sacrifice, or a representative sacrifice, or to apply the sacrifice of Christ by such means as God hath appointed. But for any sacrifice that is meritorious or propitiatory by its own power or virtue, distinct from the sacrifice of Christ, I hope the author will not say it.[72]

Bramhall interpreted this more precise definition of the propitiatory sacrifice that the Council of Trent had declared *extra quam non est salus*, 'necessary for salvation' as a deliberate attempt by Rome to exclude other Catholic Churches such as the English. Schismatics, he argued, will eventually have to justify their separation with new doctrine, 'So, of later times, the opinions of the lawfulness of detaining the cup from the laity, and of the necessity of adoring the sacrament, have by consequence excluded the Protestants from the participation of the Eucharist in the Roman Church.'[73]

In his *Answer to M. de la Milletièrre*, Bramhall uses a logical objection to the Roman idea of sacrifice arguing persuasively that Christ could not have sacrificed

---

69 *BW*, vol. 5, p. 27.
70 Ibid., pp. 163–4.
71 Ibid., p. 164.
72 Ibid., p. 188.
73 Ibid. vol. 3, p. 572.

himself at the last supper since this would have rendered any further sacrifice on the cross superfluous. Bramhall goes on, however, to acknowledge a commemorative sacrifice, 'a representation of that sacrifice to God', adding also that 'we acknowledge an impetration of the benefit of it: we maintain an application of its virtue.'[74] According to the twenty-second session of the Council of Trent the mass was not a repetition of the expiating sacrifice of Calvary, but was instead an identical sacrifice in everything save *modus operandi*.[75] It was the opinion of Bramhall that this development had dramatic consequences. In perhaps his most strongly worded attack on the Church of Rome, he claimed that in a certain sense they had as a result extinguished their office of priesthood so that it remained in name only.

> ... by corrupting the doctrine of saving truth, in a manner frustrated, at least much hindered, the end of holy Orders, do therefore, as I conceive, deny them the title, not 'in sensu diviso' as if they wanted the essentials of holy Orders but 'in sensu compositio', in respect of those superstitious errors and inventions of their own, which they had mixed with the truth.[76]

This is harsh criticism indeed and an example of Bramhall seen at his most Protestant, yet it is also worth considering that elsewhere in his work he continually points out that his position is shared with moderates within the Roman Church.[77] The papal curia as regarded by Bramhall is in the hands of extremists and it is against these that his barbed comments are aimed. Besides, in the most important respect, that is, in the essence of their understanding, the two churches are, according to Bramhall, in essentials the same.

> Seeing therefore the Protestants do retain both the consecration, and consumption or communication, without all contradiction, under the name of a Sacrament, they have the very thing, which the Romanists call a sacrifice. How is the world amused with a show of empty names to no purpose.[78]

In his reply to Baxter, Bramhall gives a type of résumé of his career as a controversialist in which he says that this attitude toward the papists as set out above had been the thoughts of his younger days and had in time been confirmed and radicated in him. The controversies of the English Church and Rome were 'logomachies', scholastic subtleties and things indifferent, the use of which every Church ought to be at liberty. These differences were neither insurmountable nor an obstacle to eventual union.

> When all these empty names and titles of controversies are wiped out of the roll, the true controversies between us may be quickly mustered, and will not be found upon a serious enquiry, to be either so exclusive of salvation to those who err invincibly and hold the

---

74 Ibid. vol. 1, pp. 54–5.
75 M.A. Mollett, *The Catholic Reformation* (London, 1999), p. 60.
76 *BW*, vol. 4, p. 249.
77 Ibid., p. 221.
78 Ibid., pp. 221–2.

truth implicitly in the preparation of their minds, nor altogether so irreconcilable as some persons have imagined.[79]

For Ussher the sacrificial interpretation of the Eucharist was not only a hindrance to unification but also a reason for departure. He was therefore naturally horrified at any attempt to rehabilitate it as a concept in any form, no matter how reconstructed. In 1641 Ussher, along with Ward, Prideaux and others of a similar disposition, put their name to a House of Lords Committee report which addressed what they conceived of as growing signs of Arminianism. The sixth objection refers to those who call the Lord's supper 'a sacrifice' (naming Peter Heylin) adding that it appears now 'that we have a true altar.'[80] However sacrifice was one of those terms which Ussher, as an historian, was aware had antiquity. Given this historical precedent, Ussher was at pains to explain that there was a wide difference in the early usage and the modern Roman heresy. In their late liturgical corruption, the papists separate the sacrifice of the mass from that of the consummation. In earlier times, at least in the British and Irish Churches, they had not done so.

> For they did not distinguish the sacrifice from the sacrament, as the Romanists do now-a-days: but used the name of sacrifice indifferently, both of that which was offered unto God, and of that which was given to and received by the communicant.[81]

All this is very similar to Bramhall's argument that the essence of sacrifice is maintained by the Protestants in their consecration, consumption and communication. Both Ussher and Bramhall are reluctant to isolate any particular part of the sacrament as an independent act of sacrifice. Each argues that the term can only justifiably refer to the whole. The difference between Ussher and Bramhall appears to be in reaction. Ussher recognises the distinction and is therefore repelled by the modern usage. Bramhall recognises it and is not only prepared to use the term according to his interpretation but also to disregard it as an obstacle to eventual Christian reconciliation. For Ussher, it is a byword for heresy, for Bramhall it is *adiaphora*, 'things indifferent' or, as he would say, mere 'logomachies.'

Ussher's criticism of modern Roman interpretation is generally common to Protestant theologians of his generation and it would be an error to regard him as a Zwinglian. The Swiss reformer had taken Protestant Eucharistic theology to its most logical limits, when asking 'What then does this eating do?' His adamant reply was, 'Nothing but make it plain to your brother that you are a member of Christ, and one of these who trust in Christ.'[82] In other words it was nothing more or less than a 'communion.' The writings of Ussher on this subject convey a deeper understanding. For him the Eucharist represented more than a bonding ritual or even a commemoration; it had real mystical content. If Ussher has rejected the sacrificial aspect of Eucharistic liturgy he most certainly had not rejected the sacred aspect.

---

79   Ibid. vol. 3, p. 540.
80   Lambeth Palace Library, Ms. 1603.25.13, 'Touching Innovations in the Doctrine and Discipline of the Church of England', 1641.
81   UW, vol. 4, p. 277.
82   H. Zwingli, *Writings*, ed. E.J. Furcha (2 vols, Pennsylvania, 1984), vol. 2, p. 141.

This is most clearly displayed at Oxford in 1640 when, like Bramhall, in his 1660 Dublin sermon, he warned his congregation that to eat and drink the sacrament unworthily was a great sin. 'So that now what was ordained to life, and appointed to be a seal and confirmation of God's love and favour is now changed and become a seal and confirmation of God's anger and indignation.'[83] The reason for this is clear; it is because they have taken them deeming them 'elements not different from bread and wine', whereas they are dishes wherein Christ is served.[84] Unlike Bramhall, however, Ussher does not regard the sacrament as being so important as to make it necessary for salvation. The Eucharist as a spiritual food provides a nourishment for the redeemed soul, the worst that can happen to those who forgo this assistance is that they will miss out on the benefits of a particular source of strength. There is hardly any suggestion that this will result in spiritual starvation, because, as far as Ussher is concerned, once saved the sinner can never die, 'Such as have knowledge, grace and faith in Christ shall taste of the new wine ... which notwithstanding may eat and drink unworthily, and come unpreparedly, and irreverently whereby they lose that comfort that otherwise they might have.'[85] Elsewhere he makes this issue a point of objection in his debate with William Malone. Here he castigates Malone's Church who would send to perdition those who did not partake of the Eucharist. This, for Ussher is too harsh a doctrine, ' ... to hold that all they are excluded from life, which have not had the means to receive the sacrament of the Lord's supper is as untrue as it is uncharitable.'[86] This said, there is an interesting aberration in Ussher's position on the necessity of this sacrament.

Having made himself abundantly clear on the issue, Ussher makes a statement in one of his Oxford sermons which appears to contradict all of his previous pronouncements. In pressing the importance of the Eucharist as a sustenance on the journey of salvation he suggests that without it the soul would be in grave danger even unto a fall from Grace, 'There is such an opposition, and antipathy betwixt the flesh and the spirit, that did not God refresh the spirit now and then, it might be overborne by the bulk of our corruptions.'[87] It is difficult to understand Ussher's approach on this occasion, not only does he contradict explicit statements on perseverance found elsewhere in his work but he also manages to contradict something he has said earlier in the same sermon.[88] Knowing how painstakingly Ussher chose his words it is also difficult to assume that he was carried away with his enthusiasm for the sacrament, perhaps the only point we can make is that there is a note of conjecture in this statement. Ussher uses the words 'might be overborne' as if to suggest that so important is this sacrament that without it who knows what might occur. Such caution goes some way to resolve such an alarming inconsistency.

After describing what Ussher said the Eucharist was not, we must turn our attention to what he said it was. The sacrament is in Ussher's view, taken in its

---

83   *UW*, vol. 8, p. 194.
84   Ibid.
85   Ibid., pp. 202–3.
86   Ibid., vol .3, p. 55.
87   Ibid., vol. 8, p. 203.
88   Ibid., p. 202.

fullest extent, best comprehended as two things; firstly the outward/visible which the schools call *sacramentum* and the intangible *rem sacramenti*. Ussher explained this distinction,

> Thus in the Lord's supper, the outward thing, which we see with our eyes, is bread and wine; the inward thing, which we apprehend by faith, is the body and blood of Christ: in the outward part of this mystical action, which reacheth to that which is *sacramentum* only, we receive this body and blood but sacramentally; in the inward, that containeth *rem*, the thing itself in it, we receive them really: and consequently the presence of these in the one is relative and symbolical, in the other, real and substantial.[89]

It is precisely the confusing of these two separate states which has, according to Ussher, caused all the mischief and is made the principal occasion of that 'woeful distraction which we see amongst Christians at this day, and the very fuel of endless strifes, and implacable contentions.[90] It is interesting to see this opinion echoed in the twentieth century by the renowned modern Catholic scholar Edward Schillebeeckx. In his work on the sacraments he makes a very similar point pinning the blame for confusion at the door of Peter Lombard and the medieval scholastics. These, claims Schillebeeckx, were so concerned with constitutive elements that they melded together the previously distinct concepts of *materia* (Ussher's *sacramentum*) and *forma* (*rem sacramenti*).[91] Ussher would have been somewhat bemused had he been able to hear his own understanding emerging from so prominent a Catholic some four centuries later. He would not have been surprised, one feels, that Schillebeeckx had his license to teach revoked by the Vatican for this and similar statements.

This confusion by Catholics of *sacramentum* and *rem sacramenti* is what Ussher believed had lead them to their most heinous of sacramental heresies, that is, transubstantiation. The belief that after consecration nothing was left of the bread and wine was a mistake which emerged precisely from the confusion of visible and non-visible elements.[92] However, given Ussher's predisposition to Rome and his apocalyptic leanings, he was always unlikely to regard the issue as merely an error of theology. There were far more sinister reasons for the confusion and Ussher claimed to have discovered their real origin in witchcraft. In a tale from Irenaeus a necromancer and idol maker called Marcus was by the use of black magic able to make wine in a chalice transform into blood. This abomination, claimed Ussher, was brought first into the Eastern Church and then the Roman 'and for those Romish fornications and inchantments wherewith the whole West was corrupted by that man of sin whose coming was foretold.'[93] This explanation, together with his previous high scholarship is a fine example of how Ussher combined technical theology and expert philology with an almost demotic apocalyptical outlook. It also explains something of his contemporary popularity, as an author he could present

---

89   Ibid. vol. 2, p. 427.
90   Ibid.
91   E. Schillebeeckx, *The Sacrament of the Encounter with God* (London, 1977), pp. 92–3.
92   *UW*, vol. 3, p. 52.
93   Ibid., p. 75.

fine scholarship together with popular prophetics which assured him a very broad appeal.

As already mentioned, Bramhall regarded transubstantiation, along with the notion of propitiatory sacrifice, as doctrine that was primarily responsible for the divisions that now blighted the Christian world. Bramhall regarded himself as an English Catholic and he saw his Church as one of many Catholic Churches whose independence was an essential part of the overall unity. He looked to the Coptic and Ethiopian Churches of North Africa as examples of autonomy and union. Transubstantiation had first been voiced four hundred years before Bramhall at the Lateran council; this had precipitated a split that finally rent Christendom when Trent had declared those who denied it anathema.[94] When M. de la Milletièrre, hoping to convert Charles II, had asked Protestants why they had not denounced transubstantiation earlier, Bramhall's reply was simple, 'But if we had rejected it four hundred years sooner, that had been a miracle. It was not so soon hatched. To find but the word 'Transubstantiation' in any old authors; were sufficient to prove him a counterfeit.'[95] There is much truth in this argument and it is a truth which is admitted, albeit tacitly, within the canons of the Council of Trent itself. The initial draft of canon two, on the Eucharist, had spoken of the doctrine which 'our fathers and the universal Catholic Church have very suitably called Transubstantiation.' This was later amended to become more simply and more truthfully that 'change the Catholic Church very suitably calls transubstantiation.'[96] Furthermore, some of the Catholic bishops present at Trent had wanted it suppressed as a modern construction, the term was eventually accepted precisely because Luther had rejected it. It might be seen as a theological version of throwing down the gauntlet, it was a political banner of the orthodox faith suitably proclaiming, in the sixteenth-century situation, the difference between the Reformers' and the Roman Catholic view of the Eucharist.[97]

There is something that must be added to this historical interpretation. It is true up to a point that transubstantiation was defined, along with other eucharistic doctrine, by a Church that had decided that confrontation rather than accommodation was the surest way to deal with the Reformation. However, another facet of theology informed those who formulated such canons and this has more to do with the numinous motif. The theology set out in the idea of transubstantiation is more full of mystery, more suggestive of miracle than other explanations such as consubstantiation. The transformation defies human explanation and in this way conveys the awe of the divinely inexplicable. Such a formulation served a Church which was anxious to promote a new mode of worship which was the adoration of the exposed sacrament. Michael A. Mullet indicated a close link between this mystery and the new liturgical forms.

> The formula of transubstantiation that Trent adopted implied a much more complete and miraculous transformation of the bread and wine ... and acceptance of the exclusive totality of Christ's presence in the Eucharist made the host a fitting object for Eucharistic

---

94 Mullett, *Catholic Reformation*, p. 48.
95 *BW*, vol. 1, p. 55.
96 E. Schillebeeckx, *The Eucharist* (London, 1980), pp. 36–8.
97 Ibid., pp. 40–41.

adoration, especially the 'special veneration and solemnity' shown annually in the feast of the 'Blessed Sacrament', Corpus Christi.[98]

As much as Bramhall was drawn to the numinous motif, he is unwilling to go as far as the Catholic Church of this period, and in this way he remains within the Reformed tradition. However, it is significant that though Bramhall voices clear objections to transubstantiation there is nowhere to be found among his writings a detailed refutation. Nor is there anywhere a detailed description of the alternative spiritual presence which Bramhall would have considered more satisfactory. This approach is entirely in keeping with the mainstream of high churchmen that made up the Durham House Group. Though they rejected the doctrine, they did so in much more reserved terms than their contemporaries. Anthony Milton calls this the *mysterium tremendum* argument, which upheld the reality of sacramental presence but was 'agnostic' over the nature of the presence. In this way, transubstantiation might be represented simply as an unnecessary attempt to define a mode of presence when this was beyond human capacities.[99] It would appear that Bramhall, in keeping with the rest of his circle, was not attracted enough to the numinous motif to endorse its most profound of Christian statements, that is, transubstantiation. Yet he was attracted enough to consider the real mystical presence of the sacrament. His muted response to this issue is an indication of this attraction and the awe it inspires; it is quite simply a respectful silence.

Penance

The attendant five sacraments of Roman Catholicism did not survive the Reformation as sacraments within the Protestant Churches. One such, penance, obtained a new-found meaning with the Roman Church since it was now considered as fundamental to the preparation of a soul about to receive the blessed sacrament.[100] Luther read Christ's call to repent (Matthew, 4:17) as an invitation to nothing less than a life of repentance.[101] Calvin on the other hand rejected confession to a priest alone, opting for the more scriptural instructions to 'confess your sins one to another.'[102] Nevertheless in spite of this general rejection of auricular confession, old habits prove hard to die and a good many practitioners among the Protestant Churches clung to some form of non-sacramental confession. In England, as Keith Thomas points out, the Book of Common Prayer required those whose consciences troubled them to repair to the minister for 'ghostly counsel, advice and comfort.'[103] Nor was this confined to the less reformed wing of the Church, 'The fact was that most of the clergy felt wistful about the disappearance of the confessional. The practice of confessing to a minister,

---

98 Mullett, *Catholic Reformation*, p. 49.
99 A. Milton, *Catholic and Reformed* (Cambridge, 1994), p. 197.
100 Mullett, *Catholic Reformation*, p. 51.
101 Wriedt, 'Luther's theology,' pp. 94–5.
102 Calvin, *Institutes*, III, iv, 10–11.
103 Thomas, *Magic*, p. 157.

on special occasions at least, was defended by Latimer, Ridley, Jewel, Ussher and many other pillars of the Anglican Church.'[104]

Thomas may have been surprised to see an old Calvinist like Ussher endorsing such an apparently Catholic practice but part of the reason for this is to be found once more in his historical research. In yet another instance, Ussher is too aware of early Christian precedent to dismiss penitential rites as mere innovations. The task for Ussher is to make such early practice compatible with Reformed doctrine. Ussher manages this in two ways: firstly, he argues that early practice was distinct to present Roman abuses; and secondly, he claims that there are theological differences of understanding between the two. In the case of penance, he maintains that the early Irish and British did not have regular recourse to the confessional but used it sparingly so as not to abuse it.

> ... but upon special occasions they did, no doubt, both publicly and privately make confession of their faults, as well that they might receive counsel and direction for their recovery, as that they might be made partakers of the benefit of the keys, for the quieting of their troubled consciences.[105]

Ussher goes on to take issue with the modern concept that absolution of sin follows any such confession, after which 'some sorry penance is imposed, which upon better consideration may be converted into pence.'[106] The point Ussher is making is that it is a theological abuse to precede penance with absolution. Such an ordering suggests that the priest has the power to absolve sins regardless of the confessor's contrition or penance. In the early practice, Ussher claims that absolution only came after long acts of penance.[107] This point touches on the whole meaning of confession as well as on the spiritual power of the clergy. If the absolution is the final part of the penitential rite then it is declaratory, the repentant sinner has absolved himself through an appropriate act of contrition. In his petition, *Touching Innovations*, numbers four and five of the objections make precisely this point decrying the way in which confession had come to be seen as not only necessary, but absolution was more than declaratory.[108] Ussher's theological interpretation is drawn straight from the Reformed tradition, Luther realised that Christian liberty required the subjugation of the outer man. The focus of his theology is the forgiveness of *culpa* [blame], not the remission of *poena* [penalty].[109]

The practical aspects of the practice are stressed by Ussher. In his *Answer to Malone*, he claims that it is profitable only as an instruction and comfort to the penitent. Ussher's preferred option is that the individual made a private plea for forgiveness to God, however if this is not considered by the individual as sufficient they may repair to Church.

---

104 Ibid.
105 *UW*, vol. 4, p. 288.
106 Ibid., p. 289.
107 Ibid.
108 J. Ussher, *Touching Innovations*, p. 1.
109 *Oxford Encyclopedia of the Reformation*, ed. H.J. Hillerbrand (4 vols, Oxford, 1996), vol. 3, p. 243.

> ... it being found true by often experience, that the wounded conscience will still pinch grievously, not withstanding the confession made unto God in secret. At such a time as this then, where the sinner can find no ease at home, what should he do but use the best means he can to find it abroad. Is there no balm in Gilead?[110]

Ussher calls this ideal 'medicinal confession'[111] and it is a true reflection of his justice motif grounding, stressing recompense and punishment over the mystical power of the minister. However, after all this, Ussher is unwilling to divest the rite entirely of its spiritual aspects. In spite of his practical Calvinism he retains enough respect for the ministry to guard some of its spiritual qualities. The minister has, Ussher writes, the power of the keys for the 'remitting and retaining' of sins.[112] This power has been passed from the Apostles to bishops and priests. Rather ambiguously though, Ussher adds that this power in the proper sense belongs to God alone and he returns once more to the idea that their role is 'declaratory.'[113] It seems that after briefly dipping his toe in the waters of the numinous he scurries back to where he feels safest on the dry land that is the justice motif.

Bramhall in contrast was not only capable of writing and preaching enthusiastically about 'confession' but he was also quite happy to stress its mystical functions. Confession was once declared by Bramhall, to be as ancient as our first parents.[114] In his *Answer to Captain Steward* (1645) he set out his understanding of the rite. Firstly he acknowledged that sins are remitted by baptism whereby 'we are made children of God, the members of Christ and inheritors of the kingdom of Heaven.' However he goes on to say that pastors of the Church possess 'a dependent ministerial power of loosing from sin.'[115] When he carefully adds that the 'primitive imperial original power belongs to God' there is an important distinction with Ussher. For Ussher the power was, and still is God's 'in the proper sense'; for Bramhall, only the 'original' of this power belongs to God. It comes from God but is now part of the power of the ministry. In this way, the minister is more fully infused with the mystical power to remit sins. There is no mention in his work of either penance or declaratory power. The stress is instead on the 'dependent ministerial power.' Bramhall recognises that in this area of confession and penitential liturgy he is perilously close to touching a strong Protestant nerve. As if recognising this, any such defence of confession is always immediately preceded by a denunciation of the present Roman approach. Bramhall's main objections centre on its being particular and plenary, and therefore seen as necessary for salvation.[116] He is not therefore one of those Laudian divines who were causing scandal by implying that confession was both of these things.[117] Other objections concern the erroneous notion that as part of their merit system confession can attain salvation. Finally he adds that all these recent developments

---

110 *UW*, vol. 3, pp. 90–91.
111 Ibid.
112 Ibid., vol. 4, p. 290.
113 Ibid.
114 *BW*, vol. 5, p. 158.
115 Ibid., pp. 190–91.
116 Ibid.
117 Milton, *Catholic and Reformed*, p. 472.

have resulted in much political violence since, 'it is made a colour for treasons to be committed as Powder-treason.'[118]

However, these objections concern abuses, not the theological principle, of confession and absolution. This fundamental principle seems to find considerable favour with Bramhall and in his sermon *The Right way to Safety after Shipwreck*, he urged the Restoration Church in Ireland to reinstate auricular confession. Most importantly this sermon indicates that he values the rite not as a means of exoneration or self-punishment but as an important preparation of the soul for receiving the sacrament of the Eucharist.[119] This is reflective of the crucial difference between the two penitential understandings of Ussher and Bramhall, the first is practical and concerned with discipline, the second is spiritual and concerned with veneration.

Reflecting on English ecclesiastical disturbances of this period, the Georges gave this advice, 'The student who hopes to trace in English Protestantism a line of cleavage which will lead straight from the origins of the church to the decisive rift of revolution in 1640 is certainly well advised to turn first to these ceremonial and liturgical disputes.'[120] After what has been considered of the differing approaches to this issue of the bishops of Armagh and Derry, this advice may be extended to cover the Church in Ireland. Certainly such differences in perspective over the sacraments and liturgy go a long way to explaining the eventual impeachment of Bramhall and the eventual execution of Strafford. The lack of initial opposition to their programme is indicative of a weak Irish Church rather than one which was in accord with developments. What then are we to make of Sharpe's remarks quoted earlier in the chapter that the issue was one of uniformity and non-theological?[121] Certainly if one takes the wider body of Bramhall's contemporaries then the rather uneven body of work or 'patchwork of uneven sources', as Lake terms them,[122] do not constitute a systematic theology. What they do share is a driving attraction toward religious expressions of the numinous and what Sharpe calls 'uniformity' is the division of the sacred and profane; it is promotion of bodily worship and it is an overall response to the *mysterium tremendum*. Besides, it must be noted that Sharpe does his best to divest Church ritual of its theological aspect by referring to it constantly as ceremony rather than liturgy, with its more religious connotations.[123]

In the area of sacraments and liturgy perhaps the underlying question facing any of the Reformers is, when does worship become idolatry? The common repulsion of those Reformers who cleaved to the justice motif of tangible holiness (be it object, place or person) is in stark contrast to the practice and sentiments of those clergymen with numinous leanings. Ussher and Bramhall provide us with stark examples. We must not, warns Ussher in true puritan manner, let our worship slip into idolatry. The invisible God might not be made visible in metal or stone, and quoting Sedulius' general rule he declared that 'to adore any other beside the Father, and the Son, and

---

118 *BW*, vol. 4, pp. 159–60.
119 *BW*, vol. 5, p. 164.
120 Georges, *Protestant Mind*, p. 350.
121 Sharpe, 'Archbishop Laud', passim.
122 Lake, *Early Stuart Church*, p. 163.
123 Sharpe, 'Archbishop Laud.'

the Holy Ghost, is the crime of impiety.'[124] In sharp contrast to Ussher, Bramhall urged that there was a 'portionable degree of honour' due to every creature in Heaven, including the saints, ' ... to his posterity, to his memory, to his monument, to his image, to his relics, to everything that he loved, or that pertained to him, even to the earth which he did tread upon, for his sake.'[125] If Kevin Sharpe is right and the dispute over 'ceremony' in the 1640s is about uniformity of practice rather than theological differences then, judging by the writings of James Ussher and John Bramhall, the whole of the European Reformation must have been about the same issue.

---

124 *UW*, vol. 4, p. 273.
125 *BW*, vol. 1, p. 44.

Chapter 5

Ecclesiastical Histories

James Ussher and John Bramhall lived, worked and wrote in an age for which ecclesiastical history held enormous controversial importance. Since the Reformation, in which an appeal to purity of religion was synonymous with an appeal to early tradition, both sides had laboured to prove that antiquity and therefore right was on their side. As polemical weapons the witness of the Church patriarchs was considered to be second only to scripture. In this atmosphere the first comprehensive history of the Church was produced; the thirteen volume *Magdeburg Centuries* under the editorship of the Lutheran, Matthew Flacius Illyricus (1520–75), covered the first thirteen centuries of the Church. The Catholics responded with the *Ecclesiastical Annals* produced by Caesar Baronius (1538–1607).[1] The Reformers delved into the Christian past in order to uncover what they perceived as an unadulterated faith beneath the layers of corruption which passed as tradition. The Catholic hierarchy at Trent responded by beatifying that same tradition.[2] Nevertheless, it was equally important for their controversialists to prove continuity with the past. The truth of Christianity was after all supposed to be *in saecula saeculorum*.

However, it was not just the eternal nature of truth that made history important to both sides. Their respective appeals to the past were reflective of one of the fundamentals of the Christian religious response, that is, it is historic in nature. Along with much else this historic characteristic of the Christian faith had been written into its religious DNA in its near-Eastern womb. The God of the Christians is the same God as that of the Hebrews, the God who intervenes in history, the God who ordains events for His own purpose and the God who uses providence to unfold His grand design. For this reason, the Christian historian may interpret the past in a way which they can claim reveals either the approbation or the discountenance of the Creator. Thus Protestant writers in the reign of Edward VI never tired of regaling the king with cautionary tales of monarchs, 'beloved of God for their piety, and others accursed by the almighty for their false religion.'[3]

Into this confessional maelstrom, a century later, stepped Ussher and Bramhall. Ussher, the vastly erudite scholar whom John Quarles had called, 'a living library',[4] the painstaking antiquarian who would add his immense research to the Protestant

---

1 C. Lindberg, *The European Reformations* (Oxford, 1996), p. 374.
2 Mullett, *Catholic Reformation*, pp. 39–40.
3 C. Bradshaw, 'David or Josiah? Old Testament kings as Exemplars in Edwardian Religious Polemic', in B. Gordon (ed.), *Protestant History and Identity in Sixteenth Century Europe* (2 vols, Aldershot, 1996), vol. 2, p. 77.
4 J. Quarles, *An Elegie on the Most Reverend and Learned James Ussher* (London, 1656), p. 4.

cause and who would stop at nothing in order to add to this repository of knowledge. Then Bramhall, whose first biography had described him as an Aquinas among the Schoolmen, 'others might be more nice, but none more methodical and substantial ... tenacious of Catholic Tradition, bold in the defence of it, and patient in suffering for it.'[5] Less punctilious than Ussher he is perhaps more profound. Bramhall adds to his history a clear, rational argument which is persuasive and often insightful. As Henry R. McAdoo points out, this approach was to prove decisive in creating what was later to become mainstream Anglican orthodoxy.

> Combined with Scripture and the appeal to antiquity is the freedom of reason, and this triad with its inner relationship by which each element informed and illuminated the others makes up the Anglican theological approach for the writers of the period as it did later for Gore.[6]

There is a good deal of common concern in both Ussher's and Bramhall's historical interpretations. One might expect no less since they shared for the most part the joint aim of defending their national Churches. However, there are also differences which are not merely limited to style, it is these dissimilarities which indicate a divergence of theological priorities. The following chapter will examine the ecclesiastical histories of Ussher and Bramhall and argue that these points of departure can best be explained by their respective attractions to the justice and numinous motifs. Before this can be done, however, we must turn once more to the Old Testament in order to appreciate the roots of Christian denominational historiography.

The biblical roots of denominational historical perspectives

In common with their neighbouring religious groups, and indeed in common with primitive religious understanding in general, the Hebrew peoples had originally interpreted time not as linear or historical but rather in terms of cycles indicated by the seasons and marked by cultic celebrations.[7] However, sometime after Israel's emergence from a nomadic life-style into a settled civilization, this concept was to undergo a radical transformation. Festivals that had previously accompanied agrarian events came now to be associated with specific occasions in the Hebrew past such as the Passover and Exodus.[8] In other words the developing Israelite society historicized their religious identity; history became a fundamental part of their spiritual experience. According to Gerhard von Rad, we can 'scarcely over–estimate the importance of such a change.'[9] The God of Israel was unique in that He was a deity who intervened in history at decisive points of time and it was these events which shaped Jewish identity. Von Rad describes what this meant.

---

5   Vesey, *Athanasius*, p. 43.
6   McAdoo, *Bramhall* (Dublin, 1964), p. 24. McAdoo is referring to Charles Gore, the outspoken bishop of Oxford, 1911–19.
7   G. von Rad, *The Message of the Prophets* (London, 1968), p. 80.
8   Ibid., p. 81.
9   Ibid., p. 80.

Israel's faith began to take as its basis not just a single event alone, not even one as momentous as the Exodus ... but she began to think of a series of consecutive data, or, to put it in another way, she began to realise that her present was based on an earlier series of creative events, a somewhat involved historical development.[10]

All this has very important consequences for Christianity; as mentioned above, it becomes heir to this kind of religio-historical perspective. When Christians looked back they interpreted history according to the same defining moments their religious ancestors did. Their religion is the story of mankind, encapsulating the fall and the redemption through Christ and looking forward to the last days when God would judge the living and the dead. The rationale of Christianity is dependent on linear history. More recently, however, Walter Brueggemann has identified two strands of this historic understanding which the Old Testament has attempted to meld.[11] It will be argued here that this insight is not only important for biblical scholarship but may also be extended to Christian history and may afford us a better understanding of the different historical priorities which emerged at the Reformation.

The first form of Old Testament history Brueggemann identifies as the 'Mosaic-Covenantal', which he sums up as a 'radical intrusion' of Yahweh on behalf of the powerless.[12] It may be identified as an expression of Yahweh's intention for freedom and justice. This historical interpretation was pregnant with contemporary political consequences. According to Brueggemann, by championing the underdog or the underclass, it represented 'a radical critique that prevented the absolutizing' of any political arrangement, as well as promising 'an alternative social arrangement' that was yet to come.[13]

The second form of history Brueggemann calls the 'Davidic-Royal'; whereas the first history is concerned with justice, this royal history is instead concerned with order. Politically this history is in tension with the first for it serves the existing social elite, preserving their power and giving theological credence to their claims, 'The royal [sapiential] tradition, inevitably conservative, fashions a life-world that is essentially settled. What is valued – that is, true and life-giving – consists in the resources managed by the king and his regime.'[14] Paul D. Hanson, in his work *The Dawn of the Apocalypse*[15], labelled these schools as 'pragmatic' and 'visionary.' Hanson claimed that the pragmatists are those who benefit from the current set up, it follows that their role is to give the present arrangement legitimacy. The visionaries are the 'world weary' who question the present arrangement, regard themselves as unfairly treated and therefore appeal to the sovereignty of God to lead them to a new future. What results from this difference of approach according to Hanson are two distinct confessions, the one of 'preservation' the other of 'deliverance.'[16] These theories receive support from biblical, historical scholarship which points out

---

10   Ibid., pp. 82–3.
11   W. Brueggemann, *Old Testament Theology* (Minneapolis, 1992), pp. 270–96.
12   Ibid., p. 273.
13   Ibid.
14   Ibid., p. 275.
15   P.D. Hanson, *The Dawn of the Apocalypse* (Philadelphia, 1975), passim.
16   Ibid. p. 29.

that in the monarchic period David and Solomon oversaw the development of a state religion with its court theologians, high priests, cultic centre and a theology of kingship. Concomitant with this disempowered tribes expressed a resistance that found its expression in the voices of prophets such as Elijah and Elisha.[17] Voices that began railing against the state and developed with the later prophets to address a more individualised protest, chiefly toward the king.[18]

Brueggemann and Hanson have limited their analysis to their own field of interest, that is, scriptural theology. However what they have identified appears to have striking resonance for the study of Christian history. If one takes the words 'king' and 'regime' in the passage from Brueggemann and replaces them with 'Pope' and 'Church' we find an equally fitting description of the papacy at the end of the Middle Ages. The concern for preservation, order and resources that make up the Davidic-Royal history might just as well have been written to describe the driving concerns of the Roman Catholic hierarchy. Similarly the challenge to the existing order, the appeal to the higher authority of God, the looking forward to a better system that describes the Mosaic-Covenantal approach have a startling echo in the history of early Protestantism. It is further proposed here that in keeping with the arguments of Chapters 2 and 3 these two historical approaches may be identified as further expressions of the justice and numinous motifs. The Mosaic, is concerned with law and the type of judgemental intervention we have used to describe the justice motif, in a very obvious way. More subtly, but just as truly, the preservation of dynasty, power and resources are reliant on, and a product of, the numinous motif. The numinous expressly states that a place, object or person have inherent sacred qualities. Brueggemann defines resources as riches[19], but in Ancient Israel, as well as much later religious regimes, the spiritual resources were surely of equal importance, the Ark of the Covenant as much as the holy relics. In this framework we may see writers like Ussher and Bramhall working ostensibly from the same Church, for the polemical cause and yet with a different range of values. In examining their respective historical works, we may see that these values are reflective of the motifs outlined above and are received via the Mosaic and Davidic historical traditions. Perhaps the best example of this divergence may be indicated by the way they tackle that most thorny of Protestant historical problems which is how to trace their succession.

James Ussher's 'godly succession'

Ussher's earliest work was published in London in 1613. *Gravissimae Quaestionis de Christianarum Ecclesiarum in occidentis praesertim partibus ab Apostolicis temporibus ad nostrum usque aetatem continua successione et Historica Explicatio* traces the descent of the Protestant Churches of Europe. In 1631, he turned his attention to matters closer to home and brought forth his *Discourse of the Religion anciently professed by the Irish and British*. This work maintained that the religion

---

17   R. Albertz, 'Religion in Pre-exilic Israel,' in J.Barton (ed.) *The Biblical World* (2 vols, London, 2002), vol. 2, p. 93.
18   18 Preuss, *Old Testament Theology*, vol. 2, p. 68.
19   Brueggemann, *Old Testament*, p. 274.

of the Irish and British in primitive times differed as much from the present Roman Catholic position as it conformed to the present national Churches. The main body of this work is for the most part taken up with his own national Church but, as if to redress the imbalance, in 1639 he published his work on the *Antiquities of the British Churches*. Ussher's biblical chronology, *Annales Veteris Testamenti*, appeared in 1650 and it was succeeded by the voluminous *Chronologica Sacra* which was only published posthumously. The *Historia Dogmatica Controversiae* was also published after Ussher's death. Among other things, it championed the reading of scripture and pressed the point that for its first six hundred years the Church had not worshipped in an unknown tongue. Ussher's study of the history of doctrine, *Tractatus de Controversiis Pontificiis* was another work which only surfaced at the Restoration. It was a detailed answer to the renowned Jesuit scholar, Robert Bellarmine.

Such an overview of Ussher's work indicates its general polemical nature. His histories function as proofs for either the veracity of his cause or the mendacity of the Roman. Even the works of scriptural chronology function in the end to provide a biblical schema that serves Protestant providentialism. Ussher's very first outing into the academic world was no less polemical than any of his later writings. *Gravissimae Quaestionis de Christianarum Ecclesiarum* set out to address perhaps the most pertinent of historical questions posed by those who had remained faithful to the old order that is, 'Where was your Church before Luther?' Bruce Gordon writes that, 'Opponents of the Reformation never tired of drawing attention to the apparent reality that whilst the Church of Rome might have needed correction, it nevertheless formed a continuous, visible and historical link with the ancient Church.'[20] Implicit in the question is the charge that Protestants were guilty of that most heinous of crimes against Christianity which is schism. Such a charge carried with it the added recrimination that their reforms of religion were driven by more salacious motives. The Protestants were being charged, along with their cohorts in the monarchies and aristocracies, of exploiting religious credulity for material and sexual ends, disguised as religion, they were advancing their own political power, stealing the wealth of the Church and turning their backs on Christian moral code.[21] For Protestants it was clearly a question which was not just accusatory but rhetorical. The English poet John Donne clearly found his Protestant loyalty tested by the very force of the query when he asked himself, 'Sleeps she a thousand, then peepes up one yeare?'[22] In dealing with the issue, writers like Ussher were not only providing polemical retorts, they were also answering their own fundamental enquiries.

Ussher as an historian was profoundly influenced by his contemporary Anglo-Protestant historical tradition. John Foxe's *Acts and Monuments* had been published in 1563 and his interpretation of history had one striking feature, it was schematic. This type of history had been revived on the continent by the German Reformer,

---

20 B. Gordon, 'The Changing Face of Protestant History and Identity in Sixteenth Century Europe', in B. Gordon (ed.), *Protestant History and Identity* in Sixteenth Century Europe (2 vols, Aldershot, 1996), vol. 2, p. 1.

21 S.J. Barnett, 'Where was your Church before Luther? Claims for the Antiquity of Protestantism Examined', *Church History*, 68:1, (March, 1999): 14.

22 J. Donne, *Holy Sonnets*, XVIII.

Johannes Sleidanus, (1506–56) and it was to prove immensely popular. Schematic history divided the past into distinct epochs.[23] This was entirely in keeping with the general return to scripture since one of the chief characteristics of biblical history is exactly this schematic layout.[24] In the preface of his work, Foxe set out his schema which divided history since the birth of Christ into four neat sections of three or four centuries. Foxe not only interpreted events of his own age in terms of this schema (the reign of the antichrist was marked by God's purges of the true Church with 'violence and tyranny') but brought the whole to a prophetic conclusion as he looked to the final apocalypse.[25] This schema was approved and fully utilized by James Ussher.

Ussher's first work on Christian antiquity incorporates Foxe's schema; it also works as a continuation of Jewel's *Apologia pro Ecclesia Anglicana* which had concluded at the sixth century. *Gravissimae Quaestionis ... Explicatio* set the binding of Satan at either the rise of the Gospels, the incarnation or the Passion, but not later than the destruction of the temple at Jerusalem in 70 AD. The rise of the antichrist was placed at the end of the sixth century and the loosing of Satan at the end of the tenth. One thousand years after the incarnation took Ussher down to the pontificate of Sylvester II, or taken from the passion to Benedict IX, and if from the destruction of the temple to the papacy of Gregory VII. Ussher then identifies Innocent III as the Antichrist before concluding his work with a defence of the Albigensians and Waldenses.[26] Such a schema has all the hallmarks of biblical schematic history including the 'golden age' which also appears to be widespread practice in antiquity[27], but also those moments of intervention by the deity either in judgement or approval. It is surely no accident that those Christians who were most drawn to the justice motif should revive such a formula of history. What Sleidanus, Foxe and Ussher gave to the Protestant world was an historical perspective which was entirely in keeping with justice motif, containing as it did the vital ingredients of law, judgement and providence. More important than this schema was how Ussher traced the line of Christian succession. There was, according to Ussher, a pure stream of Christianity that existed in Europe outside the main body of the Catholic Church. Small protesting sects of pre-Reformation reformers such as the Waldenses or Albigensians had maintained the fountain of faith, free of the corruption that polluted the rest of Christendom. *Gravissimae Quaestionis ... Explicatio* is almost like an exercise in sectarian cartography as Ussher traces a line through the centuries to the golden age of the Church via apparent enclaves of godliness.

There was nothing original about this approach, the idea that succession could be traced out through various heretical groups is present in Foxe who claimed that the Waldensian articles were the same as those received by the majority of the Reformed

---

23   *Encyclopedia of the Reformation*, Hillerbrand, vol. 4, p. 68.
24   J. Maxwell Miller and J.H. Hayes, *A History of Ancient Israel and Judah* (London, 1986), p. 58.
25   J. Foxe, *Acts and Monuments* (1841 edition) vol. 1, pp. 4–5.
26   *UW*, vol. 2, pp. 7–20.
27   Miller and Hayes, *History of Israel*, p. 58.

movement.[28] In turn Foxe acquired the schema during his Marian exile when he had come under the influence of the Calvinistic historical approach.[29] Theodore Beza had not held complete sympathy with the doctrine of the Waldenses but in his *Histoirie ecclésiastique des églises réformées* (1580) he had informed his readers that they had opposed papal superstition and corruption as far back as 120 AD[30] and were therefore to be considered Protestant forerunners. In *Gravissimae Quaestionis ... Explicatio*, Ussher dismisses the assertion that Valdes had founded the Waldenses tracing their origin like Beza into antiquity.[31] By ignoring the body of evidence gleaned from inquisitions (on the reasonable grounds that they could be liable to falsification) he uses late Bohemian sources as well as Protestant influenced confessions from the 1540s and thereby rehabilitates the Waldenses into the orthodox tradition. Ussher also creates in them a paradigm for other medieval heretics.[32]

There are two striking aspects of this type of history which seem to be in keeping with both the justice motif and the Mosaic-Covenantal history. Firstly, Ussher's primary concern is the protection, maintenance and promulgation of a basic truth which is the Word of God. The Albigensians and Waldenses adhere to this Word of God which is the means by which they gauge membership. The Word of God or their gospel of truth is the new *Torah* [law] by which inclusion or exclusion is measured. This word or law is the great religious resource of these groups since the other resources, the Churches and the iconographic paraphernalia are in the hands of the main polity of the orthodox faith. They are groups almost literally built on law. Secondly, there is the biblical form of the oppressed servant of God railing against the powerful tyrant with only truth and God on their side. William G. Naphy described the self-image of Swiss Reformers between 1530–55 in a way which is remarkably in keeping with Brueggemann's Mosaic-Covenantal history and Ussher's image of the godly underdog in *Gravissimae Quaestionis… Explicatio,*

> They are the new Israel enslaved in idolatry, led out of captivity and exile by new prophets. Moses, the law-giver, Hezekiah, the good king, and Elijah, Jeremiah and Isaiah, the prophets of old are brought to life in the persons of the preachers and magistrates of their day. The Protestants are also the remnant saved from the clutches of Antichrist and Babylon by God's intervening power. They are God's servants and champions cleansing Israel of idols, marching victoriously over the wreckage of the Beast's Babylon.[33]

Ussher is convinced that unity of faith is the fundamentally important principle in Christian history. The assent to a few basic principles (not a Protestant concept originally) was what lay at the heart of true faith, ' ... ad verae visibilis Ecclesiae constitutionem illus requiri religionis professionem que possit hominem sapientem

---

28 J. Foxe, *The Book of Martyrs*, ed. W. Bramley-Moore (London, 1865), pp. 56–8.
29 Barnett, 'Before Luther?': 17.
30 Ibid. p. 20.
31 *UW*, vol. 2, pp. 209–11; E. Cameron, *The Reformation of Heretics* (Oxford, 1984), p. 248.
32 32 E. Cameron, *The Waldenses* (Massachusetts, 2000), pp. 290–91.
33 W.G. Naphy, ' 'No history can satisfy everyone': Geneva's chroniclers and emerging Religious Identities', in Gordon (ed.), *Protestant History and Identity*, vol. 2, p. 36.

reddere ad salutem (for the continuity of the true visible Church requires the profession of that religion which is able to make a man wise unto salvation).'[34]

As an ecclesiastical historian such a principle served Ussher well since it allowed him to pursue a continuous line of subterranean Protestant existence through some quite disparate forms of Christianity. Ussher was clearly not alone in this respect. As Anthony Milton pointed out, others were equally tempted, 'Jacobean conformists appealed to all these different ancestors simultaneously, with no sense of contradiction, or fear that the different groups might be incompatible.'[35] Such scrambles for relations, no matter how distant, in order to construct a pedigree did not sit well with later generations of Anglicans. Writing at the beginning of the last century, E.W. Watson claimed that *Gravissimae Quaestionis ... Explicatio,* actually undermined the Church of England's claims to historical continuity. According to Watson, Ussher had followed completely the wrong track,

> These protests were intermittent and inconsistent, often ambiguous and often of dubious orthodoxy; but he had to make the best of them. The result, it must be confessed, was a failure; antiquarianism, however learned, is no match for history, however perverted.[36]

In Ussher's defence, it must be said that he did not accept wholesale the entire plethora of unorthodoxies which the Christian centuries had thrown up. Some he dismissed as corrupt.[37] There is no doubt, however, that on occasions, particularly his dating of the foundation of the Waldenses, he is not as critical as he is elsewhere. However, the real problem Ussher has as an historian for later Anglicans has more to do with theological trends than historical accuracy. Watson's own explanation for Ussher's fault was clearly tinged with his own high Church theology when he stated that the Primate had been raised 'among men who had no reverence for the Church as a society possessing, whatever its faults, a venerable and sacred history.'[38] Which is an indication at least of the roots of their differences. R.J. Tollefson points out in his doctoral thesis on Ussher the idea of sacred or holy is the key to the issue. Ussher, in spite of his expertise in textual criticism did not follow the etymology of the Hebrew word 'kadosh.'[39] That is, he did not recognise the essential 'separated unto' meaning,'Holiness was not always evident in the visible Church therefore not as significant as the Roman Catholics maintained. The issue of continuity of the Church was settled instead by reference to basic doctrine.'[40] This is the core of the difference between the two genres of Christian history, the one takes as its foundation sacred holiness, the other, like Ussher's is based upon a basic principle of belief. To put

---

34 *UW*, vol. 2, p. 21.

35 A. Milton, *Catholic and Reformed, The Roman and Protestant Churches in English Protestant Thought 1600–1640* (Cambridge, 1995), p. 272.

36 E.W. Watson, 'James Ussher', in W.E. Collins, *Typical English Churchmen* (London, 1902), p. 64.

37 *UW*, vol. 2, pp. 21–2.

38 Watson, 'Ussher', p. 64.

39 R.J. Tollefson, 'A Study of the Church in the Life and Thought of Archbishop James Ussher', unpublished Ph.D. Thesis, Iowa University, 1963, p. 123.

40 Ibid., p. 126.

it crudely it is, once again, a question of awe versus law. We must now turn our attention to the idea of succession in Bramhall whose own perspective when laid against Ussher's work is something of an exemplar of the second approach.

John Bramhall's 'holy and apostolic succession'

This question of succession split the Church in England around the beginning of the seventeenth century.[41] How English Protestant historians reacted to the question of their antiquity depended on their particular shade of Protestantism. The 'Puritan-Anglicans' influenced by returning Marian exiles favoured a claim to commonality with the early Church. They were increasingly disdainful of the intermittent periods of history and they were, like Ussher, inclined to use a series of proto-Protestant groups to work out their link with the pure, apostolic Church. This caused a good deal of alarm among their conservative contemporaries. These episcopalian Anglicans felt the need to defend the historical legitimacy of the episcopate. Authors like the chaplain to Elizabeth I and James I, Richard Field (1561–1616), countered such criticism by claiming that only a faction of the medieval Church had erred. Stephen Barnett describes this reaction.

> The Foxeian tradition of proto-Protestant forebears was thus progressively abandoned by some Anglican writers as a polemical tool fraught with danger. This was a tendency most evident in the 1630s ... For Laudians, an identification of proto-Protestants in medieval radical sects was too much like the Puritan position: subversive of episcopacy.[42]

The historical approach of John Bramhall fits very much into this category. Nowhere is there the Ussherian concern for doctrinal purity, nor is there anything approaching the same enthusiasm for continental Protestantism, either pre- or post-Reformation. Indeed, to employ a modern expression, Bramhall's version of Christianity is entirely Euro-sceptic. When he comes to deal with the issue of succession, Bramhall finds the answer to the problem in the natural independence of his national Church. Furthermore, the great schism which has divided Christendom is less about conflict over credal issues and more about the over-imposing authority of the Roman Church.

Such a lack of international Protestant identification or indeed doctrinal Reformation zeal might lead to the assumption that Bramhall was not in the real sense a Protestant since he appears to lack some of the important prerequisites. This is, according to one biographer a mistake. The word, according to Sparrow-Simpson, has two historical meanings. The first signifies those Christians who reject the traditional institutional, ministerial and sacramental principles of the Roman Church. Another describes those Catholics who reject papal claims and it is into this camp that we must place Bramhall.[43] For this reason, labels like Protestant or Catholic can be equally applied to Bramhall and yet on their own they are misleading.

---

41   Barnett, 'Before Luther ?', p. 19.
42   Ibid.
43   Sparrow-Simpson, *Bramhall*, p. 249.

As Sparrow-Simpson writes, 'It is therefore quite impossible to appreciate aright Bramhall's acceptance of the name Protestant without remembering that he balanced it by a most tenacious adherence to the name Catholic.'[44]

Much more recently it has been claimed that this new movement, which was made up chiefly of Henry Hammond, Bramhall and Jeremy Taylor more or less fashioned an approach that was to become known as 'Anglicanism.'[45] According to Ian Green, this constituted a more Catholic understanding of the historic nature of their Church.

> ... a new moral theology which reacted against the downgrading of the human role implicit in double predestinarian teaching, and a new stress on the rich devotional life available to the faithful through the devout use of the Church's liturgy and sacraments.[46]

For Bramhall, and other writers of his persuasion, the answer to the dilemma of succession was not to be found outside of the established Church; on the contrary, it ought to be located in the very bulwarks of organised hierarchical Christianity, the bishops. In his controversy with Richard Baxter, Bramhall warned his adversary of the 'odious consequences' that flow from attacks on the episcopacy. Bramhall states boldly that 'Catholic' and 'anti-Episcopal' are contradictory terms, though it is hard to imagine Baxter losing much sleep over that particular admonishment. Bramhall goes on to tax him to show one Western Church in the first fifteen hundred years that was without a bishopric.[47] There was certainly something original in this approach in its 'grandeur' and 'confidence' of exposition. There was also something new in its logical backbone, the claim that episcopacy was of 'apostolic origin and rested on divine authority, that it possessed *jus divinum*.'[48] Bramhall's starting point for succession was the episcopate and it is through these that he traces the true course of succession. The contrast with Ussher is vividly displayed here in these sets of historical priorities. Bramhall's true succession was based less on maintaining the integrity of the Word or law, nor is it a case of upholding a covenant; it is founded instead on the mysticism of a blessing that had been transferred by the laying on of hands directly from those blessed individuals of the early Church, the twelve apostles. This is nothing short of an historical expression of the numinous motif.

Such an historical move in the episcopal direction represented something new in Protestantism; neither Lutheran superintendents, Scottish Reformers nor the Elizabethan bishops claimed any such continuity through the bishoprics. This controversial standpoint engendered a great debate which 'burst into life' in England in the 1620s.[49] J. Davies argued that the belief of Laud that bishops were the essential link with the primitive past, the severing of which would cause confusion, was held

---

44 Ibid.
45 J. Spurr, *The Restoration Church of England* (Yale, 1999), p. 10.
46 I. Green, 'Anglicanism in Stuart and Hanoverian England', in Gilley and Sheils (eds), *History of Religion in Britain*, p. 176.
47 *BW*, vol. 3, p. 531.
48 P. Collinson, *The Religion of Protestants* (Oxford, 1982), p. 16.
49 P.G. Lake, 'Calvinism and the English Church 1570–1635', *Past and Present*, CXIV (February, 1987): 43.

by only a few in the English Church before or after him. Indeed, Davies points out that it was precisely these views which landed Laud in hot water in Oxford in 1602.[50] However, although this episcopal succession may have been a novel idea in English circles it did have very respectable antecedents. The roots of such an idea lie in the Conciliar movement which had been thrown up in the Great Schism of the fifteenth century when the papacy was split between Rome and Avignon, writers such as Lancelot Andrews, John Bukeridge and Richard Field drew on the event to add weight to their theories. During the ideological tussles of the English Civil Wars there was a revival of interest.[51] The argument of the Conciliarists may be summarised as follows: Power had been given originally to the bishops, in turn they had delegated their authority over to the pope and now wanted it restored to them.[52]

Bramhall takes his historical lead from the Conciliarists, indeed he identifies the root of the entire Christian division in this single issue. The Roman Catholics maintained that ecclesiastical power was imparted from Christ to Peter and henceforth was to be derived from him and his successors as bishops of Rome. This interpretation Bramhall calls a 'drowsy dream'[53], repugnant to the doctrine of the fathers who made bishops to be vicars and ambassadors of Christ. Bramhall disarmingly quotes Cardinal Bellarmine to the same effect as if to show that even their own doctors were of similar opinion. '"As My Father sent Me, so send I you", our Saviour endowed them with all the fullness of power that mortal men were capable of. And therefore no single Apostle had jurisdiction over the rest ... '[54] Bramhall stresses that far from setting up any kind of universal monarchy in the Church, Christ had passed on ecclesiastical power to all the Apostles and through them to their bishops each in their individual Churches. After such historical analysis comes Bramhall the logician and legalist. If there is disagreement over this interpretation, he argues, then it is up to the Roman Catholics to furnish the rest of the Christian world with scriptural proof for their claims. 'In this controversy, by law, the burden of the proof ought to rest upon them, who affirm a right, and challenge a jurisdiction; not upon us who deny it.'[55]

It is important to note that Bramhall does not entirely dispense with the idea of primacy, indeed he claims that the English Church has 'no controversy' about supremacy of power; St Peter had a fixed Church in Antioch and then Rome. He also had primacy of order among the Apostles, this is the unanimous voice of the primitive Church.[56] Bramhall's objections are more concerned with what this primacy meant. The confusion Bramhall identifies is a result of confounding primacy of order with supremacy of power. The distinction is important because it perilously mistakes human and divine right. Unlike Ussher, who saw the dangers for Christendom lurking

---

50   J. Davies, *The Caroline Captivity of the Church* (Oxford, 1992), p. 55.
51   F. Oakley, *The Conciliarist Tradition: Constitutionalism in the Catholic Church 1300–1870* (Oxford, 2003), p. 153.
52   V. Green, *A New History of Christianity* (Gloucestershire, 1996), pp. 97–8.
53   *BW*, vol. 1, p. 153.
54   Ibid.
55   Ibid., p. 158.
56   Ibid., vol. 3, pp. 549–50.

in the divine schema, Bramhall identified the peril as purely legal, though the threat is every bit as alarming.

> Against Divine right there is no prescription, but against human right men may lawfully challenge their ancient liberties and immunities by prescription. A Papacy by Divine right is unchangeable, but a Papacy by human right is alterable, both for person and place and power. So a human Papacy, if it grow burdensome, is remediable but a pretended Divine Papacy, when and where and whilst it is acknowledged, is irremediable.[57]

In pursuing this line of spiritual ancestry, Bramhall runs off in a contrary direction to Ussher. The Reformation of England is clearly not to be associated with those of the continent who lack this episcopal credential. The Protestant Church of England was not to look to the sixteenth-century Reformers for their parentage because they already had an impeccable pedigree which bypassed Luther and Calvin and went instead directly to the Apostles. In spite of Davies's remarks that few after in the Anglican Church held such views, they appear to be more enduring than he makes out. Writing in 1914, Alfred J. Mason is typical of the inheritors of the historical tradition created by Bramhall and Hammond. Mason echoes their claim for Anglican antiquity. 'It does not start with a constitution drawn up for the first time in the sixteenth or seventeenth century. It claims continuity with the Church of apostolic times. It inherits the vast store of earlier traditions.'[58]

Bramhall is, however, careful not to point an accusing finger across the Channel, he nevertheless makes an uncategorical distinction between foreign Reformed Churches and his own. They have claimed an 'extraordinary calling' because they lack true succession. This charge can never be levelled against the English Church which claims an ordinary vocation, 'But they plead thus for some foreign Churches of Protestants, who pretend to an extraordinary calling; and either out of necessity, as some, or out of election, as others, do want a personal succession of bishops to impose hands. We wish it were otherwise.'[59] Bramhall is quick to add, unless he appear rather ultramontane, that the blame for this lies with Rome who had taught them that presbyters with a papal delegation could ordain.[60] This aside, such aloof outbursts against the European Churches are hardly examples of Protestant solidarity and elsewhere when he talks of emergency non-episcopal ordinations he verges on gloating, 'But God be praised, this was not the case in England, where there was not any such necessity, nor needed any such remedy. Whether it was so in some foreign parts or not, I dispute not. They must "stand or fall before their own Master."'[61]

Such ecclesiastical isolationism was a far cry from Ussher's approach which had been quite happy not only to regard the continental Churches as siblings but also, according to his theory of succession, as religious progenitors. Bramhall, as well as other Laudians, were less inclined in both theory and practice to such close communion. During Laud's tenure of office foreign Protestants in England were

---

57 Ibid., pp. 548–9.
58 A.J. Mason, *The Church of England and Episcopacy* (Cambridge, 1914), pp. 1–2.
59 *BW*, vol. 4, p. 247.
60 Ibid.
61 Ibid., p. 254.

forced into conformity and abroad they cut off relations.[62] Viscount Scudamore refused to receive the Eucharist in the Reformed Churches preferring instead to partake of it at the English Embassy.[63] This was exactly the course of action taken by Bramhall during his exile.

This new theory of succession in the English Church raised some interesting questions with regard to Rome. If English Protestants were no longer heirs to the Reformers and proto-Reformers who had railed against the Vatican, then what was her relationship with the Church of Rome? John Morrill indicates that the revised historical perspective resulted in a radically different interpretation of the papacy. According to Morrill just as Charles and his ecclesiastical advisers played down England's status as a member of the Protestant family they also, ' ... played up her status as a Church which combined an unbroken apostolic tradition parallel to that of the Church of Rome ... They viewed Rome not as an anti-Christian Church, a force of evil in the world, but as an errant sister-Church.'[64] Bramhall's own perspective on the papacy was no less revolutionary. The possible danger for Bramhall's history was that all episcopal roads would eventually lead to Rome, it was difficult if not impossible for a serious ecclesiastical historian to deny the Roman origins of episcopacy. Bramhall solves this problem by arguing that Rome was not the fountain from which holy orders sprang; it was rather the 'conduit pipe by which they are conveyed to us.'[65] This is a huge step for any Protestant historian to make, the idea that Rome could have maintained the line of succession which kept Christianity alive would have been an alarming proposition for most other Reformed writers. As if to assuage their fears Bramhall makes it clear that such an historical perspective does not involve Protestants in a more appreciative appraisal of Rome, nor any debt of gratitude. 'The poor were not to thank Judas for that alms which he conferred upon them by the appointment of Christ; neither were the alms the worse, because Judas who kept the bag was a thief.'[66]

One might imagine that the author of *Gravissmae Quaestionis ... Explicatio* would be appalled at the type of ecclesiastical succession laid out in the works of Bramhall and others. However, the situation, as usual with Ussher, was not so clear cut. Indeed after 1640 there is a distinct shift in emphasis in Ussher's writing and we find in his *The Original of Bishops and Metropolitans* the apparently Calvinistic Ussher declaring that the Council of Chalcedon had decreed 'there had been a continued succession of seven and twenty bishops all of them ordained in Ephesus.'[67] During this turbulent decade when events had a polarising effect on most people who cared about the Church, Ussher threw his intellectual weight not behind the sort of independent groups most akin to his beloved Waldenses, but behind the episcopal party. Some authors such as Peter Brooke have even made the rather strong claim

---

62   H. Trevor-Roper, *Catholics, Anglicans and Puritans* (London, 1987), p. 208.
63   C. Cross, *Church and People 1450–1660* (London, 1976), p. 188.
64   J. Morrill, *The Nature of the English Revolution* (London, 1993), p. 9.
65   *BW*, vol. 4, p. 251.
66   Ibid.
67   *UW*, vol. 7, p. 47.

that he instigated their movement with his various defences of the bishopric.[68] Others such as Jonathan Spurr are more restrained but claim that in particular Ussher's discovery of the Ignatian letters with their 'bold and even extravagant' claims for episcopal power gave their defenders a new coherence. 'As a result, apologists such as Hammond were able to mount a far more confident argument for episcopacy based on the practice of the Early Church.'[69]

In his article on Ussher and the Church of Ireland, Buick Knox confesses that he is perplexed by this theological shift in Ussher. The content of his early work, that doctrine is more important than apostolic or episcopal succession is something, says Knox which sits uncomfortably with the contents of later work. Knox's general assessment of Ussher (which is a strong feature of his biographical work) is of a mind quite capable of entertaining contrary doctrines, as he puts it to 'keep various views in different compartments of his mind without trying to reconcile them.'[70] Buick Knox notes that Ussher did not complete *Gravissimae Quaestionis...Explicatio* which could possibly indicate a distaste for his earlier line of argument; however, he was personally more inclined to conjecture that lack of enthusiasm for the medieval period had more to do with it.[71]

A more likely explanation of Ussher's shift in the approach and content of his work might be the very different political circumstances in which the works were penned. In 1613, Ussher was anxious to validate the history of Protestantism in a comparatively irenic Church atmosphere. In the 1640s the *Marprelate Pamphlets* were branding all bishops antichrists and demanding their removal.[72] It is not a question of Ussher having different compartments of his mind, it is simply a question of the all-important theological device of stress. Theologians such as Ussher knew very well which keys to press in order to sound the right notes. It must also be added that there is nothing theologically contradictory between Ussher's early history and his later episcopal defence. *Gravissmae Quaestionis ... Explicatio* has for its heroes independent Christian groups, but it is not an anti-episcopal work; Ussher even made the specific point that many bishops emerged from out of the Albigensians who always observed episcopal ordination.[73] Furthermore if we examine closely what Ussher is saying about the bishopric, it might be observed that it lacks the spiritual content of works such as Bramhall and Hammond. In spite of some highly eulogistic language comparing bishops with the seven stars of Revelations, Ussher's idea of the episcopacy remained in essence legal rather than mystical.

---

68   P. Brooke, *Ulster Presbyterianism* (Dublin, 1987), p. 24.

69   Spurr, *Restoration Church*, pp. 39–40.

70   R.B. Knox, 'James Ussher and the Church of Ireland', *Church Quarterly Review* (April–June 1960): 155.

71   Ibid.

72   P. Christianson, 'Reforms and the Church of England under Elizabeth I and the Early Stuarts', *Journal of Ecclesiastical History*, XXXI, (October, 1980): 473.

73   *UW*, vol. 2, pp. 387–8.

With what shew of reason then can any man imagine, that what was instituted by God in the law, for mere matter of government and preservation of good order [without all respect of type or ceremony] should now be rejected in the Gospels, as a device of Antichrist[74]

Ussher and Bramhall might have found themselves in the same party in the 1640s but they had both arrived there from different directions. Ussher defended Church hierarchy because he saw it as the most efficient way of maintaining the sort of unity which comes from the law. Bramhall on the other hand was defending a mystical institution at the very heart of the Church. Ussher and Bramhall's apologies for the episcopacy were each in their own way perfect expressions of the justice and numinous motifs. Ian Green in his work on Anglicanism claimed that this intellectual defence of hierarchy under Laud was a result of more earthly consideration, and 'assertion of rights and property' which they felt had been wrongly alienated during the Reformation. Such an assertion was pressed home with claims for the historic nature and divine right of episcopacy.[75] However, such an analysis places the cart somewhat before the horse; there is no reason to doubt that there were genuine religious considerations behind works like Bramhall's. This is indicated precisely by the contrast between Bramhall's theological plea and Ussher's more utilitarian justification. If, as Green suggests, the issue was solely concerned with reclaiming certain rights, then there would be no need for anything more than a legal justification, the Laudians knew more than anyone how to avoid unnecessary theological debate. At the centre of the conflagration in the 1640s was a genuine theological tussle. In this instance Ussher, with his legalistic case for the bishopric, is very much an exception that proves the rule.

Ecclesiastical nationalism

One area of ecclesiastical history which interested both writers was the national history of their Churches. Both placed considerable importance on the independence of their country's ecclesiastical tradition and both used history as a polemical tool in order to prove both their right to self-determination, and their theological compatibility with their religious forefathers. It might be imagined that in this area, there would be quite a considerable theological and historical common ground since both have similar motives, and this is in fact the case. There is evidence that Bramhall used and approved of Ussher's research. However, there are also interesting points of departure when different religious priorities take them in different directions. Following on from the above argument, the convergence and divergence of Ussher and Bramhall's lines of national Church histories will be examined and explained as further expressions of their pull toward the justice and numinous motifs.

---

74 Ibid. vol. 7, p. 45.
75 Green, 'Anglicanism, Stuart and Hanoverian', p. 176.

A religion anciently professed: the nationalism of Ussher

Ussher finishes his monolithic work on Protestant succession with the dispersal of the Albigensians, some eastward toward Bohemia and Poland, '*alii, ad occidentem versi, in Britannia perfugium habuerunt*', [some turned West and found a refuge in Britain].[76] Thus, in his first major work, he set the scene for what was to be his next historical preoccupation, the Churches of Ireland and Britain. One is left with the sense that the major concern of Ussher's meticulous mapping of a Protestant lineage was to bring the reader to this point which would mark the triumph of his national Churches. As Hugh Trevor-Roper wrote, 'the stage was set for the appearance of Wycliffe and his disciples, and the emergence of England as "the elect nation"'.[77]

Ussher had been interested in the early history of his Church since his days as a student. The undated letter he wrote to his uncle, Richard Stanihurst, expressing an interest in the subject is certainly early[78] and in 1618 he was writing to William Camden informing him that he had been requested by the Archbishop of Armagh, Christopher Hampton, to write a treatise on the topic.[79] The first three decades of the seventeenth century witnessed in Ireland a spate of historical and devotional writings on Irish subjects. This was both encouraged and facilitated by the new availability of medieval manuscripts from the dissolved monasteries.[80] The revival of interest in antiquarian history spanned the Old English, Old Irish divide as both tried to justify their own positions in the changing political order.[81] Ussher's major work on this theme was published in 1631 under the title, *A Discourse on the Religion anciently professed by the Irish and British*. It first appeared as an appendix to Christopher Sibthorp's *A friendly Advertisement to the Pretended Catholics of Ireland* and was clearly intended to provide antiquarian clout to a polemical work. Ussher's treatise, in spite of its title, was almost entirely concerned with Irish history and more precisely how his own country's history fitted into the Protestant schema as set out in *Gravissimae Quaestionis ... Explicatio*.[82] The work also set out to show that the religion of their early Christian forefathers differed substantially from the position of the papacy. The purpose of such a demonstration was not as Ussher rather disingenuously purported in his preface to prove 'a special motive to induce my poor countrymen to consider a little better of the old and true way from whence they have hitherto been misled.'[83] Rather, Ussher set out to prove with the use of

---

76   *UW*, vol. 2, p. 413.
77   Trevor-Roper, *Catholics, Anglicans and Puritans*, p. 135.
78   *UW*, vol. 15, p. 34.
79   Ibid., p. 135.
80   W.O. Sullivan, 'Ussher as a Collector of Manuscripts', Hermathena, LXXXVIII (1956): 35.
81   B. Cunningham, 'Seventeenth-century interpretations of the past: the case of Geoffrey Keating', *Irish Historical Studies*, XXV, no. 98 (November, 1986):116.
82   As John McCafferty points out, the title of this work is making the point that the religion of the Britannic Churches was in fact of the same essence. This was of course a contemporary issue. J. McCafferty, 'St Patrick for the Church of Ireland, James Ussher's Discourse', *Bullán*, vol. 3, no.2 (Winter, 1997): 37.
83   UW, vol. 4, p. 237.

ancient text that his own Church was the same in spirit and practice and doctrine to that of their predecessors. It is a work of justification which is preoccupied not with evangelization, but refuting Catholic claims.

Besides, a little later in the preface, Ussher declares his real feelings on the subject of a wider Irish Reformation; those who would not listen to Moses and the prophets would not be persuaded by one who rose from the dead.[84] The effectiveness of his work is clearly already impeded by God's predestined judgement.

> ... that heavy judgement mentioned by the apostle, 'because they received not the love of the truth, that they might be saved, God shall send them strong delusion, that they should believe lie.' The woeful experience whereof, we may see daily before our eyes in this poor nation.[85]

Seamus Deane, in his work on Irish literature, linked Ussher's *Discourse* with the earlier diatribe of Edmund Spenser, *A View of the Present State of Ireland* (1596). Spenser's view had defended the severity of the measures taken in Munster against the native population as a means of civilizing the degenerate Irish. According to Deane, Ussher's *Discourse* offers a similar justification, providing, ' ... the Protestant planter with a crude predestination theology which seemed to justify their presence in Ireland as a providential attempt to rescue the Catholics from their benighted state or to reveal that it was no more than a proof of their outcast condition.'[86]

The *Discourse* has also been described as constituting part of the 'second Reformation' in Ireland. The first under Henry VIII had been basically legal and administrative, the second in the late sixteenth and early seventeenth centuries was aimed at doctrine, and works like *Discourse* were part of the confession building. However, as U. Lotz-Heumann explains, their audience was severely limited as the programme initiated by the Prince was 'embraced only by a ruling elite in the state and church ... this ruling elite was a colonial elite, the so-called New English.'[87] To this restricted audience Ussher argued that the early Irish Church had retained a purity of Christian doctrine in the same way that the Waldenses had preserved it in Europe. In this way they are held up as a type of Protestant mirror in which the Reformed Churches of his generation might view their own reflection. In both practice and doctrine, Ussher unearthed examples of congruity. Their ancestors, even as children, studied the Bible in their native tongue.[88] From their scriptural canon they excluded the apocryphal writings, excepting the book of Solomon.[89] They also, and perhaps most importantly to Ussher, held firmly to the doctrinal strictures of predestination. Apart from the regrettable period when the Irish were inflicted by that 'Pelagian poison', their ancestors were the very embodiment of pre-Reformation Calvinism. Ussher writes, 'The doctrine which our learned men observed out of the scriptures

---

84 Ibid.
85 Ibid., p. 238.
86 S. Deane, *A Short History of Irish Literature* (London, 1986), p. 17.
87 U. Lotz-Heumann, 'The Protestant interpretation of history: the case of James Ussher', in Bruce, (ed.), *Protestant History*, p. 107.
88 *UW*, vol. 4, pp. 243–4.
89 Ibid., pp. 249–51.

and the writings of the most approved fathers, was this, that God "by his immovable counsel ... ordained some creatures to praise him, and to live blessedly from him and in him, and by him:" namely "by his eternal predestination"'.[90]

Alongside this explication of dogma and practice, Ussher sets out his own understanding of the chronology of the Irish Church. This version of events can be summed up as follows: Patrick was sent by Rome to convert Ireland. However Rome, subsequent to dispatching the saint, had little to do with the nascent Church. Ussher contends that no papal legate was ever sent to exercise spiritual jurisdiction before Malachi and Lawrence (these papal emissaries arrived in Ireland in the twelfth century).[91] Before their arrival there existed in Ireland the 'golden age' required of the biblical historical formula which Ussher employs. In these halcyon days, apart from the foreign ports of Dublin, Waterford and Limerick which came under Norman influence, the main body of Irish Churches enjoyed an unrestrained independence.[92] On the potentially sticky problem of St Patrick's occasional deference to Rome, Ussher was unperturbed. Patrick, he argued, undoubtedly had a special regard for the Roman Church since it was the place from where his mission had sprung.[93] Besides, Ussher says, he too would have sent to Rome in those days for at the time of Patrick the papacy still had integrity. The Irish apostle was blameless in his action since he was not aware of the divine schema and the inevitable fall of Rome, according to Ussher, 'But that St Patrick was of opinion, that the Church of Rome was sure ever afterward to continue in that good estate, and that there was a perpetual privilege annexed unto that see, that it should never err in judgement ... that will I never believe.'[94]

All this represents the first major attempt at forging a Protestant history of Ireland, its relative lateness can be explained by the delay in a confessional Reformation in the country.[95] As indicated above, *Discourse* represented an academic effort to construct a religious posterity and a greater self-awareness. There was, however, an important ancillary purpose to the work. Ussher was seeking to prove that the Church of Ireland originated from St Patrick and not out of England. This is not to say that they were not sister Churches, or that their faith was different, but the sibling, not progenitive, nature of their relationship is important to Ussher. There are important contemporary political implications for this as John McCafferty has pointed out. 'Thus his own Church of Ireland was autonomous under its Primate, answering only to Charles I – but Charles as king of Ireland, not king of England.'[96]

The timing of Ussher's publication could not have been more expedient; only three years later his Church was to experience the overbearing style of the Laudian government at the 1634 Convocation where the English Articles of Faith were

---

90   Ibid., p. 252.
91   D. Attwater, *The Penguin Dictionary of Saints* (London, 1965), p. 226, pp. 215–16.
92   *UW*, vol. 4, pp. 319–25.
93   Ibid., p. 330.
94   Ibid.
95   Lotz-Heumann, 'Protestant Interpretation', p. 109.
96   McCafferty, 'St Patrick' p. 2.

pressed upon them. It is hard to resist the conclusion that Ussher was aware of the pertinence of his claim to independent ancestry. In accordance with his move toward a greater stress on the historical nature of the episcopacy, the real heroes of the *Discourse* are the Irish bishops. Ussher describes a strongly autonomous Church hierarchy in which independent bishops of Ireland are certainly civil toward the Church of Rome but by no means servile, ' ... the bishops of Ireland did not take all the resolutions of the Church of Rome for undoubted oracles; but when they thought that they had better reason on their sides, they preferred the judgement of other churches before it.'[97] Ussher pointedly observes that it is precisely the debate over Pelagius in which the Irish bishops show their true mettle.[98] According to Ussher they rose up jointly with other groups in Italy and Africa after Rome refused to condemn the three chapters of Pelagius' work under scrutiny. Later they were to blame the famine, war and pestilence in Italy on Rome's prevarication.[99] It is clear that Ussher is convinced that the Irish bishops played an important part in conserving true faith and ecclesiastical autonomy. Ussher is anxious to dismiss the claim of Giraldus Cambrensis that there were no archbishops in Ireland and for this purpose he quotes a letter from Pope Hildebrand addressed to 'Terdeluachus ... the illustrious king of Ireland, the *archbishops*, bishops, abbots, nobles and all the Christians.'[100] This as well as 'other pregnant testimonies' establish an ancient precedent for episcopacy. In the same way that Bramhall traces national episcopacy through to the apostles, Ussher regards the first call of the disciples as the starting point. The imparting of episcopal power is universal; when the Saviour was posing the question of his identity, Peter was answering for all.Therefore the power of loosing and binding was given to all.[101]

Perhaps a more convincing proof for apostolic equality is provided when Ussher uses evidence from Claudius that whilst acknowledging a 'kind of primacy' calling Peter 'Ecclesiae principem et Apostolorum principem' [prince of the Church and prince of the apostles] he adds that Paul was given primacy in founding the Churches of gentiles. In this, Paul esteemed himself 'not to be inferior.'[102] By establishing this role for Paul as apostle to the gentiles, Ussher is free to trace episcopal lineage in the national Churches not to the (apparently) first Pope but to another who is his equal. Besides, Protestants were always going to be happier tracing their origins to the author of the letter to the Romans. In using the bishopric as pillars of pre-Reformation orthodoxy, Ussher is aware of the problems which face Bramhall; that is, those following the route of their episcopal ancestry inevitably find themselves at Rome. Ussher in unconcerned by such consequences; on the contrary, he is full of invective against those who see only evil in pursuing such a course. 'Yet now-a-days men are made to believe, that out of the communion of the Church of Rome nothing

---

97 *UW*, vol. 4, p. 332.
98 Ibid., p. 95.
99 Ibid.
100 Ibid., pp. 320–21.
101 Ibid., p. 316.
102 Ibid., p. 99.

but hell can be looked for.'[103] The consequences of such wholesale antagonism would be disastrous for the proud heritage that belongs to the national Churches. Though it may 'go current for good divinity' it would cause us to forget the twelve hundred monks who were martyred at Bangor as well as St Aidan and St Finan, 'who deserve to be honoured by the English nation.'[104]

Ussher urges his readers to recognise that there were better, more harmonious times in Church history. Antagonism to the present corruption does not necessitate an antagonism to the original. Even in that most heated contest which was the Synod of Whitby no side was so disparaging of the other as to declare them false.

> Neither is it here to be omitted, that whatsoever broils did pass betwixt our Irish that were not subject to the see of Rome, and those others that were of the Roman communion in the succeeding ages, they of the one side were esteemed to be saints, as well as they of the other.[105]

Ussher's *Discourse* with its pivotal role for the bishopric has much in common with Bramhall's historical perspective. However, the essential difference remains: Ussher's bishops are essentially non-sacerdotal. They are the great leaders, the organisers and brave defenders of true faith but there is in Ussher's work a silence on the mystical properties of their office. In an otherwise lionising tribute to Ussher, W.E. Watson lamented the fact that he seemed incapable of distinguishing 'the essential' and 'the accidental' attributes of episcopacy. Here Watson elaborates on the distinction.

> If the administrative powers, necessarily concentrated in the bishops' hands in ancient times of persecution were withdrawn; if the dignity of high civil rank in which the Roman Empire, after conversion had clothed him, and the feudal rights with which the Middle Ages had invested him were also removed ... then there would remain the primitive work and status of the bishop.[106]

Ussher's theological understanding, rooted as it was in the justice motif, equated this 'work and status' of the bishop precisely with the administrative power, the civil rank and the feudal rights. Ussher might have traced their origin to apostolic times, but unlike Bramhall, he is not inclined to explore the mystical connotation of this human link to the incarnation. We shall see that this link was important to Bramhall because it preserved the integrity of a blessing, it is important to Ussher because it established a hierarchy that would spread and preserve the word of God.

Ussher may have dealt with the Roman origins of episcopacy in a satisfactory manner but ultimately his Irish ecclesiastical history fails because he does not successfully manage to marry it to the Protestant schema which he has already established. *Discourse* is meant to serve as the Irish piece in the European Protestant jigsaw but Ussher cannot get it to fit. This is seen most clearly in his awkward and not to say contradictory handling of the twelfth century Norman invasion. Ussher tells us on the one hand that this signalled the end of the golden age since it meant

---

103 Ibid., p. 357.
104 Ibid.
105 Ibid., pp. 356–7.
106 Watson, 'Ussher', pp. 74–5.

an introduction of the Roman rites which have blighted the Church of the majority in Ireland since.[107] On the other hand, Ussher argues that English sovereignty comes from this very conquest.[108] If this is the case, then it follows that Ussher is indicting the Old English (his own ancestors) for facilitating the Antichrist and at the same time using them to legitimize the crown and government which he served. Ussher has hoisted himself on his own schematic petard and as John McCafferty indicates he is on this point vulnerable to criticism. 'He was wide open to the taunt that Antichrist and English rule came very close to one another, as well as to the more mundane charge that the title of the English king had been dependent on the papacy.'[109]

For the Primate of Ireland there is also another consideration. On the last page of his *Discourse*, he claims that he is at pains to convert the Old English. If this claim is to be taken seriously, one can only assume that any such missionary efforts would be severely handicapped by Ussher's depiction of them historically as the pawns of Satan. Nor indeed is it easy to envisage any greater success outside the confines of his own ethnic group. The New English would have found little that was appealing in an account of an Irish Protestantism rooted in a Gaelic past that was synonymous for them with barbarism and backwardness.[110]

A schism guarded against: the ecclesiastical nationalism of Bramhall

John Bramhall's portrait of his national Church's history must be seen as part of what Patrick Collinson referred to as the 'blunt instrument' of the new and confident episcopalian ideology which had assumed shape in the 1590s and early 1600s.[111] In terms of formulating an apologetic account of national ecclesiastical autonomy it achieved its purpose in a less brutal fashion than the Reformed visionaries. Collinson argued that it accomplished this task by erecting 'more delicately balanced edifices' based on two principles, 'For the purposes of these polemics it was necessary on the one hand to deny that the will of the prince was the only rule of faith, and on the other to explain the nature and limits of ecclesiastical obedience.'[112] Bramhall never produced any purely historical works per se, but there is a good deal of historical referencing in his Anglican apologetics. In his most celebrated work on the subject, *The Just Vindication of the Church of England* (1654), his main concern is to refute the charges of schism and, as Collinson expresses it, to outline the limits of obedience. Bramhall's appeal to history might be summarised as follows: The Britannic Churches are greater in antiquity than the Church of Rome, 'being planted by Joseph of Arimathea in the reign of Tiberius Caesare, whereas it is confessed that St Peter came not to Rome, to lay the foundation of that Church, until the second

---

107 *UW*, vol. 4, p. 276.
108 Ibid., p. 367.
109 McCafferty, 'St Patrick': 95.
110 A. Ford, 'James Ussher and the creation of an Irish Protestant identity.' in B. Bradshaw and P. Roberts (eds), *British Consciousness and Identity: Tthe Making of Britain, 1533–1707* (Cambridge, 1998) p. 206.
111 Collinson, *Religion of Protestants*, p. 11.
112 Ibid., p. 12.

year of Claudius.'[113] British bishops were autocephalous, that is self-governing, and ordination took place in Britain among themselves without reference to Rome. Bramhall points to an instance of this autocephalous nature when St Augustine of Canterbury, as Pope Gregory's legate, failed to persuade the English bishops to either conform to Rome's customs, submit to Roman bishops or to join in a preaching mission to the Saxons.[114] English kings, previous to the thirteenth century enjoyed the same rights and privileges of all Christian emperors in matters of ecclesiastical discipline, regulating laws concerning revenue of the Church, calling councils, dissolving or confirming these councils and regulating law concerning Holy Orders, benefices, and the suspension of bishops and priests.[115] Then as the papacy began to assert a greater power than it was entitled to, problems grew between the sister Churches. According to Bramhall, events took a serious turn for the worst in the reign of King John. ' ... taking advantage of King John's troubles, they attempted to make the royal sceptre of England feudatory and tributary to the Crosier-Staff of Rome at the annual rent of a thousand marks.'[116]

Nor was it solely the ruling powers who were affected; the people of England generally suffered because of the Roman drain on their resources.

> ... they cheated and impoverished the people by their dispensations, and commutations and pardons, and indulgences, and expeditions to recover the Holy Land, and jubilees, and pilgrimages, and Agnus Deis, and a thousand pecuniary artifices so as no sort of men escaped their fingers.[117]

Various kings between 1200 and 1300 objected, though mostly in vain, at such treatment until the reign of Henry VIII when it was as if the English monarchy had said that enough was enough, and the break was made. This was not therefore a breach that was taken capriciously but one that had been building up for centuries. Bramhall refers to earlier English monarchs as the first Reformers, 'So what was threatened and effected in part in the days of Henry the Third and Edward the Third, was perfected in the reign of Henry the Eighth; when the jurisdiction of the Court of Rome in England was abolished, which makes the great distance between them and us.'[118]

In keeping with his position in other works, the *Vindication* shows no inclination to integrate national Church history with the histories of other Protestant Churches. Indeed, in an attack on the work printed in Paris in 1655, the Catholic writer John Sergeant noted with glee Bramhall's lack of confessional camaraderie.

> Moreover, he professeth only to clear the Protestant Church of England from the crime of schism, as if either other Protestant Churches were guilty of schism, or it were too hard

---

113 *BW*, vol. 1, p. 160.
114 Ibid., p. 163.
115 Ibid., p. 171.
116 Ibid., p. 188.
117 Ibid., p. 190.
118 Ibid., p. 196.

for him to defend them from it. Surely, this seems either to argue his little charity toward other Protestant Churches, or his little skill to defend them.[119]

For this reason, Bramhall does not fall into the same schematic trap as Ussher, he is neither attracted to that form of providential history or to fitting the English Reformation into the broader European reform. Bramhall's Reformers are not Luther and Calvin but the English kings, and then not so much the kings as individuals, but as representatives of government. Bramhall has no taste for prophetic heroism, and he is anxious to claim the English Reformation for the establishment. Elsewhere he elaborates, the founders of Protestantism 'were not our Reformers', instead Bramhall looks to the 'synods proposing, the Parliament receiving, the king authorizing.' In defining the English Reformation in this way Bramhall is by implication condemning other less ordered movements. When we read that the events in England were not 'seditious, tumultuous, not after a fanatical or enthusiastical way', we are left in no doubt that others were.[120] This is a classic example of the Davidic-Royal history. The primary purpose of this history is to sustain the presence on behalf of 'legitimated political-cultural institutions' especially the 'royal house.'[121] Bramhall fulfils this obligation by establishing them and their institutions as the instigators of English Christian reform.

Bramhall betrays a sense of urgency in his attempts to win the rewards of Church history for the English kingship and this occasions him to portray them at once as the abused victims of Rome and the lion-hearted heroes who refuse to cow. This was a slip that was immediately picked up on by John Sergeant. In another treatise against Bramhall he pointed out the contradiction.

> All this while he would persuade the World that Papists are most injurious to Princes, prejudicing their crowns, and subjecting their Dominions to the will of the Pope. He has scarce done saying so, but with a contrary blast drives as far back again confessing all he had said to be false[122]

In fairness to Bramhall the contradiction is not as strong as there suggested, and he would no doubt have countered the objection by saying that in order to rebel one must first be oppressed. Nevertheless Bramhall's account of Anglo-Papal relations has a slightly jumbled analysis of the power struggle.

A problem of greater proportion thrown up by Bramhall's history (a problem that, to his credit, he recognises) is that it is an undeniable account of his Church severing relations with another Church. The charge of schism rings in the ears of authors like Bramhall who did not deny that Rome was indeed a Church. Bramhall deals with the problem in his usual deft manner. Firstly, he argues that England has withdrawn

---

119 British Library, main collection, 3935.a.a.2, R.C., *A Brief Survey of the Lord of Derry* (Paris, 1655), p. 5. This R.C. is John Sergeant who was educated at St John's College, Cambridge. He became a Catholic at the age of twenty-one and spent the rest of his life as a controversialist against the Anglicans including Casaubon, Jeremy Taylor, and Hammond.

120 *BW*, vol. 1, p. 21.

121 Brueggemann, *Old Testament*, p. 273.

122 S.W., *Schism Disarmed* (London, 1655), p. 320.

sovereignty from the papacy but they have had total schism thrust upon them. In other words, because they have reclaimed a measure of their independence, Rome has expelled them completely from their communion. It is for this reason, according to Bramhall, that the Vatican and not England is the real guilty party. 'If the Court of Rome will be humorous, like little children, who, because they cannot have some toy that they have a mind to, do cast away all that their parents have given them, we cannot help it.'[123] Bramhall does not dismiss papal authority in its entirety, and in this he goes as far as any member of the Protestant community may. There is, argues Bramhall, a spiritual power which the Pope has, 'I accept always that jurisdiction which is purely spiritual, and an essential part of the power of the keys, whereof emperors and kings are not capable.'[124] However, it is precisely because the papacy usurped a secular jurisdiction over the other national Churches that the present problems and divisions have erupted. This interpretation of relations and events carried potentially dangerous implications suggesting as it does that servants might sit in judgement of their masters. Once more, Bramhall's legal mind extricated him from the difficulty. 'I confess, inferiors are not competent judges of their superiors; but in this case of a subordinate superior, and in a matter of heresy or schism already defined by the Church, the sentence of the judge is not necessary.'[125]

Secondly Bramhall claims that this separation is not from Rome, or from any other Church, it is instead from her errors. This neat use of semantics is enough to exonerate the Reformed generation of the English Church but Bramhall is concerned that it might be seen to condemn their forefathers. Like Ussher, he is reluctant to lose such posterity; once more, Bramhall employs a clever piece of casuistry to solve the dilemma.

> We do not condemn them, not separate ourselves from them. Charity requires us both to think well, and speak well of them .... We believe our fathers might partake of some errors of the Roman Church, we do not believe that they were guilty of any heretical pravity, but held always the truth implicitly in the preparation of their minds, and were always ready to receive it when God should be pleased to reveal it.[126]

It should also be noted that this was the closest Bramhall comes to introducing a note of providential history into his account of events. His English ancestors it seems were only waiting for the time when the divine hand would remove the scales from their eyes. Bramhall does, however, avoid any specific reference to the Protestant schema by way of explanation and it would seem that his brush with providentialism is only slight.

Placed together, Ussher's and Bramhall's accounts of Christian succession and the progress of their national Churches show some remarkable distinctions. Two leading ecclesiastics of the same Church writing about the same events and institutions have approached their subjects from what appears to be very different

---

123 *BW*, vol. 1, p. 176.
124 Ibid., p. 171.
125 Ibid., p. 262. 'Subordinate superior' here refers to the pope being subordinate to the council of bishops in true Conciliarist fashion.
126 Ibid., p. 264.

perspectives. In the epic of Ussher's Christian history, it is the underdog who is held up for tribute; even when he draws on the hierarchy of his own Church for champions, they are boy David's struggling against the Goliath of Rome. Bramhall's bishops are no such thing. They are the conduit pipes of succession, the guarantors of the apostolic line and the bulwarks of national Church independence. Bramhall does not seek the down-trodden hero who tilts at the establishment because his hero is the establishment. These two interpretations of events are seventeenth-century examples of the two strands of biblical history that are the Mosaic-Covenantal and the Davidic-Royal, and further behind these two schools of history lie the justice and numinous motifs.

Chapter 6

Secular Politics

James Ussher and John Bramhall found themselves in paradoxically similar and opposite positions during the political turmoils that were the English Civil Wars. Both were exiled from Ireland, but whilst Ussher was feted as a refugee, Bramhall was tainted by his close association with Laud. One seems to have represented the acceptable face of episcopacy while the other, the very epitome of all that was wrong with it. Both were employed within the royalist propaganda machine, but only Bramhall appears to have excited the full force of Parliamentarian wrath for doing so. The Bishop of Derry was forced to flee the country after Marston Moor, the archbishop of Armagh continued to live and work in London until his death. On the face of it their respective experiences during these traumatic years appears to colour the two bishops with rather distinct political hues. Ussher the compromising moderate in sharp contrast to the zealous hard-line Arminianism of Bramhall. Yet, as this chapter will set out to demonstrate, this gulf is largely an artificial one based more on perceptions than concrete political ideals. By comparing two of their most important political works, *The Power of the Prince* and *The Serpent Salve*, it will be shown that their fundamental divine-right absolutism had much in common, though if anything it is Bramhall's which reflects a more modern, more tempered style of scholarship. Lastly this chapter will examine the current debate on absolutism in light of the politics of Ussher and Bramhall in order to show that, contrary to modern revisionist scepticism, the English version of *de jure divino* did exist and that the works before us provide two examples of this political genre.

Ussher: the reluctant politician

If Archbishop Ussher showed a marked disinclination to become involved in the necessary practicalities of high office in the Church then he displayed even more antipathy to the machinations of the political world. This was not always easy and because of his great reputation others were often keen to employ his voice in their cause, even when this voice was unsolicited. The manuscript evidence we have available contains numerous examples of political tracts purporting to be by Ussher, nearly always followed by a petition from the supposed author to have the tract suppressed. On 9 February, 1640 he appealed to the Commons to stop the dispersal of a pamphlet entitled, *The Bishop of Armagh's directions to the Houses of Parliament, concerning the Liturgie of Episcopall Government* which he claimed had been 'injuriously fathered upon him.'[1] The following year he was 'humbly requesting' the House of Lords call in a published sermon called *Vox Hiberniae*, which he said was taken from 'some rude and incoherent notes' of a sermon he had preached.[2] The pamphlet warned the English people that they would soon fall prey to the same judgement visited on the Irish in 1641, unless the nation repent. 'God hath overthrown that land especially the best of the land, according as he did to Germany; And now he is come nearer to us.'[3] It is significant that Ussher nowhere objects to the sentiments expressed in these works, although in the case of *Vox Hiberniae*, he bemoans the fact that it is in many places 'void of common sense'; he is talking of grammatical errors in the sermon notes. It is clear from the petitions that he is more concerned that these publications have neither been prepared nor authorised by himself, something that would have caused obvious pain to such a meticulous scholar. He is also perturbed that words intended for a private audience might be the cause of public strife at such politically sensitive times. However, there is nothing in the petition to suggest that Ussher's words had been falsified, nor does he attempt to disown their message. This clearly implies that such examples of pamphlet sermons appearing under his name may well be crude but they are not entirely inaccurate and they can provide a useful insight into the thoughts of an otherwise reluctant politician.

As reluctant a politician as Ussher was, he was also far too big a name to be allowed the rare luxury of neutrality. By the late 1630s the Primate found himself a conscript in the propaganda war that had arisen out of the prayer book rebellion. The Scottish Kirks had produced and dispersed numerous tracts insisting on their natural rights, claiming divine support and denigrating Charles's government. The King, a man not naturally at home in the medium of words, was impelled to reply; in 1637 he declared their printing to be a traitorous act and thus embarked for the first time in his life on a war of words. Kevin Sharpe describes the significance of this event. 'The Prayer Book rebellion ended the authority of silence in Caroline England and instigated a new politics of discourse in which power depended upon the articulation of the royal voice.'[4]

In Ireland, Sir George Radcliffe garnered Ussher's opinion on the matter. The Archbishop committed his thoughts to paper and dispatched it forthwith; meanwhile, he set out for Dublin. On arriving in the capital, Wentworth requested that he should make his views public and Ussher complied with two sermons before state in Christ Church. The text of his homily was taken as, 'I counsel thee to keep the King's commandment, and that in regard of the oath of God.'[5] Shortly after, Wentworth communicated to the archbishop that it was not only his wish, but also the King's that these sermons should be printed or else he might write a treatise based on them.

---

1   Dr Williams Library, Ms. 12.55.8, 'Petition from James Ussher to the House of Commons', 1640.

2   Dr Williams Library, Ms. 12.55.9, 'Petition from James Ussher to the House of Lords', 1641.

3   J. Ussher, *Vox Hiberniae*, (London, 1642), Thomason Collection, E 132(32), p. 3.

4   K. Sharpe, 'The King's Writ: Royal Authority in Early Modern England', in K. Sharpe and P. Lake (eds), *Culture and Politics in Early Stuart England* (London, 1994), p. 134.

5   Bernard, *Clavi*, p. 47.

Ussher opted for the latter and produced *The Power of the Prince as communicated by God and the subject's duty*. It represents Ussher's only attempt at political writing, though it is of course highly theological. Since it is unique among Ussher's writings in this respect it will occupy the majority of our attention when dealing with him in this chapter.

Even before this Royal commission there is evidence that Ussher was being talked of as a useful ally for the King against the Scottish Presbyters. Ussher was not only an academic heavyweight but his name carried much kudos among the Calvinist Scots who would have regarded him as theologically sound. Bishop Hall recognised this and in a letter to Laud he proposed Ussher as head of a team that might take on the objectors.

> If there, in Ireland, the Lord Primate, the bishop of Kilmore, the bishop of Down and Conor, men as you know of singular note in the Church ... shall be enjoined by you to express their judgments fully concerning these two heads of episcopacy and lay presbytery, and to print them together, it will be a work that will carry in it such authority and satisfaction as will give great contentment to the world and carry in it a strong rebuke of the adversaries.[6]

In another letter to Laud, Bishop Hall states his belief that such names behind such opinions would have a profound effect, and would 'certainly confound these heady and ignorant opposers of government and good order.'[7] In the event, Ussher was to serve the cause not by putting his name to a joint declaration but by lending the full weight of his own considerable learning to the King's cause. *The Power of the Prince* does not address the situation especially but rather offers a much more fundamental endorsement of the King's divine authorisation and the subject's Christian obligation to passively obey. The treatise works as both an affirmation and a warning. It testifies to the Godly power of the prince and cautions those who might fail in their duty to recognise it.

In spite of his efforts Ussher's treatment of monarchical government was never published during the crucial years of political turmoil that it set out to address. Though royally commissioned, *The Power of the Prince* never made it to the printing press until after the author's death. Robert Lincoln (the publisher) spins a rather dubious yarn in his introduction which hints at foul play.

> Whereupon the author, being not then at London himself, sent up the aforesaid transcript copy thither, to the intent it should be there printed; which, notwithstanding, whether by the negligence or unfaithfulness of the party, to whose care and trust it was committed, was not done; but the copy itself finally lost ... The original copy in the mean time by the author ... negligently laid aside, and so at length mingling with some papers ... that it never was his hap to meet with it again all his lifetime.[8]

Whatever the reason, in 1640 Ussher's text was not printed, and the royalist cause was championed in a more conciliatory language. Whether it was sabotage, the hand

---

6   *Cal.S.P.Dom., 1639–1640*, p. 30.
7   *Cal.S.P.Dom., 1639*, p. 527.
8   *Power of the Prince*, pp. 229–30.

of fate or an act of royalist self-censorship which prevented the publication no one will perhaps ever know for certain. However by looking at Ussher's stance a little more closely one is able to observe a curious paradox which tends to lend itself to the latter explanation. Ussher held a somewhat unusual political position throughout the 1640s. Whilst an ardent royalist he was naturally an intellectual recruit to their cause, yet his position geographically and theologically endeared him to those of a more puritanical disposition. His less dogmatic form of Church government also caused William Prynne to enquire as to why England did not enjoy similar toleration.[9]

Herein lies the paradox. As the political strife intensified Ussher was obviously seen as a more palatable representation of ecclesiastical authority, just as more problematical individuals were being jettisoned. Kevin Sharpe describes these developments, 'Laud was not of great importance in the politics of the winter of 1640. In part, this was because Charles showed his willingness to desert him, to elevate Williams and Ussher and to promise to restore the Church to the primitive purity of Elizabeth's time.'[10] Ironically, just as Ussher the man grew in prominence, Ussher the thinker became more and more at odds with both sides. Though he was a 'low Churchman' with Calvinist tendencies, he was always going to be an uncomfortable bedfellow for the parliamentarians for obvious reasons. When he arrived in England in 1640 he did so as a refugee, a hero of the outpost war, and he was welcomed as such. Yet as ultra-Protestant as he was, he was one of the Irish mould and therefore fundamentally different on the question of loyalty. Buick Knox sums up the predicament this left Ussher in.

> When he came to England in 1640 he found himself in a painful dilemma. Much as he sympathised with those who feared the Roman Catholic Church he found that he could not countenance them when at the same time their policy proved to be a threat to the Monarchy and the Establishment.[11]

Therefore Ussher was unusually placed; his prestige as a scholar and his heroic escape meant that he was lionised by people against whom he was diametrically opposed. That the author of such a trenchant piece of royalism as *The Power of the Prince* survived the Civil War and its aftermath is testimony to the ambiguous way he was perceived. Such was the turmoil of the 1640s that men could find themselves very quickly in and out of favour, and in some cases they were in favour yet strangely irrelevant. Ussher found himself in a political limbo, accepted and rejected by both sides. The cause he did embrace found him increasingly useful as a figure of stature but eventually useless as a propagandist. The document that Charles took pleasure in reading in 1639 was neglected, possibly suppressed, in 1640. *The Power of the Prince* is uncompromising just when Charles wanted to build bridges. James Ussher's brand of ideology always at variance with the English mainstream, was to become impractical during the exigencies of war. To the question, what impact the work had on the immediate situation? The answer is none, and this is probably because its tone was deemed to be alienating. Ussher went the way of Robert Filmer; he was

---

9 W. Prynne, *Anti-Arminianisme* (London, 1630), p. 20.
10 K. Sharpe, *The Personal Rule of Charles I* (London, 1995), p. 935.
11 Knox, *Ussher*, p. 55.

put on political dry ice until such time as the royal appeal need not be so appeasing. In the event, this was exactly what happened when Ussher's political theories were resurrected in 1660 along with ideas of divine right monarchy as a whole. The horrors of the conflict and their aftermath came to be associated with the Commonwealth, and royalism enjoyed a revival. The Restoration followed and along with it, the political justifications of monarchy. *The Power of the Prince* enjoyed a posthumous vogue as a scholarly attempt to seek such justifications in the word of God.

Bramhall: the resolute politician

Compared to Ussher's marked reluctance for dirtying his hands with the business of Church and State affairs, Bramhall's approach displayed all the opposite qualities, he was the consummate politician. When appointed to high office he threw himself headlong into his duties and the enormous tasks that faced him. Just as Ussher was happy to relinquish the reins, Bramhall was equally keen to grab them. When circumstances beyond his control forced him from the seat of power, he refused to languish in idle dejection, nor did he let his reduced circumstances better him, but rather he wrote voluminously on all the current issues of the day. If Ussher may be described as a conscript to the political battleground, then Bramhall was the most eager of volunteers. Ussher, it appears, had politics thrust upon him, in the case of Bramhall he was most assuredly born to it.

Throughout the early 1640s Bramhall was also an exile from Ireland, residing in Yorkshire for the most part with William Cavendish, the Marquess of Newcastle. Cavendish was an officer in the King's army and Bramhall provided spiritual support for his northern campaign. From here he sent to the King his plate.[12] Deprived of any real official power, he returned to his earlier world of scholarship and preaching. In a similar fashion to Ussher also, he became part of an ecclesiastical and scholarly body of apologists for the royal cause. In this capacity, he made a not insignificant contribution, though Arthur Hadden is probably stretching the point somewhat when he claims that by these means 'he put considerable life into the King's affairs.'[13] In 1642 Bramhall published his most important political study which he entitled *The Serpent Salve; or a Remedy for the biting of an Asp*. The work was anonymous and it represented a robust defence of *de jure divino* government, as well as a defence of the origins of episcopacy. It was also a reply to the Parliamentarian Henry Parker who had penned the challenging volume entitled *Observations upon some of His Majesties late Answers and Expresses*. These publications marked the end of the manifesto war of early 1642, which had seen the Royalists victorious, and began the Civil War pamphleteering.[14]

At the time of his writing *Observations*, Parker was secretary to the army under Robert Devereux, a prolific pamphleteer. He had already published *A Discourse concerning Puritans, The Question concerning the Divine Right of Episcopacie truly*

---

12 *DNB*, (1968), vol. 2, p. 1113.
13 *BW*, vol. 1, p. x.
14 J.W. Daly, 'John Bramhall and the theoretical problems of Royalist moderation', *Journal of British Studies*, XI (1971): 27.

stated, and *The Altar Dispute*. *Observations* proved his most controversial work and, aside from Bramhall, it was answered by Dudley Digges, John Jones, and most significantly the crown in *The King's Answer to the Nineteen Propositions* (1641).[15] *Observations* stated that political power residing in the King could only be seen as divine in origin in the most general sense. In fact the power he exerted through his office ascended from the people and did not descend from the heavens. Parker's own slant on history had important political implications. He argued that post-Eden mankind found peaceful society difficult to maintain, yet the monarchical government they turned to was little better than the anarchy they had left. The answer was some form of people's representation which would both secure peace and avoid tyranny, 'The people then having intrusted their protection into the King's hands irrevocably, yet have not left that trust without all manner of limits, something they have reserved for themselves out of Parliament, and some things in Parliament.'[16] Parker's defence of representative government was unabashed, going so far as to elevate the institute of Parliament over the institute of monarchy, 'for in truth, the whole kingdom is not so properly the author as the essence it self of Parliaments.'[17] As representative of the whole community, Parliament was therefore obliged by the laws of nature to preserve itself, this single assertion was the complete mirror image of the King's position in the ship money trial.[18] However, it was when Parker boldly asserted that Parliament ultimately possessed 'arbitrary power' because of its representative nature[19] that the parliamentary cards were finally and shockingly placed on the table. John Sanderson shows that up until *Observations* such a contentious statement had never been openly advanced. It proved royalist suspicions were well founded that whilst protesting about innovation it was the parliamentarians that were the innovators; Bramhall seized upon it 'To Bramhall the great innovation of the parliamentarians was to endeavour to establish in themselves an arbitrary power over the Commonwealth; but now, with the publication of Parker's pamphlet, 'the mask is off ... .'[20]

Bramhall's rejoinder convincingly argued that Parker was not describing monarchy, but rather democracy, something he took for granted that nobody wanted. *The Serpent Salve* defended the descending theory of monarchical power and the work rests on the assumption that men cannot take back what was never theirs to give. Besides he lambasted the parliamentarians for their basic hypocrisy. They were men who called for liberty and yet would impose their own form of tyranny, they cried out for liberty of conscience and would yet impose their own heavy yoke on the consciences of men. Later Bramhall was to call this their 'disciplinarian humour' the 'very quintessence of refined Popery.'[21] *The Serpent Salve* argued that of all forms of government the absolutism of a single ruler was to be preferred. On a purely

---

15   *DNB*, (1968), vol. 15, pp. 240–41.
16   H. Parker, *Observations upon some of His Majesties late Answers and Expresses* (London, 1642), p. 8.
17   Ibid., p. 5.
18   D. Hirst, *Authority and Conflict in England 1603–1658* (London, 1986), p. 223.
19   Parker, *Observations*, p. 34.
20   J. Sanderson, 'Serpent Salve 1643, The Royalism of John Bramhall', *Journal of Ecclesiastical History*, XXV (1974): 9.
21   *BW*, vol. 3, pp. 242–3.

practical level, setting aside divine injunction, autocracy functioned better than the confusion that resulted from any dispersal of power.

> ... one physician may see more into the state of a man's body than many empiracs, one experienced commander may know more in military affairs than ten freshwater soldiers, and one old statesman in his own element is worth many new practitioners; one man upon a hill may see more than a hundred in a valley.[22]

Bramhall acknowledges the dangers of tyranny that might result from such a focus of power, but he found them far less alarming than the dangers of anarchy that would certainly result from any deprecation of sovereign rule. The binding of the whole kingdom, he allows, 'is of no great virtue against the evils of tyranny, but is a sovereign remedy against the greater mischiefs which flow from ochlocracy.'[23] Besides one need only look to France, where according to Bramhall, the people are miserable now under the burden of their monarchy but were even more so in times of sedition.[24] Bramhall's work was greeted with a chorus of approval from the royalist party and after reading it James Ussher wrote to him expressing his delight.

> I cannot sufficiently commend your dexterity in clearing these points, which have not been so satisfactorily handled by those who have taken pains in the same argument before you, and I profess I have profited more thereby, than any of the books I have read before, touching that subject.[25]

It would appear from its immediate publication and circulation that *The Serpent Salve* was regarded as more useful in terms of propaganda than Ussher's effort. This was no doubt due to its attempts to portray monarchy as self-regulating and therefore a less perilous political avenue than some were suggesting. Bramhall is also careful to appreciate the role of parliament, albeit secondary in function to the crown. *The Serpent Salve* makes genuine attempts to be persuasive, where *The Power of the Prince* is homiletic. In his work on constitutional royalism, David L. Smith argued that the importance of Bramhall as an example of tempered royalism is underestimated.[26] John Daly also cites Bramhall as the best known of a group of eight royalist writers among whom we find the names Sir Charles Dallison, Dudley Digges (the younger), Henry Ferne, and Sir John Spelman.[27] This cabal of moderate monarchists printed much of their work at Oxford during the first Civil War. Smith contrasts them with absolutists like Filmer, John Maxwell and Hobbes, and he gives a summary of their approach.

> The shared attitudes may be briefly characterised as a belief that royal powers should be guided and limited by the rule of law, and that Charles I's action posed less of a threat to

---

22 *Serpent Salve*, p. 407.
23 Ibid., p. 416.
24 Ibid., p. 324.
25 Vesey, *Athanasius*, p. 27.
26 D.L. Smith, *Constitutional Royalism and the Search for Settlement c.1640–1649* (Cambridge, 1994).
27 Daly, 'Royalist Moderation': 14.

legality than those of the Houses: the combination of a respect for Parliament's place in the constitution with and abhorrence of the Junto;[28]

They defended the existing Church of England 'as by law established', and the discretionary powers of the King to appoint Privy Councillors, senior officers and legal and military; together with the overriding conviction that resistance ran contrary to both God's law and the common law.[29] All of which had a certain popular appeal and it is not difficult to see why the likes of Bramhall were considered more suitable to promote the King's cause than the likes of Ussher. As an example of this group's work, Smith claims that *The Serpent Salve* is by far the most important.[30]

The broad appeal of the so-called 'moderate' could however only be so broad and amongst the unconverted it made Bramhall a 'marked man.'[31] The next time Bramhall wrote, it was under very different circumstances, exiled this time (and somewhat more painfully) from his native country, and indeed from his wife and children. In 1649, the bishop was leading an itinerant life on the continent when he wrote *A Fair Warning to Take Heed of the Scottish Discipline*. In this work Bramhall describes a situation which has developed for the worse since *The Serpent Salve*. Those in England who now cried justice had taken their cue from the Scottish Covenanters, both their claims based on the dangerous notion that sovereignty rested with neither King nor his government but with the godly elect. Bramhall was repulsed by what he saw as their claims to infallibility and he predicted disaster if they were allowed to 'obtrude their dreams, not merely upon their fellows but also upon their King.'[32] If *The Serpent Salve* described the root of this evil then *The Fair Warning* was describing its fruits. Once more the subject was where power was to be located and if the parliamentarians had previously attacked the King's prerogative then now they had learnt from their Scottish mentors to challenge, on religious matters, even that of the civil magistrates.[33]

Bramhall was still an exile when he wrote his third most important commentary on politics. *The Catching of the Leviathan*, (1658) was written after his meeting with Thomas Hobbes. Though this work does not deal exclusively with matters of government, nevertheless there is, concurrent with his defence of freedom and choice, an attack on the kind of tyrannical absolutism as advocated by the great philosopher. The work has done much to enhance Bramhall's reputation as a moderate. Just as Bramhall was appalled by the philosophical notion that personal freedom does not exist and that we are dictated to by a series of desires and circumstances, so too he abhorred the idea that no political freedom exists and that we ought to be dictated to by an all–powerful monarchy. In spite of his fervent royalism, Bramhall found it difficult to believe that anyone might want to live in the sort of realm that he claimed

---

28 Smith, *Constitutional Royalism*, p. 220.
29 Ibid.
30 Ibid.
31 McAdoo, *Bramhall*, p. 14.
32 *BW*, vol. 3, p. 242.
33 Ibid., p. 243.

Hobbes espoused where 'the sovereign may lawfully kill a thousand innocent every morning before his breakfast.'[34]

The Catching of the Leviathan demonstrates an unusual quality in Bramhall, that is he is able to fight his religious and political battles on two approaches. Just as he conducted a confessional tussle against reformed Protestants at the rear, and Roman Catholicism at the front, so too he is able to maintain a political war against those who challenge royal power and those who wanted to exaggerate it. In terms of royal apologists this puts Bramhall in a rather unique position and J.W. Daly is suitably impressed writing, 'No other royalist argued on two such different fronts, refracting the rays of his party's conviction through two very different lenses, and consequently revealing more sharply its primary colours.'[35] Bramhall's previous reputation has probably suffered from his close association with Laud; however, more recently, there has been with John Daly and John Sanderson a process of rehabilitation. Bramhall is now regarded as an early example of high Toryism, and if he was not exactly a martyr for this cause then Daly and Sanderson would have us believe that he was at least some kind of Tory patristic scholar. It will be part of the function of this section to examine this reputation in light of Bramhall's most important political work, *The Serpent Salve*.

The Power of the Prince: James Ussher's theory of divine right and absolutism

Perhaps the first thing that needs to be said about Ussher's political theory is that it proposes both an absolutist monarchy and it defines the prince's rights as divine. This may seem at first like a rather obvious statement in view of the author's unequivocal pronouncements; however, it needs to be made for two reasons. Firstly, there is a need to explore not just the meaning of the term but its practical implications. Divine right as a theory presents us with a mixture of the political and religious which our post-enlightened and secular minds do not always immediately appreciate. Pursuing this idea, it will be argued that only through a clearer theological understanding will we have a holistic picture of what was ostensibly a religious concept.

Secondly, there is a need to identify instances of seventeenth-century British absolutism, since a historical tradition, primarily Whig and latterly revisionist has sought to deny that an English equivalent existed of what is seen as a continental phenomenon. This argument will be taken up at the end of this chapter, it is however argued here from the outset that Ussher's treatise is as pellucid an example of Anglo-absolutism as could be wished for.

Writing over one hundred years ago, John N. Figgis provided the first serious and thorough elucidation of divine right theories. In his seminal work *The Divine Right of Kings* (1896), he laid down four criteria for the theory in its most complete form, criteria which are still generally accepted and used. As an exercise in identification it is helpful to use Figgis's points as a yardstick in order to ascertain whether the four propositions are met with in Ussher's work.

---

34   Ibid., vol. 5, pp. 560–62.
35   Daly, 'Royalist moderation': 27.

Firstly, divine right monarchy by its very nature is to be conceived of as an institution ordained by God.[36] Not only does Ussher deal with this on the first page of *The Power of the Prince*, but he addresses it in his choice of title. The power is communicated not by man but rather by God. Later Ussher states, 'For the kingdom being God's own, and by him given to whomsoever he will, it will follow, that unto our Prince, who beareth the place of God, we are to be subject as unto God himself.'[37] This is an interesting departure from classical Calvinism as one biographer of the Reformer illustrates. Calvin accepted that all-powerful monarchs played an important part in establishing order but he does not seem to regard them as the ideal form of government, 'He accepted it only as the most effective form of government for most states and for the time being.'[38] Besides, as the last chapter of *Institutes* shows, Calvin's own particular preference was for an aristocratic republic.[39]

The second point of Figgis's criteria deals with the indefeasibility of hereditary right. God has appointed the monarch by birth and his position cannot be usurped no matter how unworthy he might later prove to be. A prince's behaviour was a matter that concerned God and himself and was not related to the amount of honour due.[40] When Ussher preached to the King at Newport in 1648, it was the occasion of Charles's forty-eighth birthday and he chose the subject of monarchical primogeniture. Unusually Ussher traced primogeniture back not to Adam, or even to patriarchy in general, but rather to the death of Jacob.[41] Genesis 49 tells us that the dying patriarch assembled his sons and with a blessing appointed the head of the twelve tribes of Israel. The sermon also makes an important contemporary point, 'The Regal power which comes by descent is described by a double Eminency. The excellency of Dignity, and the excellency of Power. By Dignity you understand, all outward glory; by Power, all Dominion, and these are the two branches of majesty.'[42]

It was clear from this explicit statement that Ussher was not prepared to countenance the more moderate royalist concession that whilst the power came from God, the title or dominion might be from men. For Ussher the power of monarchy comes via God through an hereditary line and its double quality was indivisible, he was not prepared to share any part of it for the sake of agreement. Here Ussher provides a clear example of the descending theory of government most closely associated by Walter Ullman with the clerical mind of medieval Europe.[43] On the point of the prince's worthiness Ussher maintained that it was irrelevant, God ordained Nero as well as Solomon and obeisance was as much an obligation to the former as it was to the latter, 'We being not herein so much to look into their

---

36   J.N. Figgis, *The Divine Right of Kings* (London, 1896), p. 5.
37   *Power of Prince*, p. 340.
38   W.J. Bouwsma, *John Calvin: A Sixteenth Century Portrait* (Oxford, 1988), p. 207.
39   Calvin, *Institutes*, IV(XX), 8.
40   Figgis, *Divine Right*, p. 5.
41   Huntington Library, San Marino, California, printed collection, 243329, J. Ussher, *The rights of primogeniture* (London, 1648), p. 3.
42   Ibid., p. 3.
43   W. Ullmann, *A History of Political Thought* (Baltimore, 1970), pp. 12–13. Francis Oakley takes issue with what he regards as an over-simplified analysis, for an overview of this debate see S. Ozmet, *The Age of Reform, 1250–1550*, (New Haven, 1980), pp.135–8.

persons as into the ordinance of God, who hath placed them over us; and wisely to consider, that in respect of that dignity and power received from above, not their personal virtues, all this honour is due unto them.'[44] Ussher goes further; honour is not only unrelated to the personality of the monarch, but also to the religion that they professed. Christ recognised the heavenly source of Pilate's power even as he was about to condemn him. So too did the Church in Rome recognise Caesar as God's appointed, even as he persecuted it. Ussher quotes the deacon Hilary to this effect, 'that we give honour unto a Pagan, if placed in authority; although he be in himself most unworthy of it, who, holding God's place, gives the devil thanks for it.'[45] This point had been an important part of Ussher's argument in a speech he made in Dublin Castle which attempted to persuade reluctant Old English Catholics to contribute to the King's army in spite of their religious differences. It was not, said Ussher 'a thing left to your own discretion either to do or not to do; but a matter of duty which you are bound in conscience to perform.'[46] He also reminded the gathering of Romans 13 affirming that we must be subject to higher powers. On this occasion his powers of persuasion were ineffective and the King did not receive his money. It seems clear that many, unlike Ussher, at this period in history, were preferring to follow their political conscience and not their political duty.

The third of Figgis's points states that kings must be held accountable only to God.[47] Again Ussher supports this proposition with numerous quotations. One from Optatus, 'There is none above the emperor but God alone', from Cassidorus, 'if any of the people commit a fault ... he sinneth to God and the King, but when the King offendeth he standeth guilty unto God alone', and St Ambrose, 'kings are tied by no laws, because they are not called to punishment by them, being warranted by the power of their empire.'[48] Behind this theory lay the politico–religious understanding that comprehended society, nature and the universe in terms of a stratified hierarchy. The 'great chain of being' meant that men were neither free nor equal; in common with the heavens a triangle of subordination existed in ever increasing layers of worth until it reached a single pinnacle of importance. Andrew Sharp explains how this worked.

> God was the master of the universe and beneath him were ranged all creatures intellectual, animal and inanimate. In the heavens, a hierarchy of subordination did his will: Archangels, Angels, Cherubims, Seraphims, and Powers. On earth there were Emperors, Kings, Princes, and all the rulers of nobility ... .[49]

With such a system great stress was laid on public virtue and duty, the principal of which was obedience to superiors; the commandment applied to all authority. In this system, men were answerable only to their superiors. Since the prince was at

---

44 *Power of Prince*, p. 346.
45 Ibid., p. 347.
46 Trinity College Dublin Ms. 842, 'A Speech by James Ussher at Dublin Castle, 1627', p. 174.
47 Figgis, *Divine Right*, p. 5.
48 *Power of Prince*, p. 310.
49 A. Sharp, *Political Ideas of the English Civil War 1641–44* (London, 1983), p. 10.

the apex of this social triangle, there existed none, in this realm anyway, that could judge him, he was neither bound by any civil code nor was his power subject to any legal limitations. He was in a very real sense above the law of men with only the law of God to restrain him. As Shakespeare put it 'kings are earth's gods ... And if Jove stray, who dares say Jove doth ill'[50] Ussher confirms such notions in *The Power of the Prince*.

> ... the King who as St Hierom [Jerome] also noteth, stands not in fear of any other. This difference herein he observes between him and his people, that they in occasion of offence have the judge to fear, and the laws to curb them: the King hath nothing but the fear of God and the terror of hell.[51]

Relying on the world view that is the great chain of being was something of a departure for Ussher who instinctively preferred to see the world in terms of saved and damned, chosen and reprobate, his Ramist training (see Chapter 1) predisposed him to regard this contrast before all others. In his sermons, even those before royalty, Ussher made no use of the idea of natural hierarchy but rather emphasised the gulf between the godly and the ungodly.[52] Nevertheless he employs this notion very clearly in *The Power of the Prince* and one can only assume that he, like many at that time, were forced to statements and conclusions that they might not otherwise have made because of the very seriousness of the situation.

Lastly, Figgis stated that the praxis of non-resistance and passive obedience are to be enjoined by God.[53] Once more, Ussher's text provides an abundance of quotations endorsing this last requirement, and therefore completing the very fullest account of divine right theory. Ussher often uses the early Church as an example of turning the other cheek and in doing so he is making a very pressing comparison. If the holy fathers suffered the abject cruelties of attempted genocide, then how much more were their early-modern descendants forsworn to suffer the comparatively lesser tyrannies of their own rulers. In a sermon at Oxford in 1645, the archbishop advised his congregation, 'Remember that he is still thy prince, and since thy conscience may not yield to his command, shew thy self his subject in yielding to his punishment.'[54] Ussher stated that there were only three exceptions to this otherwise universal dictum. When ordered, a subject might not, with impunity, execute the command if it was either physically impossible, beyond their material means, or contrary to the laws of God.

> Now among such things as cannot be done are reckoned not only those which are in their own nature impossible [as that a man should pull down the moon] or in respect of one's particular condition fall to be such, [as to pay a greater sum of money than his ability or

---

50   W. Shakespeare, *Pericles*, Act. I, Sc. I.
51   *Power of Prince*, p. 311.
52   H. Kearney, *Scholars and Gentlemen, Universities and Society in Pre–Industrial Britain 1500–1700* (London, 1970), pp. 67–8.
53   Figgis, *Divine Right*, p. 5.
54   Lambeth Palace Library, 1609, 15, 10, J. Ussher, *The Sovereignes power and the subjects Duty* (Oxford, 1644), p. 29.

credit can reach unto] but those also that are repugnant to the law of God and the known rules of piety and honesty.⁵⁵

This represents Ussher's only measure of qualification to the otherwise unquestioned authority of the monarchy. This said, it must be noted that such restraints were highly hypothetical and benign to say the least. Ussher was writing with his own particular royal house in mind. His frame of reference is the Christian kingdoms of Europe. It would have been hard for him to envisage such thrones issuing illogical or evil commands. Knox recognised this in his biography of Ussher commenting, 'Such qualification did not amount to much more than a hypothetical restraint since Ussher did not anticipate that the kings who he had in mind would issue orders contrary to the will of God.'⁵⁶ For this reason, they were not genuine qualifiers in any real sense since they provided no tangible restrictions. Ussher affords all authority to the monarchy save that which is God's. That there were three grounds for exception provided reassurance to the devout subject but represented no real handicap to the power of their lords.

If then we are to accept the definition proposed by Figgis, it is difficult to argue that Ussher's description of royal power and civil duty does not come under its terms of definition. Ussher's work is a classic of orthodox divine right theory. Nor does the author attempt his own interpretation or modification to suit the theory to any new circumstances. Ussher is an elucidator; he is explaining something that he believes exists as a type of metaphysical truth, as real as God himself. Divine right was perceived to have been imparted by history and was not thought of as a human ideology, but as a revealed truth. Andrew Sharp writes:

> It was not so much that they did not see politics as a human activity, the rules of which are constructed by men ... it was more that given their view of customary arrangements as embodying a divinely established order as it emerged through time, they found it hard to imagine that the laws which governed them might be better.⁵⁷

Ussher portrays this theory of monarchy as part of the natural order of God's universe and a defining feature of creation. He does however admit that other forms of government are possible. *The Power of the Prince* names three types, that is the investment of power in a group, 'which is called an aristocracy'; and sometimes in the whole body of people 'where ariseth a democracy.' However, nature being what it is, it eventually seeks out an individual in an almost evolutionary way to form the purest form of autocratic rule. This is not only natural but, as mentioned above, also a reflection of the heavenly constitution in which, 'there is represented unto us an image and superscription of that high eminency.'⁵⁸ Besides, Ussher points out, this is the best possible system since it allows for a legal stopgap should the rigour of lesser authority be too stern. It not typical of Ussher to use practical considerations as a justification and this idea of the King as a type of appeal judge is a rather

---

55   *Power of the Prince*, p. 351.
56   Knox, *Ussher*, p. 150.
57   Sharp, *Political Ideas*, p. 13.
58   *Power of Prince*, p. 265.

uncharacteristic example of a concern for the functions of state. Previously Ussher's only aim was to provide scholarly endorsements from scripture, patristics and classical literature. However, one of the main features of *The Power of the Prince* is its insistence on this judicial nature of monarchy. Kings are judges appointed by the Saviour ruling in 'his name, in his room.' They are His ministers 'their judgment is His judgment' and Ussher provides numerous texts from the Old and New Testaments to show that they are appointed 'magistrates.'[59] Then in his nod towards a utilitarian defence he cites the example of the man who receives a penalty that is too harsh, who then might appeal to the supreme governor with whom the final word rests 'and while the laws do stand in force it is fit that sometimes the King's clemency should be mingled with the severity of them.'[60]

John Allen has written that Ussher's silence on the ability of the prince to make law is pregnant with meaning, implying 'that he did not attribute such power to the King.'[61] Nothing could be further from the truth; in fact, a primary function of Ussher's prince is as a judicial monarch to make and pass laws. As *The Power of the Prince* plainly states, 'For the making of the law, whereof the force and penalty doth generally reach unto the whole kingdom, must be an act of the prince ... The αρχον [*archon*], or the prince, makes the laws, not to himself, but to his subjects.'[62] Ussher even made another of his rare forays into the world of logical considerations to justify this idea. There is, he claims, nothing that is perpetual and all things must change with time. So too with the law. What is just before may prove unjust and unprofitable now. For the moderating and changing of law to suit the present conditions it is necessary to have a prince 'who is Lord of the laws.'[63] Elsewhere Ussher claims that it is precisely in this role that the monarch most resembles God, 'the most high and absolute monarch of this whole universe.'[64] This practical point leads Ussher to conclude that it is necessary that the prince is above the laws of the land. Since he is to provide a type of safety clause in the legislative programme, it stands to reason that he must not be bound by it. Ussher is careful to draw a distinction here between three types of law, 'the law of God, the law of the King, and that which is God's and the King's together.'[65]

The first of these is the law of nature to which the King like all men is bound. The second type is the civil laws of the King and that he should be tied to these was not only wrong according to Ussher, but also illogical. To support this idea, he points out that there is no first person imperative in grammar; it is an unnatural device, 'As no man is superior to himself so no man hath jurisdiction over himself; because none can oblige a man against his will, but only his superior.'[66] The third, which is of God and the King, concerns those things which offend nature but are punished by the

---

59 Ibid., p. 256.
60 Ibid., p. 307.
61 J.W. Allen, *English Political Thought 1603–1644* (London, 1967), p. 487.
62 *Power of Prince*, p. 291.
63 Ibid., p. 316.
64 Ibid., p. 279.
65 Ibid., p. 301.
66 Ibid., p. 304.

King's sanctions, such as murder and stealing. Again the King is bound, though only God may be considered worthy to check him. Punishment came from a superior to an inferior; a servant could not chastise his master. For breaching this category of law, the King was answerable only to his maker. Ussher does not however advocate a Machiavellian kingship, though the prince is free to have this if he chooses, but rather he urges them to submit to their own legislation as a matter of good example to their subjects. This self-subjection is entirely voluntary and might be, but ought not to be, revoked. J.W. Allen describes this as '*legibus solatus*', bound by the law, but not absolutely.[67] Quoting St Ambrose to his own emperor Valentinian, Ussher proves the antiquity of this tradition, 'What thou has prescribed unto others, thou has prescribed also unto thyself, for the emperor maketh laws which he himself should keep first.'[68] Once more in all of this Ussher is making a departure from mainstream Calvinism. The *Institutes* provided for active resistance to any authority that was deemed to be ungodly or unruly. An aberrant ruler 'must be brought to order', though Calvin is careful to add that this must be by lesser magistrates and not by individuals.[69] No such provision is to be found in Ussher, in keeping with Lutheran and early English Reformers, wicked rulers are to be regarded as part of a just God's punishment and this must be accepted with patience accordingly.[70]

Often, in terms of this period, what an author does not say is just as interesting as their expressed opinion. In the case of Ussher's most important political treatment, the most deafening silence is on the issue of Catholicism. As indicated in Chapter 1, Ussher remained throughout his life an unreconstructed anti-papist of the old school. Indeed during the Civil Wars his first impulse was to detect the papist hand stirring up discord amongst the Protestant community, time and again he urged his congregations not to succumb to the Catholic wiles. There is however not a trace of his antagonism in his work on monarchy. This is even more surprising given the strong tradition among Protestant absolutists of accusing Catholics of disrespect for regal authority. In England, Bishop Jewel had charged various popes with letting monarchs kiss their feet, chaining the King of Crete, and putting Emperor Frederic's neck underfoot. Jewel states, 'This rather is our profession ... to call the emperor his lord and master, which the old bishops of Rome, who lived in times of more grace ever did.'[71] In *The Power of the Prince* the Catholic Church is replaced by a different dark force, that of chaos; the antichrist exchanges his papal vestments for the dark cloak of anarchy. Quoting Rabbi Hanniah, Ussher spells out the threat, 'Pray for the peace ... of the kingdom; for if it were not for fear of authority, every one would swallow down quick his neighbour.'[72] This new emphasis in Ussher is possibly

---

67   Allen, *Political Thought*, p. 487.
68   *Power of Prince*, p. 272.
69   Calvin, *Institutes*, IV(XX), 8.
70   *Power of Prince*, p. 417.
71   Bishop Jewel, *The Works of Jewel*, ed. J. Ayre (4 vols, London, 1845), vol. 3, p. 76.
72   *Power of Prince*, p. 264. This is Hannia Segan Ha-Kohanin (*c*.50–90). In spite of the destruction of the Temple in Jerusalem, where he was deputy High Priest, he declared that one should pray for the peace of the authorities. *The Oxford Dictionary of the Jewish Religion*, eds R.J. Zwi-Werblowsky and G. Wigoder (Oxford, 1997), p.229.

the only example of his bowing to the political zeitgeist. At the time of writing, a new trend among the English ruling elite was moving away from the old religious paranoia and replacing it with a more sociological fear. Throughout the sixteenth and seventeenth centuries the imminence of dark forces had played an important part in knitting the socio–political fabric in what has been called 'the prevalence of what another age has come to know as conspiracy theory.'[73] The nefarious twins of Catholicism and anarchy had provided an important adhesive to a potentially discordant society. However at the court of Charles I, a Catholic match had been made and Rome came increasingly to be perceived of as less of a threat.[74] At the same time, an anxiety developed to replace the old phobia, this time it concerned the perceived challenge to the established order. For Charles I the bogeyman had become the insubordinate plotters who threatened disorder with their ideas of rights and liberties. In response, the establishment rallied. A favourite text to be read out in place of sermons at Church addressed the issue, 'Take away kings, princes, magistrates, judges and such estates of God's orders, no man shall ride or go by the highway untroubled, no man shall sleep in his own house or bed unkilled.'[75]

Whilst the threat of chaos was as old as the Judaeo-Christian tradition (Lucifer had been the first rebel and Adam had been thrown out of paradise for disobedience), in Caroline England such abstract ideas of disorder were fast becoming manifestly real. James Ussher was one of those defenders of order that rallied to the flag. *The Power of the Prince* makes a veiled reference to the contemporary troubles, 'An anarchy is an evil thing indeed ... and the ground of the subversion of a state. But the disobedience of those that are under government is an evil no less than that; and bringeth the matter to the self same pass.'[76] In this text at least, Ussher the erstwhile foe of the Vatican, suspends his preoccupation; he has received a royal commission and he deals with issues that concern the throne. However, *The Power of the Prince* does not represent a political U-turn for the archbishop, he continued to see Rome as the source of all unrest, he left Oxford when the King engaged with Catholic soldiers, and his last utterances before his death were ribald anti-Catholic prophesies. Rather this is an example of self-censorship, Ussher had never previously written at the behest of an individual, or to serve an individual's cause; when he does so, he is faithful to his duty. By focusing on the King's immediate enemy, the Catholics were, for the time being, out of the picture. However, for James Ussher they were never entirely out of the frame.

Perhaps an even more important omission in *The Power of the Prince* is the overlooking of Parliament in the governing of the state. In this instance there is not a total silence but Ussher's treatment is severely muted to say the least. The single time that Parliament is mentioned by the Primate it is to dismiss the idea that their existence represents any form of mixed rule; this, claims Ussher, is a misconception.

---

73   Hirst, *Authority and Conflict*, p. 102.
74   J. Morrill, *The Nature of the English Revolution* (London, 1993), p. 9.
75   A. Hughes, *The Causes of the English Civil War* (London, 1991), p. 64.
76   *Power of Prince*, p. 326.

... in our high court of Parliament, although the knights, citizens and burgesses [representing the whole body of the commons] bear the shew of a little democracy among us, and the lords and nobles, [as the optimates of the kingdom] of an aristocracy; yet our government is a free monarchy notwithstanding: because the supreme authority resteth neither in the one nor in the other, [either severally or jointly] but solely in the person of the King, at whose pleasure they are assembled, and without whose royal assent nothing they conclude on can be a law forceable to bind the subjects.[77]

In this respect, Ussher's silence is representative of a more closely held conviction. The entire premise of his political treatise rests on the assumption that God has given the power of regal government directly to the single individual who is the monarch. For proof Ussher turns to classical art which depicted 'a single hand crowning the heads of kings.'[78] Turning to the writers of the ancient world he tells his readers that Sophocles called government 'παντελης μοναρχια' [*panteles monarchia*], an absolute monarchy, and according to Marcus Aurelius, 'an absolute kingdom, not subject to the control of any.'[79] Ussher implies that since monarchy is a gift from God, one of the greatest conferred on man[80], it is almost blasphemous to impinge on such a heavenly tribute. Ussher does not explore the role of representative government simply because to him it is irrelevant in the discussion of the source and focus of power. Ussher takes it as axiomatic that all power in society has its source in the divine and it would be oxymoronic of him to talk about non-religious power. Certainly the parliaments are never seen as having any type of restraining influence, for how could men restrain what was from God. If any constraint at all was to be placed on the King, it was limited to God's word and right reason, to which he must be 'obsequious.' All this puts Ussher at the extreme end of the royalist politicians during the Civil War years. *The Power of the Prince* bears an interesting comparison with Henry Ferne, the future bishop of Chester, who had written *A Conscience Satisfied* in 1643 at the height of the conflict where he stated, 'I want to take off that false imputation laid upon the divines of this kingdom and upon all those who appear for the King in this cause, that they endeavour to defend an absolute power in him.'[81] There had, as discussed earlier, been a conscious move to a centre ground amongst the writers and thinkers on the King's side. It is a move that Ussher seems to be blissfully ignorant of and it almost certainly cost his work the royal license during those sensitive years.

Another aspect of *The Power of the Prince* is also indicative of the extremes to which Ussher was prepared to take his religio-political ideology. He alone of his contemporaries seems to be able to refer to the god-like characteristics of monarchy without any indication of self-consciousness. The famous precedent for this was of course James I whose statement that 'kings are called Gods by the prophetical King

---

77 Ibid., p. 278.
78 Ibid., p. 298.
79 Ibid., p. 279.
80 Ibid., p. 294.
81 H. Ferne, *A Conscience Satisfied* (London, 1643), p. 3.

David, because they sit upon God his throne in the earth'[82] was closer to deification than the majority of even the most ardent royalists were prepared to go. It is worth considering that Ussher refers to King James almost alone among the writers of his age, drawing on him to state 'the chief princes, invested with the glory and power of God, are styled gods ... so the princes and judges of the earth have frequently the title of gods in holy Writ: and in one place of gods, and the sons of God both together.'[83] For good measure he quotes Tertullian to suggest that this deification might have a literal interpretation, 'We worship the emperor as a man next unto God, and who hath obtained of God whatsoever he is, and is less than God only.'[84] Then in his Newport sermon, Ussher elaborates on the divine properties of kingship and he warns that movements afoot against the monarchy were sacrilegious, 'The King is not only Glorious, but Glory; Not only Powerfull, but Power. In Judges the wicked are described as those who 'despise Dominion that make no conscience to blaspheme the foot-steps of the Lord's Anointed. Those men dare do what Michael durst not doe.'[85] By employing the past King's most ultra-royalist of statements and by adding his own theological interpretations on regal authority, Ussher shows that he is prepared to push at the boundaries of Christianity in order to give royalism its fullest enunciation. With his lack of appreciation for the non-monarchical government bodies, Ussher demonstrates that he is an absolutist of the extreme kind, with his semi-empyrean portraits of kingship he proves that though he may be a reluctant politician, he is a most fervent divine-right monarchist.

A royalist anti-venom: John Bramhall's theory of divine right and absolutism

The snake referred to in the title of John Bramhall's work is the two-headed monster unleashed by those who sought a mixed monarchy. From the outset, Bramhall's work decries the folly of such a course which would imperil the estate, liberty and life of the English subject, 'Of all heretics in policy, they are the most dangerous, which make the Commonwealth an amphisboena, a serpent with two heads; who make two supremes without subordination one to another, the King and the Parliament.'[86] Once the monster is identified Bramhall sets about prescribing a balm for its poison, throughout he refers to his opponent directly as the 'observer', (in references to Parker's own work) and he deals with him point by point, often in the catechetical form of questions and answers. Perhaps the most pressing of these questions was the one which dealt with the source of monarchical power. On the opening page of his treatise, Parker had strongly objected to the King's references to the *jure divino* nature of his rule, 'The King attributeth the original of his royalty to God and the law, making no mention of the grant, consent, or trust of man therein ... .'[87]

---

82   James I, *King James VI and I: Political Writings*, ed. J.P. Sommerville (Cambridge, 1994), p. 77.
83   *Power of Prince*, pp. 268–9.
84   Ibid., p. 298.
85   Ussher, *Primogeniture*, p. 3.
86   *Serpent Salve*, p. 297.
87   Parker, *Observations*, p. 1.

As mentioned previously, Parker set out an ascending theory of political power in which the prince has power invested in him from below in order that there might be stability. This argument has antecedents, ironically in the medieval period royalist such as John of Paris had used an ascending theory of power to defend Monarchical rights against the popes.[88] Bramhall is naturally horrified by such analysis which he called a 'cockatrice egg', and he implies that it is the source of all the present troubles.

> Then the mystery began to work closely, but shortly after it shewed itself openly, when his succesor did publish to the world that 'if kings observe not those pactions to which they were sworn, subordinate magistrates have power to oppose them, and the orders of the kingdom to punish them if it be needful till all things be restored to their former estate.[89]

Aside from dissecting the proposals of Parker, Bramhall sets out a theory of monarchy in his usual reasoned and persuasive prose. It is a striking example of the sort of rational royalist apologetics which were beginning to emerge at this point in Charles's reign. The new wave of royalist theorists were less scriptural, less mystical and they relied more heavily on both practical justifications and concrete warnings than the old school. J.W. Allen roughly divided all royalist political thought of this period into two camps. Firstly there were the biblically rooted group, in which he placed Ussher. These, according to Allen, have little to say except that forcible resistance to the King is forbidden by God.[90] The other less scriptural group started from a definite conception of the legal constitution in England, 'Royalists conceived that constitution to be defined explicitly or implicitly, in the recognised law and custom of the land.'[91] The emergence of this new trend has been traced to the Conciliarists with whom Bramhall was linked in Chapter 5. It has been argued that from these a 'new divine right orthodoxy had begun to develop which, despite that perhaps misleading label, continued the practice of grounding governmental authority in the natural law rather than in the revealed word of God.'[92]

This more modern, more rational approach is certainly striking when Bramhall's political work is compared to Ussher's; however, one must be careful not to exaggerate the distinctions. Whilst it is important to recognise this development it can be overplayed and the use of analogies as well as scriptural citations by absolutists was still happening well into the 1660s.[93] This is certainly true of Bramhall and whilst he does not reach for his Bible with quite the alacrity of Ussher, he is at the same time not adverse to doing so. Besides, Bramhall's theory, for all its modernity, is still anchored in a spiritual understanding of ordination. In a clear refutation of Parker's ascending theory, and in keeping with Figgis's first definition, Bramhall's

---

88   Ozmet, *Age of Reform*, p.136.

89   *Serpent Salve*, p. 316.

90   Allen, *Political Thought*, p. 485.

91   Ibid., p. 494.

92   F. Oakley, 'Anxieties of Influence: Figgis, Skinner, Conciliarism and Early Modern Constitutionalism', *Past and Present*, CLI (May 1996): 102.

93   J.P. Sommerville, 'Absolutism and royalism', in J.H. Burns, *Cambridge History of Political Thought, 1450–1700* (Cambridge, 1990, Cambridge University Press) p. 352.

descending theory traces all power in society firstly to the throne and then ultimately to the heavens. Sommerville terms this concept 'designation theory', as opposed to 'translation' theory. Though the term was first used by Catholic theologians after the French revolution, Sommerville argues that it was anticipated by the Stuart absolutists.[94] The implications were obvious, the people could not, according to Bramhall, give what they had never possessed, that is, the power of life and death.[95] Sommerville indicates that this was the most commonly used argument against the consent theory, 'For the power of governing included the right to execute criminals, and by nature no individual possessed this right.'[96] By employing this justification Bramhall displays just one example of his desire to construct his defence on a platform of logic.

On the same issue of the source of political power, Bramhall demonstrates another aspect of his more rational style. In refuting Parker, *The Serpent Salve* does not turn instinctively to sacred text for endorsement, but rather to the actualities of world history. What, he asks, are we to make of sovereignty won by the sword, the first owners of wastelands, those who had planted remote parts in America, or the fathers of great families, 'In all these cases there is no grant of the people.'[97] All of which is very telling. Ussher did not completely refrain from practical point scoring but he clearly considered it of much less importance to the revealed will of God that can be found in the pages of scripture. In these wars of words the choice of weapons lets us know a good deal about the combatants. Bramhall's account of royal power in *The Serpent Salve* is much more detailed than Ussher's since he does not set out to provide a theological or biblical overview but rather to tackle specific issues which were surfacing in 1642. A typical objection to royalist claims is voiced by Parker when he insists that royal power is no more of God than the power of the aristocracy or the magistrate. Since all power may be said in some sense to originate from God they carry the same authority. Bramhall flatly refutes this idea arguing that these people are fond of leaping over intermediaries to get straight to God, thereby they destroy all beauty in the world.[98] It is interesting to note that James Ussher made a very similar point a year later in a sermon at Oxford. It was clearly a popular refrain from the parliamentarians and Ussher claimed it was a theory used by those 'who secretly labour to curb kings.'[99] Bramhall does not abjure that all commands are from God, yet not so immediately or firmly as the sovereign. Then he provides one of those vivid analogies typical of his work likening them to 'a row of iron rings touching one another, and the first touching the loadstone, in their several degrees, some more loosely, some more remotely than others.'[100] Both of these points from

---

94 J.P. Sommerville, *Politics and Ideology in England, 1603–1640* (London, 1986), p. 20.
95 *Serpent Salve*, p. 318.
96 Sommerville, *Politics and Ideology*, p. 20.
97 *Serpent Salve*, pp. 318–19.
98 Ibid.
99 Ussher, *Sovereignes Power*, p. 5.
100 *Serpent Salve*, p. 319.

Bramhall and Ussher shed some light on the current debate on the nature of divine right theory which will be returned to at the end of this chapter.

For Bramhall the most fatal error of the Observer is a natural consequence of this misidentification of the source of royal authority. This leads him to the logical conclusion that usurped is the same as established power. The point Parker is making is that both are of human origin, an argument Bramhall cleverly inverts until it means the exact opposite allowing him to feign horror at the heretical implications, 'Much less dare we say with the Observer that power usurped and unlawful is as much from God as power hereditary and lawful. If it be so, cough out, man, and tell us plainly, that God is the author of sin.'[101] On this issue of the divine authority, Bramhall appears to be slightly less hard-line than Ussher in that he is prepared for the sake of argument to concede that the people are the originators of regal authority, though he prefers to regard God as the fount.[102] However, even if we allow this, the people have given up their power and may not take it back, 'To take your case at the best, they have put the staff out of their own hands, and cannot without rebellion and sin against God undo what they have done.'[103] Bramhall makes the brief point that there is no biblical text which allows subjects to reduce their sovereigns but his real defence is once more practical. Even if we had once had the power to say which laws governed us, we never had power to say we would obey only the ones we wanted, 'This were to make our sovereign, not a great and glorious King, but a plain Christmas lord.'[104] Such an allowance is however highly qualified and admitted only to show that it had no significance. Even if it were the case that Bramhall agreed with the ascending nature of power, he would have had good company amongst the absolutists. In spite of this being the first of Figgis's criteria, such godfathers of divine right as Jean Bodin allowed that sovereign power might have been conferred by the people, though they could not now place restrictions on it.[105] Grotius too, claimed that natural liberty had been lost in the mists of time.[106] Bramhall, unlike Ussher, acknowledges this interpretation but ultimately, like Ussher, he does not accept it.

The whole topic of sourcing royal power did of course throw up an obvious problem for British royalists in that they had to account for the apparent usurpation that was 1066. Parker had leapt on this to attack the royalists arguing that William and his successors had in part disinherited by violence and perjury the people of their free customs and laws.[107] Bramhall diverts the barb of this objection instead using it as a weapon in his defence. The conquest proves, if nothing else, that the

---

101 Ibid., p. 320.
102 Ibid., p. 324.
103 Ibid., p. 330.
104 Ibid., pp. 323–4. The 'Lord of Misrule' was elected to lead the revels at Christmas, *Oxford English Dictionary*, 2nd edition, eds J.A. Simpson and E.S.C. Weiner (Oxford, 1989), vol. 3, p. 182.
105 P. Kléber Monod, *The Power of Kings, Monarchy and Religion in Europe, 1589–1715* (Yale, 1994), p. 73.
106 Ibid., p. 109.
107 Parker, *Observations*, p. 3.

people of England were not the authors of their monarch's regal dominion.[108] 'Just conquest', argues Bramhall, is consistent with universal opinion and practice and being common to all nations it is infallible. It is also, he adds, testified in scripture.[109] It is interesting to compare Bramhall's analysis of the Norman conquest with previous royalists. Johann Sommerville points out that prior to 1640 authors such as Hayward, Fulbeke and Cowell had used it to justify tax without consent.[110] The argument roughly stated maintained that since the Conqueror had obtained the land and then graciously restored it to its former owners, there existed certain intrinsic obligations. Nowhere does Bramhall use the conquest in this way to justify the most extreme forms of absolutism. Bramhall's interpretation of events follows an idealised path in which the law since Hastings has developed into what Candide would have called the 'best possible of worlds.' John Sanderson described this rose-tinted view of British constitutional history.

> Bramhall, then, had a strong sense of the evolution of the English Constitution, which he saw as becoming increasingly liberalised since the absolutism of 1066, and thus rejected the vision of the parliamentarians of a polity in the process of grim descent into popery and continental style despotism.[111]

Ferne and Spelman among the more modern royalists employed the conquest in this same way.[112] Such an idealisation also has much in common with Ussher. In his short work, *Of the first establishment of English Laws and Parliament*, he treated the constitution of England as a gift to Ireland[113], though he adds that 'all enjoyed not this privilege appeareth plainly.'[114] Though it is hard to imagine that Ussher would have regarded recent developments in the English establishment as part of this continued refinement.

On the second of Figgis's criteria, that is the indefeasibility of hereditary right, Bramhall makes an interesting contribution. As far as this is concerned all rights and privileges of the land are present through the King and may be obtained only after humble petition, 'In a word, he is the head, not only of the hand or of the foot, but of the whole body. These things are so evident, that all our laws must be burned before this truth can be doubted of.'[115] However, as part of the general perfection that described the English system, Bramhall agreed that a certain diffusion of power had been granted freely and generously by a succession of good monarchs. These do not, as Parker suggests, represent concessions bargained over and agreed upon mutually but 'acts of grace and bounty.' J.W. Daly describes these benefits as 'prescriptions'[116] and in keeping with the Elizabethan world picture they are based on the assumption

---

108 *Serpent Salve*, p. 319.
109 Ibid., p. 340.
110 Sommerville, 'Absolutism and royalism': 369.
111 Sanderson, 'Serpent Salve': 8.
112 Ibid.
113 *Power of Prince*, p. 449.
114 Ibid., p. 452.
115 *Serpent Salve*, p. 328.
116 Daly, 'Royalist moderation': 29.

that every right was in proportion to a duty. The King had rights, but he also had to respect the self-imposed limitations in the same way that he demanded his subjects respect super-imposed limitations.[117] Daly argues that in its historical context, the idea of prescription had a much firmer resonance being linked to fundamental notions of property right.

> The argument that what the King or his ancestors had solemnly and voluntarily given he could not take back was reinforced by the reminder of the role of time setting everyone's property rights. If the King could not take back alienated royal lands, why should men fear his ability to take back alienated royal powers[118]

J.W. Daly and J. Sanderson have done much to rehabilitate Bramhall as an essentially moderate politician largely based on his ideas of prescriptive rights. Bramhall has emerged from under his reputation as a hard-liner until he has become something of a constitutional monarchist, a precursor of high-Toryism whose monarchy is explicitly limited. Yet it is difficult to avoid the conclusion that modern commentators on Bramhall are in danger of making rather a lot out of very little. Bramhall's 'prescriptions' do not strike one as being all that much more than Ussher's injunction to 'prescribe also unto thyself.'[119] It must also be added that whilst Daly is correct in stating that Bramhall uses the self-imposed restrictions to reassure, there is also no denying that the original purpose of prescription theory is that it defended (at the very least theoretically) just this ability to reclaim any such graces. These liberties are based on largesse, not natural rights and for this reason they can hardly be used to elevate Bramhall into the pantheon of great English constitutionalists.

The third of Figgis's criteria, which holds that kings must be held accountable only to God, also forms a major part of Bramhall's political understanding. It is an 'undeniable principle' claims Bramhall that kings can do no wrong. Parker had obviously tried to get around this maxim by arguing that he can do no wrong 'de jure' but 'de facto' he may. This was, according to Bramhall, the:

> Drowsiest dream that ever dropped from any man's pen ... that in the intendment of law, his person is sacred, he is freed from all defects [as, though he be a minor or and infant, yet in the eye of the law he is always of full age], he owes account of his doing to God alone, the law hath no coercive power over him.[120]

On this issue Bramhall does not go as far as Ussher by saying explicitly that it is the king's function to create laws. The regal image that Bramhall portrays is less legal than Ussher's; though the magisterial qualities of the office are certainly present, there is less stress on this Solomon-like characteristic. When listing the Kings' prerogatives there is no mention of his right to frame new legislation and this is an important difference which sets the *Serpent Salve* in a somewhat more moderate tone than *The Power of the Prince*.

---

117 Ibid., p. 38.
118 Ibid., pp. 30–31.
119 *Power of Prince*, p. 272.
120 *Serpent Salve*, pp. 383–4.

There is in Bramhall another aspect of his royalism entirely in keeping with his idealisation of English monarchy which adds to this tempered and reassuring quality of his work. Compared to the absolutists of the old school such as Ussher, there is much greater stress on the self-imposed limitations of royal authority. These benevolent gestures have provided the essence of the English system and a good King cannot with impunity flout them and in this respect Bramhall is even prepared to talk of them as 'limits and bounds' to royal authority. The King has 'by his charter granting new liberties and immunities to the collective body of his subjects or to any of them, he hath so far remitted of his own right, and cannot in conscience recede from it.'[121] This goes a degree further than Ussher's mild injunction to kings that they ought to obey their own laws. Bramhall uses these limits to underscore the entire constitutional history of England. Ussher's advice reads like a personal motto for the King, whilst Bramhall's is more like a definition of the relationship between crown and country. This type of self-regulation has been picked up on and it is claimed that it is a 'duality' which is fundamental to so-called absolutist regimes 'and one of the most underplayed.'[122] It is further argued that this common feature makes something of a misnomer of the term absolutism since it describes something that had clearly defined limitations. The debate on what constitutes absolutism or divine right government will be discussed more fully later, it is perhaps sufficient to say here that Bramhall's own idea of this 'duality' may represent a regal step away from political omnipotence, but it must always be remembered that it was a voluntary step.

Lastly Bramhall complies with the fourth of Figgis's defining characteristics when he states that there are no circumstances when a subject may actively resist their monarch. When Henry Parker makes the common parliamentary distinction between the person and office of the King he is making the point that subjection is due to the authority of the King and not to his person. Here Bramhall quotes from him.

> ... that this authority resideth 'in his courts and in his laws;' that the power which St Paul treateth of, is in truth 'the kingly office:' that to 'levy force' or to raise arms 'against the personal commands of a King, accompanied with his presence', is not levying war against his authority residing in his courts.[123]

Bramhall allows that the person and office of the King are distinguishable, 'A good man may be a bad King; and a bad man a good King.'[124] However, this does not excuse revolt because though the person and office are distinguishable it is not right for the subjects to do so, indeed to divide the King's person from his authority is a 'Platonical idea.'

> ... as if the King of England were nothing but Carolus Rex written in court hand, without flesh, blood, or bones. To what purpose then are those significant solemnities used at the

---

121 Ibid., p. 360.
122 N. Henshall, *The Myth of Absolutism* (London, 1992), p. 127.
123 *Serpent Salve*, p. 350.
124 Ibid., p. 351.

coronation of our King? Why are they crowned, but to shew their personal and imperial power in military affairs?'[125]

Following Ussher, Bramhall uses the example of the early Christians passively suffering under persecution. He adds acerbically that had they the ingenuity of the Observer then they might have avoided any such hardship, 'How dull were the primitive Christians, that suffered so much, because they were not capable of this distinction.'[126]

> Some desperate ruffian or two or three ragamuffins, sometimes [but rarely] out of revenge, most commonly upon seditious principles, and misled by some factious teachers, may attempt upon the person of the prince; but all grand conspiracies are veiled under the mask of reformation, of removing greviances and evil counsellors.[127]

Here Bramhall shows his readiness to refer the argument specifically to the political situation, something *The Power of the Prince* is much more coy about. The idea that Charles was under the malevolent influence of his councillors was a common excuse for what otherwise might be rebellion.[128] Bramhall acknowledges that if the King was captive, his commands forced from him by duress, they would like a forced marriage be null. Bramhall asserts that this was most assuredly not the case with Charles Stuart.[129] Once more like Ussher, Bramhall goes on to list the usual set of circumstances when a subject is not bound to obey their sovereign. Also like Ussher they are circumstances so extreme as to be hardly envisaged by any sane commentator. The subject is not bound to break the law of nature; here Bramhall uses the same sentence of exoneration as Ussher, 'pardon me, O Sovereign, thou threatenest me with prison, but God with hell.'[130] To this Bramhall adds two other circumstances: if the command is against the law of the land or an injury to a third person. It is significant that Bramhall includes a proviso on national law which is not present among Ussher's exceptions. This certainly represents a development which should not be underestimated. Bramhall binds his prince much more to the legal system than Ussher considers necessary. This no doubt reflects the high esteem in which Bramhall holds English law; it is a national treasure and it is only fitting that it be included. However, Bramhall is aware of the dangers of allowing individual considerations into the political equation and he adds a stern warning, ' ... to disobey the King upon surmises, or probable pretences, or an implicit dependence upon other men's judgments, is to disobey both God and man; and this duty [as the Protesters say truly] is "not tied to a King's Christianity, but his crown."'[131]

Finally Bramhall poses the question of a recourse for the Christian subject against the abuses of an evil ruler, for which he offers three remedies. Firstly to cease from

---

125 Ibid., pp. 355–6.
126 Ibid.
127 Ibid.
128 M. Bennett, *The English Civil War* (London, 1995), p. 19.
129 *Serpent Salve*, p. 355.
130 Ibid., p. 351.
131 Ibid., p. 352.

sin since, 'Rex bonus est dextra, mala sinistra Dei', a good King is God's right hand, a bad his left hand, a scourge for our sins. Secondly Bramhall offers the same passive consolation that can be found in Ussher that prayers and tears were the weapons of our fathers, 'St Naziansen lived under five persecutions, and never knew other remedy; he ascribed the death of Julian to the prayers and tears of the Christians.'[132] Lastly there is flight, 'This is the uttermost which our Master hath allowed; "When they persecute you in one city, fly to another"'. And if all this made grim reading for a troubled Christian, Bramhall advised them that it was good to suffer since the blood of martyrs are the seeds of the Church.[133]

These injunctions for passive obedience are almost identical to those found in *The Power of the Prince*. However, it is when we get to the topic of the subject's duty, or more precisely the role of the subject with regard to their representative bodies that there is a radical departure. Ussher is cursory in his treatment of the parliaments, leaving his reader with the assumption that they were of little significance when it came to the government of absolute monarchy. Bramhall on the other hand devotes a considerable space in *The Serpent Salve* to defining the nature of the relationship between prince and parliament and it is somewhat surprising to find that his assessment of parliament's role is far from negative. At the very start of his treatise Bramhall announces in gushing prose that his work most emphatically should not be interpreted as wishing to prejudice the lawful rights and privileges of parliament, the 'very name of a Parliament was music in our ears; at the summons thereof our hearts danced with joy.'[134] However, he adds more soberingly that the present difficulties have arisen precisely because we have idolised Parliament. They had now reached the deplorable situation when it was observed, 'the father of our country threatened and vilified by a common soldier.' It was enough, exclaimed Bramhall, 'to make a dumb man speak, as it did sometimes the son of Craesus.'[135] Parker had boldly suggested that as institutions of government the Houses might be held in greater esteem than the Crown, 'Parliaments have the same efficient cause as monarchies, if not higher, for in truth, the whole kingdom is not so properly the author as the essence it self of Parliaments.'[136] One of the first tasks for Bramhall then was to establish the correct order of precedence. The King does not, claimed Bramhall, derive his powers from parliament, a fact which is demonstrated in history since monarchy preceded parliaments.[137] Indeed the opposite is true, the King is the source of any extra-monarchal power, 'That the King is the cause of the Parliament, is as evident as the noon-day light. He calls them; he dissolves them, they are his council; by virtue of his writ they do, otherwise they cannot sit.'[138]

---

132   Ibid.
133   Ibid., p. 353.
134   Ibid., p. 299.
135   Ibid. Licinius Crassus (*c.*112–53 BC) had joined his army with Pompey to obtain a consulship of 70 and overthrow the dictator Sulla, thus putting an end to his reform.
136   Parker, *Observations*, p. 8.
137   *Serpent Salve*, pp. 378–9.
138   Ibid.

In keeping with Bramhall's idea that liberties and privileges had been gifted, not negotiated, he viewed Parliament as just one of these endowments owing their very existence to royal benevolence.

> When the great representative body of Parliament are assembled, they are yet but his great council; not commanders. He calls them, he dissolves them; they do not choose so much as a speaker without his approbation; and when he is chosen, he prays his Majesty to interpose his authority and command them to proceed ... .[139]

According to Bramhall, Parliament must be understood not as an authoritative but as a consultative power, to advise the King or at the very most act in an approbative manner, assenting to the laws already propounded, 'he having limited himself to make no laws without them.'[140] Parker grumbles that some of the King's papers have made statements which have lessened and injured Parliament, denying that the Lords and the Commons may rightly be named Parliament or have the power of a court, or indeed be anything more than a convention of men.[141] Bramhall reminds him that the King must only uphold the laws of the Triennial Parliament.[142] Then, more importantly, he brings Parker back once more to his original point that if the King made the Houses more than his councillors he would be making them his 'commanders and controllers.'[143] Yet Bramhall is not completely hard-nosed in his response to this accusation and he adds a more placatory, if unconvincing explanation of the King's words.

> So the body is sometimes contradistinguished to the soul, and includes both head and members; sometimes it is contradistinguished to the head, and includes the members only. It is one thing to be a true Parliament, and another to be a complete Parliament, complete to all intents and purposes, and particularly in respect of the legislative power. In this latter sense only his Majesty denies it.[144]

The working ideals of King and Parliament encapsulated above have led commentators in the past to regard Bramhall as representative of the most extreme form of absolutism, little different to the likes of Ussher. William Sparrow-Simpson summed up Bramhall's political approach as pushing monarchical principles to 'despotic and irresponsible extreme.'[145] However, further reading of his position of Parliament's function reveal a slightly different picture. After establishing the origin of Parliament and its position in the hierarchy of government, Bramhall is happy to allow it a positive and not to say influential role in the body politic. There is, claims Bramhall, a threefold body of state, the essential body, the representative body, and the virtual body.[146] The essential body is described as the diffused company

---

139 Ibid., p. 327.
140 Ibid., p. 329.
141 Ibid., p. 392.
142 Ibid., p. 393.
143 Ibid., p. 397.
144 Ibid.
145 Sparrow-Simpson, *Bramhall*, p. 103.
146 *Serpent Salve*, pp. 380–81.

of the whole nobility, the representative body as the Lords, citizens and burgesses in Parliament assembled. The virtual body is the King 'in whom rests the life of authority, and power legislative, executive, virtually.'[147] Parliament is not therefore essential; however, Bramhall indicates that a necessary requisite to this state is the 'consent and concurrence of the representative body.' Then after what has been an exercise in parliamentary containment Bramhall makes the somewhat startling announcement that Parliaments, functioning correctly, acts as a palliative to bad monarchy.

> The ends of Parliament is to temper the violence of sovereign power; the remedy must needs be later than the disease, much more than the right temper. Degenerate monarchy becomes tyranny, and the cure of tyranny is the mixture of governments. Parliaments are proper adjuments to kings.[148]

Later in *The Serpent Salve*, Bramhall describes the function of Parliament in no less laudatory language when he compares the King to the *primum mobile* and the Houses to the 'lower spheres.' These spheres by their 'vincible motions' allay the violence of the highest orb and preserve the universe. 'Where there are no such helps and means of temper and moderation, there liberty is in danger to be often trodden under foot by tyranny.'[149] Such statements appear unusual after what have been some rather uncompromising assertions of monarchal absolutism but Derek Hirst argues that we should not be so surprised. To our logically inclined modern mind absolutism would exclude any other claim to authority, but this would not be so apparent to the early modern way of thinking. Educated contemporaries were persuaded of the harmonious nature of the universe. The world was created of opposites and dissimilarities working in a fruitful tension according to Plato's *concordia discors*.[150] It was therefore less difficult for politicians like Bramhall to think simultaneously of a sovereign King and a sovereign common law.

Francis Oakley traces this type of dualism back to scholastic ideas of *potentia dei absoluta et ordinata*. During the twelfth and thirteenth centuries, thinkers such as Duns Scotus had formulated a 'power distinction' between the omnipotent power of God to do as He wishes (*potentia absoluta*) and the power that he has ordained for himself (*potentia ordinata*), self-imposed limits by which he may act.[151] Rather like a divine version of the self-denying ordinance. Such theological conceptions survived the Reformation and inevitably moved into politics and by the early seventeenth century the legal version of this distinction had established itself among practitioners of English common law. According to Oakley it moved to centre stage during the great Stuart trials such as Bates, Darnel's, and Ship Money cases.[152] It was also to find revived expression in the work of William Perkins, Hugo Grotius, René Descartes

---

147 Ibid.
148 Ibid.
149 Ibid., p. 404.
150 Hirst, 'Authority and conflict': 87.
151 F. Oakley, 'The Absolute and Ordained power of God – and Seventeenth Century Theology', *Journal of the History of Ideas*, vol. 59, no. 3 (1998): 437–61.
152 Oakley, 'Anxieties of influence': 683.

as well as John Bramhall.¹⁵³ Oakley's identification of Bramhall as a Conciliarist adds to his modern reputation as an essentially moderate royalist. Certainly if one is to compare him with Ussher he emerges as someone who was prepared to envisage certain limitations on absolutism, yet we must be cautious about overstating this moderation. On the issue of conciliarism, Bramhall very quickly dismissed any suggestion from Parker that such a system was applicable to the English situation. Bramhall calls this a 'woeful argument' since it confused the elective papacy with hereditary kingship, free ecumenical councils with the sworn subjects and arbitrary proceedings with action which is grounded in law.¹⁵⁴ The English people did not have the rights, power and privileges as a General Church Council, and the election of the pope by men was not the same as the election of a king by God.

We must also consider Bramhall's positive statements on representative government alongside his forthright rejection of any form of mixed government. Bramhall denigrates such government as aristo-democracy, nicknamed monarchy, circumscribed, conditionate and mock-monarchy. For good measure he reminds Parker that after suffering the defects of popular government the Romans fled to the 'sacred anchor' of a dictator and absolute prince.¹⁵⁵ Bramhall's idea of parliament was an institution to facilitate the workings of absolute monarchy, he never really recognises the independence of their power. It is a fundamental weakness of Bramhall, and other royalists, that they never manage to get beyond a series of broad statements to formulate anything concrete. At a time when the opposition were looking for specific legal or political solutions they were offering only blandishments and general assumptions. As J.P. Sommerville writes, they were very imprecise in just exactly how they saw such curbs to regal sovereignty working and it is arguable that if pressed most of them would have agreed with Filmer.¹⁵⁶ Bramhall never set out the working arrangement in clearly defined specific terms and it is arguable that in spite of his modernity and in spite of his lip-service to Parliament that there is little in *The Serpent Salve* to distinguish it from *The Power of the Prince*. Certainly there was nothing in it that could have provided any reassurance to the opposition. As Henry Parker observed, 'For where no remedy is, there is no right.' In the end, Bramhall's prescription for the serpent's bite is little more than a placebo.

De jure divino aut non de jure divino: the question of absolutism

Our historiographical tradition has rarely been comfortable with British absolutism, preferring to see it as uniquely foreign. A general run through Whig history emphasises a distinct island culture which was anti-authoritarian. The Saxons import with them their democratic institutions, and whilst the rest of Europe falls victim to papal domination, the waters of the English Channel protect Albion from any such yoke. Liberties were of course threatened in 1066 but the forces of liberty that coursed through English veins could not long be suppressed and John is made to guarantee

---

153 Ibid., p. 681.
154 *Serpent Salve*, p. 316.
155 Ibid., p. 428.
156 Sommerville, 'Absolutism and royalism', p. 368.

this freedom at Runnymeade in 1215. In the ensuing centuries the megalomania of individuals may have threatened this freedom, but the people were stoutly championed throughout by the mother of Parliaments. Though much of Whig history has now been challenged ideas of a separate English political tradition have proved resilient. Indeed modern scholars have often taken up the baton of English political uniqueness from their Whig forerunners and have been equally uncomfortable with ideas of Anglo-absolutism. John Miller sums up an interpretation he largely accepts. Mainland Europe is a cradle of absolutism where scattered groups sacrificed their independence for security reasons under the extended power of the monarch. England had no need to resort to such measures since the structures were already in place for strong government without repression.

> Under the Tudors, monarch and Parliament co-operated in extending the crown's function and powers and the monarchy was eventually able to secure many of the aims of absolutism ... without recourse to authoritarian methods and the sacrifice of traditional liberties or local self-government.[157]

The idea that England fought against or indeed never had an absolute monarchy seems initially to receive a good deal of support from evidence of the period, though as J.P. Sommerville points out, absolutist writers such as Bodin and the German jurist Christoph Besold took it for granted that the King of England held absolute sovereignty as they defined it.[158] Yet, in practice, even King James I assured his government 'We at no time stand so high in our estate royal as in the time of Parliament, when we as head and you as members are cojoined ... .'[159] James I suppressed the absolutist writer John Cowell in 1610 when his book *The Interpreter* upset Parliament, and during delicate negotiations there appears to be a lot of Royal and Parliamentary give and take. The two bodies of government were mutually dependent, the monarch needed money and their subjects depended on Royal support to advance their cause. It would therefore seem that even as the Stuarts espoused their own unquestionable authority they acquiesced in reality to a more practical and realistic duality. However, a closer examination of divine right as praxis may reveal that such apparent power-sharing arrangements do not in actual fact undermine the overall theory. Divine right is an ideal, something to be held up as a defining principle which should serve as an ultimate aim. If in practice this is not always possible then no matter, so long as the ideal remains intact. J.N. Figgis described divine right as a 'chimera' representing for him the last attempt to achieve an immutable system of government; henceforth politics would be determined by more attainable goals.[160] Indeed it is perhaps not until centuries later that the Bolsheviks in Russian attempted to construct society on such an idealistic basis. The fact that James or Charles did not always act like divine righters does not mean it never represented their fundamental philosophy. Lenin

---

157 J. Miller, *Absolutism in Seventeenth Century Europe* (London, 1990), p. 195.

158 J.P. Sommerville, 'The English and European political ideas in the early seventeenth century: revisionism and the case of absolutism', *Journal of British Studies*, April 1996, XXXV, no. 2: 189.

159 James I, *Writings*, p. 22.

160 Figgis, *Divine Right*, p. 162.

introduced his New Economic Policy in 1921 in order to give communism time to breathe; this did not mean that he was not a socialist. Charles Stuart called the Long Parliament in 1640; this does not mean that he would have preferred to have done without it.

It is one thing to deny that anything like an absolute monarchical system ever existed on these islands, it is a step further to refute the existence of any real divine right theorists. Yet just as ideas of an absolutist court in England prove indigestible, examples of British divine right thinkers stick in the throat. In *English Political Thought*, J.W. Allen grudgingly recognises only one.

> If there were any Royalists who, in 1643 regarded the King as an absolute monarch able to make law as he pleased, they must have been exceedingly few. I find no definite assertion to that effect before 1647; unless the unpublished and unfinished *Patriarcha* of Sir Robert Filmer is to be counted.[161]

Such a strong statement does not go unqualified. Allen goes on to illustrate that prominent royalists tempered their claims with legal restraints. However, in a volume that deals at some length with Ussher and also deals with Bramhall's claim that the King may disregard laws *pro bono publico*, it appears to be oddly dismissive. Allen makes numerous references to exceptions and atypical examples (he feels able to dispense with a whole set of opinion because it was clerical) until one is left with the impression that it must have been difficult to move in the royalist camp without falling over an unorthodox ally. It appears incongruous that Allen's conclusion overrides these examples, especially after he has taken pains to describe them.

Conrad Russell makes similar claims as Allen, though from the opposite angle. In *The Causes of the English Civil War*, he holds that far from no one holding divine right opinions in the seventeenth century, it is a commonly held assumption. He adds however that the term is to all intents and purposes meaningless, ' ... the basic proposition that kings ruled by divine right was a proposition almost universally accepted, not particularly controversial, and utterly uninformative about the extent of the King's powers.'[162] Russell goes on to argue that it does not matter that power was seen to be descending from God or rather ascending from the people since all power was seen to be of God. Whether ordained or elected, all authority was godly and therefore the parish constable, who was chosen, held his position by divine right in the same way as the King. For this reason, ascending and descending theories of power could be held together and often merged to form a balanced conception of man and God working together. That God chose the constable did not mean that the King's power was conceived of as different.

> To me, it appears a normal proposition that power was derived from God, and an equally normal one that God works through second causes, so divine and human origins of power appear to me not to be mutually exclusive, and divine right appears to me to be perfectly capable of being combined with legal limitations.[163]

---

161   Allen, *Political Thought*, p. 482.
162   C. Russell, *The Causes of the English Civil War* (London, 1990), p. 147.
163   Ibid., pp. 145–6.

If one pursues Russell's line of reasoning, the works of Ussher and Bramhall we have examined might easily have been written to describe the power of the sheriff, the magistrate or the father, since it refers to an identical authority. It would seem that rather a lot of time and effort had been squandered by the bishops in specifically referring to the monarch. However, Russell's theology would not appear to be on a par with his history; a simple example illustrates the flaw. Most religious people today would describe God as the creator of the world and all that is in it. If asked, a Christian would claim that God made the oak tree, but he would also say that God made the chair sitting beneath it, even if he knew personally the carpenter who constructed it. It makes reasonable theological sense to claim that God created all things even those made by carpenters, mechanics and builders. It also makes perfect religious sense to hold those things created immediately by Him in a special, elevated place. Seventeenth-century man was just as capable of making a similar distinction and whilst all power may have come from God, the constable was as different from the King as a chair is from an oak tree. Besides, both *The Power of the Prince* and *The Serpent Salve* provide proof that not only were their authors capable of making the distinction but also that it was very important to them. When Ussher compares the power that magistrates derive from the King (in order to execute his laws) and the power that belongs to the monarch, he tells us that the latter represents to us, 'the image of God, the most high and absolute monarch in this whole universe.'[164] Bramhall is less metaphysical but no less conclusive when he states, 'God and the law operate both in kings and Parliaments, but not in both alike. God is the immediate cause of kings, the remote cause of Parliaments.'[165]

J.P. Sommerville makes a further criticism of the revisionist position. Sommerville states that even if the monarchy was instituted indirectly, it did not matter, as a popular contemporary analogy dealt with the issue.

> They argued that her own consent is necessary to make a woman a wife but that the power of her husband over her comes to him directly from God. Similarly, they proceeded, kings might at first have been instituted by popular consent, but monarchs derive their powers not from the people but from God alone.[166]

It is perhaps another indication of Bramhall's general modernity when compared to Ussher that he uses this device, calling God the 'principal agent' and man the 'instrumental.' Bramhall insists that God is always the root, the foundation, the essence of the power even if the existence is 'sometimes from God, sometimes from man.'[167]

There are numerous examples of the apparently mythological creature, the English absolutist. Sir Thomas Fleming in the Bates case (1606) expressed absolutist views. Judge Berkeley did the same in the Hampden case (1637–38) and Davies in *The Question Concerning Impositions* claimed the King could tax without consent. Far from being radical or eccentric, these people lay at the heart of English political

---

164 *Power of Prince*, p. 279.
165 *Serpent Salve*, p. 386.
166 Sommerville, 'Political ideas': 189.
167 *Serpent Salve*, p. 318.

life and cannot easily be overlooked.[168] Nor can the theoreticians such as Cowell and Gentelli, (*Regales Disputationes Tres* recognises the 'extraordinary' and 'free' power of the King) not to mention Filmer. Into this tradition we must fit Ussher and Bramhall who were as absolutist as any continental author. *The Power of the Prince* and *The Serpent Salve* provide useful reminders, despite recent popular trends, of a thriving divine right tradition in the seventeenth century on this side of the strait of Dover. As J.P. Sommerville writes, ' ... if there were no English absolutists then there were also none in France or elsewhere on the continent. Either way it is impossible to distinguish between England and the rest of Europe on the grounds that the former alone was an absolutist-free zone.'[169]

---

168 Sommerville, 'Political ideas': 191.
169 Sommerville, 'Political ideas': 190.

Chapter 7

Ecclesiastical Politics

The following chapter sets out to explore the respective ecclesiastical politics of our two Primates. Under three subheadings it is the intention to examine Ussher's and Bramhall's attitudes to Church government, relations with the Church of Rome and finally their visions of future unity among the post-Reformation Christian world. In both cases it is fair to say that their reputations precede them. Uşsher is most often regarded as a pulpit thumping Protestant, left-wing in leaning with a ribald anti-papism to match. Bramhall is portrayed as the lover and enforcer of hierarchical church structure, hard on dissenters and soft on Rome. Indeed there is much in their outpourings to substantiate such preconceptions, however there is also much that contradicts them. There is evidence in Ussher's work that he was more inclined toward the traditional institutions of the Church than he is often credited with, nor is his aversion to Rome completely unqualified. Whilst Bramhall emerges as a staunch defender of his national Church's independence and heritage. These points will be considered and it will be argued that they are best seen and interpreted in light of what we have previously called the justice and numinous motifs.

Ussher on church government

In 1625 when Ussher was made archbishop of Armagh his primacy of Ireland was by no means beyond dispute; indeed since the reign of Edward VI there were grounds for the archbishop of Dublin to stake his claim to the stewardship. The lengths to which Ussher went to establish not only his supremacy over Dublin but the supremacy of all future incumbents at Armagh says much about how he valued hierarchy and order as well as a sense of history within the Church.

The problem had its source in the policy of the Edwardian Lord Deputy, Sir James Croft. After experiencing some trouble with Archbishop Dowdall of Armagh he procured an Act of the King and Council of England depriving Armagh of the Primacy and transferring it to Dublin.[1] Ussher resolved the long running argument by using his patronage along with a minutely researched vindication of his rights. In a letter to Laud he plucked on what he knew to be Laudian heartstrings, claiming that the issue had obvious implications for the King's majesty, 'And it would peradventure be not altogether unworthy the consideration, whether it would not make somewhat for the Dignity of his Majesties kingdoms and the splendor of our Church that we should have not only Metropolitans, but patriarchs also within ourselves as in the

---

1 J.T. Ball, *The Reformed Church of Ireland* (London, 1886), p. 39.

days of old.'² Wentworth summoned the two archbishops along with a retinue of lawyers before the council and their cause was heard over two days, after which they found in favour of Ussher and Armagh.

It is clear from this incident that Ussher's theological disposition may have been informed by Calvinism but his views on ecclesiastical government were certainly not based on Presbyterianism. In fact Ussher's reputation in this area is probably as more of a mediator than a member of either of the two main schools. This largely bases itself on one particular pronouncement on the subject of Church government. Designed as a balm for the problems which beset the Church of the early 1640s it was a manuscript entitled, *The Reduction of Episcopacy into the form of synodical government received in the Ancient Church*, latterly it came to be known as *The Reduction Manuscript*. Ussher's aim was to provide a scheme, based apparently on the primitive Church, which would place a bishop at the head of a synod, whilst making him answerable to elected elders. He was attempting to appeal not only to both sides in the English dispute but as the document's marginalia indicates, the Scottish as well.³ Jonathan Spurr has written that Ussher's plan was deliberately vague allowing people to read into it what they wanted.⁴ Samuel Gardiner argued in his *History of England* that it set out to deal reasonably with the unreasonable⁵ and Conrad Russell repeated this assertion, 'It was a brilliant attempt at squaring the circle, though it was perhaps to be expected that Charles should regard it as reducing bishops to ciphers, and that Henderson should regard the little matter of a permanent president as the crack in the door that let in the principle of popery.'⁶ *The Reduction Manuscript* received some airing, though in the end it excited more opposition than support.⁷ Those who had suffered the full weight of Laudian heavy handedness had developed an aversion to episcopacy even in its most innocuous form.

W.M. Abbot in his 1990 article on Ussherian episcopacy makes some interesting and convincing observations on this issue. Rejecting the notion that Ussher's proposal failed because of the unwillingness of both parties to move from their entrenched positions, he argues instead that it was the subject of self-suppression.⁸ By 1641 Ussher had 'come to view the Reduction plan as too dangerous to propose formally', and that it was his own withdrawal of the scheme 'that robbed it of

---

2   A. Ford, 'The correspondence between Archbishops Ussher and Laud', *Archivium Hibernicum*, XLVI (1991–92): 17.

3   C. Russell, *The Fall of the British Monarchies, 1637–1642* (Oxford, 1991), p. 250.

4   J. Spurr, *The Restoration Church of England, 1646–1689* (Yale, 1999), pp. 26–7.

5   S.R. Gardiner, *The History of England 1603–1642* (10 vols, London, 1890), vol. 9, p. 387.

6   Russell, *Fall of Monarchies*, p. 250.

7   Not least from the poet John Milton who wrote *Of prelactical Episcopacy and whether it may be deduced from Apostolic times, by virtue of those testimonies which are alleged to that purpose in some late treatise, one whereof goes under the name of James, Archbishop of Armagh* (London, 1641).

8   W.M. Abbot, 'James Ussher and the "Ussherian" Episcopacy, 1640–1656: The Primate and His Reduction Manuscript', *Albion*, XXII, (1990): 237–59.

political support.'⁹ Abbot points out that there is no mention of the proposals in contemporary sources,¹⁰ nor in Ussher's own correspondence.¹¹ This was because the manuscript, post-Root and Branch petition, had changed in character, it would now be a 'stepping stone' towards unacceptable alterations, rather than a 'cap-stone' to an acceptable programme of reform.¹²

This hypothesis is entirely in keeping with Nicholas Bernard's contemporary account of events. Rounding on Ussher's critics who confused *The Reduction Manuscript* with Ussher's own ideals, he asks them to remember 'what was that which caused it, even the pressing violence of those times, with the sole end of it, a pacification.' In this Ussher was like Jonah 'willing to cast himself into the tempest in order to still it.'¹³ Bernard adds later on the same subject, 'What he did, or was willing to have, yielded into out of a calm temper of moderation in such times of extremity, to preserve the unity and peace of the Church ... ought not in reason so to be stretched, as to infer it was his absolute desire.'¹⁴ Abbot's theory seems to be vindicated by contemporary evidence, but arguably it does not contradict Gardiner and Russell. It is feasible that Ussher, sensing that the parties were polarising to such an extent that moderate appeal was useless, ditched the unifying scheme. If at this early stage he had a foot in both camps, by 1641 his feet were firmly planted on the royalist side. As a consequence the proposal, which had been referred to as 'eirenicon'¹⁵ was not only irrelevant but a potential embarrassment. Ussher, like the majority of the body politic, had by then become a part of the general polarisation. By this time Ussher had been recruited by Bishop Joseph Hall into an episcopalian cabal, a type of seventeenth-century Tractarian movement who would propagandise the bishops' cause.¹⁶ Ussher was clearly no reluctant conscript and his contribution was prolific, three volumes all appeared in 1641 in which he not only defended episcopacy as integral to Church government but identified bishops with the stars of Revelation. Included among these were *A Geographical and Historical Disquistion touching Asia properly So-Called, The Original of Bishops and Metropolitans*, and *The Judgment of Doctor Rainoldes touching the original of Episcopacy*. All these works are included in Elrington's collection and they have left something of a legacy within the Anglican Church. A.J. Mason, writing at the beginning of the last century, described them along with similar works by Joseph Hall and Jeremy Taylor as 'a constellation.'¹⁷ In the *Original of Bishops* Ussher declared firmly that the episcopacy derived firstly from the pattern prescribed by God in the Old Testament wherein government was committed to priests and Levites (with priests in superiority) and secondly, ecclesiastical hierarchy is in imitation of the same institution as it was

---

9   Ibid., p. 245.
10 Ibid., p. 247.
11 Ibid., p. 251.
12 Ibid., p. 253.
13 Bernard, *Clavi*, pp. iii–iv.
14 Ibid., p. 57.
15 Carr, *Life*, p. 271.
16 *Cal.S.P.Ire., 1639–40*, p.30.
17 A.J. Mason, *The Church of England and Episcopacy* (Cambridge, 1914), p. 118.

confirmed by Christ.[18] Throwing down the gauntlet Ussher challenges, 'With what shew of reason then can any man imagine, that what was instituted by God in the Law, for mere matter of government ... should now be rejected in the Gospel, as a device of Antichrist'[19] This view was repeated in a report requested by the House of Commons; completed in 1642, it addressed liturgy and episcopal government.[20]

What was to prove the most important volume of Ussher's episcopalian works appeared three years later and in it he skilfully settled a long hermeneutical debate concerning the first-century letters of St Ignatius. The contention concerned which, if any of the letters, were genuine. In 1623 the Genevan Calvinist Vedelius had rejected more than half of them. Ussher's new collection was based on manuscripts he had uncovered in Cambridge at Bishop Montagu's library, with them he was able to prove that six of the epistles were genuine.[21] It is an assessment that still stands (barring one) and is in fact probably Ussher's only lasting scholastic achievement.[22] It is easy to overlook the contemporary significance of what appears on the surface to be a purely academic matter. In fact the political and ecclesiastical implications were profound. The Ignatius letters are the earliest extra-canonical Christian writings and they are a very early witness to the existence of a bishopric in the primitive Church. Ignatius urges the people to submit to their bishop as Christ had done to his Father.[23] Furthermore the letters distinguish between bishops and presbyters, who must be obeyed as one would obey the Apostles.[24] From this Ussher concludes that the distinct institution of episcopacy can be traced back to the Apostles. In the currency of theological debate such early validation was of rare and valuable coinage; Ussher had unearthed a priceless endorsement. The significance was not lost on royalist Oxford who presented Ussher with a eulogy which was intended ever after to precede his name.[25]

The footnote to Ussher's contribution to the English debate on Church organisation is interesting. In spite of its failure to make an impression during the conflagrations of 1641, *The Reduction Manuscript* was placed into suspended animation rather than killed off. In 1649 it was revived at Newport when it was offered to the King who 'having perused it, liked it well, saying it was the only expedient to reconcile the present differences for his Majesty.'[26] The tide had by then turned so much against the Royal camp that Ussher's scheme appeared once more as a cap to extreme proposals. By this time it was too late to seek concessions, but the plan experienced several revivals, re-emerging during the Interregnum in 1656 when it was printed

---

18   *UW*, vol. 7, p. 43.
19   Ibid., p. 45.
20   J. Ussher, *Opinions on Church Government*, Thomason Tract, E109 (10), p. 4.
21   Spurr, *Restoration Church*, pp. 139–40.
22   J.B. Lightfoot, *St Ignatius* (London, 1885), vol. 1, pp. 315–18.
23   *UW*, vol. 7, p. 47.
24   Ibid.
25   Parr, *Life*, pp. 100–101. The eulogy ran, 'Jacobus Usserius, Archiepiscopus Armachanus Totius Hiberniae Primas, Antiquitatis primaerae pertissimus, Orthodoxae Religionis vindex άγαγπρρη Errorum Malleus. In Concionado frequens, facundas, praepotens vitae inculpate exemplar spectabile.'
26   Ibid., p. 66.

for the first time and dispersed among Presbyterians by Bernard, Ussher's one time chaplain and now almoner to Cromwell. The idea sank once more as the Lord Protector drove on toward a more conservative and authoritarian religious regime.[27] There was however one final gasp of life from the manuscript before it expired; it was presented by Richard Baxter at the Restoration as a scheme for establishing a united, inclusive and peaceful Church. This time it was the episcopalians' turn to reject its compromises.[28]

Ironically Ussher's edition of the Ignatian letters also received a post–Restoration revival when Henry Hammond was able to use them to build his defence of episcopacy at the Savoy Conference in 1661.[29] Ussher may perhaps have been amused had he known that the English Church under the restored Stuart dynasty would set about settling the volatile issue of Church government with either side employing two of his own contributions to the debate. One cannot help but feel that he would have been happy to have seen the *Ignatian letters* winning over the *Reduction Manuscript*. As his other works on the subject illustrate and as his great efforts during the primacy controversy show, the former corresponded much more closely to the Ussherian ideal of Church government.

Bramhall on church government

In agreement with Ussher, Bramhall believed that the bishopric as an institution was rooted and established by Christ. Quite simply it was Christ's gift to the Church, the redeemer had not left His bride as the ostrich her eggs in the sand without provision for governing. To do so would have been to have consigned it to anarchy in order and dogma, like Cyclop's cave where no man heard or heeded another.[30] Similarly Bramhall traces episcopal government through history to the primitive Church. As mentioned above, writing in defence of himself and the English episcopacy in general against Ussher's would-be disciple, Richard Baxter, Bramhall challenges his opponent to show him one Church in the first fifteen hundred years of Christianity that had been formed without a bishop. Confident that such historical enquiry would prove fruitless he states,

> I will shew him the proper and particular names of Apostles, Evangelists, Bishops, Presbyters, Deacons, in Scripture, in Councils, in Fathers, in histories; if he cannot name one particular lay-elder, it is because there never was any such thing *in rerum natura* for fifteen hundreds years after Christ.[31]

Adding to this he brings the historical argument to more modern times, in case Baxter thought that Church government was a Reformation issue Bramhall observed that the

---

27   Spurr, *Restoration Church*, pp. 26–7.
28   Knox, *Ussher*, p. 143.
29   H. De Quehen, 'Politics and scholarship in the Ignatian controversy', *The Seventeenth Century*, vol. XIII, no. 1 (Spring, 1998): 73.
30   *BW*, vol.3, p. 521.
31   Ibid., p. 53. That is before Calvin's return to Geneva.

first Reformers had all approved of the institution. The Waldenses and the Bohemian Brethren had both retained their episcopacy.[32] Next the Lutherans in Sweden and Denmark had kept bishops 'name and thing', in Germany; they called them 'superintendents.'[33] Bramhall remarks, 'There cannot be a more luculent testimony for the Lutherans' approbation of bishops than the Augustan [Augsburg] Confession itself.'[34] As for the second wave of Reformers Bramhall is at first disparaging, however, they eventually appear to him as too valuable a weapon to dismiss entirely, instead he uses them as a stick with which to beat his Presbyterian accuser. The 'next reformation' according to Bramhall was Zwinglian and whilst they may have erected no new bishops they did not pull down any either.[35] As for Calvin he subscribed to the Augsburg Confession (which is pro-episcopal) and further to this in his 190th Epistle, which was to the King of Poland, he represented episcopal government as the fittest for monarchies. Bramhall quotes directly from the letter. 'Indeed the ancient Church instituted Patriarchs, and gave certain Primacies to particular provinces, that bishops might remain bound one to another by this bond of concord.'[36] Bramhall's assessment of the Reformers' contribution to episcopal issues is of course distinctly selective, not to say shrewd. His use of them is purely tactical knowing as he does that an enemy is best beaten with his own weapon.

Aside from the shared base on which Ussher and Bramhall constructed their defences of Church hierarchy there are two distinctive features of Bramhall's carefully worked apologetics. The first of these is the centrality of nationalism to Bramhall's understanding. Baxter had made a shrewd assertion by labelling Bramhall's ecclesiology 'Grotian' since its ideal is rooted in the work of the Dutch humanist and Calvinist bogeyman, Hugo Grotius (1583–1645). Grotius had been called the 'miracle of Holland' because of his precocious intelligence but later as a supporter of Oldenbarnevelt he became embroiled in the politico-religious conflict of the Remonstrants and Gomarists which resulted in a daring flight from his native country.[37] In exile Grotius wrote a series of tracts including *De jure belli et pacis* (1625) which set out as a type of founding principle the idea that a sovereign state was subject to no human authority outside of itself.[38] Grotius further stated that this ideal was based on natural law, drawing as it did on human reserves of conscience and reason,[39] nothing could be further from the Calvinists' analysis of the human condition. A point of departure for the Grotian ideal was its strong Erastian tendencies, a logical consequence of his high esteem for national autonomy and human government. In a series of works from 1611 to 1617 which included *Ordinum Pietas* and *Defensis Fidei*, Grotius defended the rights of state governments to exert full authority (*jus magistratus*) over the full range of ecclesiastical affairs

---

32   Ibid.
33   Ibid. p. 532.
34   Ibid.
35   Ibid., pp. 532–3.
36   Ibid., p. 534.
37   *Encyclopaedia of the Reformation*, Hillerbrand, vol. 2, pp. 197–8.
38   G. Treasure, *The Making of Modern Europe, 1648–1780* (London, 1985), p. 185.
39   Ibid., p. 193.

including doctrinal controversies, the appointing of ministers and the prohibition of national synods.[40] Bramhall's work takes up these themes and uses them to justify the independence of his national Church. The English Church did not break with Rome, rather it reasserted its natural autonomy. In fact it was the papacy which caused the rift by violating the authority of another sovereign state.[41] Bramhall also strongly defends the rights of the prince to call synods and appoint bishops in his own territory.[42] In exile, Bramhall wrote that in appointing persons to the rejuvenated restoration bishopric, he preferred the Irish system in which the King made the selection.[43]

By comparison, Ussher also liked to exert the independence of his national Church but in doing so he preferred to rest his argument on antiquity rather than modern assertions of statehood. In his *Discourse of the Religion Anciently Professed* he argues that the world was originally divided into three, that is Asia, Africa and Europe. In turn Europe was divided into four, Rome, Constantinople, Ireland, 'now translated to England' and Spain, 'whereby it appeareth, that the King of England and his kingdom are of the more eminent ancient kings and kingdoms of all Europe, which prerogative the kingdom of France is not said to obtain.'[44] This mattered more to Ussher than any of the natural rights claimed by Bramhall. In addition it is difficult to find anything quite as Erastian as Bramhall's formula for Church state relations in the work of Ussher. Indeed in a speech before the Castle Chamber in Dublin he categorically stated that God created two powers on earth, the one of the keys, the other of the sword.[45] Drawing on the classic division of Moses' commandments into worldly and godly he states, 'And howsoever by this means we make both prince and priest to be in their several places *custodes ultriusque tabulae*, keepers of both God's tables: yet do we not hereby any way confound both of their offices together.'[46]

The second distinction between Ussher and Bramhall's ecclesiology concerns the breadth of their vision. For Ussher the episcopacy is the best institution to serve the national Church, for Bramhall it was the best institution to serve the universal Church. Bramhall's argument goes much further than the pro-episcopal, anti-episcopal feud that polarised the English Church of the 1640s. It stretched far beyond a defence of national Church hierarchy. Bramhall so idealised the institution that he saw it as the basis for not only ecclesiastical government but an international Church community, which in principle could lead to the reunion of the whole Church. Bramhall's vision is of a unified Church made up of autocephalous national Churches and based on a mutual understanding and respect. The Bishop of Rome would be reduced from his universality to his *principium unitatis*, a unifying principle.[47] Churches would be presided over by an oligarchy of bishops who would in turn preside over the Church

---

40   *Encyclopaedia of the Reformation*, vol. 2, pp. 197–8.
41   *BW*, vol. 1, p. 97.
42   *BW*, vol. 2, p. 404.
43   *Calendar of the Clarendon State Papers*, ed. W. Dunn (Oxford, 1869), vol. 3, p. 253.
44   *UW*, vol. 4, p. 370.
45   *UW*, vol. 2, p. 462.
46   Ibid., p. 464.
47   *BW*, vol. 3, p. 545.

mundial via the ancient system of ecumenical councils. By this means would be preserved national Church sovereignty.[48] Here again Bramhall locates the source of the problem in modern politics. In an almost mirror image of his secular politics of kingship he sees the papacy as deriving its power from human origins, but claiming them from God. The consequences of this confusion are disastrous since it means the Pope may draw a million souls into hell, give his *non obstante* to the canons of the Fathers, and yet none may depose him.[49]

Bramhall was not entirely averse to drawing upon ancient history for support but the strongest basis for his claim came from the fifteenth century. In April 1415 as the Church suffered the humiliation and confusion of division and dual papacy an ecumenical council gathered at Constance. Frustrated by the intransigence of both Popes the council of bishops moved to remedy the situation by declaring themselves the supreme government of the Church.[50] Five decrees were passed dealing with Church government, the first, '*Haec Sancta*', ran, 'this Council holds its power direct from Christ; everyone, no matter his rank or office, even if it be Papal is bound to obey it in whatever pertains to faith.'[51] Denys Hay explained the monumental significance of such a development, 'In this way the Fathers of Constance reversed the thousand-year-old process which had turned the pope into an absolute monarch. The Church was given a written constitution.'[52] Conciliarism had to all intents and purposes established itself in Western Christendom, however a papal bull in 1460 declared it anathema and it was consigned to the dust bin of history.[53] Outside of the Church establishment however the tradition proved to be more enduring. In Germany, Poland, France, Scotland and even Italy, Conciliarist ideologies survived throughout the late fifteenth and sixteenth centuries and they were reanimated to a marked degree in the early decades of the seventeenth century.[54]

Bramhall, writing in 1654 indicated four ways in which the popes might be charged with schism, the third of these refers explicitly to the Council of Constance. The papacy, as it now stands above the council, with its power to confirm or reject sanctions, argued Bramhall, is the biggest cause of the rift in Christendom. This ran contrary to the decrees of the ecumenical councils which had stated specifically 'the Pope is subject to a general Council, as well in matter of Faith, as of manners; so as he may not only be corrected, but, if he be incorrigible, be deposed.'[55] Bramhall was adamant that the Pope, who undoubtedly constituted a 'Patriarch', was made so by the Church and not by Christ. Besides, he urged, the present claims of the papacy were incompatible. You cannot be a Patriarch and a universal bishop, it is

---

48   Ibid.
49   Ibid., pp. 548–9.
50   *The History of the Church*, ed. H. Jedin (10 vols, London, 1980), vol. 4, p. 465.
51   *Oxford Dictionary of the Christian Church*, eds F.L. Cross and E.A. Livingstone (Oxford, 2005), p..407.
52   D. Hays, *Europe in the Fourteenth and Fifteenth Centuries* (London, 1989) pp. 308–9.
53   Ibid., p. 312.
54   F. Oakley, 'Anxieties of influence', *Past & Present*, 151 (May 1996): 81.
55   *BW*, vol. 1, p. 253.

inconsistent.⁵⁶ In identifying this papal self-elevation as a source of much of the conflict within the Christian world Bramhall is chiefly concerned with its implied relegation of the episcopal office. The popes have appeared great by reducing those around them, they have increased their authority by grasping the power of their bishops. In the fourth of his charges Bramhall rails against the papacy for limiting the power of bishops by exemptions and reservations. Holding themselves to be bishops of every particular see, making all jurisdiction flow from them and thus taking away apostolic succession. Ultimately this was a confounding of the source and order of power, implying that all bishops drew their power from the pope where in fact it was he who drew his power from them.⁵⁷

There is almost certainly nothing here that would cause Ussher much trouble, there is nothing in either of their theories which contradicts. Indeed Ussher and Bramhall stoutly defended the episcopal office for the same primary reasons that it was constituted by Christ and it would provide order. Their differences are ones of stress and scope. Whilst Ussher was more inclined to look to the distant past to justify episcopacy and provide pedigree for his English national Church, Bramhall employed the events of the recent past to justify his vision of a universal Catholic Church.

Ussher and Roman Catholicism

Ussher's theological conclusions on the issue of the Roman Church was part of the well-established tradition that drew heavily on the apocalyptic verses of scripture. His understanding of Revelations 17 and 18 identified the seven headed beast as Rome with its hills; the Vatican was 'Pontificalibus' in which dwelt the 'Pontifex Romanus', waited on by the false prophets whom Ussher terms the 'Clerus Romanus.'⁵⁸ Elsewhere he draws on the same verses to formulate a prophetic vision of the future, 'Whereby it is most evident that Rome is not to cease from being Babylon, till her last destruction shall come upon her: and that unto her last gasp she is to continue her spiritual fornications, alluring all nations unto her superstition and idolatry.'⁵⁹ In a sermon from 1620 Ussher warns his congregation that one might also be guilty by association. Reminding them of the Angel who followed those who similarly worshipped the beast and he 'received his mark in [sic] his forehead or in his hands the same shall drink of the wine of the wrath of God.'⁶⁰

We can gain a picture of how this theological antipathy translated into political practice from examining the early career of Ussher when he was at his most politically

---

56   *BW*, vol. 2, pp. 322–3.

57   *BW*, vol. 1, p. 253.

58   J. Ussher, *The Judgement of the Primate (wrot by him long agoe in answer to a request of a learned friend) what is meant by the beast that was, and is not, and yet is*, Thomason Tract, E1783, pp. 14–17.

59   N. Bernard, *The Judgement of the Late Archbishop of Armagh and Primate of Ireland of Babylon, Revelations 18:4* (London, 1658), p. 8.

60   Bodleian Library, Oxford, Ms. Perrot 9 (9774) 'Notes taken from Doctor Ussher's sermon at Temple Church, 2 July 1620.'

active. In 1619 Ussher visited England and was presented at Court, shortly afterwards he was appointed by James I to the position of the King's personal chaplain. He remained at Court until 1621 and, according to Alan Ford, these years represent the period when Ussher 'crossed over the subtle boundary between scholarship and politics.' His anti-Catholicism, coupled with his Calvinism made him useful to Sir Thomas Roe and the anti-Spanish circle around the Earl of Pembroke.[61] Two sermons preached in London are indicative of the apocalyptic line that Ussher was furiously pressing. At the Temple Church, 2 July 1620 he discoursed on the text of Revelations 19:20 in which the false prophet was cast into brimstone. He pressed the clergy with their inescapable duty to warn of the dangers of Romanism. He was, according to A. Ford, 'Well aware of mounting royal concern about the inflammatory and disruptive impact of political sermons.'[62] In the second sermon before Parliament in 1621, Ussher launched an attack on idolatrous practice, in particular the adoration of the consecrated bread during the mass. At this time James I was planning the marriage of his son to a Catholic, Alan Ford points out that Ussher was unequivocal in warning of the dangers posed to the state,[63] perhaps a somewhat polite adjective since Ussher had actually asked his congregation to consider, 'What peace, so long as the whoredoms of thy mother, Jezebel, and her witchcrafts are so many?'[64] Nor was such invective the result of youthful zeal; early in the reign of Charles I, Ussher was once more venting his disapproval of royal policy toward recusants. This time the implications were more serious since he was doing so in his new capacity as Primate of Ireland. Charles's crime was to offer the Catholic population of Ireland the various Graces that he hoped would secure their loyalty. Feeling was high amongst them that full toleration would soon follow. Ussher gathered twelve prelates together to discuss the matter, their response was a strongly worded letter of protestation the opening lines of which declared;

> The Religion of the papist is superstitious and idolatrous, their faith and Doctrine erroneous, and Heretical. Their Church, in respect of both, Apostatical. To give them therefore a toleration or to concent that they may freely exercise their Religion and confess their faith and doctrine, is a grievous sin ... .[65]

The letter continues that such toleration made them 'accessories' to idolatry and 'set religion for sale.'[66] Later Anglican biographers were censorious of Ussher's brand of anti-Catholicism as displayed in *The Protestation* because it was, as they saw it, based solely on the assumption that Catholicism was a false religion. The only legitimate excuse for such action would have been the Roman Catholics' own intolerance. J. Aiken makes the point 'the archbishop and his suffragans acted

---

61 A. Ford, 'James Ussher and the godly prince in early-seventeenth-century Ireland', in H. Morgan (ed.), *Political Ideology in Ireland 1541–1641* (London, 2000), p. 212.
62 Ibid., p. 214.
63 Ibid., p. 215.
64 *UW*, vol. 2, p. 456.
65 *The Protestation of the Archbishops and bishops of Ireland, 26 Nov. 1626* (London, 1641), no pagination.
66 Ibid.

according to the principles of the extremest intolerance, for they did not found their reasoning upon maxims of state ... but solely upon the nature of the Roman Catholic worship, without making mention of its persecuting spirit.'[67] The language of *The Protestation* might certainly be described as incendiary and might also be considered to be based on the crudest of theological reasons, yet two things need to be taken into account before we take this outburst at face value. Firstly, the Primate was careful to temper the group's proceedings in order to avoid scandal. In a letter to the Archbishop of Canterbury he explained that he took measures to keep the dispute internal.

> I procured a meeting of all the prelates at my house, who with one voice protested against these courses and subscribed this protestation with their hands. But forasmuch as we knew that the project was wonderful distasteful to the papists themselves, we continued ourselves in public and suffered the breach to come from their side.[68]

Ussher may have wanted to placate Archbishop Abbott after what was without doubt a rather accusatory protest, nevertheless it demonstrates that the arrows of the Archbishop's invective were often not as barbed as they might appear.

Secondly, and even more significantly, was what followed immediately after the bishops' protest was issued. When the throne pressed upon Lord Deputy Falkland that Catholic contributions were absolutely necessary in order to build a standing army, he called upon the Lord Primate 'in regard of the great esteem in which he was held by both parties', to pronounce on the urgency before the whole assembly.[69] Under such an injunction from the royal representative Ussher performed a *volte face* and the outspoken demonstrator turned into a plaintiff for official crown policy. In his speech in Dublin Castle the Primate made a distinction between loyal and rebellious Catholics, describing the difference in racial terms. Ussher appealed to the Old English who had always been safely 'counted on against a foreign invader.' They had withstood Spain (though the pope had held up England as an infidel enemy) and in this they had been 'supported by a loyal Catholic clergy of the Pale.' Therefore they were to be distinguished from the Gaelic, Old Irish 'who have nothing at all to lose' and 'are very likely to join any foreign invader.'[70] The speech failed but a copy was duly dispatched to Charles I who 'expressed in strong terms his approbation of the zeal and fidelity which it displayed.'[71]

It might at first seem incongruous that Ussher executed such an apparent U–turn in so short a time. It has been interpreted as a sign that Ussher had matured since his early outbursts.[72] However as early as the 1620s the young firebrand had been persuaded to qualify his remarks and tow the party line. Alan Ford crucially points out that at the close of the 1621 homily there comes a type of post scriptural

---

67 J. Aiken, *The Lives of John Selden, esq. and Archbishop Ussher* (London, 1812), pp. 234–5.
68 *Tanner Letters*, ed. C. McNeill (Dublin, 1943), p. 73.
69 Elrington, *Life*, p. 78.
70 *Cal.S.P.Ire., 1625–32*, p. 229.
71 Elrington, *Life*, p. 86.
72 V. Treadwell, *Buckingham and Ireland* (Dublin, 1998), p. 281.

compromise. Ussher demands no new policy against Catholics; after venting his spleen with denunciation upon denunciation he appears after all satisfied with the present legislation. 'God's laws there are already enacted to this purpose which if they were duly put in execution we should have less need to think of making new.'[73] Ford indicates the significance of this, 'In other words he neither called for fiercer measures against Catholics nor for the suspension of all proceedings against them; rather he opted for James's traditional formula of distinguishing between those engaging in treachery and open idolatry and the mass of quiet and loyal Catholics.'[74]

Alan Ford is right to make this assertion; Ussher was capable of combining the most apocalyptic demonization of Romanism with a more pragmatic approach toward Catholics. This does not represent a new and more reasoned departure in the mature Ussher, indeed we can find examples as early as 1612. In a letter dated that year Ussher refers the Catholic priest Francis Barnaby to the Oath of Allegiance he had persuaded him to take. Ussher grumbles that similar efforts to cajole Bishop Conor O'Devany to do the same were unlikely to succeed, 'I would willingly know what effect your persuasions have taken with that miserable old man, who is not able, or rather not willing ... to distinguish the cause of conscience and religion toward God, from the cause of open rebellion and treason against his Prince and Country.'[75] It seems clear from this that far from a general evolution in Ussher's thinking he was ever able to distinguish between Roman rebel and the benign papist, just as he was always willing to dilute his polemics with a healthy dose of practicality. However incongruous this appears Alan Ford points out that it is by no means unique. Indeed condemnations of royal policy were not inconsistent with general royalism, rather they identify Ussher with a long line of clergy who expressed concern at their Prince's failure to pursue his godly duties. Nor indeed is this tradition limited to puritans; in fact, it had a much broader base.[76] If Ussher can be characterised as someone who consistently maintained an amalgam of left wing theology and staunchly conservative politics, he was not alone in doing so. Besides, in public life at least, it was clear which took precedence.

Bramhall and Roman Catholicism

Just as Ussher's reputation as a scourge of Romanism needs some qualification, John Bramhall's notoriety as a prototype Anglo-Catholic must take into account his occasional antipathy to the Church of Rome, at least in its contemporary state. Perhaps this should not surprise us since Bramhall was a product of such a Calvinist

---

73   *UW*, vol. 2, p. 457.
74   Ford, 'Godly Prince', p. 216.
75   B. Millet, 'James Ussher, Francis Barnaby, and Blessed Conor O'Devany', *Collectanea Hibernica*, no. 58 (1996): 46.
76   Ford, 'Godly Prince', pp. 224–5. It is also worth noting that Ussher's geographical position in Ireland had a significance at a time when freedom of speech was directly proportional to distance from the throne. Ford points out that Joseph Hall was imprisoned in 1623 in England for complaining that religion was being sold for Spanish money. In 1627, Ussher not only retained his see but also his place on the Privy Council.

establishment as Sidney Sussex College. Whilst a casual appraisal of his life might suggest that he imbibed nothing of its puritan ethos, closer examination shows that in some respects at least his lessons were not lost on him. The title of Bramhall's doctoral thesis describes the papacy, '[as it was challenged and usurped in our native country] as either the procreant or conservant cause, or both of all the greater ecclesiastical controversies in the Christian world.'[77] Bramhall later provided John Vesey, his first biographer, with information on the thesis for which he gives us this summary.

> ... in the seas of controversy, that he looked on him [the Pope] as either a mother or the nurse that gives life or nourishment to all or most of those doctrines, that have so long disquieted the Christian world, and by pretending to give life and safe conduct to uncertain travaillers, has engaged them among Rocks and Quick-sands.[78]

This aspect of Bramhall's life tends to be eclipsed by his career as what would later be regarded as a high-clergyman but as one commentator warned in the 1930s, 'Any sketch of Bramhall's life would be incomplete if it failed to draw attention to his vehement anti-papal activities.'[79] The seeming incongruity of this has been remarked upon; it caused some scholarly head scratching as the editor composed an edition of Bramhall's works for the Library of Anglo-Catholicism. He commented, 'It is curious to observe how early and how continually his attention was turned to the subject of his subsequent treatises against the Romanists.[80]

Bramhall's polemic was by no means confined to scholarship, in 1623 he mounted the public stage for the first time to take up a challenge from two Catholic priests in the neighbourhood of Northallerton, Yorkshire.[81] Vesey predictably described the encounter in triumphant terms as Bramhall 'managed both the shield and sword of controversy with such dexterity.' As with Ussher's debate in Dublin the boy David parallels proved too good to ignore; Vesey writes, 'not enduring to see his brethren so dispirited, while those Goliahs [sic] were blaspheming the Armies of the living God, as inspired with a great zeal and indignation, undertook the combat.'[82] The subject was transubstantiation and despite his age, it appears that Bramhall won the day quickly cutting to the chase he opened with a logical attack on the Roman practice of denying the cup to the laity, 'Amen, Amen I say to you unless you eat his flesh and drink his blood you shall not have life in you ... If we eat this flesh and

---

77   SparrowSimpson, *Bramhall*, pp. 5–6.
78   Vesey, *Athanasius*, p. 5.
79   C. Nye, 'John Bramhall', *The Church Quarterly Review* (CXVII, 1934): 267–8.
80   *BW*, vol. 1, p.iv.
81   Collins, *Typical Churchmen*, p. 83. The names of these priests are usually given as Hungate, S.J. and Houghton, yet W.E. Collins could find no trace of them in Gillow's *Bibliographical Dictionary of English Catholics*. He concludes, 'Perhaps ... Bramhall's opponents cannot be considered as definitely determined.'
82   Vesey, *Athanasius*, pp. 3–4.

drink this blood under one kind only, it follows that eating is drinking and drinking is eating. But the consequence of this is absurd.'[83]

Vesey could not resist embellishing the episode by extending the victory to the point of death. This passage of the biography ends with the author gleefully relating that during the course of the debate Bramhall got the priests to say that eating was drinking and drinking was eating. This error had fatal consequences for one of them who afterwards found 'that he could not quench his thirst with a piece of bread, he reflected sadly on the dishonour he had suffered, that not being able to digest it, in ten days he died.'[84] Vesey's version of events must clearly be taken with a pinch of salt but what is certain from the incident is that in the 1620s Bramhall was just as eager to enter the confessional fray as Ussher, even in times when it was contrary to the prevailing mood of the country. Making the same point about himself that A. Ford made about Ussher he was quick to remind Richard Baxter that the Conference at Northallerton took place in 1623 when the Prince was in Spain negotiating a marriage, 'I adventured, with more zeal than discretion when the religion of England seemed to be placed in *acquilibrio*.'[85] The renowned Presbyterian sympathiser had written an attack on Arminianism entitled, *The Grotian Religion Discovered*, in 1658.[86] In this work he accused the Laudian wing of the Church in general, and Bramhall in particular, of attempting to bring the Church of England into the Roman fold. Bramhall countered that the Conference proved that he was neither a crypto-Catholic nor an opportunist but rather that he had ever been a stout defender of their common faith. He might well have added to these anti-Roman credentials a sermon he preached three years after Northallerton, this time to the Northern Synod. There Bramhall chose as his subject 'the pope's unlawful usurpation of jurisdiction over the Britannic Churches.'[87]

Whilst these similarities with Ussher's enthusiasm for anti-papist rhetoric are worth observing, proving as it does that there was more common ground between the two wings of the English Church than one might expect, nevertheless a significant distinction has to be made. Of course we have to be careful since we have no copies of Bramhall's earlier discourses but it does appear from the title of his doctoral thesis and his Northern Synod sermon that he is stressing the illegality of over–inflated papal claims, or else the controversy and schism caused by usurping power illegally. What seems to be missing are the apocalyptic or biblical references to the prophetical or to the use of antichrist imagery that appear in the work of Ussher. This would be in keeping with later work which never drew prophetically on scriptural passages and made no habitual use of the term antichrist with reference to the papacy. Indeed Bramhall only refers to the term in order to clear up the matter of its abuse.

---

83 Bodleian Library, Oxford, Ms. Rawlinson, D320, 'The Summe of the Conference between Mr Bramhall and Mr Houghton at Allerton, sincerely related by John Danby who was at it an enemy to neither, and a friend to the truth.', p. 1.

84 Vesey, *Athanasius*, p. 4.

85 *BW*, vol. 3, p. 540.

86 R. Baxter, *The Grotian Religion Discovered, at the invitation of Mr. Thomas Pierce in his Vindication* (London, 1658).

87 Wright, *Yorkshire Divine*, p. 4.

According to Bramhall the term has two meanings, one general and one specific. Generally or largely it refers to every opposer of Christ. 'In this sense we believe the Pope to be an antichrist: that is, an opposer of Christ's prophetical office, by presuming to add his own patches to the doctrine of this great Prophet ... .'[88] The term also has a stricter sense as the man of perdition found in 2 Thessalonians 2:3. This, Bramhall maintains, is a matter of dispute amongst Protestants and whilst many of the signs may correspond with the prophecy, he sits on a temple, his city is on seven hill, he shows himself around the year 666 but doubtless 'these marks do all agree to the Turk.'[89]

It is tempting to see Bramhall's anti-Roman Catholicism as an early aberration in an otherwise Laudian career but there seems to be little evidence to suggest that there were any great fundamental theological differences between the younger and more mature English Church apologist. In common with Ussher he was concerned with winning the confessional argument, in common perhaps with everyone who cared about religion. Also in common with Ussher, he was more worried about Rome than Romanists, though as indicated in previous chapters he was less inclined to trace the root of the problem as far back into history as Ussher. Unlike Ussher he was not theologically disposed to imposing a biblical and millenarian trajectory onto his understanding of events. As far as Bramhall was concerned the present trouble in Rome, the split in Christendom and the Reform movements, had more to do with overweening popes than with any cosmological timescale. Rome was a corrupt city not Babylon, and the papacy was an institution that had overestimated itself, it was not the throne of the antichrist. This appears to be true of Bramhall's earlier pronouncement as it does of the considered writings of the bishop in exile. If there is a distinction between the earlier and later positions it can probably be explained by mitigating circumstances. In spite of Bramhall's allusions to the Spanish match it was both easier and more in keeping with a general trend to attack Rome in the England of the 1620s. Besides, the aspiring cleric was working under the episcopal directorate of Tobias Matthew in Yorkshire, a prelate noted for his zealous approach to religious controversy and his dogged pursuit of rescusants.[90] We must also take into account that the doctoral thesis was produced to please his masters at Sidney Sussex and that the Northern Synod was traditionally a forum in which to present anti-Catholic papers. In the 1630s with the rising influence of the Durham House group not only were such sentiments viewed as unedifying they were actually seen as pejorative to the cause of the English Church. In Laudian eyes anti-popery no longer seemed an acceptable form of religious expression, but rather was increasingly seen as a source of potentially seditious activity.[91] Bramhall's theological attitude to Romanism experienced no road to Damascus transformation, it represented little more than an ability to move with the ecclesiastical zeitgeist.

---

88   *BW*, vol. 4, pp. 256–7.
89   Ibid., p. 257.
90   *DNB*, (1968), vol. 8, pp. 60–63.
91   A. Milton, *Catholic and Reformed* (Cambridge, 1995), p. 65.

Ussher and church unity

According to Ussher the Church was so hermetically linked to Christ as to constitute a part of him, 'so nearly conjoined unto him, that he holdeth not himself full without it ... but, as long as any one member remaineth yet ungathered and knit into this mystical body of his, he accounteth, in the mean time, somewhat to be deficient in himself.'[92] In the entire corpus of Protestant literature it would be difficult to find a stronger statement on the importance of Church unity. To suggest in any way that the fullness of Christ is somehow compromised without the presence of the whole Church raises the importance of Christian reconciliation to a level beyond which it is difficult to imagine. But how exactly did Ussher define this body? When he talked of the Church as Christ's bride, of what or of whom was he referring?

In the catechism written and published by Ussher in 1647 he dealt precisely with this question in a similar manner to Calvin, and indeed St Augustine, by dividing the theological concept of the Church into two parts. Firstly in respect to inward nature the Church of God is one, one head, one spirit and one final state. Outwardly however 'there be as many Churches as there be congregations of believers, knit together by special bonds of order for the religious expressing of that inward nature.'[93] The Churches inward and outward are also referred to by Ussher as the invisible and visible Churches. The former being perfect, the latter tainted by the infliction common to all the world. However Ussher is quick to point out that though less than perfect these Churches retained the pure foundations of Christian fundamentals and on this principle he urged unity, 'From Churches holding the foundation, in substance of faith and worship, though otherwise not free from blemish, we are not to separate ... farther then [sic] in dislike and refusal of that wherein they do apparently separate from Christ, in respect their manners, doctrine, or form of public worship.'[94] In his disputation with Malone, Ussher further states that it is precisely the inability or unwillingness of Rome to make this distinction that leads to the presumptions that are at the heart of Christian division, ' ... for the magnifying of that Church, to confound *urbem* and *orbem*: unless he mingle also heaven and earth together, by giving the title of that unspotted Church, which is the special privilege of the Church triumphant in heaven, unto the Church of Rome here militant upon earth.'[95] Preaching before James I in 1624, Ussher provides an alternative to this divisiveness setting out what was to become essentially his mantra on Church unity. The sermon argued that the Church ought not to be sought in any particular branch but rather in all its entirety.[96] An ecclesiological approach which came to be known among Anglicans as 'branch theory.'[97]

---

92 *UW*, vol. 2, pp. 474–5.
93 J. Ussher, *A body of Divinitie or the summe and substance of the Christian Religion* (London, 1647), p. 189.
94 Ibid., p. 398.
95 *UW*, vol. 3, p. 27.
96 *UW*, vol. 2, p. 475.
97 P. Avis, *Anglicanism and the Christian Church* (Edinburgh, 1987), p. 84.

Ussher consistently insisted that a belief in fundamentals, or 'points of religion revealed unto the prophets and apostles'[98] was the only essential of Christianity. At times he defined this with a few articles of faith, and on these he was careful not to be embroiled in dogma. Ussher's criteria is confined to principles and not statements, basic codes which might urge 'a desire to fear God's name, repentance for sins past, and a sincere purpose of heart for the time to come to cleave unto the Lord.'[99] If Ussher talks at all about creedal fundamentals he states that the 'right knowledge' was nothing more than the *Pater Noster* and the creed.[100] Ussher was an energetic sponsor of the Scot, John Drury's scheme for a *pax ecclesiae* which would have reconciled Lutherans and Calvinists in Europe in a system which avoided 'doctrines unprofitable.'[101] If salvation is dependent on membership of a Catholic Church then membership must be based on nothing which goes beyond these basic principles. This approach is reflective of a general trend among seventeenth-century Anglicans who drifted toward simplification.[102] In this way they are clearly determined to pitch their tent in the middle ground between what they saw as Roman innovation and those Protestants more inclined to precisian dogmatics. In the case of Ussher at least, it also reflected a deep seated dismay caused by ecclesiastical discord. It is clear from his passionate sermons on the subject that the strife among continental Protestants that was finding its way into the English Church was to be utterly regretted. In a sermon in 1627, once more before the King, there is a tangible sense of tragedy as he urges his congregation to cast their eyes to the Netherlands from where they might observe those who cause dissensions and division contrary to the doctrine they have learned. Ussher lambasts them as such that 'serve not the Lord Jesus Christ but their own belly.'[103] Of course the finger of blame here is pointed squarely at the Arminians but no-one who considers his own record of co-operation and compromise could doubt the veracity of the sentiments which conclude this sermon when Ussher declares that if he were an Arminian he would keep his knowledge to himself rather than disturb the peace of the Church.[104]

It is perhaps not surprising that given his Irish background, in which he appears to have developed a type of Protestant compound mentality, Ussher was of necessity less fussy than some about the sort of ecclesiastical company he kept. What is surprising, considering his 'mother of harlots' and 'abominations of the earth'[105] statements, is that he by no means excluded the Roman Church from his pantheon of Churches. Ussher's ecclesiology placed so great an importance on fundamentals

---

98 *UW*, vol. 3, p. 41.
99 *UW*, vol.2, p. 483.
100 Bodleian Library, Oxford, Ms. Rawlinson, 'Theological and historical extracts by Ussher', D. 280.
101 101 E. Boran, 'Propagating religion and endeavouring the reformation of the whole World: Irish bishops and the Hartlib circle in the mid-seventeenth century' in V.P. Carey and V. Lotz-Heumann (eds), *Taking sides? Colonial and confessional mentalites in early modern Ireland* (Dublin, 2002), p. 169.
102 *Anglicanism*, eds P.E. More and F.L. Cross (London, 1935), pp. xxvi–xxvii.
103 *UW*, vol. 13, p. 343.
104 Ibid., p. 350.
105 Ibid. vol. 2, p. 457.

that he was forced to conclude that the essence of these remained in place as a foundation within Rome. Unlike Foxe therefore, and the majority of Jacobean churchmen, Ussher did not regard Rome as a false Church. The Christian foundation of Rome remained even though the Antichrist has raised his own building upon it, an edifice not of 'hay and stubble only, but far more vile and pernicious matter, which wrencheth and disturbeth the very foundation itself.'[106] What, according to Ussher's interpretation, the Antichrist does not do however is destroy the groundwork, for as Ussher points out the light of truth is so strong that the power of darkness cannot extinguish it, nor the gates of hell prevail against it.[107] These sentiments are echoed elsewhere, in his own private notebook in which the differences in essentials are markedly downplayed.

> The decision of them that have departed from the Church of Rome unto the Church of Christ is not in articles of faith nor such, but that they are all brethren, that unfeignedly profess the doctrine of salvation; although they dissent in the matter of the sacraments, in orders, rites and ceremonies. Their variance is in no greater matters, then that between two godly martyrs of the primitive church Cornelius of Rome and Cyprian of Carthage.[108]

In his 1625 discourse with Malone, Ussher is similarly disarming in his treatment of Rome declaring that it is not every spot that taketh away the beauty of a Church, nor every sickness its life, he concludes 'there is no necessity, that hereupon presently she must cease to be our sister.'[109] More remarkable still is Ussher's statement before the throne in 1624 that this conviction that Christian fundamentals had an overriding significance led him in Ireland to propose a joint mission with the Catholic Church to 'teach those main points, the knowledge whereof was so necessary unto salvation; and of the truth whereof there was no controversy betwixt us.'[110] It was of course a common polemical tactic at this time to use such devices in order to show that the non co-operation of the 'other side' resulted in a loss for Christianity, yet this is not the case with Ussher who blames both parties for the projects failure. In a pronouncement so full of liberal self-deprecation it would not have been out of place at a modern day ecumenical forum he declares, 'But what for the jealousies, which these distractions in matters of religion have bred among us, and what for other respects, the motion took small effect, and so betwixt us both the poor people are kept in miserable ignorance neither knowing the grounds of one religion or the other.'[111] That is not to say that there was not a certain amount of hyperbole in this statement and it is impossible to know if Ussher ever made such an offer (certainly no evidence remains) however the significance of these sentiments lie more in the fact that they were said at all, and said in the presence of the monarch.

---

106 Ibid., p. 490.
107 Ibid., p. 492.
108 Bodleian Library, Oxford, Ms. Rawlinson, C.919, 'Theological commonplaces of Archbishop Ussher.'
109 *UW*, vol. 2, p. 28.
110 Ibid., p. 499.
111 Ibid.

It is at first difficult to juxtapose the inflammatory nature and vitriolic content of some of Ussher's anti-Rome outpourings with these eirenic and conciliatory statements. Indeed Paul Avis argues that in this respect Ussher is something of a phenomenon. Ussher, he concludes, differs from the radical Protestants in that he includes Rome in the Church Catholic, and from the extreme high Churchmen in that he includes the Churches of the Reformation.[112] However Ussher is far from unique in this respect, Hooker and even George Downam and Thomas Beard all accepted that the Pope was antichrist but rejected the notion that this implied Rome was not a true Church.[113] There is a tendency among historians to put people into anti-Catholic straitjackets from which they are either unable or unwilling to escape. It was rare for Protestant polemicist to deny absolutely that Rome was a Church of Christ, it was more often argued, even by Puritans, that it was a particular Church.[114] Nevertheless Ussher's treatment of the Roman Church often sits awkwardly together as if there is a type of dualism in his ecclesiology which at once condemns in the fiery apocalyptic diatribes of the prophet, and considers with the moderate appreciation of the academic historian. It is probably fair to say that these reflect aspects of a theology which might express itself in either form depending on the perceived need. If at times it appears incongruous it must be placed in the historical context of incongruous times. It might also be added that incongruous though it may be it is never self-contradictory. Firstly Ussher is too fond of antiquity to consign so many of the patriarchs to perdition by damning completely their Church. Ussher's solution is to distinguish the papacy and the Church in the way he claims the apostle distinguished the Antichrist and the Temple. Our ancestors were preserved by God, from what Ussher calls the 'mortality of popery.'[115] Ussher explains, 'For popery itself is nothing else but the botch or the plague of that Church, which hazardeth the souls of those it seizeth upon, as much as any infection can do the body.'[116] Like any other disease the effects are in the very least debilitating but a strong body can survive infection, just as a worthy soul can survive corruption.

Secondly, in spite of Ussher's political misgivings about Roman plots and machinations it is clear that he is most exercised in his writings and sermons by a fear of crypto-Catholicism rather than by the overt presence of the Roman Church. In spite also of his torrid denouncements and prophecies it is worth noting that these look to a time when the antichrist sat in a true temple. Ussher's prophetic vision relies on Rome being a true Church. Besides Ussher is far too wedded to the notion that the foundation is set in Christ and the essence of membership based on a few fundamentals of faith to damn the Church of Rome in its entirety. This he knew would contradict the systematic basis of his ecclesiastical policy but as Janus-headed as his approach appears it never slips into inconsistency.

---

112   Avis, *Anglicanism*, p. 84.
113   Milton, *Catholic and Reformed*, p. 106.
114   A. Milton, 'A qualified intolerance: the limits and ambiguities of -arly Stuart anti-Catholicism', in A.F. Marotti (ed.), *Catholicism and Anti-Catholicism in Early Modern English Text* (London, 1999), pp. 88–9.
115   *UW*, vol. 2, p. 490.
116   Ibid., p. 493.

Bramhall and church unity

When Ussher considered the holiness of the Church, like Luther and Calvin, he attributed it to the invisible Church in its heavenly perfection and in the visible Church it might only be encountered within degrees of righteousness. Such spiritual and physical demarcation is not present in the theology of Bramhall, indeed his concept of holiness was entirely informed by the biblical concept of *kadosh* which we have previously referred to as the numinous motif. In turn this forms a central plank in Bramhall's ecclesiastical policy. In a sermon preached on the coronation of Charles II the new Primate of Ireland sums up the previous years of turmoil with direct reference to the Old Testament. The exile of the King and his Church is characterised in a strong biblical metaphor full of import and reverence for the visible Church.

> First, the temple, which was the glory of Sion, was demolished. Then, the ceremonies, and sacrifices and ordinances of Sion were abolished. Thirdly the holy vessels and garments and other utensils and sacred ornaments were exported. Lastly, the Priests, and Levites, and people of God were all carried away captive. These were the living Sion; without these, Sion was but a dead carcass of itself.[117]

Earlier the letters of Bramhall to Laud written during the first days of his arrival in Ireland were full of shocked displeasure at the casual deprecation of churches that he encountered in his journeys. Laud's envoy was particularly incensed by the tomb that Richard Boyle, the Earl of Cork, had erected in place of the altar in St Patrick's Cathedral.

> I cannot omit the glorious tomb in the other Cathedral Church of St Patrick, in the proper place of the Altar, just opposite to his Majesty's seat, having his father's name superscribed upon it, as if it were contriv'd a purpose to gain the worship and reverence which the Chapter and the whole Church are bound by special statute to give toward the East.[118]

Bramhall adds acidly, 'Credimus esse Deos ?'

Because this type of ecclesiological perspective is informed by the numinous motif it does not see the Church in terms of invisible perfection and visible imperfection. Bramhall declares himself much more inclined to the distinction between the nature and essence of the Church, what he terms its 'integrity and perfection.'[119] This is a similar concept to the visible/invisible dichotomy but the change of emphasis has meaning. For Ussher the visible Church was part of the fallen world and forever tainted with its sin. Bramhall approaches from a different angle saying that the Church in nature contains something of the very essence of God. Its integrity is vouchsafed by the presence in some degree of God's perfection. This was the theological reason why the Church and also the churches are to be considered separate and holy, they are *kadosh*. Interestingly Bramhall credits Thomas Stapleton with the nature and essence distinction. Stapleton (1535–98) was the most pre-eminent English, Roman

---

117   *BW*, vol. 5, p. 114.
118   *BW*, vol. 1, pp. lxxix–lxxx.
119   *BW*, vol. 1, p. 24.

Catholic controversialist of his generation whom Anthony Wood was later to call 'the most learned Roman Catholic of all his time.'[120]

In his *Vindication*, written against Richard Baxter's accusations of popery Bramhall argued that his ideas on Church unity were 'from my Lord Primate', obviously referring to Ussher. Bramhall explained their shared principle that 'agreement in the high and necessary points of faith and obedience ought to be more effectual to unite us than our difference in opinions divide us.'[121] Ostensibly the basis of Church unity was raised on this fundamental principle, a core of central truths ought, in theory, aid unity to a greater degree than differences in practice cause separation. It would have been difficult in this era to find a Christian who did not at least pertain to espouse such a view, schism was generally considered an indictment. However, further reading of Bramhall indicates that underneath this façade of shared aspirations there lay an utterly different vision to Ussher of what exactly constituted the universal Church. The starting point of this different vision may be traced to their respective notions of what exactly their national Churches represented.

Underscoring Bramhall's ecclesiology of the English Church is an overt appreciation of an essentially Catholic nature. In his *Answer to S.W.*, Bramhall categorically denies that the English Reformers were Protestant.

> What then, were Warham, and Heath, and Thurlesby, Tunstall, and Stokesley, and Gardiner, and Bonner, &c., [*Henrician bishops*] all Protestants? Did Protestants enjoy Archbishoprics and Bishoprics in England, and say Masses, in those days? Will he part so easily with the greatest patrons and champions of their Church, and opposers of the Reformation?[122]

In other places Bramhall claims that the English martyrs died as 'Roman Catholics' maintaining the Six Articles of faith.[123] They did so according to Bramhall 'for faith not faction.'[124] Elsewhere he begs his correspondent not to 'perplex' his country's Church with other Protestant Churches with their 'heterogeneous disputes.'[125] The same treatise describes these 'other Protestants', in terms reminiscent of Ussher's anti-papist outpourings, as 'like those misshapen creatures which were produced out of the slime of Nilus by the heat of the sun, which perished soon after they were generated, for want of fit organs.'[126]

Bramhall is prepared to use the word Protestant self-descriptively, but only occasionally. His answer to John Sergeant accepts the term reluctantly if it means those who deny the 'absolute universal monarchy' of the Pope, and in this case then he adds that the Greeks and Russians must be Protestants also.[127] Bramhall indicates that the essential difference between the English and Protestant Churches

---

120 A.A. Wood, *Athenae Oxonienses* (London, 1820), vol. 1, p. 669.
121 *BW*, vol. 3, p. 571.
122 *BW*, vol.2, p. 295.
123 Ibid., pp. 98–9.
124 *BW*, vol. 1, p. 577.
125 *BW*, vol. 2, p. 43.
126 Ibid., pp. 47–8.
127 Ibid., vol. 1, p. 295.

is their lack of succession. England has, he proudly asserts, 'an ordinary vocation.' Unlike the newly emerged creatures of the Nile who lack history and therefore organs, the English Church is part of a living breathing tradition. Like the Churches of antiquity Bramhall's Church is not new 'for then we must produce new miracles, new revelations.'[128] Like the independent Churches of Africa and the East they can trace autonomy to an apostolic tradition.[129] Bramhall does so for the English Church through Joseph of Arimathea, who he argues was only technically not an apostle.[130] It follows from this that when Bramhall refers to other Churches, when he calls for unity with these bodies, he is not looking North, as Ussher does, but South and East. Bramhall, shares Ussher's desire to end separation, he departs from Ussher in seeing this separation exclusively in terms of the pre-Reformation Churches. Ussher may not be the ribald anti-Romanist that is often suggested but for all his rhetoric the disunity in the Church which hurt him was Protestant disunity. Ussher despaired at the growing disharmony among the Reformed Churches of the continent and England, Bramhall displays no concern for the former and precious little for the latter. Whilst Ussher wants to paper over cracks in Protestantism Bramhall wants to build bridges to the old Churches of Russia, Greece, Antioch, Jerusalem, Ethiopia, the Coptic and Armenian Churches, and above all to the Church of Rome.[131] For Bramhall these Churches contained some of God's essence and they therefore had integrity. Because they were repositories of God, they were real Churches.

Bramhall made his position clear on Rome very early on in his Irish career, on 4 August 1633 he preached on the text 'thou art Peter' arguing that the church of Rome was only 'schismaticall' and that the Pope was a patriarch.[132] He shares Ussher's view that the separation of the English Church from Rome was not over fundamentals of faith. However, Ussher's reputation appears to have afforded him a certain ecclesiological license, Bramhall did not get away with it so lightly. The Scottish Presbyterian Robert Baille railed against 'Dr Bramhell' the 'pretended bishop of Londonderry' for this very theological issue.[133] From the Catholic side 'R.C.' concludes that Bramhall's position was contradictory since at the same time as arguing that Rome was a true Church he attempted to say that it was legal to separate from her, 'Talk therefore no more of any cause, which the Roman church may have given you to depart from her communion, till you have proved she is no true Church of God in substance, which you can not say, because you teach she is the same Church in substance with yours.'[134] Bramhall's riposte was that the Church of Rome and not the English Church had been guilty of schism since it was they who had separated from the other Catholic Churches.[135]

---

128   Ibid., p. 199.
129   Ibid., vol. 2. p. 453.
130   Ibid., p. 299.
131   *BW*, vol. 1, p. 100, vol. 3, p. 557.
132   *DNB* (2004), vol. 7, p. 313.
133   R. Baylie, *A Review of the seditious pamphlet lately published in Holland by Dr Bramhell pretended bishop of Londonderry* (London, 1649), p. 5.
134   R.C., *A brief survey of the Lord of Derry* (Paris, 1655), pp. 141–2.
135   *BW*, vol.. 1, p.97. This produced at least one outraged response which pointed out that since the breach came via Henry VIII, Rome could not be imputable to subsequent

Like many of his contemporaries, including Laud and Cosin, Bramhall accepted Rome as a true Church (as indicated with Ussher this was not uncommon) however what appears in Ussher and others as a general acceptance comes across in Bramhall as something akin to a predisposition. It has been argued that there is nothing new in the approaches of the Laudians to the Church of Rome, any apparent distinctions were merely ones of stress.[136] However, in one respect this analysis is incorrect, in terms of hierarchy among the Churches the Laudians represented a new departure. A study in 1982 pointed out that the Laudian stress on collegiality of bishops seems to have led to a logical progression.

> ... when we come to the question of a simple Rome primacy we find instances of flexibility which arise from the writers' knowledge of Church history and from the fact that there is no inbuilt resistance in Anglicanism to the concept of primacy per se. It is noticeable that ... Anglicans such as Field, Bramhall, Cosin and Laud could conceive of a primacy of order or dignity within a strongly collegial setting.[137]

Several times Bramhall indicates that he is prepared to accept the primacy of Rome declaring that the Pope had priority of order, he was 'omni praesidet creature', above every creature. In the Council he was styled 'Ecumenical or Universal.' Though when Bramhall argues this he adds that it is in 'care' and not 'power.'[138] 'That is no more than to say, that the Bishop of Rome, as successor to St Peter, is 'principium unitatis' – the beginning of unity, or hath a principality of order (not of power) above all Christians.'[139] To the objection from Richard Baxter that the Eastern Churches would not accept this primacy, Bramhall cleverly points out that they did so at the great Council of Nicea.[140]

As mentioned before, Bramhall is by no means the only voice in the English Church affected by such ultramontanism, but he has been called the most noteworthy because he is the most theological.[141] Richard Montagu has been singled out as the sole representative of an English desire to reconcile with Rome. In Montagu's discussion with the Papal nuncio, Parzani, Milton ponders how much support the Laudians would have given him concluding that Laud himself appears to have been indifferent.[142] A reading of Bramhall strongly suggests that he would have found an ally in the bishop of Derry. Bramhall himself cites not only Richard Montagu as a supporter but rather optimistically Lancelot Andrews and even King James I in his *Apology for the Oath of Allegiance*. Bramhall quotes Montagu's *De Originibus Ecclesiasticis Commentationes* (1636). The words in parenthesis are his glosses.[143]

---

excommunication, 'Tis plain, since the effect cannot be before the cause.' Anonymous, *Twenty-one Conclusions* (Oxford, 1688), B.L. 222.e.4.

136 Georges, *Protestant Mind*, p. 387.
137 J.C.H. Aveling et al., *Rome and the Anglicans* (Berlin, 1982), p. 166.
138 *BW*, vol. 3, pp. 144–5.
139 Ibid.
140 *BW*, vol. 3, p. 557.
141 J.C.H. Aveling et al., *Rome*, p. 275.
142 Milton, *Catholic and Reformed*, p. 371.
143 BW, vol. 3, pp. 568–9.

> Let the Bishop of Rome have delegated unto him [that is, by the Church] a power or order, direction, counsel, consultation, conclusion [or pronouncing sentence] and putting in execution; but let that power be subject to the Church, let it be in the Church's power to take it away seeing it is not instituted in the Holy Scripture, not tied personally unto Peter.[144]

Herein lies Bramhall's remedy to the problem of disunity which he elsewhere sets out in three clear 'conditions for peace and reunion.' Firstly, the Bishop of Rome would be reduced from his universality to his *principium unitatis*; secondly the necessary points of faith would be reduced to what they were at the first four ecumenical councils; and thirdly 'things' which caused offence 'but did not weigh half so much as Christian unity' would be removed.[145] Bramhall's agenda is thus clear through these measures he sets out a programme of reconciliation, but one which seeks to reconcile the pope to the English Church and not the other way around.[146] The fundamental difference between the respective visions of Ussher and Bramhall of a unified Christendom once more reflect their inclinations toward the justice motif and the numinous motif. Ussher is concerned with the word and law of God, in reducing this to its most basic formula he hoped to gather the Churches around the minimum of unifying principles or laws. Bramhall is more concerned that the holy and apostolic Churches, those which represent the *kadosh* idea of separate and blessed institutions, ought to unite around their spiritual home. In this sense Rome was the Christian equivalent of the Jerusalem Temple, the Holy of holies. Crucial to the future of this working relationship was the papal acceptance that you can only be a centre if you are part of a whole, Rome was not greater than the sum of its parts, or as Bramhall put it, 'The World is greater than the city.'[147]

---

144 Ibid.
145 Ibid., p. 545.
146 Ibid., p. 546.
147 Ibid., vol. 2, p. 295.

Chapter 8

Practical Policy

Thus far it has been the purpose of this book to examine the ideological and theological make-up of Ussher and Bramhall. For this reason it has been largely confined to the realm of the mind. However the question remains; how did their respective, and somewhat differing mindsets translate in terms of praxis? There is sometimes quite a divergence between the written word and the actions of men of letters. Did Ussher and Bramhall remain true to their own often precise formulas? This final chapter sets out to examine their respective careers as high officers in the established Church. It will be demonstrated that the justice and numinous motifs which provided the mainstay of their theological speculations also informed their practical activities. Ussher is driven by the law of God located in the word of God and it is not much of a generalisation to say that he built the entire framework of his practical policy on this motivation. Conversely Bramhall seeks to establish, or more correctly as he sees it, re-establish a Church whose splendour and formality will promote the sacred mysteries. In this way the bishop of Derry believed he was recreating a Church worthy of its name and one which would be numbered among the ancient Churches of the world. It might be presumed that such diverse visions would almost certainly produce the kind of internecine conflict between the two bishops that their counterparts in England were at this time experiencing, this was not the case. As diametrically opposed as their theological tendencies may have been, Ussher and Bramhall were united by an overriding loyalty and sense of service to the English crown. Whatever tangents of policy they respectively pursued they were always joined at their base to the throne and its established Church. It seems Bramhall was in the end right, they may have burnt their lights at opposite ends of the Levitical candle but its solid base was what held them aloft, and it also held them together. We will now discuss the practical policies of Ussher and Bramhall prior to, during, and after what was perhaps the most important event of their careers, the 1634 Irish Convocation of the established Church.

Ussher's practical policy pre-Convocation

On 2 December 1622 James I nominated his royal chaplain, Ussher, to the bishopric of Meath and he was consecrated the following June at St Peter's, Drogheda.[1] He was, at that time, presented with an anagram of his name, 'James Meath, I am the

---

1   Elrington dates this at June 1621, he does, however, admit that this is only probable and that he has no evidence. Elrington, *Life*, p. 56; Buick Knox gives it the correct dating, showing that June 1621 was when he was nominated. Knox, *Ussher*, p. 28.

same', but the words he chose for himself, to be inscribed on his episcopal seal, were *Vae mihi, nisi evangelizarero,* Woe to me if I do not evangelise.[2] One nineteenth-century study expressed surprise that Ussher was considered at the time because after the Synod of Dort James I was gravitating more toward the Arminians. It concluded that Ussher's standing and the personal esteem of the King, 'entirely outweighed the objections which the doctrinal view he advocated may have caused.'[3] If Kenneth Fincham is correct this could have been part of a scheme that James maintained of equiliberal representation among his episcopacy. Composition of the bench was 'intimately linked to ... attempts to construct a united national Church incorporating a wide spectrum of theological opinions.'[4] Conrad Russell is more specific. He saw the appointment as part of an underhand plan by the throne in which they sought to keep the Scots on side by promoting a 'believer in a severely limited episcopacy very like what had been approved at Linlithgow in 1606.'[5] However, this is placing the Ussherian compromise far too early; as already stated there is no indication that Ussher maintained such a system until he proposed it as a compromise during the very turbulent situation that developed in 1641.

Ussher's episcopal career was characterised by absenteeism and lack of interest. From the outset the fledgling bishop already had the appearance of the bookish academic, ill-equipped for the finely balanced world of politics in which diplomacy was considered a higher virtue than the pursuit of eternal verities. There are some signs that Ussher felt that he had strayed too far from his more familiar surroundings. In 1623 he applied for and was granted unlimited leave of absence by the Irish Privy Council in order to pursue his studies. Ussher left for London where he was charged by the King to collect antiquities of the British Church.[6] He was also commanded to reside at one of the universities but during his long periods of time in the capital he lodged with George Montaigne, then bishop of London.[7] Ussher remained absent from Ireland until 1626, that year Primate Hampton died and James was elevated to the see of Armagh.[8]

Shortly after his appointment the new Primate was embroiled in the controversy surrounding the Irish bishops' protest. As already indicated in the previous chapter the incident not only illustrates a certain lack of political subtlety in Ussher, it also

---

2   *Two Biographies of William Bedell,* ed. E.S. Shuckburgh (Cambridge, 1902), p. 161.

3   J.T. Ball, *The Reformed Church of Ireland* (London, 1886), p. 107.

4   K. Fincham, *Prelate as Pastor* (Oxford, 1990), p. 25.

5   The General Assembly of Linlithow had made bishops permanent moderators of the presbyteries. C. Russell, *The Fall of the British Monarchies, 1637–1642* (Oxford, 1991), p. 33.

6   E.W. Watson, 'James Ussher', in W.E. Collins (ed.), *Typical English Churchmen* (London, 1902), p. 60.

7   Montaigne provides another example of the eclectic nature of Ussher's associates. The bishop of London belonged very much to the high Church party, he was an ardent ally of Laud. He preached, like Ussher, passive obedience and received the commendation of Charles I when he allowed the erection and adoration of images in his churches. *DNB,* (1968), vol. 13, pp. 723–4.

8   Knox, *Ussher,* p. 35.

proves that when it came to the crunch the Primate was more than willing to kowtow. It also proves one other point, that is Ussher, in the first years of his tenancy as Primate had obviously resolved to play more of a proactive role. In the summer of 1628 this new approach bore some early fruit. Charles I wrote to his Lord Deputy in Ireland (in response to representation from Ussher) to order 'that further encouragement' be given to the Irish Church. The King commanded that escheated lands in Munster pass immediately to the clergy, lands given for maintaining free schools were to be passed to the Archbishop of Armagh in trust. Further Ussher's office was to be awarded more power to appoint surrogates, register and pursuivants 'as is done by the Archbishop of Canterbury.'[9] If these measures were designed to shore up the established Church in Ireland then it would appear that, initially at least, Charles envisaged his Irish Primate as playing a key role in any improvement. By 1631 however Charles' correspondence with Ussher has an air of dissatisfaction with the slow progress. The King informs Ussher in no uncertain terms that he must require his clergy 'remove all pretences of scandal in their lives.'[10] Ussher promptly issued this injunction and even went so far as to present a less hostile façade to the recusant population inviting them to discuss their religious differences.[11]

Not everyone was so negative in their assessment of the situation in Ussher's Ireland. Indeed the Irish Church was something of a religio–political litmus test. Depending on which way you inclined in the 1630s and 1640s your view of Ireland would either be positive or negative. The Arminians saw it as a shambolic failure and the Calvinists as a working example of a godly Church. Sir Thomas Barrington wrote enviously about the tough regime that Ussher imposed on recusants.

> Neither public mass is said nor any of this rabble presumes to walk abroad with their former confidence, so that there is great hope of much better times in that kingdom, thanks be to God. The Lord Primate hath bled lately with such violence in his tongue, as that he was compelled to have it seared twice ... but God be praised he is perfectly well and hath begot a wonderous reformation in his northern parts of Ireland, where the light of trueth is broken forth in great lustre.[12]

In 1628 Ussher began what has been described as his 'voluminous correspondence' with William Laud who was acting as a type of surrogate Primate in England.[13] Their relationship got off to a auspicious start as Ussher confided to his good friend Samuel Ward, 'For my L[ord] Primate, he useth me with as much respect as I could desire, and I take him to be as you describe him, a marvellous good and true hearted man.'[14] Hugh Trevor-Roper drew a picture of the two prelates as philosophically opposed and mutually mistrusting. He writes, 'In Laud's eyes, Ussher, to buy puritan support, was prepared to sacrifice some of the essentials of episcopacy; to Ussher,

---

9   *Cal.S.P.Ire. 1625–1632*, pp. 3634.
10   W.A. Philips, *A History of the Church of Ireland* (3 vols, Oxford, 1933), vol. 3, p. 8.
11   Ibid.
12   *The Barrington Family Letters, 1628–1632*, ed. A. Searle (London, 1983), p. 138.
13   Carr, *Life*, p. 223.
14   *William Bedell*, Shuckburgh, p. 294.

Laud, in his campaign against Puritanism, was sacrificing some of the essentials of Protestantism.'[15] In reality the two managed, in spite of some stormy incidents, and despite two quite different theological perspectives, to maintain a reasonable friendship if not affection. Undoubtedly Ussher fell foul of Laud on occasion, but then few people did not; and when the Archbishop of Canterbury was finally executed, Ussher was genuinely devastated exclaiming that he 'did believe 'twould spoil all.'[16]

An incident in 1631 involving the two Primates indicates that the success of their relationship rested to some extent on Ussher's willingness to acquiesce to the will of Laud. In that year George Downham, the bishop of Derry, had injudiciously entered the theological fray centred on the predestination debate by publishing a book setting out his Calvinistic soteriology. Since the book was published in Ireland Ussher must have endorsed it, indeed it has been argued that the Primate furnished Downham with material for the work.[17] However, in the ensuing agitation he unashamedly passed the buck. Writing to Laud, Ussher declared, 'What did pass here before in the press at Dublin, I had no eye unto, because it was out of my province, and the care I suppose did more properly belong unto my brother of Dublin.'[18] In order to prevent further trouble Ussher appointed William Bedell to overlook the press and ensure that it gave no further offence.[19] This is not an incident from which Ussher's reputation emerges completely unblemished. Not alone did he backtrack but he appears to have been less than honest. J.S. Reid, whilst otherwise an Ussher enthusiast, found the affair distasteful.

> It is truly painful to find the venerable Primate betrayed into servile compliance by his timid and irresolute spirit. Through fear of displeasing this haughty and powerful prelate, Ussher meanly lent himself to the violent suppression of a work, which was not only in perfect accordance with his own sentiments, but also with the accredited standards of the Church of which he was the high officer.[20]

Once more it is clear that for Ussher, theological principles, as well as personal political convictions were all eclipsed by the overriding obligation that was service to the English crown. In addition to this sense of duty Ussher appears to be impressed by the strength of Laud's character and conviction, he clearly believed that this would be a useful force in Irish ecclesiastical life. In 1631 he wrote with obvious

---

15   Roper, *Catholics, Anglicans and Puritans*, p. 143.
16   *The Journal of Thomas Juxon, 1644–1647*, eds K. Lindley and D. Scott, Camden Society, 5th Series, vol. 13, (Cambridge, 1999), p. 41.
17   N. Murphy, 'Archbishop Ussher', *Irish Ecclesiastical Record* (February 1897): 154.
18   W. Prynne, *Canterburies Doome* (London, 1646), pp. 17–18. This letter was eventually to haunt Laud as Prynne recovered correspondence with Ussher from his study to prove that he had 'exercised a kind of Patriarchal jurisdiction, for suppressing all orthodox books against the Arminians both in England and Ireland.' It was noted by Prynne that his commands were 'punctually executed' by those Archbishops who 'should have most stoutly opposed his Arminian innovations.' Ibid.
19   J. Collier, *An ecclesiastical history of Great Britain* (London, 1707), p. 750.
20   Reid, *Presbyterian History*, vol. 1, p. 164.

relish to Laud about the effect his reputation has, 'You strike such a terror into the hearts of those who wish to despoil the Church that if I merely mention your name at the Council table it is like the Gorgon's head to some of them.'[21] Tellingly, in the same letter, Ussher is trying to hold on to his influence in the internal affairs of the Irish church. He conveys to Laud his frank displeasure at hearing that the Arminian Henry Leslie had been given the see at Raphoe.[22] However it is not the theological issue that concerns Ussher, indeed two years previously he had recommended Leslie for preferment to Laud as a 'great supporter of yours.'[23] Leslie's crime with regard to Ussher occurred in the ensuing years when he had forced the issue of non-conformity by bringing examples of it in his diocese to the attention not only of the authorities in Dublin, but worse still, London.[24] Ussher adds to his complaint that he hoped that John Richardson and George Andrews would be remembered when future sees fell vacant. Ussher's influence was waning as the English establishment began to tighten their grip on Irish affairs, Ussherian *laissez-faire* was about to give way to Laudian state control.

As John Morrill has indicated 'Nothing in James's reign prepared the Irish Protestant establishment for the onslaught on their Church to be mounted by William Laud.'[25] The English Archbishop involved himself in the ecclesiastical affairs of Ireland to an unprecedented degree. He told Ussher to send him the present names of bishops and deans,[26] he requested an evaluation of Church lands,[27] and he nominated his own candidates whenever any Irish sees became vacant.[28] If Ussher resented this new form of direct control he never articulated his feelings. On the contrary his correspondence gives an almost unqualified welcome to the interest Laud was taking in his Church. As mentioned above he was quite prepared to bow to England even when this ran contrary to his own dogmatic theology or ecclesiastical policy. If further evidence of this Ussherian trait is needed then it is provided by a well documented incident in the 1630s in which the Irish Primate rescinded on perhaps the most important guiding principle of his practical policy. For Ussher Protestant unity in Ireland was imperative, if his tenure of Church government could be characterised by any one axiom it would probably be 'United we stand, divided we fall.' Yet even in this he was prepared to give way to what he considered to be the higher consideration of service to the throne.

Two Scottish ministers, Robert Blair and John Livingston, both graduates of Glasgow University, had landed themselves in hot water with their bishop for 'uncanonical and schismatic conduct.' They were apparently teaching the necessity

---

21   *Cal.S.P.Ire. 1625–1632*, p. 622.
22   Ibid.
23   Ibid., September 11, 1629, p. 481.
24   A. Ford, 'The origins of Irish dissent', in K. Herlihy (ed.), *The Religion of Irish Dissent, 1650–1800* (Dublin, 1996), p. 22.
25   J. Morrill, 'A British patriarchy? Ecclesiastical imperialism under the early Stuarts,' in A. Fletcher and P. Roberts (eds), *Religion, Culture and Society in Early Modern Britain* (Cambridge, 1994), p. 222.
26   Laud, *Works*, vol. 6, p. 262.
27   Ibid., p. 261.
28   Ibid., p. 52.

of bodily pain and exciting ecstasies among their congregations.[29] The fact that Blair was later to call Cromwell a 'greeting devil' indicates something of his extreme views.[30] In the midst of their difficulties they appealed to Ussher, not only as the Primate but as someone who would be potentially disposed favourably to their plight. Blair left an interesting account of his visit to Ussher's house in which he expressed his disapprobation of the non-Calvinist worship he found, writing, 'I had expected another thing than formal liturgies in the family of so learned and pious a man.' Nevertheless he arranged a second meeting at Drogheda which appears to have fared better and after quizzing Blair on predestination and liturgy Ussher declared himself satisfied. Blair reported, 'For when I had freely opened my grievances, he admitted that all these things ought to have been removed, but the constitution and laws of the place and time would not permit that to be done.'[31] Ussher's biographers were sceptical about this account, Elrington called it 'notoriously false'[32] and W.B. Wright wrote that it ought to be taken 'cum grano salis.'[33] Nevertheless, they were objecting as established Church of England clerics anxious to claim Ussher as one of their own, and whatever Ussher did or did not say the outcome of their conference was a letter to their bishop requesting that he relax 'his erroneous censure.'[34]

Blair may have exaggerated the extent of Ussher's sympathy but it does appear that he got what he wanted from the meeting. Elsewhere Ussher was putting a very different public face on the incident. In 1631 he formally complained about their activities to the Lord Justices in Dublin and he castigated bishop Echlin for 'winking at this disorder, protesting that I would complain to the state and procure a certificate at their irregularity to be transmitted unto England.'[35] It is worth noting that when the two ministers got into trouble again in 1637 the Laudian regime had by now dug deep into Irish affairs. Their new bishop was John Maxwell, an Edinburgh minister and a hammer of Canterbury's programme. Maxwell appealed to the King and the Primate's decision to reinstate the recalcitrants was overruled.[36] After this, appeal to Ussher was not only fruitless but unwelcome, they were told curtly that the archbishop was no longer able to help them.[37] Reid's assertion that he did so with tears in his eyes seems unlikely;[38] what is certain is that whilst Ussher may have had no taste for expulsion, and he valued highly the *terra firma* of a broad Protestant common ground, his empathy was never going to be allowed to compromise his deep sense of duty.

---

29   Reid, *Presbyterian History*, vol. 1, p. 135.
30   Lady Burghclere, *Strafford*, vol. 1, p. 93.
31   Reid, *Presbyterian History*, vol. 1, pp. 136–7.
32   Elrington, *Life*, pp. 148–9.
33   W.B. Wright, *The Ussher Memoirs* (London, 1889), p. 94.
34   Reid, *Presbyterian History*, vol. 1, p. 137.
35   Ford, 'Origins of dissent', p. 22.
36   H. Trevor-Roper, *Archbishop Laud*, p. 233. Blair was to later assert that the direct intervention of Bramhall prevented an extension to this reprieve. M. Perceval-Maxwell, 'Ulster Scots': 525–6.
37   Elrington, *Life*, p. 149.
38   Reid, *Presbyterian History*, vol. 1, pp. 142–3.

Bramhall's practical policy pre-Convocation

The Laudian policy with regard to the Churches of the three Kingdoms has engendered some debate among historians. Conrad Russell has argued that there existed a determined will to enforce uniformity throughout the realms.[39] Julian Davies agrees adding that Charles was eager to pursue an impulsive programme that would lead to British conformity.[40] On the other hand John Morrill holds that the Laudian idea of conformity (saving the areas of restoring and jurisdiction) was much more personal than institutional.[41] Whilst Kenneth Fincham maintains that Charles sought uniformity throughout his realms simply because he held that the English Church came 'nearest to the purity of the primitive doctrine and discipline.'[42] Whatever their motives it is certain that in the 1630s the English administration was determined to have a much more 'hands on' approach when it came to the affairs of Ireland. When Bramhall was selected to accompany Wentworth to Ireland it is hard not to believe that they saw in him an antidote to Ussher's pedestrian style.

The official royal agenda as articulated by Charles (after a conference with Laud) was double pronged. Wentworth was to restore the Irish Church to a position in which it would be able to evangelise the Catholic population. He would also provide it with a surer foundation by consolidating the union of the two established Churches.[43] This meant essentially scrapping the Irish Articles of Faith as well as their distinct canons, and replacing them with English Articles and canons, though Charles was prepared to make the concession that English models 'were to be adapted to fit the constitutions and customs of the country.'[44] In fact the idea of replacing the Irish Articles had come from Bramhall who first suggested it to Laud in a letter in 1633. Bramhall wrote,

> I doubt much whether the clergy be very orthodox and could wish both the Articles and Canons of the Church of England were established here by Act of Parliament or state; yet as we live all under one kingdom, so we might both in doctrine and discipline deserve an uniformity.[45]

Initially perhaps the most conspicuous aspect of the new policy was its approach to recusants. Alan Ford has written, 'As Bramhall, Laud and Wentworth saw it, the main problem for the Church of Ireland was not the Catholic threat, or recusancy, but

---

39   C. Russell, 'The British problem and the English civil war', *History*, 72 (1987): 399.
40   J. Davies, *The Caroline captivity of the Church, Charles I and the remoulding of Anglicanism, 1625–1641* (Oxford, 1992), passim.
41   Morrill, 'British patriarchy?', pp. 223–7.
42   K. Fincham, 'The ecclesiastical policies of James I and Charles I', in Fincham *The Early Stuart Church*, p. 49.
43   A. Ford, 'Dependent or independent: the Church of Ireland and its colonial context, 1536–1649', *The Seventeenth Century*, X, no. 2 (August, 1995): 174.
44   Laud, *Works*, vol. 7, p.66.
45   *BW*, vol. 1, pp. lxxx–lxxxii.

the non-conformity, theological extremism, abuses and poverty of the established Church itself.[46] Reminiscing about his time in office Bramhall wrote;

> I remember not one Roman Catholic that suffered in all that time, but only the titular Archbishop of Cashel. We did our work by more noble and more successful means than penal laws – by building of Churches and mansion houses for ministers, by introducing a learned clergy, by enjoining them residence, by affording them countenance and protection and means of hospitality, by planting and ordering schools for the education of youth ... .[47]

This is not meant to imply any predisposition of Bramhall or Wentworth towards the Irish Roman Catholics; it was merely a question of priorities. Wentworth himself distrusted Catholics, he hated their religion, but he judged that for the present purposes, it was expedient to leave them alone.[48] Writing to Laud early on in his Irish campaign Wentworth informed him that once he had reformed the administration he would deal with 'the over-growth of Popery.'[49] Meanwhile because of the parlous state of the Church this was put on a very long finger. Besides Wentworth knew that he was treading on a lot of Irish toes, for the time being he did not need to make any more enemies than he already had.

The contrast with Ussher's approach to reforming Ireland could not be more stark. The Primate believed implicitly in the message of the gospels as sufficient to win souls, Bramhall insisted that without a disciplined and efficient Church, any such mission would be predisposed to failure. One Irish ecclesiastical history wrote of the new addition to the Church, 'Bramhall was a great stickler for rites and ceremonies. He had an intense antipathy to Calvinism, and he believed that religion could be best propagated, not so much by the preaching of the word, as by discipline enforced by state authority.'[50] Bramhall's methodology was typical of the new wave of Laudianism in the English Church. Whereas Calvinist elements in the past had tended to place all their eggs in an evangelical basket, the Laudians reaction to this was that loss of material splendour resulted in spiritual impoverishment. In terms of the biblical motifs the Calvinists were prophetical voices pressing their listeners to embrace the law of God, whilst the Laudians echoed Solomon who cut down the cedars of Lebanon in order to raise a splendid edifice to the glory of God. Anthony Milton summed up the difference.

> The emphasis was now not on the liberating force of *sola scriptura* to convert the papists to the true religion, but rather on the need to sustain an elaborate liturgy and ceremonial sufficient to rival the drawing power of the counter-Reformation in order to prevent members of the Church of England defecting to Rome.[51]

---

46 A. Ford, *The Protestant Reformation in Ireland* (Dublin, 1997), pp. 214–15.
47 *BW*, vol. 2, p. 124.
48 A. Clarke, 'The Government of Wentworth, 1632–40', in T.W. Moody et al. (eds), *A New History of Ireland* (8 vols, Oxford, 1976), vol. 3, p. 252.
49 *The Earl of Strafford's Letters and Dispatches*, ed. W. Knowler (2 vols, Dublin, 1740), 'Wentworth to Laud, 31 January 1634', vol. 1, pp. 187–9.
50 W.D. Killen, *The Ecclesiastical History of Ireland*, (2 vols, London, 1875), vol. 2, pp. 17–18.
51 Milton, *Catholic and Reformed*, p. 82.

In 1633 an order of Wentworth regarding Christchurch in Dublin is indicative of this new ideal. The order prohibited any house adjoining the Church to be used as a 'tippling house' or 'tobacco shop.' Any building erected against the church or encroaching on the churchyard would be viewed and if necessary removed. No persons 'what degree soever' would presume to put a hat on during service, and no person 'presume to make urine against the walls of the Church.'[52] All these measures were designed to restore the hallowed nature of the holy building by protecting it from profane use and by making it *kadosh*, separate to God.

Where was Ussher going to fit into the Wentworth–Bramhall rearrangement? According to Amanda Capern, nowhere at all. On theological matters, Ussher was, in Capern's view, bracing himself for conflict as he prepared to fight a rearguard action.[53] This attitude meant that Ussher was at best uncooperative and at worst underhand in his dealing with the Lord Deputy. Capern is damning in her assessment of their relationship 'from the time Thomas Wentworth arrived to take up his duties as Lord Deputy of Ireland, Ussher got under his feet.'[54] In fact there is a good deal of evidence to the contrary, that Ussher welcomed the force and energy the Laudian duo brought to his country. There may have been differences of opinion over approaches to recusants, and there were obvious theological points of departure, but the Primate seemed to appreciate that they were generally speaking a force for the good of the Irish Church. In an undated letter to Laud, Ussher mentions the arrival of the new Lord Deputy and reports how 'honourably affected' he was on making his acquaintance. He adds that Wentworth 'every day showeth himself so zealous for the recovering of the dissipated patrimony of the Church, that mine eye never yet beheld his match in that land.'[55] Besides Ussher did very well out of various statutes that were forced through by the new regime. One statute regulated the letting of Church land and fixed them for limited periods; this halted further alienation of bishop's land. Another provided for the restoration of impropriations to parishes.[56] In these years working together Wentworth, Bramhall and Ussher seem to have formed a sincere friendship which, judging from their later correspondence, and their mutual support in less auspicious times, was as enduring as it was genuine. Cicely Wedgewood described their characters and abilities as naturally complementary. 'Ussher was the spiritual, as Bramhall was the practical partner in this triple alliance.'[57] Ussher also gave due recognition to the efforts of his junior partner. In 1635 he wrote to Bramhall,

> ... not only myself but all my successors likewise shall have cause to honour the memory as well of my Lord Deputy as of yourself, who God has used as an instrument to bring his work to such perfection. In the mean time with my most hearty thanks for your

---

52   *Cal.S.P.Ire.*, 1633–1647, pp. 31–2.

53   A. Capern, 'The Caroline Church: James Ussher and the Irish dimension', *Historical Journal*, XXXIX (1996): 64.

54   Ibid., p. 69.

55   *UW*, vol. 15, pp. 571–2.

56   J.T. Ball, *The Reformed Church of Ireland* (London, 1886), p. 121.

57   C.V. Wedgewood, *Strafford, 1593–1641* (London, 1935), p. 179.

extraordinary pains taken in the Church's cause and mine, I recommend you to God's blessing and rest.[58]

One of Bramhall's first duties in Ireland was a regal visitation in his capacity as one of the King's Commissioners.[59] On these occasions he gave Laud full and graphic accounts of the material, moral and spiritual decay he was forced to witness. One such letter reported that this demoralising picture was not confined to the hinterland beyond the Pale, but infected the heart of anglicized Ireland.

> It is hard to say whether the churches be more ruinous and sordid, or the people irreverent; even in Dublin, where any reformation would begin the parochial church was converted into the Lord Deputy's stables, a second had become a nobleman's dwelling, and a third was used as a tennis court.[60]

Bramhall went on to relate with a mixture of disgust and self-righteous delight, 'In Christ's Church, the principal Church in Ireland, whither the Lord Deputy and Council repair every Sunday, the vaults from one end of the minster to the other are made into tippling–rooms, for beer, wine and tobacco, demised all to Popish recusants ... .'[61] Laud replied, 'But in earnest my Lord cannot serve God better, nor do himself more honour, than by making his government famous in the vindicating of God's houses from such abominable abuses.'[62] But in case the English Primate thought that it was only the buildings that were in such a lamentable state, Bramhall was no less disdainful of the clergy. One particular journey to Ussher's 'reformed' Ulster elicited a horrified response.

> I found almost the whole resident clergy absolute irregular, the very ebullition of Scotland, but conformists very rare, and those rather in judgment than in practice ... in place of it [an altar] a table ten yards long, where they sit and receive the sacraments together like good fellows ... They disclaim in their pulpits ... against kneeling at the sacrament, as the sign of Jeroboam, and run away from a priest's coat with high sleeves as the Devil from the sign of the Cross.[63]

However, it was the material well-being of the Church that immediately preoccupied Bramhall and along with his Lord Deputy he set out to recover lost ecclesiastical wealth. It is worth noting that there was a precedent for the Irish campaign. Laud had conducted a very similar programme of renovation in England where parish churches had been allowed to fall into decay. Nor indeed were improvements only at a parochial level, in 1631 Laud set up a commission which included himself, bishop Neile and representatives of the City of London, to address the dilapidated state of St Paul's Cathedral. The ruinous condition had according to their report, been brought about by 'the neglect and sufferance of the dean and

---

58   Vesey, *Athanasius*, p. 13.
59   Ibid., p. 7.
60   *BW*, 'Bramhall to Laud, 10 August 1633', vol. 1, p. lxxix.
61   Ibid.
62   *Hastings Ms.*, 'Laud to Bramhall, 16 August 1633', vol. 4, p. 55.
63   Trinity College Dublin Ms. 1697, paper VI.

chapter in times past.'[64] Laud, like Bramhall after him, set about raising funds with his usual energy.

In Ireland Bramhall initiated a number of schemes which appeared to return dividends in a very short space of time. A statute rushed through Parliament addressed the Act of Mortmain which prohibited the established Church from receiving gifts or bequests. The Act was altered.[65] Bramhall also acquired a grant from Laud and the King for 'pious use.'[66] Also out of England he secured loans from wealthy men, subscriptions from friends of Wentworth, and money from others who died intestate.[67] It is also claimed that he used his own money when necessary and he also managed to persuade 'many persons possessed of tithes to restore them or sufficiently to endow the vicarage, or to grant a proper salary at least to the curates.'[68] In addition, he tirelessly set himself to the reappropriation of ecclesiastical lands which had, over the years, been allowed to erode the fabric of the Church. His first biographer was fulsome in his praise of these achievements, 'By these and other means [not come to my knowledge] he regain'd for the Church in the space of four years time, thirty, some say, forty thousand pounds per annum, whereof he gave account at his going into England to the Archbishop of Canterbury ... .'[69]

It would be erroneous to regard this early economic campaign as solely secular, there was an underlying theological concern that was the recreation and protection of the sacred. There is a sense that appropriations, the dereliction of God's houses, the siphoning of money intended for the holy Church were all part of a general violation that defiled what was consecrate. Wentworth made this point during the opening stages of the trial against Richard Boyle when he declared, 'I held it one of the crying sins of this nation that men had laid sacrilegious hands upon the patrimony of the Church.'[70] Bramhall repeated these sentiments when on his arrival in Derry he was told by Dr Walker that impropriation had impoverished the clergy. The new bishop assured him that the Lord Deputy was on their side 'especially if it had the least tincture of sacrilege.'[71] This is the defining feature of Laudianism, which refuses to be reduced to a series of dogmatical points, it is instead the attempt to redraw the line between the sacred and the profane.[72] According to Jeremy Taylor, Wentworth was the Zerubbabel who rebuilt the temple of Jerusalem, and Bramhall was his Jeshua. He pointed out that their achievements were not universally appreciated, he knew

---

64 R. Lockyer, *The Early Stuart Church, A Political History, 1603–42* (London, 1989), p. 316.
65 Philips, *Irish Church*, vol. 3, p. 32.
66 *BW*, vol. 1, p. vii.
67 Vesey, *Athanasius*, p. 15.
68 *BW*, vol. 1, p. vii.
69 Vesey, *Athanasius*, p. 16.
70 J. McCafferty 'John Bramhall and the reconstruction of the Church of Ireland, 1633–1641', unpublished Ph.D. Thesis, University of Cambridge, 1996, p. 17.
71 Vesey, *Athanasius*, p. 10.
72 P. Lake 'The Laudian style, uniformity and the pursuit of the beauty of holiness in the 1630s', in Fincham, *The Early Stuart Church*, p. 163.

'there could not in all time be wanting too many, that envied to the Church every degree of prosperity, so Judas did to Christ the expense of ointment.'[73]

It is difficult to criticise the intentions of the Laudian entourage, they worked very hard in what was ostensibly a good cause. However their best efforts were ultimately to make a bad situation worse. John Morrill comments that their policy toward recusants, though sophisticated, was flawed, allowing as it did the Catholic hierarchy time to evangelise and 'further secure their immunity to Protestantism.'[74] In addition, a doubly negative effect of Bramhall's economic drive has been indicated; not only did it mean that evangelism received little encouragement but it created a rift between the planters and the Church. This was because endowment could often only take place at the expense of Protestant landowners who had procured doubtful rights over Church property.[75] Finally it has been noted with regard to Laud's restoration policies in England, that although there was a certain amount of good reason behind such projects the way they were executed often caused resentment, 'They had logic on their side, but they affronted and alienated the leaders of the local communities.'[76] This was a lesson that John Bramhall would have done well to absorb.

The Convocation of 1634

On 14 July 1634 Parliament assembled in Dublin in tandem with the first Church convocation since 1615. Ussher preached to the gathered a sermon whose title was pregnant with meaning, 'The sceptre shall not depart from Judah.'[77] The unrelenting pace that the Wentworth regime set for itself was about to reach a crucial stage when it set its face to the troublesome issue of the Irish Church Articles and canons. The records of this convocation are not available to us now, having almost certainly perished in the 1641 rebellion. Surviving records include two very terse letters from Ussher, an account from Nicholas Bernard of the proceedings of the Lower House, a statement from Bramhall concerning the Upper House as well as something from Strafford which fills some of the gaps in Bernard's account.[78]

The Laudians, using Bramhall as their main agent, set themselves the task of building a new doctrinal framework in order to provide a foundation for not only raising the established theology but also facilitating a more general Anglicization by erasing the kind of independence that they saw as fertilising disloyalty. The Irish party were determined if not to halt any Canterburian impositions then at least to salvage some of their distinctiveness and independence in a type of damage limitation exercise. As the two sides squared up, the mutual rallying points were their respective articles of faith. Besides representing a symbol of what remained of

---

73 *BW*, vol. 1, p. lx.
74 Morrill, 'British patriarchy?', p. 229.
75 M. Perceval-Maxwell, *The Outbreak of the Irish Rebellion of 1641* (Dublin, 1994), p. 24.
76 Lockyer, *Early Stuart Church*, p. 317.
77 Elrington, *Life*, p. 166.
78 *Ms. Book of Common Prayer for Ireland*, ed. A.J. Stephens (3 vols, Belfast, 1849), vol. 3, p. lviii.

Irish Church self dominion, the 1615 Articles had also recently provided something of a flag of convenience for discontented English parties. William Prynne had used the Irish Articles in 1630 to justify his party's theological stance. He reasoned that since the Churches of England and Ireland are under one sovereign, since most of the bishops who framed the Articles were English, 'trained up in the doctrines of the Church of England', since they were licensed by James and printed in England, 'we may hence infallibly collect that our Anti-Arminian assertions are the established, the received doctrine of the Church.'[79] By dealing with them in a summary manner, Wentworth and Bramhall would be killing two birds with one convocational stone. This issue between the two Churches had some history, as early as 1613 Ussher had written to Dr Challoner admitting to the defects in the Irish Church and expressing a wish to improve the Church in the eyes of the Archbishop of Canterbury, but he warned, 'I pray you be not too forward to have statutes sent you from hence, Dictum Sapienti.'[80] It remained to be seen whether Ussher had lost any of this old resolve.

Convocation finally began proceedings in October 1634. In the Upper House Bramhall immediately took the initiative and urged the acceptance of the Thirty-nine Articles, reasoning that not only did they allow greater latitude in things not essential, but also that a public agreement with the English would afford obvious practical benefits.[81] There would be strength in unity, and as discord was a gift to their enemy, they must endeavour to seek uniformity. Jeremy Taylor was later to summarise these motives as two nations 'populus unius labii.' The bishop of Derry had laboured to take away 'that shibboleth which made his Church lisp too indecently, or rather in some little degree to speak the speech of Ashod, and not the language of Canaan.'[82] Bramhall's opening gambit displayed all the classical traits of Laudian *modus operandi*. Though it is implicit, he never attempts any theological justification but relies instead on this practical defence. When the indigenous clergy argued that the essential meanings of the articles were the same, Bramhall side stepped the looming quagmire of inter-Protestant semantics, and moved to the firmer ground of a functional discussion. Sparrow-Simpson described this tactic.

> ... Bramhall was not to allow himself to be drawn into the debate. He contented himself with the reply that though the sense might be the same, yet the common complaint of the opponents of the Church was that they were dissonant confessions. It was only reasonable to remove this offence, when it might be easily done.[83]

However, as John Vesey wrote, the convocation was not without its 'Sanballats and Tobiahs, who with the people of the land endeavoured to weaken them and hinder the Building.'[84] Whilst Bramhall was promoting the English Articles in the

---

79   W. Prynne, *Anti-Arminianisme* (London, 1630), p. 20.
80   Parr, *Life*, p. 42.
81   Watson, *Typical Churchmen*, p. 91.
82   *BW*, vol. 1, p. lxii; the prophet Nehemiah berated the Jews who had married wives from Ashod with the result that their children could not speak the Jewish language, Nehemiah 13:23–4.
83   Sparrow-Simpson, *Bramhall*, p. 41.
84   Vesey, *Athanasius*, p. 12.

Upper House, events in the Lower House were not going in his favour. There the godly majority had ordered, without consulting the bishops, that the canons of the Church of England be examined noting in the margin either 'A' for allowed, or 'D' for deliberandum.[85] Even more offensively, they had inserted into the 5th Canon that the Irish Articles, were to be received 'under pain of excommunication.'[86] Hereupon Wentworth stepped in, he sent for the select committee who had undertaken the examination and rebuked them as only he was capable. In the presence of Ussher and four bishops he told them, 'how unlike Clergymen, that owed canonical obedience to their superiors, they had proceeded in the committee; how unheard of a part if was for a few petty clerks to presume to make Articles of Faith, without the privity or consent of state or bishop; what a spirit of Brownism and contradiction I observed in their Deliberandums.'[87] If Ussher objected it seems that he did so in silence. Wentworth then ordered that the English Articles be voted on, for or against, and he directed Ussher to draft a canon for this purpose. The Primate obeyed but in doing so he tried to slip in a final clause which would have 'deprived' clerics of their benefices (rather than excommunicate them) for not accepting the Irish Articles. This failed to satisfy the Lord Deputy and he decided to draft his own causing Ussher to attempt a last ditch effort to have his own accepted. He was not successful.[88]

Alan Ford argues that Ussher was obstructing the passage of the Articles acting on the firm belief that the Irish Articles represented 'the purity of our ancient truth.'[89] The evidence supports this argument and it seems that this obstruction had a certain furtive quality. Only gradually was the Lord Deputy becoming less convinced that Ussher was as firmly committed to the programme as he had obviously led him to believe. In a letter to Laud he related an incident in which he informed Ussher of a scheme to bring upon the Irish clergy the 39 Articles and have their own silenced. Wentworth claimed that Ussher 'grew fearful he should not be able to effect it, which awakened me, that had rested hitherto secure upon that judgment of his, and had indeed leaned upon that belief so long ... .'[90] This is all the more significant since when the Canon was eventually presented to Convocation the Upper House voted it through unanimously and in the Lower House it passed with only two votes against it.[91] It seems that Ussher's pessimism masked what was in actual fact an aversion.

The result was 'sudden and decisive' and caught the supporters of the Irish Articles by surprise. Wentworth had presented them with a *fait accompli* and only when it was over did they begin to wonder at the implications.[92] If the Irish party had

---

85   Wills, *Distinguished Irishmen*, vol. 4, p. 171.
86   Ibid.
87   *Strafford Letters*, 'Strafford to Laud, 16 December 1634', vol. 1, p. 343.
88   J. McCafferty, 'God bless your free Church of Ireland, Wentworth, Laud and Bramhall and the Irish Convocation of 1634', in J.F. Merritt (ed.), *The Political World of Thomas Wentworth, Earl of Strafford, 1621–1641* (Cambridge, 1996), p. 193.
89   Ford, 'Independent': 19.
90   *Strafford Letters*, 'Wentworth to Laud, 16 December 1634', vol. 1, p. 342.
91   McCafferty, 'God Bless', p. 196.
92   Sparrow-Simpson, *Bramhall*, p. 42. The canon composed by the Lord Deputy read, 'For the manifestation of our agreement with the Church of England, in the confession of the same Christian faith, and the doctrine of the sacraments; we do receive and approve the

thrown up their collective hands at the inevitability of acceptance, then the English party was privately breathing a sigh of relief. During their tussle Bramhall had done much to play down to Laud the extent of their differences writing, 'It is true that there were some unbeseeming passages, as I conceived among us, about the introduction of the Articles, but of so small moment that I shall beg leave of your Grace to forget them, since we are all here in peace and perfect amity.'[93] When some of the dust had settled he came clean with Laud and confessed that their passing was a close run thing, probably much closer than the Irish opposition had supposed. He did not demur at taking a large slice of the credit.

> Never any escaped a danger more nearly than we did, to have the Articles of Ireland obtruded upon in the House of the Bishops, before ever they were viewed, or the committee had returned their opinion ... I was the means to stay it, and the business being represented to my Lord, he hath so well ordered it that the Articles of England solely are received by all clergy ... except two.[94]

There is among the surviving accounts an impression of Ussher as a man caught between two stools. His loyalty to the Crown is unquestioning and yet his theological beliefs, as well as his own involvement in their formulation, would have made him attached to his own Church's tenets. Add to this the responsibility he must have felt on the one hand of being head of the King's Church in Ireland and on the other the leading representative of the Irish ecclesiastical body, Thomas Carte was right in the eighteenth century when he wrote that the bishops and clergy depended on Ussher's judgment.[95] In the end it is clear that whatever obstacles he was putting in the way of the English Articles were abruptly removed once the Lord Deputy had drawn up his canon. A clue to why Ussher did so can be found in a letter from the Irish bishops, signed by Ussher, from early in the same year as Convocation. Ussher writes that in all the Christian world there is not a rural clergy 'reduced to such extremity of contempt and beggary.' He adds that if Charles settled a clergy endowed competently then, 'it will most surely bring upon your Majesty and this Kingdom, barbarism and superstition will be expelled, the subject shall learn his Duty to God and to his sovereign, and true religion be propagated.'[96] The Primate knew, as well as his bishops and ministers, that their established Church owed its existence now, and in the future, to the support of English crown and government; Ussher's Church was embryonic and he was not about to cut the umbilical cord. Any amount of prevarication and grumbling in Convocation was never going to disabuse them of this sober reality.

---

book of Articles of religion, agreed upon by the archbishops, and the whole clergy in the convocation, holden at London, in the year of our Lord 1562, for the avoiding of diversities of opinions, and for the establishing of consent touching true religion.' The canon went on to excommunicate non-subscribers; Wills, *Distinguished Irishmen*, vol. 4, p. 171.

93   *Papers relating to the Church of Ireland*, ed. E.P. Shirely (London, 1874), 'Bramhall to Laud, 20 December 1634', p. 41.
94   Trinity College Dublin Ms. 1697, paper VI.
95   T. Carte, *The Life of Ormonde* (London, 1736), p. 78.
96   *Strafford Papers*, 'Ussher to Laud, January 1634', vol. 1, pp. 382–3.

The Laudian victory was not quite wholesale. The Irish Articles still stood; if they had not been endorsed, then they had not been proscribed either. Bramhall's first biographer had written that there was an attempt by the Irish clergy to have their own Articles ratified along with the English. According to Vesey the counter-argument used by Bramhall rather disingenuously maintained that such an endorsement would merely diminish them and insult the 1615 Convocation by implying that they needed ratifying.[97] Documentary evidence is not, however, provided by Vesey and his version of events has been disputed as doing 'injury to the candour and honesty of Bramhall.' The author adds that it was, impossible that the bishop of Derry could have answered such a proposal in the Upper House, since it was never made there, and if it was made in the Lower House, a bishop could not have debated it.[98] Whatever the circumstances surrounding the outcome a certain ambiguity was allowed by Strafford and Bramhall in order to satisfy all parties. On the one hand, Vesey could write, 'By the passing of this Canon, the Articles of the Church of England were superinduced and consequently those of Ireland ... were now virtually repealed.'[99] On the other, certain Irish members could salve their consciences by claiming a parity for both confessions. Ussher was insisting in his correspondence that the Irish Articles still stood.[100] This said, it is probable that a certain amount of self-deception went on, although Peter Heylin was to write that Strafford had outwitted Ussher,[101] A.J. Stephens is probably more accurate when he wrote:

> If Ussher was deceived, he deceived himself, by persuading himself that the canon would not have the effect which its promoters avowed; and if any member of the Lower House were deceived, there can be little doubt that it arose from their trusting to Ussher's opinion, expressed to them in some private conference.[102]

The 39 Articles safely imposed, the Convocation then turned its attention to the canons. The standardizing of Church laws was at the heart of Laudian policy. These were the means by which the administration would mould the Irish Church into one that was more in its own image. This has been seen as central to Laud's grand plan, 'securing canonical uniformity was at the true heart of the "Laudian" Church in England, and this rather than doctrine or altar policy was what fundamentally occupied Canterbury's attention and dictated much of this course.'[103] It could, of course, be argued that this is precisely how Laud pursued his doctrinal policy. Laws are born of doctrine and in turn reproduce theological opinion. Besides, such a policy had a lot to recommend it since Church laws could be swiftly and cleanly imposed whereas doctrinal dispute were invariably long winded and fraught with danger. Enforcing policy was the Laudian preferred method of doing theology.

---

97 Vesey, *Athanasius*, p. 18.
98 *Ms. of Common Prayer*, Stephens, vol. 3, p. cvi.
99 Vesey, *Athanasius*, p. 18.
100 *UW*, vol. 16, p. 9. Ussher to Samuel Ward, 15 September 1635.
101 P. Heylin, *Respondet Petrus* (London, 1658), p. 125.
102 *Ms. of Common Prayer*, Stephens, vol. 3, p. cvi.
103 J. McCafferty, 'John Bramhall and the Church of Ireland in the 1630s', in A. Ford et al., *As by Law Established*, p. 101.

On the issue of canons Bramhall once more took to the breach. This time, the Irish contingent, having already suffered one blow to their autonomy, were reluctant to receive another. Bramhall had drawn up 'the heads of some canons necessary for the Church', which he claimed in a letter to Laud had been 'seen and allowed' by Ussher.[104] However if Ussher's opposition had previously been covert, it now became more open. Bramhall's early biographer was sympathetic, 'To this the Primate opposed himself with great earnestness, and some think he had reason on his side: for it looked like betraying the privileges of a national Church which his Grace was by his place to defend.'[105]

Ussher was clearly corresponding with Canterbury at this juncture, with some success. In his correspondence to Bramhall, Laud, informed him that he had compared Ussher's canons with the English and advised that the addition of a 'some few canons is very necessary for that kingdom.' Probably recognising Ussher's overall service to their cause he also pressed the bishop of Derry to be 'a little softer to the Primate.'[106] The difficulty was not merely confined to national pride; there were theological sensibilities within the Irish Church which were likely to be offended by some of the higher Church practices of the English. The eighteenth-century *Life of Ormonde* pointed out that this would have touched a particular nerve with Ussher.

> The main difficulty was to engage the Primate Ussher, upon whose judgment most of the bishops and clergy depended, whose honour might be touched by a repeal of Articles which he himself had drawn, and who, being horribly afraid of bowing at the name of Jesus, and some other reverences prescribed in the English canons which he neither practised nor approved ... .[107]

Wentworth reported the situation to Laud advising him that this 'crotchet put Ussher into an alarming agony, as you cannot believe so learned a man should be troubled withal.' The Lord Deputy seemed to regard the matter as purely a point of honour, 'left Ireland might become subject to the Church of England, as the Province of York is to that of Canterbury.' Though he did recognise enough theology in the affair to opine that 'some puritan correspondents of his had no doubt infused these necessities into his head.' In the end Ussher was only placated when Wentworth agreed to his writing to Laud in order to ascertain his opinion.[108] In the Upper House Bramhall's chosen line of argument was ill-judged as he attempted to use their first decision as a precedent. They would, he claimed, no more be surrendering their self-government than they had done by voting in the Articles. However, the members were already licking that particular sore and they were little persuaded that another would mend it. As one of the earliest sources comments, 'this was but an ill argument to them who had so repented their having done so much that they resolved not to cure themselves by a second wound.'[109]

---

104 *Hastings Ms.*, 'Bramhall to Laud, 21 August 1634', vol. 4, p. 61.
105 Vesey, *Athanasius*, p. 19.
106 *Hastings Ms.*, vol. 4, p. 66.
107 Carte, *Ormonde*, vol. 1, p. 149.
108 *Strafford Letters*, 'Strafford to Laud, 10 March 1634', vol. 1, p. 381.
109 Vesey, *Athanasius*, p. 19.

Throughout the proceedings Bramhall was acting as Laud's agent, though even in this role, he abided, to some extent, by the rule of secrecy. This perhaps had more to do with an anxiety to paint a rosy picture than any loyalty to the Irish Church. In a letter to Laud in August he explained, 'I am tied by promise not to acquaint you with the passages in the Convocation House.'[110] For his part, Laud was accepting of this situation, knowing that whatever details he failed to receive, he would have full knowledge of the most important deliberations. His reply is untypically sanguine, and a measure of his trust in his charge, 'And for your business in Convocation since you are tied by a promise of secrecy, I shall be very well content to be ignorant, either altogether or at least till such time as you may speak more freely.'[111] In spite of the moratorium on passing information Bramhall kept up a regular correspondence with the English Primate in which he gave him a good, if somewhat upbeat, digest of events. In February 1635, his optimistic prognosis for the passage of the canons in the Houses betrays not only a certain naivety but also a messenger's desire to deliver to his master only good news. He reported that opposition to them was weak, 'six maybe three opponents in both Houses.' He adds, 'I can not doubt but that the addition of some few canons fitted properly for this meridian will be harmful. But I must confess diverse of those will not [missing] as canons. I have persuaded my Lord Primate to send them to your grace and take your advice ... .'[112] What transpired was a compromise which, even more than the first vote, allowed both parties to take away with them a certain claim to victory. A committee headed by George Andrews modified the proposed canons to include even a subscription to the beloved Irish Articles.[113] The Irish canons were an unusual theological hybrid in which something of the Calvinistic past was married to Laudian innovations. John McCafferty explained how this came about.

> In their final form the Irish canons were the product of a clash between Bramhall, trying not only to ensure the greatest conformity with England but also to target specific Irish abuses and improve on the English canons, and Ussher, who was seeking to preserve the broader more godly base of the Irish Church and trying to ensure that some marks of independence were included in the canons. In the event Bramhall went far beyond a grudging acceptance of some canons necessary for 'that meridian' and Ussher secured something other than total defeat.[114]

McCafferty has done much excellent work on the canons and indicated various important points of departure. Canon 18 maintained the English order during service, it does however omit directions for kneeling, standing, and bowing at the name of Jesus. The English canon prescribing the use of copes never got past Andrews and his committee.[115] Yet, some went further than the English, and could only cause Laud

---

110 *Hastings Ms.*, vol. 4, p. 61.
111 Ibid., p. 62.
112 Huntington Library, California, Huntington Ms., HA 14048, 'Bramhall to Laud, 18 February 1635.'
113 McCafferty, 'God bless', p. 199.
114 Ibid.
115 Ibid., pp. 199–200.

to gaze enviously across the Irish Sea. Canon 19 exhorted the people on hearing the church bell to examine their consciences and if they were much troubled to seek out a minister not only for advice but absolution. Canon 94 placed the communion table at the east of the church and provided a silver cup for communion.[116] In May, Laud wrote to Bramhall thanking him for the canon concerning confession and congratulating him on acquiring additional powers for the Church.

> It is very well gained by my Lord, if he hath gotten a confirmation for coercive power to the clergy to take off the canons of excommunication, whereas all Parliaments here have complained of the one and yet would never grant the other. By which they made plain their endeavour was to take off all power from the Church, but to grant none.[117]

Laud added jokingly, but ominously, that he desired to be granted land in Connaught or Ormond that he might come to live in Ireland when 'they are weary of me in England.'[118]

All in all the canons managed, in spite of the committee, to make the Irish Church more altar centred; the Laudian regime was determined to make adoration an important ingredient in general worship. As J. McCafferty has indicated, 'Within the church, the altar was to be the focus of attention and in the hearts of the communicants, absolution provided a way up to the altar – an altar at which the priest administered the sacramental wine in a precious cup.'[119]

Aside from the theological and liturgical parrying, another canon of a more secular nature caused much internecine struggling. Historians have counted as the potentially the most important of the drafted canons, the one which provided for a clerk to read parts of the service in Irish if the minister was English.[120] One of the most interesting aspects of this canon's passage is just how much it caused Ussher and Bramhall to lock horns. Much work has been done in the last few years to rehabilitate Ussher with regard to the Irish language. Whilst previously he had been largely regarded as antagonistic[121] it has now been largely demonstrated that he was by no means averse to Gaelic,[122] though recent descriptions of him as 'a fine Irish scholar' are probably going too far. [123]Beyond an antiquarian interest Ussher displayed little appetite for the Irish language, however there are some examples of gestures made in promoting its cause. In 1628 an edict from Charles stipulated that the Bible and Book of Common Prayer in Irish ought to be used in parishes where there were Irish speakers. This mandate is clearly a response to an appeal from

---

116　Ibid., pp. 200–201.
117　*Hastings Ms.*, 'Laud to Bramhall, 11 May 1635', vol. 4, p. 68.
118　Ibid.
119　McCafferty, 'God bless', p. 201.
120　Philips, *Irish Church*, vol. 3, p. 21.
121　N. Sykes 'James Ussher as churchman', *Hermathena*, LXXXVIII (1956): 70–71; Elrington in, *UW*, vol.1,118.
122　J. Leerssen, 'Archbishop Ussher and Gaelic culture', *Studia Hibernica*, XXII–XXIII (1982–83), passim.
123　C. Lennon, 'Religious wars in Ireland: plantations and martyrs of the Catholic Church', in B. Bradshaw and D. Keogh (eds.), *Christianity in Ireland* (Dublin, 2002), p. 92.

Ussher.[124] Elsewhere however Ussher shows little interest in employing the native tongue as a means to promote the word of God. However, in Convocation he seems to have experienced something of a late conversion and it is hard not to conclude that this was part of a reaction to the imperious nature of the new English party. Whatever the case, when William Bedell brought up the issue, he found support in his Primate.

According to one Presbyterian historian, Bedell's proposal brought out the worst in Bramhall's prejudiced nature and he objected, 'on the absurd principle, the application of which had already been so fatal to the progress of truth – that the native Irish were a barbarous and degraded people, unworthy and incapable of civilization.'[125] This attitude is illustrative of Bramhall's general approach to the reforming of Ireland which was less to do with effective proselytising than a concerted effort to raise the native Church in the most effective manner, which to him meant Anglicization. This and his general attitude to the independence of the Irish Church display an ecclesiastical imperialism which does not sit comfortably with what is, after all, the nub of his ecclesiastical ideology, national autonomy. As it turned out this issue was one of the ones on which the Irish were victorious and Canon 94 made some nod toward recognising a certain amount of Irishness within the established Church. However Reid was almost certainly right when he described it as a gesture of little significance, for it was 'vain to expect any practical advantages to result from this solitary and unsupported enactment.'[126]

The conclusion of Convocation in 1635 seemed to have left all parties more or less contented, in spite of Amanda Capern's assertion that relations between the main partners were irreparably damaged.[127] A long tradition propounded a conspiracy theory that Ussher so nursed a grudge against Strafford that he took revenge some years later when he managed to persuade Charles I that he could keep his crown and a clear conscience by signing the Bill of Attainder against Wentworth. Lord Campbell's account credits Ussher with the type of skulduggery that would have shamed Titus Oates when he has him reason that 'since his Majesty refers his own judgment to his judges, and they are to answer to it if any innocent person suffer.'[128] There is a good deal of contemporary evidence to suggest that relations between the two remained cordial, even warm. Even when others conspired to cause difficulties, such as the gossipping Lord Nithsdale, who reported some disparaging remarks apparently made by Ussher about preferments Wentworth was supposed to have conferred on his sister.[129] The Lord Deputy called Ussher and Bramhall together and once more 'talked ourselves friends.'[130] The temporary rift may have been related to an incident which must have occurred only shortly before when the Primate had

---

124 *Cal.S.P.Ire., 1625–1632*, King Charles to Lord Deputy, 8 July 1628, p. 364.
125 Reid, *Presbyterian History*, vol. 1, p. 176.
126 Ibid.
127 Capern, 'Caroline Church': 70.
128 Lord Campbell, *The Lives of the Chancellors* (2 vols, London, 1869), vol. 2, p. 494.
129 Burghclere, *Strafford*, vol. 1, p. 93.
130 Sheffield City Archives, Fitzwilliam Ms., 'Wentworth to Coke, 12 July 1637.'

castigated Wentworth for opening a theatre in Dublin. Though significantly the Lord Deputy was hurt precisely because a few days previously Ussher had told him that he had done more to aid him than all his council.[131] There were inevitable, though remarkably few, differences between two men playing such leading roles in the affairs of the same state. For his part Ussher told Laud that 'he never knew any layman in all his life that so well and fully understood matters of divinity as the Earl.'[132] Perhaps the ultimate testimony to the enduring nature of their friendship is the fact that Strafford spent his last days with Ussher when he was denied access to Laud. Later Ussher related that he had 'never known a whiter soul.'[133]

As to the Irish Primate's relations with his English counterpart, it has recently been argued that these were 'permanently poisoned.'[134] However, contemporary evidence does not substantiate this assessment. Laud was phlegmatic to say the least about surrendering what little they did to the Irish and he wrote to Ussher congratulating him on the well-ordered ending which afforded no advantages to the Irish recusants by terminating on a discordant note. Or as Laud put it, 'rising in heat.'[135] On the issue of the canons, he expressed his satisfaction.

> And for your canons, to speak truth, and with wanted liberty and freedom, I cannot but think the English Canons entire ... would have done better; yet since you, and that Church, have thought otherwise, I do very easily submit to it, and you shall have my prayers that God would bless it.[136]

Laud it seems, in spite of some small reservations, to have been favourable to the Irish Church's new regulations, but what of Ussher? According to J. McCafferty his 'nightmare had come true.'[137] Writing in the seventeenth century Bedell's biographer Gilbert Burnet claimed that Ussher deeply regretted their passing and 'confessed that the tolerating those abominable corruptions that the canonists had brought in, was such a stain upon a Church, that in all other respects was the best reformed in the world, that he apprehended it would bring a curse and ruin upon the whole constitution.'[138] However, there is no evidence to suggest that the Primate was so averse to the new innovations, and since he had a hand in drawing them up and was indeed one of the 'canonists' it hardly seems likely. The most immediate effect of the Convocation was however, Ussher's virtual retirement to Drogheda. There were of course obvious rumours that he did so in a fit of pique and Laud was obliged to write to Strafford to reassure him that he would ignore any such gossip in circulation that pointed the finger of blame at him. 'As for that, or anything else that is causelessly laid to your charge, you must [as I know you do] scorn and go on.'[139] More likely than

---

131 Ibid., 'Wentworth to Laud, 10 July 1637.'
132 Burghclere, *Strafford*, vol. 2, p. 340.
133 *Hastings Ms.*, vol. 2, p. 82.
134 Capern, 'Caroline Church', p. 70.
135 Laud, *Works*, 'Laud to Ussher, 10 May 1635', vol. 6, pp. 396–7.
136 Ibid.
137 McCafferty, 'God Bless', p. 207.
138 G. Burnet, *The Life of William Bedell* (Dublin, 1736), p. 67.
139 Laud, *Works*, 'Laud to Wentworth, 23 January 1635', vol. 7, p. 235.

Ussher's move being attributable to umbrage is that he was only too happy to escape to the more sedate world of scholarship after the gruelling fray of Convocation. The evidence suggests strongly that this is the case, in a letter to Samuel Ward, Ussher was in very high spirits about the arrangement declaring, *'redire in gratiam cum veteribus amicus'*, [I retire in thanks with old friends].[140]

For Bramhall, who had previously manifested no qualms about acting as the *pontifex maximus* in Ireland, this meant that he was now Primate in everything but name. Once again it appears that Ussher was quite happy to sign over his responsibility, even on occasions taking the initiative in designating his authority. In a letter from Drogheda Ussher thanks Bramhall for procuring a dispensation for his absence and added, 'I entreat you to be further mindful that the patent for the High Commission may be so drawn up that my presence be not necessary in the execution thereof.'[141] The following month he wrote concerning the draft legislation to deal with tenantry waiving his responsibility to Bramhall declaring, 'wherein what ever is done by you, I shall most willingly give mine assent to.'[142] In an undated letter but from the same year Ussher instigated a move to have the Church leadership pass from his hands when he wrote, 'Having referred the whole settlement of the temporal state of the Primacy into your care and circumspection.'[143] It might well be argued that Ussher acted in this way because he would not have had any stomach for the activities of the new church order as they were about to set about their strict policy of enforcement. In this way Ussher might be seen to be withdrawing his services for ideological reasons. However, one comment in the letter concerning the formation of the new High Commission gives the lie to such an interpretation. Regarding the make up of the Commission Ussher is clearly concerned that it will be effective, he urges, 'withall I should advise, that the commission should be every way as large as those which have been erected heretofore.'[144] Whatever the reasons for the Primate's lack of involvement they should not be interpreted as disapproval.

Bramhall was able to assist with the Primate's internal exile and he made numerous efforts to do so. Primarily the new locum was of great financial assistance to Ussher. In October 1635, he had received a letter from Drogheda in which the archbishop bemoaned his impecunious circumstances. Bramhall was quick to respond and a second letter dated in February the following year thanks the bishop of Derry for augmenting a doubling of rents in Ussher's archbishopric.[145] It has been calculated that this represented an annual income of £1,200 a year.[146] A figure made even more significant when one takes into account Hugh Kearney's statement that Ussher retired in 1635 for financial reasons.[147] Bramhall was clearly determined to make the unofficial retirement as trouble free as possible and it is hard not to conclude that

---

140   *Tanner Letters*, ed. C. McNeill, (Dublin, 1943), 'Ussher to Ward, 15 September 1635', p. 113.
141   Huntington Ms., HA 15950, 'Ussher to Bramhall, 27 October 1635.'
142   Huntington Ms., HA 15951, 'Ussher to Bramhall, 23 November 1635.'
143   Huntington Ms., HA 15953, 'Ussher to Bramhall, undated, 1635.'
144   Huntington Ms., HA 15950.
145   Huntington Ms., HA 15954, 'Ussher to Bramhall, 25 February 1636.'
146   Burghclere, *Strafford*, vol. 1, p. 296.
147   H. Kearney, *Strafford in Ireland*, (Manchester, 1959), p. 116.

this was based on the simple premise that the less Ussher had to complain about the less he was going to interfere in the affairs of state. In any event he need not have worried, henceforth the Archbishop of Armagh played little part in his Church's proceeding. As he swung shut the library door in Drogheda and settled down to the altogether more congenial life of a scholar it is also difficult to conclude that he would have been nothing but grateful to the Laudian triumvirate for facilitating the arrangement.

Ussher and Bramhall, post-Convocation

The passage of the Irish articles and canons through the 1634 Convocation was the single biggest and most lasting of all the activities of the Laudian regime in Ireland. Ussher may still have insisted on double-subscription to both English and Irish Articles at ordination,[148] but this has been aptly described as 'quixotic' since the Irish Church's tenets and regulations were now redundant in everything but name. If proof was needed of this we need only look at the Church Bramhall inherited at the Restoration, the 1661–65 Convocation no longer considered the Irish Articles to be of the slightest importance.[149]

The initial victory for Bramhall and his party must have appeared to be more or less resounding. By 1635 it seemed that they had established a firm foundation in terms of faith and structure in the Irish Church and were apparently making substantial progress on financial affairs. However with every triumph they were sowing seeds of disaster. Convocation may well be counted as the Laudians lasting endowment to the established Irish Church but the immediate implications were revolutionary. Not alone did it introduce novel and unpopular innovations that were unrepresentative of Irish Protestant opinion, but its whole Catholic emphasis was entirely inappropriate to the Irish situation.[150] If this was one of the immediate effects then Laud for one was relishing it since he believed that it usefully drew out the enemy. The English Primate had already marked the card of dean Andrews, and he expected a similar advantage for Bramhall, 'What opposition was, it may be, 'tis better now than if there had been none, and for my part, I think so. For now you are as certain as you could any way [have] been, and yet you know what enemies you may expect upon like occasions; and perhaps know who those enemies are.'[151] For the rest of his acting primacy Bramhall was devoted to purging the Irish Church of these 'enemies.' For this purpose a High Commission was established

---

148 Some controversy surrounds Ussher's attitude to the Irish Articles post-Convocation. A.J. Stephens shows that this argument centres on the evidence of Peter Heylin and John Vesey. Both claimed that Ussher and several other Irish bishops required of their ordinands double subscription. However as Stephens indicates both authors are relying on Nicholas Bernard who maintained in his *Judgement of James Ussher*, that this was the case. However Bernard's evidence is often doubtful and with regard to this rather sensational text it must be considered even more untrustworthy. *Ms. Book of Common Prayer*, Stephens, vol. 3, cix.
149 C. Hardwick, *A History of the Articles of Religion* (London, 1890), p. 186.
150 Clarke, 'Government of Wentworth', p. 257.
151 *Hastings Ms.*, 'Laud to Bramhall, 16 January 1635', vol. 4, p. 64.

which was to concern itself with the central supervision of diocesan courts and the enforcement of state policy, for this end it was provided with powers of amercement and imprisonment.[152] Ussher was placed at its head but more out of procedure than any expectation that he might fill the position. When it first met in February 1636 Ussher was, true to form, absent.

One major incident during its first year involving five Presbyterian ministers in the north (including Blair and Hamilton, who had sought and received succour from Ussher) gives us an insight into Bramhall's method of dealing with non-conformity. The bishop was present at the public conference in Belfast in which the newly appointed Laudian bishop Leslie was deposing the clergymen for non-subscription to the new canons.[153] The accused ministers recorded that Bramhall's words were at times 'rather bitter than to the purpose.' Hamilton had enquired where in scripture kneeling at communion was enjoined, to which the bishop of Derry allegedly retorted, 'Give him Scripture for a peck of oats to his horse.'[154] The ministers were deprived and recognising the hopelessness of their cause in the face of the new administration, Blair and Hamilton, along with one hundred and forty followers, set sail for New England in September of the same year.[155] By the middle of 1637 the campaign against ministers was so successful that the High Commission was able to turn its attention to laymen.[156] A success rate that made his English superior comment that he wished the Scottish were 'as able, and had as good means to purge these tumours, as [God be thanked] you in Ireland have.'[157] On one of these occasions, a Mr. Bayley was presented to the High Commission and once more Bramhall was gaining notoriety with his forthright comments. According to Reid, Bayley was a 'despoiler' and a 'puritan', the bishop publicly addressed him as 'a young devil.'[158] Bramhall was later to find himself in some hot water with the Star Chamber in England for the use of 'unguarded' language. It would appear from these accounts that his tongue was also never particularly fettered whilst he was in Ireland.

In all his activities, Bramhall kept in close contact with the Archbishop of Canterbury, not only informing him of measures that had been taken but also feeding him with alarming tales of nonconformity. There were particular problems in Down and Connor which had a large Scottish population. In February 1637 Bramhall related how he feared that this diocese would contaminate others.

> How had this contagion lately spread itself over the face of the whole counties of Down and Connor, and some adjacent places. In mine own diocese, I have had anabaptistical

---

152 Clarke, 'Government of Wentworth', p. 257.
153 Watson, *Typical Churchmen*, p. 96.
154 Reid, *Presbyterian History*, vol. 1, p. 539.
155 Perceval-Maxwell, 'Ulster Scots': 527.
156 Ibid., p. 528.
157 *Hastings Ms.*, 'Laud to Bramhall, 27 June 1637', vol. 4, p. 75.
158 Watson, *Typical Churchmen*, p. 96; in 1637 Bramhall was the recipient of charges brought by a Mr. Beacon that he had used 'yeomanly' language whilst serving at Star Chamber. The charges came to nothing. *BW*, vol. 1 Appendix, p. xx.

prophetesses come gadding up and down, and the doors of churches barricaded up for a quarter of a year together in despite of all ecclesiastical jurisdiction.[159]

Such reports were clearly designed to excite a response and tacked on to the end of this scandalous account is an almost desperate appeal, 'My Lord, I beseech you, be a means that a well begun and almost settled reformation be not thus destroyed. Save me and my chancellor from this insolent madness of the lay elders.'[160]

Around this time Bramhall seems to have made a personal commitment to the Irish Reformation. After travelling to England he sold his entire estate for £6,000 and began a plantation in Omagh.[161] Laud now had a man in Ireland who was fully focused on the task at hand, the Archbishop kept up a barrage of letters, commanding, pressing, and encouraging his plenipotentiary. In August of 1638, he set out his instructions in no uncertain terms, informing Bramhall that he expected 'an exact account' of the Church of Ireland as promised, nor must it be 'only a beginning, but a full account.' He adds that Bramhall is 'not to think of a private life.'[162] In a letter in October the same year, it is clear that even the industry of Bramhall was not always enough to satisfy his task master, 'I shall expect your account concerning the Church preferments when you can be ready. But I confess the sooner I have it, the better. And though Mich[elmas] term be begun, yet I hitherto hear not of your first part.'[163] Generally speaking however Laud's correspondence indicates that he is eminently pleased with the general progress in Ireland and somewhat surprisingly there is at least one occasion when he has to rein in the bishop of Derry for his over-zealous handling of a deprived minister in his own diocese. A Mr. Yorke had written to Laud complaining of his treatment at the hands of Bramhall who had deprived him of a benefice that he had held in commendium. Laud intervened and pointed out to Bramhall that the minister had a large family and he added 'I am very confident you will use no act or power to the undoing of any poor man and therefore I pray, if his faults be not grievous to serve him merely for my sake, and I shall thank you heartily for it.'[164] The reply is full of backtracking as Bramhall claims that he believed the complaint had come from Wentworth and he assures Laud that he is now satisfied, conceiving of no 'danger in the man that way for the future.'[165]

During these years Bramhall was playing a dual role; primarily he acted as a Laudian enforcer, but he also performed the important function of acting as an informer. In an undated letter, but one clearly written after the deprivation of the northern ministers, Bramhall sent 'according to your command' a list of the names and surnames of all the judges and King's Council and the 'ringleaders of our non-conformists.'[166] Laud makes a direct connection with incidents of religious

---

159 Trinity College Dublin Ms. 1697, paper XI.
160 Ibid.
161 *BW*, vol. 1, p. viii.
162 Lambeth Palace Library, Ms. 2872, f. 204.
163 Huntington Ms., HA 15168.
164 Huntington Ms., HA 15161, 'Laud to Bramhall, 3 October 1635.'
165 *Papers relating to the Church of Ireland*, Shirley, 'Bramhall to Laud, 1 April 1636', p. 46.
166 Huntington Ms., HA 14039.

independence in Ireland and his own growing trouble at home. In a dispatch to Bramhall in 1637 he tells him that 'no other business is greater than this', as there had arisen a similar struggle recently in England.[167] Laudian logic clearly supposed that if any such tendency could be crushed in Ireland it would facilitate a similar suppression in his back yard. Typically he was never able to grasp that using a sledge hammer to smash such small fruits of unorthodoxy often scattered its seed. One very immediate result of Bramhall's heavy handedness was to have serious future repercussions in that many of the Scottish ministers were driven back to their own country adding to the growing discontent and preparing the way for the crowds of laity whom Wentworth's later policy was to force from Ulster.[168]

By the late 1630s Bramhall was ruling the established Church in Ireland with an iron fist. He had settled the northern counties and was providing shelter for anti-Covenanter pamphleteers, and the refugee John Corbet.[169] In his own diocese he attempted to procure permission to extend the plantation scheme, but though he managed to get Laud's approval, that of the King's was less forthcoming.[170] Nevertheless further control was taken in 1639 when Wentworth wound up the Londonderry company, recalling all their land to the King. It was to be administered by a commission headed by the bishop of Derry.[171] These years saw Bramhall as a fully committed, hard working and fastidious stand-in primate whose industry appeared to be paying dividends. Events were about to overtake him but it must have appeared to him in 1639 that his star was firmly on the cusp.

Whilst Bramhall was tightening his grip on the Irish Church Ussher felt less need to involve himself in ecclesiastical affairs. For the present at least he seemed content to let the Laudians have their day, and if this meant sacrificing the occasional separatists then it appears that this was a price Ussher was prepared to pay for a stronger, more financially secure Church. However the Irish Primate did not completely roll over before Laudian direct control, one area of Irish life was still dear to him and for this he was prepared to resist. Prior to Convocation Laud had targeted Trinity College Dublin for reform. As the seminary of the Irish Church the English Primate recognised its importance, he must also have been aware of the distinctly Calvinist ethos which had permeated the College since its foundation. Laud removed Ussher's cousin, Robert as Provost and replaced him with the Arminian, William Chappel.

---

167 Huntington Ms., HA 15162, 'Laud to Bramhall, 5 April 1637.'

168 R. Bagwell, *Ireland under the Stuarts and during the Interregnum* (2 vols, 1909, London), vol. 1, p. 232.

169 McCafferty, 'Bramhall and Church of Ireland', p. 104.

170 Huntington Ms., HA 15165, 'Laud to Bramhall, 28 March 1638.' Laud replied that in spite of his best efforts with the King he was unable to get approval, though he himself was very favourably disposed to the idea.

171 N. Canny, *Making Ireland British, 1580–1650* (Oxford, 2001), p. 297. Nicholas Canny has argued that Bramhall was part of a policy of Wentworth to introduce complete conquest of Ireland via plantation. There is, he argues, a close association of plantation and Reformation amongst their faction. However, there is no evidence for this with regard to the bishop of Derry. The only proof N. Canny could provide was Bramhall's desire to name the Cathedral in Derry after St Columba, 'who was the first planter of faith in those parts', ibid., pp. 277–8.

One of Ussher's biographers, Richard Elrington rightly points out that Ussher had instigated his cousin's removal on the grounds that he was clearly unsuitable for the position,[172] he is, however, wrong in assuming that the Irish Primate was content with Laud's replacement.[173] The recommendation was secured by Wentworth in his usual blunt fashion when he went to the College and informed the fellows that they would stay until they understood the King's pleasure.[174] Charles Elrington is keen to argue that it was this heavy-handedness, rather than Chappel himself, that Ussher objected to. Besides, he argues, Chappel never in his entire incumbency introduced a single Arminian statute to the College.[175] However, the conflagration which the new Provost's swearing in caused, indicate that the circumstances were a lot more fraught than Elrington suggests.[176] Chappel had lost no time instigating a reform of Trinity immediately insisting on daily chapel and the wearing of the surplice on Sundays. Nor were his innovations confined to liturgical life, Chappel also established a Roman Commonwealth among the students, complete with a dictator, censors and other officers.[177] This could only be interpreted as an assault on the Ramist culture at the College with its leanings toward egalitarianism. In addition the Provost, seen through Protestant eyes, was a thorough-going papist, and the implications of his appointment were clearly understood as inauspicious. The Protestants understood that what could be forced upon Trinity would more than likely become the rule for the whole Church.[178] They were not going to allow this without a struggle.

Chappel's relationship with Ussher had started badly when he refused to wait on the Primate at Drogheda as had been the custom of his predecessors.[179] When trouble arose among the fellows Ussher immediately involved himself as Vice-Chancellor and visitor.[180] One of the fellows named Nathaniel Hoyle had refused to don a surplice declaring it to be 'a rag of popery.'[181] Four of the fellows then appealed to the visitors; an appeal which Chappel declared illegal. He compounded this by committing an illegal act himself manoeuvring his own candidate into a fellowship.[182] Ussher wrote a three page letter to Laud complaining of Chappel, a communication which was received according to Lady Burghclere 'with many groans.'[183] The situation worsened after two senior fellows were expelled and in August 1636 Wentworth was writing his own letter to Laud confessing that he did not know how to resolve the problem. Interestingly the Lord Deputy maintained that

---

172 Elrington, *Life*, p. 155, f.n.
173 Ibid., p. 156.
174 *Strafford Letters*, 'Wentworth to Laud, 23 August 1634', vol. 1, p. 289.
175 C.R. Elrington, *An Answer to Dr Reid's Animadversions upon the Life of Archbishop Ussher* (Dublin, 1849), pp. 15–16.
176 Elrington, *Life*, p. 156. Chappel clearly blamed the delay on Ussher. Ibid.
177 C. Maxwell, *A History of Trinity College, Dublin* (London, 1946), p. 50.
178 D. Bowen, *The History and the shaping of Irish Protestantism* (New York, 1995), p. 87.
179 Carr, *Life*, p. 233.
180 Burghclere, *Strafford*, vol. 2, p. 69.
181 Carr, *Life*, p. 232.
182 Burghclere, *Strafford*, vol. 2, p. 69.
183 Ibid.

the matter had been dealt with too 'sharply.'[184] It is also worth noting that Wentworth clearly still trusted Ussher after their differences, he was unable to perceive him as the instigator of the trouble, tracing it instead to Dr Martin the bishop of Meath rather than 'the mild and gentle disposition of the Primate.'[185] At first Laud lent a sympathetic ear to Ussher's protest, writing to Wentworth he stated 'let him be punished in God's name as a man that attempts to break the peace of the Church.'[186] However, the apparently caring response soon evaporates as Laud loses his patience and turns against Ussher. Later in the letter he exclaims, 'I see the Primate [is] all content to sacrifice honest men for [his] humour, and to lose any friend to be revenged upon not an enemy, but an opinion. Is this your saint?'[187] The vociferous campaign headed by Ussher was only resolved by promoting Chappel out of the College to a less volatile position as bishop to the see of Cork.[188] In April 1637 Laud was writing to Bramhall expressing his satisfaction that the matter between the Primate and the Provost had been concluded 'charitable' rather than 'legal.' This was especially so since Wentworth had told him that he was 'without all hope of any accommodation.'[189] The incident was not however a resounding success for Ussher; he had by this time been usurped from his role as primary visitor which he had enjoyed as Vice-Chancellor. The affront was all the more poignant since it came from Laud, the very man he had requested to be Chancellor. Ussher took no further interest in the College.

It might be tempting to interpret Ussher's silence in matters of Church and state as a resentful one. That he wisely stayed out of the way of the new regime, though an attack on his beloved *alma mater* was more than he could bear. However this was not the case. Ussher may have supported the fellows at his College and there can be no doubt that he would have been resistant to the programme that Chappel was trying to implement, yet his loyalty and commitment to the English regime never wavered. One incident in 1638 involving Ussher and Bramhall does much to show that the Primate, far from brooding beneath his silence, was a supporter of the post-1634 establishment. On occasion he was even prepared to defend it. In 1638 the somewhat maverick bishop of Kilmore, William Bedell, had held a diocesan synod based on what Bramhall described as 'some obsolete canons.' The synod had passed various acts and canons among which one forbade the public catechising of women.[190] Bramhall reported to Laud that he had told the bishop 'How opposite to his Majesty's prerogative and laws of the Kingdoms. How inconvenient some of them are for this Church ... .' Bramhall was particularly anxious about one which prohibited burying inside churches, he told Laud that this was offensive to the Irish 'who are mightily addicted to their fathers sepulchres ... .'[191] This aside, the bishop of

---

184 *Strafford Letters*, 'Wentworth to Laud, 9 March 1635', vol. 2, p. 26.
185 Ibid.
186 Laud, *Works*, 'Laud to Wentworth, 8 September 1636', vol. 7, p. 281.
187 Ibid.
188 Carr, *Life*, p. 237.
189 Huntington Ms., HA 15162, 'Laud to Bramhall, 5 April 1637.'
190 Trinity College Dublin Ms. 1697, paper XV, 'Bramhall to Laud, 2 November 1638.'
191 *Shirley Papers*, 'Bramhall to Laud, 12 January 1638', p. 65.

Derry seems untroubled and a letter to Laud later that year even requests that some forbearance be allowed at least for a time.[192]

Ussher on the other hand, declared himself with 'some passion' against Bedell's canons, and he earnestly entreated Bramhall to be his delegate when the matter was brought before the High Commission. Remarkably, Bramhall is unable to oblige, since he had already agreed to represent Bedell.[193] Meanwhile Ussher wrote to Laud advising him to tell Bedell to 'forbear the Execution of them: as far as they are singular, and different from the canons of the National Synod confirmed here by his Majesties supreme Authority.'[194] Bedell had at the time fallen out with his Primate when he charged him with permitting excessive exaction and corruption in his ecclesiastical courts. Ussher had replied tartly 'that if men stood not more in fear of the fees of the court than of standing in a white sheet, we should have here among us another Sodom and Gomorrah.'[195] This may shed some light on the force of Ussher's reaction, nevertheless it is illuminating to compare the attitude of this latitudinarian with that of the draconian Bramhall. The bishop of Derry does of course insist that the canons be declared void but as he was counselling moderation his Primate was becoming more heated. Finally, only when Bramhall intercedes with him on behalf of Bedell does Ussher agree to an *amnestia*, though he asks, 'was not the hand of Joab in all this.'[196] On this occasion Bramhall is in an uncharacteristically forgiving mood, even when the bishop of Kilmore is castigating him for his role in the commission's decision, he takes the attack lying down, deciding 'out of the uprightness of mine own conscience, to make myself a garland of his invective flowers.'[197] Generally speaking Ussher and Bramhall's Church leadership may be characterised as one trying to make the Church as eclectic as possible whilst the other attempted to make it as uniform as possible. The above incident may only prove that some times they both acted out of character; yet it does establish one other important point. In spite of what has been written to the contrary Ussher approved, supported and defended the new ordinances that he had helped to construct in 1634.

Two incidents at the end of the 1630s were more in keeping with Bramhall's general tactics, though in one of them (which was to haunt him in later years) his part was significantly exaggerated by his now gathering enemies. Both events did little to endear him to the theological lower end of the Church. The first however saw Bramhall play the significant part. This was the deprivation of Bishop Adair of Killala. He was brought before the High Commission in Dublin after remarks he made betrayed a certain sympathy for the Covenanters. He was duly deprived unanimously by the bishops and once again Bramhall found it necessary to give free

---

192 Trinity College Dublin Ms. 1697, paper XV.

193 Ibid., paper XVI.

194 A. Ford, 'Correspondence between Archbishops Ussher and Laud', *Archivium Hibernicum*, XLVI (1991–92): 19.

195 Murphy, 'Archbishop Ussher': 154.

196 Huntington Ms., HA 15957, 'Ussher to Bramhall, 28 February 1639.' Joab was a general in David's army. In spite of misdeeds he had a mysterious hold over David who confessed that he was unable to punish him, 2 Samuel 3:38.

197 Trinity College Dublin Ms. 1697, paper XVI.

reign to his tongue declaring that Adair was 'fit to be thrown into the sea in a sack, not to see sun, nor enjoy the air.'[198]

Much more serious than this incident in the eyes of the Ulster Scots was Bramhall's close association with the Black Oath. The Oath was proposed and drawn up by Wentworth in January 1639, in it the Scots living in Ireland would be 'gently persuaded' to swear to a rejection of the Covenant.[199] Ussher wrote to Bramhall warning him that he saw that trouble was 'like to arise' from the oath 'which, God knoweth, this time had little need of.'[200] Yet for the royal household the Oath had greater significance and it was too important to set aside. The idea was that Ireland would once more act as a policy testing ground with a view to introducing a similar oath in England and Scotland.[201] Strafford's correspondence at the time suggests that the bishop played no part in the composition of the Oath.[202] Nevertheless he was very active in enforcing it and he was ever afterwards indelibly linked to it by those it most offended. To add insult to the Scottish injury, Bramhall had during these years offered hospitality to Catholic leaders such as the Archbishop of Dublin, they became convinced that he was an Irish Richelieu whose main endeavour was to establish royal autocracy.[203] It was also this incident which earned him Cromwell's sobriquet of the 'Irish Canterbury.'[204]

Ussher left his native country in 1640 never to return, he did however continue to work with Bramhall particularly as Ireland lunged into a state of crisis. The bishop of Derry sent his Primate a petition for examination which called for the abolition of episcopacy in Ireland. Ussher replied that he would be able to get 'half of those hands to sign a contrary petition', and add to it a further 50,000 names. Ussher claims that he mentioned this twice to the King who requested that he get Bramhall to organise it.[205] No trace of such a petition exists and we cannot know if Bramhall ever got around to the task.[206] If he did it would have represented the last time the two prelates worked together. In 1642 Bramhall was also in England, his world in Ireland that he had laboured so hard to create, had collapsed around him. He had no choice but to take his cause to England. Once there he would find that Ussher, in spite of a perceived ambivalence in some quarters, in spite also of his theological sympathies, would be contesting along side him once more.

It would be easy to assess the change in direction the Irish Church experienced as the tenure of Ussher passed, almost surreptitiously to Bramhall, as one based on

---

198 *House of Lords Journal Ireland*, vol. 1, p. 112; E.W. Watson claimed that this statement may not be applicable to Adair given the short hand in which it is written. In spite of this, it is difficult to see in its present context who else it could be referring to. Watson, 'Typical churchmen', fn. p. 98.
199 Perceval-Maxwell, 'Ulster Scots': 536.
200 *Hastings Ms.*, 'Ussher to Bramhall, 29 July 1640', vol. 4, p. 89.
201 Perceval-Maxwell, 'Ulster Scots': 537.
202 *Strafford Letters*, vol. 2, pp. 344–6.
203 Bowen, *Irish Protestantism*, p. 87.
204 McCafferty, 'John Bramhall', p. 104.
205 *Rawdon Papers*, 'Ussher to Bramhall, undated', p. 82.
206 Perceval-Maxwell, *The Outbreak of the Irish rebellion of 1641*, p. 114.

issues of materialism and order.²⁰⁷ Certainly the principal basis for the activities of the New English cortege seemed to be restoring the physical wealth and structure of the established Church. It must also be said that there is a good deal of primary evidence to show that Bramhall personally was not averse to enriching himself in the process. However, underscoring these highly practical endeavours was a deeper theological significance. Ussher made the occasional, limp effort to fortify his visible church, but this area of policy never enjoyed his full attention simply because compared to the word of God it was not a priority. When Luther compared the Word of the Old Testament with that of the New he wrote of the latter being 'cut short.' The former was of necessity elongated that it might be perceived of the senses. The Word now is perfect, cleansed of contamination, it cannot share in the visible world, it is cut off from these things and they are no longer necessary.²⁰⁸ This Reformed theology finds a reflection in the policy of Ussher. If the word of God could not reform Ireland then nothing else would; and if Ussher talked of improving the economics of his Church he did so in order to provide it with a solid preaching ministry. For Bramhall, and the other Laudians who valued the numinous, creating a house fit for God and a sanctuary of holiness would restore to Ireland a valid Church. The buildings they refurbished would reflect the numinous and the land they retrieved would be made holy and separate once more. This was in their eyes, not only sound policy, but failure to do so would amount to nothing short of sacrilege. The recovery of ecclesiastical wealth and jurisdiction was perhaps the only Stuart/Laudian policy common to all three kingdoms.²⁰⁹ Laud explicitly used the term 'sacrilege' to describe lay appropriations.²¹⁰ As mentioned previously this is characteristic of a Laudian preferred theological method, their forte was to express their convictions in the short, sharp world of policy decisions, rather than the convoluted arena of polemics.

It would perhaps be even easier to regard the policy shift from the Ussherian regime to the Laudian takeover as purely an exercise in Anglicization. It has been argued that Laud was seeking out a 'lowest common multiple' an ideal to which all Churches must aspire, the Church of England corresponding most closely to it, 'the Churches of Scotland and Ireland had to abandon much false practice even before they began to join the English Church in the final striving after perfection.'²¹¹ Another study adds that with regard to the Reformation in Ireland there was not a 'mission strategy' but rather an 'anglicizing one.'²¹² In terms of Ussher and Bramhall this implied for the former sacrificing the small portion of independence for the sake of survival. For the latter it meant improving the Irish Church on the basis of the working model Church he had grown up in, the English Church. However,

---

207 Certainly Iain Mackenzie sees order as the driving force behind Laudianism. I.M. Mackenzie, *God's Order and Natural Law: The Works of the Laudian Divines* (Aldershot, 2002), p. 915.
208 G.W. Bromiley, *Historical Theology: An Introduction* (Edinburgh, 1978), p. 211.
209 Morrill, 'British patriarchy?', p. 224.
210 Ibid.
211 Ibid., p. 226.
212 McCafferty, 'John Bramhall', p. 111.

this represents only part of a much fuller ecclesiological understanding. Whilst both Ussher and Bramhall kept an immediate eye fixed on their domestic Churches, both kept another eye focused on the wider family of international Churches. If it was the intended purpose of the 1615 Articles to be all encompassing the very obvious omission of Episcopal ordination must also be seen as an attempt to embrace the majority of continental Protestants. Any insistence on *de jure divino* episcopacy effectively unchurched most of the European Reformers. As mentioned in the previous chapter Bramhall also has a wider vision, he wanted the English Church to join in communion with the family of Catholic Churches World wide. In these circumstances being joined at the hip to a deformed twin in Ireland (not to mention Scotland) was something of an obstacle. If we are to take into consideration Bramhall's later writings on the future of the Catholic Churches then we must regard his policy in Ireland as being based partly on raising the Church theologically in order to Catholicize the Church of the three kingdoms. Then it might be prepared to take its place among the great quorum of old Episcopal Churches.

Perhaps we cannot know if this represented official Laudian policy. The Primate was notoriously taciturn concerning his ultimate intentions. However a short passage in a letter to Ussher gives us a tantalizing glimpse of what might have been his bigger picture when he writes, 'And while I use the word conformity, I pray your Grace to understand, that his Majesty's meaning is not conformity to or with the Church of England, but with the whole Catholic Church of Christ ... .'[213] It was Peter Heylin writing in 1658 who first maintained that subscription to the Irish Articles had meant easy subscription to all the Reformed Churches. One recent commentary suggests that the imposition of the 39 Articles allowed no such 'continental drift.'[214] This is true, but it is only part of their purpose, their primary intention may have been to prevent a drift North, but their secondary, long term, intention was to set a more Southerly and Easterly course into what were obviously regarded as the warmer, more congenial waters of Catholicism.

---

213 Laud, *Works*, vol. 7, pp. 291–3.
214 McCafferty, 'God Bless', p. 189.

Conclusion

When John Bramhall used the Levitical Candle as a metaphor for his relationship with James Ussher[1] he was following a long allegorical tradition. The kabbalah, a mystical medieval Jewish sect, regarded the menorah as symbolising the tree of life, the seven branches represented the seven planets and the seven days of creation.[2] More orthodox interpretations were more intellectual; the stem was symbolic of the Torah [law] and the branches the sciences, all seen as rooted in the law.[3] Bramhall employs the same stem and branch imagery, making clever use of the fact that the candelabrum diverges from one source to several. The symbolism is obvious, he and Ussher may have had theological points of departure, they may have appeared to some (such as Richard Baxter)[4] as ecclesiastically inimical, yet in truth they were rooted and held aloft by the solid base of the one Church.

Has this assessment of their relationship stood the test of this examination? After all we have seen many authors from opposing camps posthumously claiming and counter-claiming Ussher as a fellow traveller for centuries. We have throughout this study offered the biblical justice and numinous motifs as a means of gauging theological, and consequently political, perspective. This approach has produced consistent conclusions which indicate that Ussher gravitated toward the justice pole with its leitmotifs of law and judgement. Chapter 3 showed that in terms of dogmatic theology he was pessimistic, regarding man as fallen and incapable of his own redemption. He is fundamentally logocentric and Chapter 4 indicated that the Primate viewed the sacraments as important, but secondary to the reception of the Word. Concomitant with this, Chapter 5 pointed out that Ussher's pursuit of history followed, if subconsciously, the Mosaic tradition of the biblical prophets who look to direct divine intervention (judgement) into human events. Leaving aside Chapter 6 for a moment, if we consider the ecclesiastical politics of Chapter 7 we see that the word (law) is once more central. Ussher's world would have a Church, or Churches, held in unity by a set of minimum Christian tenets, as pure as they were basic. This in turn translated into a practical policy that was based on latitudinarian, Reformed principles.

In these chapters we have also seen that in all these areas what emerges from Bramhall's writings, sermons and policy is an ecclesiastic who is drawn, just as strongly as Ussher, but in the opposite direction toward the numinous motif. Bramhall is optimistic in his assessment of the nature of man. He goes as far as the boundaries of orthodoxy permit by saying that man is able to choose good and, by implication, salvation. The sacraments, with their mystery and grace are of focal importance

---

1   *BW*, vol. 5, p. 74.
2   *Oxford Dictionary of the Jewish Religion*, eds R.J. Zwi-Werblowsky and G. Wigoder (Oxford, 1997), p. 456.
3   L. Jacobs, *The Jewish Religion: A Companion* (Oxford, 1995), pp. 341–2.
4   R. Baxter, *The Grotian Religion discovered* (London, 1658), passim.

for Bramhall's soteriology. He talks of the Eucharist in Catholic terms reflective of the leitmotifs of holiness and sacredness; he does not even demur at sacrificial associations. Bramhall's ecclesiology is underpinned by an episcopacy that has been imparted by the laying on of hands, the bestowing of sanctity. His policy in Ireland represented efforts to establish a holy and apostolic Church to rival that of the Roman Catholics. All these terms are rooted in the cultic practices of Israel and dependent for their function and effect on what Rudolf Otto called the numinous.[5]

Could such disparate understandings be held together? The answer to this question is that clearly they were. James Ussher and John Bramhall lived, worked, wrote and died as members of the same ecclesiastical organisation. It is therefore apparent that they were being held together by some sort of unifying principle. This poses a rather perplexing question, what ideological notion could have held together these rather diametric versions of Christianity? It is argued here that the answer was provided in Chapter 6, the stem and base of Ussher's and Bramhall's Levitical candle was secular politics. Both clerics were divine-right monarchists, their understanding that their prince, their secular and religious ruler, was appointed by God provided their axis. What deviated in their theology was bound together by their politics. This was no doubt given considerable impetus by the exigencies of their time. In the political storms of the 1640s they both anchored in royalist waters, though it has to be said that this would have provided a more natural harbour for Bramhall than it would for Ussher. The latter's political choice can almost certainly be explained by Ussher's perspective as a member of the Irish establishment whose *raison d'etre* was so firmly rooted in English royalty. Besides, even in biblical times the courts had their prophets as well as their priests. It seems therefore that Bramhall's metaphor holds, the Levitical candle is intact and held secure by the common base that was provided in the certainty of absolutism.

If we are allowed to pursue Bramhall's analogy, a rather interesting further question emerges. In the Temple of Solomon we are told that there were ten Menorahim, five to the right and five to the left of the holy of holies (1 Kings 7:49). If we expand on Bramhall's metaphor and regard these candelabra as separate Churches, we may position the Reformed to the left, the Catholic to the right. If we then take the Temple to represent the Christian world, the visible Church, it begs the question, where would either Ussher or Bramhall place the candelabrum that so apparently united them? From what we know of their theology and politics it is difficult to see their menorah holding when such an analogy is applied. Ussher's justice and Bramhall's numinous motifs would surely have dragged them in opposite directions, Ussher to the left and Bramhall to the right of the shrine. The former seeking out the company of those Churches built on the divine Word, whilst Bramhall would look for a home among those Churches which based their integrity on the sacred. We must conclude then that Bramhall's analogy is secure only so long as the lights were looking downward to identify their foundation. This was precisely what was happening in the 1640s in these islands as protagonists in the conflicts sought to identify the source and foundation of their secular and religious institutions. Both intimated their vision of Christendom but only as some future purpose. Had this era

---

5   R. Otto, *The Idea of the Holy* (Oxford, 1923), passim.

in English and Irish history been more eirenic, had the foundations of the National Church been more established, then the vision may have been more peripheral as they looked around them in order to fix their place in the Temple of Christendom. Under these circumstances Ussher and Bramhall would almost certainly have parted company. If this is true then perhaps we may conclude that it was time, events, and circumstances that actually held their Levitical candle together.

It has been the argument of this volume that post-Reformation theology is best gauged and identified not within categories or under labels. Indeed attempts to do so have often ended in rather confusing fudges. Perhaps the worst consequence of these ill-fitting labels is that they allow authors such as Peter White to argue that since these categories did not in reality exist, then neither did any real theological differences.[6] If, on the other hand, we release ourselves as historians from the straitjacket of compartments and apply instead a spectrum of religious impulses ranging between the justice and numinous poles we will find in its flexibility a more accurate account of the diverse range of Christian theology that made up not only Anglican tradition, but also that vast spectrum of multifarious movements, denominations, schools and individuals that is post-Reformation Christianity. James Ussher and John Bramhall defy firm categorization, their religious convictions do not rest upon any particular set of tenets. Nor indeed do the rest of Protestant and Catholic theologians from Calvin and Bucer to Borremeo and Cajetan. Rather the beliefs they espoused were expressions of a pull toward two religious motifs as old as that disparate gathering of believers that came to be known collectively as the Israelites.

As historians we have been too ready to drive a wedge between Christianity and its Semitic past. Often we have assumed that Christians have been influenced or informed by the Old Testament simply because they read it. This is a gross underestimation of the impact of Christianity's Jewish ancestry. Unless we restore Christianity as a religious tradition to its theological parents then we will only ever be able to half-understand it. The justice and numinous motifs are presented here as a method for going some small way to effecting that restoration and thereby obtaining a clearer understanding of ecclesiastical history.

---

6   P. White, *Conflict and Consensus in the English Church from the Reformation to the Civil War* (Cambridge, 1992) passim.

Bibliography

I PRIMARY SOURCES

1 Manuscripts

(i) Balliol College, Oxford

259 Volume containing 34 sermons by Ussher

(ii) Bishop Marsh's Library, Dublin

z.3.1.3 1622 visitation; Orders and directions for the Church of Ireland
z.3.2.5 Extracts from the parliamentary journals, 1623–41
z.3.2.6 Bramhall to Charles Vaughan, 12 December 1639
z.4.2.1 High Commission proceedings and fragments.
z.3.1.1 Bramhall's petition to the Lord Justices after his arrest 4 May 1641
z.3.4.24 Bishop Ussher's praediction (plus other material)

(iii) Bodleian Library, Oxford

313 Five letters of Ussher to T. Lydyat, 1617–43

Additional:
C286 Letters of Wandesforde to Wentworth, 1636–40
C287 Collection of Ussher's writings on chronology
C296 Collection by Ussher on the history of the British Isles
C299 Ussher's papers
C301 Miscellaneous papers of Ussher
A379 Ussher's writing on Easter and bishops
A380 Miscellaneous papers of Ussher

Ashmolean:
828 Briefe narrative on Ussher by N. Bernard

Barlow:
13 Theological collection and sermons on Ussher

Cherry:
19 Account of Ussher's views on justification

Perrott:
9 Notes taken from Ussher's sermon, 1620

Rawlison:
89 Letters of Ussher, 1612–30
C850 Collectanea varia Jacobi Usserii
C919 Theological commonplace of Archbishop Ussher
D224 Ussher's theological extracts and notes on his private affairs
D280 Theological and historical extracts by Ussher
D320 Bramhall's conference at Northallerton
D1290 Theological and historical extracts by Ussher

Sancroft:
18 Ussher's letters

Savile:
47 Epitaph by J. Greaves on Ussher

Smith:
21 Letters of James Ussher to John Seldon, 1625
71 Four letters of Ussher to Sir R. Cotton, 1627–29
75 Letter of Ussher to Patricius Janius, 1639

Tanner:
67 Letters of Ussher to S. Ward, 1640
70 Three letters of Ussher to S. Ward 1634
72 Four letters of Ussher to S. Ward, 1629–34
73 Letters of Ussher to S. Ward, 1625–28
74 Letters of Ussher to S. Ward, 1623–25
281 Ussher's treatise on episcopacy and ordination
458 Discourse of Ussher on imperial laws

(iv) British Library, London

Additional:
4274 Ussher to Lady Tyrreil, 1654
4763 Bramhall to Secretary Nicholas, 1662
15856 Catalogue of bishoprics in Ireland – 1655
19831 Documents relating to Richard Boyle
19831 Correspondence of the Earl of Cork, 1633–44
23113 The deduction [sic] of the episcopacy 1648
25384 Ussher to Henry Spelman 1628
33746 Memoirs of events 1530–44
34253 Ussher's evidence to the House of Commons
34599 Ussher's correspondence with Henry Spelman
34600 Letter of Ussher to Henry Spelman

Harleian:
822 Bibliothecae Theologicae-Usserii

1837 Greek codex with marginal notes by Ussher
5108 Bishop of Armach's direction to the House on Liturgy and Episcopacy

Landsdowne:
827 Copy of articles of impeachment against Bramhall

Sloane:
402 Two letters of Ussher
654 Letters from Ussher to John Dury, 1633, 1634, 1639
1012 Extracts from Bramhall on liberty & necessity
1449 The Church History of Ireland
3827 Correspondence of Falkland on Irish affairs, 1604–32
3838 A short view of the state of Ireland, 1640

Stowe:
76 Notices of Downham and Ussher
155 Document by R. Ware relating to Calvin's overtures in 1549 for Union with English churches
180 Opinions of Archbishop of Armagh on the Book of Common Prayer

(v) Dr Williams Library, London

12.4.18 Short catechism enlarged by the author, Ussher
12.55.7 A petition to Parliament by Ussher requesting the suppression of a false publication under his name
12.58.12 Copy of a most pithy and pious letter by James Ussher
3022.e.5. A discourse of religion anciently professed with the author's corrections

(vi) Henry E. Huntington Library, San Marino, California

Hastings Irish Papers Boxes 5–8, unsorted material, 1623–41
HA 14037–14080 Bramhall correspondence and papers, 1633–62
HA 14191 List of bishoprics 1660 July
HA 14192 Petition to Charles II
HA 14193 Petition to the Lords Justices 1661 June 3
HA 14668 College of Arms. Grant of arms to John Bramhall 1628, November 20
HA 15153–15173 Laud–Bramhall correspondence, August 1633–January 1641
HA 15948–15960 Laud–Bramhall correspondence, January 1634—March 1645

Other:
HM 102 Copies of letters of Strafford and others
HM 22294 Letter from Oliver Cromwell to the Commission of Parliament for Irish affairs

(vii) House of Lords Library

Long Historical Mss Examination of Ussher upon Strafford's cause
Comm 4, app., 1874

(viii) Lambeth Palace Library

2004 Ussher's letter to the Earl of Bath 1638
2413 Portrait of Ussher
2872 Letter from Laud to Bramhall, 1638
dc.170 Original Institution of Corbes
dxciv. 68 Manuscripti codices Usseriani
w.5.28 Sermon by Ussher before the King at Greenwich, 25 July 1627
w.15.28 Two sermons by Ussher at Great St Barts
Laud 943 Letters from Laud to Bramhall and Wentworth

(ix) Public Records Office Northern Ireland, Belfast

T415 (1–18) Ten letters of Wentworth to Bramhall, 1634–39
T415 (22) Two letters of Ussher to Bramhall concerning Church Affairs
T415 (26) Letter of Charles I to Bramhall, 30 July 1641

(x) Representative Church Body Library, Dublin

C2.14.2.34 Nineteenth century copy of a letter from Bishop Bramhall to Jonas Wheeler, Bishop of Kilkenny
C6.26.13 Bramhall's report on Christchurch lands, 1637
List 64 Correspondence and sketches regarding memorial to Ussher In Westminster Abbey 1903–05

(xi) Trinity College, Dublin

77.78 Letter from Ussher to W. Bedell
510 Eulogium Britanniae – Ussher
545 Ussher to Spelman, Sept. 1639
578 Ussher's proofs that laws made in England bind them in Ireland
580 Letters concerning the Church, 1620–30
581 On the antiquity of the British religion
582 Instructions for the Church, 1620; Ussher's notes on the primacy dispute
663 Some episcopal sees founded by St Patrick
672 Various papers – Ireland seventeenth century
773 Abridgement of James Ussher's 'Catechisme'
774 Collection of notes and tracts by Ussher on theological, historical and philological matters
776 Theological tracts collected by Ussher
777 Theological tracts by Ussher

778 Book by Ussher relating to logic, ethics and rhetoric
779 A transcript on the history of the Popes annotated by Ussher
780 Collection of material on canon law and history compiled by Ussher
781 Epistles of Ignatius, annotated by Ussher
782 A collection of material on Church History compiled by Ussher
783 Material relating to canon law and astronomy, annotated by Ussher
784 'A history of the Christian Churches' by Ussher
842 Speech by Ussher at Dublin Castle, 1635
853 Various documents, reign of James I
865 A brief narration concerning the primacy dispute
943 Collection of Ussher's letters
1038 Convocation journals, Dean Andrews on the canons
1067 The 1634 visitation
1073 Bishop Reeves's annotated Elrington
1173 Sermons by Archbishop Ussher on the six witnesses
1185 Ussher's Antiquities of British and Irish Churches (trans. into English)
1697 Letters of Bramhall to Laud, 1631–39, relating to the Church
2877 Transcript of cancelled pages in Parr's life of Ussher
2940 Religious treatise by James Ussher
3659 Ussher to Spelman 4 September 1639 (Copy from Pierpoint Morgan Library, New York)
Mawr Miscellaneous texts in various hands collected by James Ussher
Sc 43464 Considerations on the Book of Common Prayer by Ussher

2 Printed

The works of James Ussher

Elrington, C.E. and Todd, J.H. (eds), *The whole works of James Ussher* (17 vols, Dublin, 1847–64).
Sermon preached before the Commons House of Parliament in St Margaret's church at Westminster 18 February 1620 (London, 1631).
Briefe declaration of the universalitie of the Church of Christ and the Unitie of the Catholike faith (London, 1631).
The opinions of the Most Reverend Father in God, James Ussher (London, 1634).
Touching innovations in the doctrine and discipline of the Church of England (London, 1641).
The Protestation of the Archbishops and bishops of Ireland (London, 1641).
The soveraignes power and the subjects duty (London, 1644).
A body of divinitie or the summe and substance of Christian religion (London, 1647).
The rights of primogeniture (London, 1648).
The daily examination of sins (London, 1652).
The Principles of the Christian Religion (London, 1654).
Eighteen sermons preached at Oxford, 1640 (London, 1659).

The great necessity of unity and peace among all Protestants (London, 1688).
Tracts attributed to James Ussher
Directions concerning liturgy and espiscopal government (London, 1640).
Vox Hiberniae (London, 1641).
Letter written by Ussher to persuade the King to return to Parliament (London, 1645).
A message from the Isle of Wight (London, 1648).
Bishop Ussher's Praediction (London, undated).
Bishop Usher's second prophesie (London, 1681).
Strange and remarkable prophesies (London, 1681)
The Prophecy of Bishop Usher (London, 1687).
The fulfilling of prophecies, or the prophecies and predictions of the late learned James Ussher (London, 1689).
Europe's warning piece; or bishop Usher's life and prophesies (London, 1712).
Opinions concerning the return of Popery into England, Scotland and Ireland 1682, reprinted with a preface by H.P. Disney, (Armagh, 1843).

The works of John Bramhall

Hadden, A. W. (ed.), *The works of the most reverend father in God, John Bramhall* (5 vols, Oxford, 1842–45).
Sermon preached in the Cathedral church of York, June 30 1643 (London, 1643).
Berwick, J. (ed.), *The Rawdon Papers, Letters to and from John Bramhall* (London, 1819).

Contemporary and other primary sources

Abbott, W. (ed.), *The Writings and Speeches of Oliver Cromwell* (4 vols, Oxford, 1947).
Anonymous, *A detection of the falsehood in a pamphlet intituled – A message from the Ilse of Wight brought by Major Cromwell* (London, 1648).
Anonymous, *Twenty–one conclusions* (Oxford, 1688).
Ayre, J. (ed.), *The Works of John Jewel* (London, 1845).
Baxter, R., *The Grotian Religion discovered* (London, 1658).
———, *The autobiography of Richard Baxter* (London, 1974).
Baylie, R., *A review of a seditious pamphlet lately published in Holland by Dr Bramhell pretended bishop of Londonderry* (London, 1649).
Bernard, N., *The life and death of the most reverend and learned father of our Church, Dr James Ussher* (London, 1656).
———, *The judgement of the late Archbishop of Armagh and Primate of Ireland of Babylon. Rev. 18:4* (London, 1658).
———, *Clavi Trabales* (London, 1661).
Bliss, J. (ed.), *William Laud, Works* (7 vols, Oxford, 1847–60).
Bramley-Moore, W. (ed.), *Foxe's Book of Martyrs* (London, 1865).
Brereton, W., *Travels in Holland, the United Provinces, England, Scotland and Ireland* (London, 1634).

Burnet, G., *The life of William Bedell* (Dublin, 1736 edition).
Carte, T., *Life of Ormonde* (London, 1736).
Cavendish, M., *The life of William Cavendish, Duke of Newcastle* (London, 1667).
Clarendon, E., *The History of the Rebellion* (6 vols, Oxford, 1888).
C.R., *Doctor of divinity* (London, 1655).
De Beer, E.S. (ed.), *The Diary of John Evelyn* (6 vols, Oxford, 1951).
Ferne, H., *A conscience satisfied* (London, 1643).
Firth, C.H., (ed.), *The Memoirs of Edmund Ludlow, 1625–1672* (2 vols, Oxford, 1894).
Fuller, T., *The Church history of Britain* (London, 1665).
Furcha, E.J. (ed.), Zwingli *Writings* (2 vols, Pennsylvania, 1984).
Hammond,H., *Nineteen letters of Henry Hammond D.D.* (London, 1739).
Heylyn, P., *The answer of Peter Heylyn* (London, 1658).
Hobbes, T., *Leviathan* (London, 1968 edition).
Gardiner, S.R., *The Constitutional Documents of the Puritan Revolution, 1625–1660* (Oxford, 1909).
Gee, H. and Hardy, W.J. (eds), *Documents Illustrative of English Church History* (London, 1896).
Gower, S., *A Preface to eighteen sermons* (London, 1659).
G.R.B., *A review of Dr Bramble* (London, 1649).
Hill, G. (ed.), *Montgomery Manuscripts, 1603–1706* (Belfast, 1869).
Kendra Baker, H., *Glastonbury Traditions* (London, 1930).
Knowler, W. (ed.), *Strafford's Letters and Dispatches* (Dublin, 1740).
Lindley, K. and Scott, D. (eds), *The Journal of Thomas Juxon,1644–1647,* Camden Fifth Series, vol. 13, (Cambridge, 1999).
Luther, M., *Luther's Works* (55 vols, Philadelphia, 1960).
Malone, W., *A reply to Mr. Ussher's answere* (London, 1627).
Marvell, A., *The rehearsal transpos'd* (London, 1672).
McNeill, C. (ed.), *Tanner Letters* (Dublin, 1943).
McNeill, J.T. (ed.), *Calvin's Institutes of the Christian Religion,* (London, 1961).
Mervyn, A., *A speech made to the Upper House with certain articles of high treason Against Bramhall* (London, 1641).
Midwinter, E., *The history, life and death of that most learned and pious divine, Bishop James Usher. With his wonderful prophesies* (London, 1712).
Milner, J., *A defence of Archbishop Usher* (Cambridge, 1694).
Milton, J., *Of prelatical episcopacy* (London, 1641).
Nichols, J. and Nichols, W. (eds), *The works of James Arminius* (2 vols, London, 1825–75).
Parker, H., *Observations upon some of His Majesty's late answers and expresses* (London, 1642).
Parr, R., *The life of the most reverend Father in God, James Ussher, late Lord of Armagh* (London, 1686).
Pierce, T., *ΕΑΥΤΟΝΤΙΜΩΡΟΥΜΕΝΟΣ, The self revenger exemplified* (London, 1658).
Prynne, W., *Anti-Arminianisme* (London, 1630).
——, *History of the Tryall of Laud* (London, 1644).

———, *Canterburies doom* (London, 1646).
Quarles, J., *An elegie on the most Reverend and learned James Ussher* (London, 1656).
R.C., *A brief survey of the Lord of Derry* (Paris, 1655).
Rushworth, J., *The trial of Strafford* (London, 1680).
———, *Historical Collections of Private passages of State, Weighty Matters of law* (7 vols, London, 1701).
Searle, A. (ed.), *Barrington family letters, 1628–32* (London, 1983).
S.W., *Schism disarmed* (London, 1655).
Shirley, E.P. (ed.), *Original letters of the Church of Ireland* (London, 1851).
———, *Papers relating to the Church of Ireland, 1631–1639* (London, 1874).
Sibthorp, C., *A friendly advertisement to the pretended Catholickes of Ireland* (London, 1622).
Spalding, R. (ed.), *The Diary of Bulstrode Whitelocke, 1605–1675* (Oxford, 1995).
Stephens, A., *Ms. Book of Common Prayer according to the use of the united Church of England and Ireland* (3 vols, Belfast, 1849).
Synge, G., *Rejoynder to the reply to James Ussher published by the Iesuites under the name of William Malone* (Dublin, 1632).
Taylor, J., *A sermon preached at the funeral of Bramhall with a narrative of his whole life* (London, 1663).
Tibbutt, H.G. (ed.), *The Letter Book of Samuel Luke, 1644–45* (London, 1963).
Verdidicus, P., *A briefe confutation of certaine absurd heretical and damnable doctrines delivered by Mr. James Ussher* (London, 1627).

3 Calendars of state papers

Calendar of State Papers Domestic, 1637–49.
Calandar of State Papers Ireland, 1603–62
Calendar of the Clarendon State Papers, vols 4 and 5, ed. J. Routledge (Oxford, 1932).

4 Historical Manuscripts Commision

Cowper, ed. W.D. Fane, (London, 1888).
Franciscan Manuscripts, eds G.D. Burtchaell and J.M. Rigg (Dublin, 1906).
Hastings Manuscripts, vol. 4, ed. Harley (London, 1928).

5 Government journals

Journals of the House of Lords, vols 4 and 9
Commons Journal, Ireland, vol. 1

6 Newsbooks

A perfect summary of chief passages in Parliament, 20–27 September 1647.
The Kingdom's Weekly Intelligences, 18–25 January 1648.
Mercurius Politicus, 10 April 1656.

II SECONDARY SOURCES

1 Books

Acton, J.E.A.D., *Essays on the Church and State*, (London: Hollis & Carter, 1952).
Aikin, J., *The lives of John Seldon, esq. and Archbishop Ussher* (London: Matthew & Leigh, 1812).
Allen, J.W., *A History of Political Thought in the Sixteenth Century* (London: Meuthuen, 1957).
———, *A History of Political Thought 1603–1644* (London: Meuthuen, 1967).
Aveling, J.C.H., Loades, D.M. and McAdoo, H.R., *Rome and the Anglicans* (Berlin: W. de Gruyter, 1982).
Avis, P., *Anglicanism and the Christian Church* (Edinburgh: T. & T. Clark, 1987).
Aylmer, G.E., *The King's Servants: the Civil service of Charles I, 1625–42* (London: Routlegde, 1974).
Bagwell, R., *Ireland under the Stuarts and during the interregnum* (2 vols, London: Longmans: Green & Co., 1909).
Ball, J.T., *The Reformed Church of Ireland, 1537–1886* (London: Longmans, Green & Co, 1886).
Bardon, J., *A History of Ulster* (London: Blackstaff Press, 1992).
Barnard, T.C., *Cromwellian Ireland* (Oxford: Oxford University Press, 1975).
Barton, J., (ed.), *The Biblical World* (2 vols, London: Routledge, 2002).
Barwick, P., *The Life of Dr J. Barwick* (London: Bettenham, 1724).
Beckett, J.C., *A Short History of Ireland* (London: Hutchison, 1952).
Bennett, M., *The Civil Wars in Britain and Ireland, 1638–51* (Oxford: Blackwell, 1997).
Bernard, J.H., *Archbishop Ussher* (Edinburgh, 1895).
Berwick, E., *The Rawdon Papers* (London: Nichols & Son, 1819).
Bolton, F.R., *The Caroline Tradition of the Church of Ireland* (London: SPCK, 1958).
Bouwsma, W.J., *John Calvin, A Sixteenth Century Portrait* (Oxford: Oxford University Press, 1988).
Bowen, D., *The History and Shaping of Irish Protestantism* (New York: P. Lang, 1995).
Brachlow, S., *The Communion of Saints* (Oxford: Oxford University Press, 1988).
Bradshaw, K. and Keogh, D. (eds), *Christianity in Ireland: Revisiting the Story* (Dublin: Columba Press, 2002).
Bradshaw, B. and Morrill, J. (eds), *The British Problem c.1534–1707* (London: MacMillan, 1996).

Brady, W.M. *The Irish Reformation* (London: Longmans, Green & Co, 1867).

Brewer, J.S. (ed.), *The Church History of Britain* (6 vols, Oxford: Oxford University Press, 1845).

Bright, J., *A History of Israel* (London: SCM, 1972).

Bromiley, W., *Historical Theology: An Introduction* (Edinburgh: T. & T. Clark, 1978).

Brooke, P., *Ulster Presbyterianism* (Dublin: Gill & MacMillan, 1987).

Brueggemann, W., *Old Testament Theology* (Minneapolis: Fortress Press, 1992).

———, *The Theology of the Old Testament* (Minneapolis: Fortress Press, 1997).

Burghclere, Lady, *The Life of James 1st Duke of Ormonde* (2 vols, London: John Murray, 1912).

———, *Strafford* (2 vols, London: Macmillan, 1931).

Bush, D., *English Literature in the Early Seventeenth Century* (Oxford: Clarendon, 1945).

Campbell, J., *The Lives of the Chancellors* (2 vols, London: J. Murray, 1869).

Cameron, E., *The Reformation of the Heretics*, (Oxford: Clarendon, 1984).

———, *The European Reformation* (Oxford: Oxford University Press, 1991).

———, *Early Modern Europe* (Oxford: Oxford University Press, 1999).

———, *The Waldenses* (Oxford: Blackwell, 2000).

Canny, N.P., *The Upstart Earl: A study of the Social and Mental World of Richard Boyle First Earl of Cork*, (Cambridge: Cambridge University Press, 1982).

———, *From Reformation to Restoration, 1534–1660* (Dublin: Helicon, 1987).

———, *Making Ireland British, 1580–1650* (Oxford: Oxford University Press, 2001).

Carr, J.A., *The Life and Times of James Ussher* (London: Wells Gardner & Co, 1896).

Champion, J.A.I., *The Pilars of Priestcraft Shaken. The Church of England and its Enemies, 1660–1730* (Cambridge: Cambridge University Press, 1992).

Chappell, V., *Hobbes and Bramhall on Liberty and Necessity*, (Camridge: Cambridge University Press, 1999).

Christianson, P., *Reformers and Babylon: English Apocalyptic Visions from the Reformation to the Eve of the Civil War* (Toronto: University of Toronto Press, 1978).

Clarke, A., *The Old English in Ireland, 1625–42*, (London: MacGibbon & Kee, 1966).

———, *Prelude to Restoration in Ireland* (Cambridge, Cambridge University Press, 1999).

Collier, J., *An Ecclesiastical History of Great Britain* (9 vols, London: Straker, 1840).

Collins, W.E. (ed.), *Typical English Churchmen* (London: SPCK,1902).

Collinson, P., *The Elizabethan Puritan Movement* (Oxford: Clarendon Press, 1967).

———, *The Religion of Protestants, The Church in English Society 1559–1625* (Oxford: Clarendon Press, 1982).

Coonan, T.L., *The Irish Catholic Confederacy and the Puritan Revolution* (Dublin: Clonmore & Reynolds, 1954).

Copleston, F., *A History of Philosophy*, vol. 3 (London: Doubleday, 1993).

Coward, B., *The Stuart Age: England 1603–1714* (London: Longman, 1980).
Cressy, D. and Ferrell, L.A. (eds), *Religion and Society in Early Modern England: A Source Book* (London: Routledge, 1996).
Cross, C., *Church and People, 1450–1660* (Oxford: Blackwell, 1976).
Cuming, G.J., *A History of Anglican Liturgy* (London: Macmillan, 1969).
Cust, R and Hughes, A (eds), *Conflict in Early Stuart England: Studies in Religion and Politics, 1603–1642* (London: Longman, 1989).
Davies, G., *The Early Stuarts, 1603–1660* (Oxford: Clarendon, 1959).
Davies, G. and Keeler, M.F., *Bibliography of British History, Stuart Period, 1603–1714* (Oxford: Clarendon, 1970).
Davies, H., *Worship and Theology in England* (Cambridge: Cambridge University Press, 1975).
Davies, J., *The Caroline Captivity of the Church, Charles I and the Remoulding of Anglicanism, 1625–1641* (Oxford: Clarendon, 1992).
Day, M.F., *Lectures* (Dublin: Hamilton and Co, 1862).
Deane, S., *A Short History of Irish Literature* (London: Hutchinson, 1986).
De Vaux, R., *Ancient Israel, Its Life and Institutions* (London: Darton, Longman & Todd, 1961).
Dickens, A.G., *The English Reformation* (London: Batsford, 1964).
Dix, G., *The Shape of Liturgy* (London: Dacre Press, 1942).
Dixon, W.M., *Trinity College, Dublin* (London: F.E. Robinson, 1902).
Dowden, J., *James Ussher* (Edinburgh: Peplographia Dublinensis, 1895).
Doyle, R.C., *Eschatology and the Shape of Christian Belief* (Carlisle: Paternoster Press, 1999).
Drysdale, A.H., *The History of the Presbyterians in England* (London: Publication Committee of the Presbyterian church of England, 1889).
Dunn, J.D.G. and Rogerson (eds), *Eerdman's Commentary on the Bible* (Grand Rapids: W.B. Eerdman, 2003).
Duncan-Jones, A.S., *Archbishop Laud* (London: Macmillan, 1927).
Dudley-Edwards, R., *Church and State in Tudor Ireland* (Dublin: Talbot Press, 1935).
Edwards, D.L., *Christianity, the First Two Thousand Years* (London: Cassell, 1997).
Elrington, C.R., *An Answer to Dr Reid's Animadversions upon the Life of Archbishop Ussher* (Dublin, 1849).
Figgis, J.N., *The Divine Right of Kings* (Cambridge: Cambridge University Press, 1914).
Fincham, K., *Prelate as Pastor: The Episcopate of James I* (Oxford: Clarendon, 1990).
——— (ed.), *The Early Stuart Church* (London: Macmillan, 1993).
Firth, K.R., *The Apocalptic Tradition in Reformation Britain, 1530–1645* (Oxford: Oxford University Press, 1979).
Fitzpatrick, B., *Seventeenth–Century Ireland: The War of Religions* (Dublin: Gill & Macmillan, 1988).
Feltcher, A. and Roberts, P. (eds), *Religion, Culture and Society in Early Modern Britain* (Cambridge: Cambridge University Press, 1994).

Ford, A., *The Protestant Reformation in Ireland, 1590–1641* (Dublin: Four Courts Press, 1997).
Foster, R.F., *Modern Ireland, 1600–1972* (London: Penguin, 1988).
Fraser Mitchell, W., *English Pulpit Oratory from Andrews to Tillotson* (London: SPCK, 1932).
Gammie, J.G., *Holiness in Israel* (Minneapolis: Fortress Press, 1989).
Gardiner, S.R., *The History of England, 1603–1642* (10 vols, London: Longman, Green & Co, 1890).
Garstin, J.R., *The book of Common Prayer in Ireland: Ist Origin and History* (Dublin: Hodges & Foster, 1871).
George, C.H. and George, K., *The Protestant Mind of the English Reformation, 1570–1640* (Princeton: Princeton University Press, 1961).
Gillespie, R., *Devoted People, Belief and Religion in Early Modern Ireland* (Manchester: Manchester University Press, 1997).
Grell, O.P., *Calvinist Exiles in Tudor and Stuart England* (Aldershot: Scolar Press, 1996).
Green, V., *A New History of Christianity* (Gloucestershire: Sutton, 1996).
Gribben, C., *The Irish Puritan: James Ussher and the Reformation of the Church* (Darlington, 2003).
Haller, W., *The Rise of Puritanism* (New York: Harper, 1957).
Hanson, P.D., *The Dawn of the Apocalypse* (Philadelphia: Fortress Press, 1975).
Hardwick, C., *A History of the Articles of Religion* (London: G. Bell & Son, 1895).
Hay, D., *Europe in the Fourteenth and Fifteenth Centuries* (London: Longman, 1989).
Hazlett, W.I.P., *The Reformation in Britain and Ireland* (London: T. & T. Clark, 2003).
Heal, F., *The Reformation in Britain and Ireland* (Oxford: Clarendon, 2003).
Henshall, N., *The Myth of Absolutism* (London: Longman, 1992).
Hill, C.P., *The Intellectual Origins of the English Revolution* (Oxford: Clarendon, 1965).
———, *The English Bible and the Seventeenth–Century Revolution* (London: Penguin, 1994).
Hillerbrand, H.J., *The World of the Reformation* (London: Dent, 1975).
Hirst, D., *Authority and Conflict in England, 1603–1658* (London: Edward Arnold, 1986).
———, *England in Conflict, 1603–1660* (London: Oxford University Press, 1999).
Holmes, F., *The Presbyterian Church in Ireland* (Dublin: Columba Press, 2000).
Hone, R.B., *The Lives of Eminent Christians* (London: J.W. Parker, 1839).
Hughes, A., *The Causes of the English Civil War* (London: Macmillan, 1991).
Jedin, H., *History of the Council of Trent* (4 vols, London: Nelson, 1965).
——— (ed.), *The History of the Church* (10 vols, London: Burns & Oates, 1980).
Johnston, T., Robinson, J.L. and Jackson, R.W., *A History of the Church of Ireland*, (Dublin: APCK, 1953).
Jones, E., *The English Nation the Great Myth* (Gloucestershire: Sutton, 1998).
Karant-Nunn, S.C., *The Reformation of Ritual: An Interpretation of Early Modern Germany* (London: Routledge, 1997).

Kearney, H.F., *Strafford in Ireland, 1633–41: A Study in Absolutism* (Manchester: Manchester University Press, 1959).
———, *Scholars and Gentlemen* (London: Faber, 1970).
Kendal, R.T., *Calvin and English Calvinism to 1649* (Oxford: Oxford University Press, 1979).
Killen, W.D., *The Ecclesiastical History of Ireland* (2 vols, London: Macmillan, 1875).
Kishlansky, M., *A Monarchy Transformed: Britain 1603–1714* (London: Penguin, 1996).
Knox, R. B., *James Ussher: Archbishop of Armagh* (Cardiff: Cardiff University Press, 1967).
Kretzmann, N. and Kenny, A., *The Cambridge History of Later Medieval Philosophy* (Cambridge: Cambridge University Press, 1982).
Lamont, W.M., *Marginal Prynne* (London: Routledge & Kegan, 1963).
Laslett, P. (ed.), *Filmer's Patriarcha and Other Writings* (Oxford: Blackwell, 1949).
Leland, T., *The History of Ireland from the Invasion of Henry II* (3 vols, Dublin: B. Smith, 1814).
Lennon, C., *Richard Stanihurst the Dubliner, 1547–1618* (Dublin: Irish Academic Press, 1981).
———, *The Lords of Dublin in the Age of Reformation* (Dublin: Irish Academic Press, 1989).
———, *Sixteenth Century Ireland: The Incomplete Conquest* (Dublin: Gill & Macmillan, 1994).
Lightfoot, J.B., *St Ignatius; St Polycarp* (2 vols, London: Macmillan & Co, 1885).
Lindberg, C., *The European Reformations* (Oxford: Blackwell, 1996).
———, *The Reformation Theologians* (Oxford: Blackwell, 2002).
Lockyer, R., *The Early Stuarts; A Political History of England, 1603–1642* (London: Longman, 1989).
Lydon, J., *The Making of Modern Ireland* (London: Routledge, 1998).
McAdoo, H.R., *John Bramhall and Anglicanism, 1663–1963* (Dublin: APCK, 1964).
MacCulloch, D., *The Later Reformation in England, 1547–1603* (London: Palgrave, 2001).
McGrath, A.E., *Intellectual Origins of the Reformation* (Oxford: Basil Blackwell, 1987).
———, *Reformation Thought* (Oxford: Basil Blackwell, 1988).
———, *A Life of John Calvin* (Oxford: Basil Blackwell, 1990).
———, *Iustitia Dei: A History of the Christian Doctrine of Justification* (Cambridge: Cambridge University Press, 1998).
———, *The SPCK Handbook of Anglican Theologians* (London: SPCK, 1998).
MacKenzie, I.M., *God's Order and Natural Law: The Works of the Laudian Divines* (Aldershot: Ashgate, 2002).
McKim, D.K. (ed.), *The Cambridge Companion to Luther* (Cambridge: Cambridge University Press, 2003).

MacLysaght, E., *Irish Life in the Seventeenth Century* (Cork: Cork University Press, 1950).
McNeill, J.T., *The History and Character of Calvinism* (Oxford: Oxford University Press, 1962).
Mahaffy, J.P., *An Epoch in Irish History: Trinity College, Dublin, 1591–1640* (London: Fisher Unwin, 1903).
Mant, R., *A History of the Church of Ireland from the Reformation to the Revolution* (2 vols, London: J.W. Parker, 1840).
Marshall, P. and Ryrie, A. (eds), *The Beginnings of English Protestantism* (Cambridge: Cambridge University Press, 2002).
Mason, A.J., *The Church of England and Episcopacy* (Cambridge: Cambridge University Press, 1914).
Maxwell-Miller, J. and Hayes, J.H., *A History of Ancient Israel and Judah* (London: SCM, 1986).
Maxwell, C., *A History of Trinity College, Dublin* (Dublin: Dublin University Press, 1946).
Meigs, S.A., *The Reformations in Ireland; Tradition and Confessionalism 1400–1690*, (Dublin: Gill & Macmillan, 1997).
Milton, A., *Catholic and Reformed. The Roman and Protestant Churches in English Protestant Thought, 1600–1640* (Cambridge: Cambridge University Press, 1994).
Moberly, R.W.L., *The Old Testament of the Old Testament* (Minneapolis: Fortress Press, 1992).
Moody, T.W., *The Londonderry Plantation, 1609–41* (Belfast: W. Mullan, 1939).
Moody, T.W. and Simms, K., *The Bishopric of Derry and the Irish Society of London 1602–1705* (Dublin: Irish Manuscript Commission, 1968).
Morley, J., *Oliver Cromwell* (London: Macmillan, 1900).
Morrill, J., *Critical Bibliographies in Modern History, Seventeenth–Century Britain, 1603–1714* (Folkstone: Dawson, 1980).
―――― (ed.), *Oliver Cromwell and the English Revolution* (London: Longman, 1990).
――――, *The Nature of the English Revolution* (London: Longman, 1993).
Murphy, H.L., *The History of Trinity College* (Dublin: Hodges, Figgis, 1951).
Naphy, W.G., *Fear in Early Modern Society* (Manchester: Manchester University Press, 1997).
Neal, D., *The History of the Puritans* (5 vols, London, 1822).
Oakley, F., *The Conciliarist Tradition: Constitutionalism in the Catholic Church, 1300–1870*, (Oxford: Oxford University Press, 2003).
Oberman, H.A., *The Reformation,Rroots and Ramifications* (Edinburgh: T. & T. Clark, 1994).
O'Day, R.O., *The English Clergy: The Emergence and Consolidation of a Profession, 1558–1642* (Leicester: Leicester University Press, 1979).
O'Grady, H., *Strafford and Ireland*, (2 Vols, Dublin: Hodges, Figgis, 1923).
Otto, R., *The Idea of the Holy* (Oxford: Oxford University Press, 1923).
――――, *Mysticism East and West* (London: Wheaton, 1932).
Ozmet, S., *The Age of Reform, 1250–1550*, (New Haven: Yale University Press, 1980).

Pelikan, J., *Reformation of Church and Dogma, 1300–1700* (Chicago: University of Chicago Press, 1984).
Pennington, D.H., *Europe in the Seventeenth Century* (London: Longman, 1989).
Perceval-Maxwell, M., *The Outbreak of the Irish Rebellion of 1641* (Dublin: Gill & Macmillan, 1994).
Pettegree, A. (ed.), *The Reformation World* (London: Routledge, 2002).
Philips, W.A. (ed.), *The History of the Church of Ireland* (3 vols, Oxford: Oxford University Press, 1933–34).
Phillipson, N. and Skinner, Q. (eds), *Political Discourse in Early Modern Britain* (Cambridge: Cambridge University Press, 1993).
Preuss, H.D., *Old Testament Theology* (2 vols, Edinburgh: T. &.T. Clark, 1996).
Reeves, W., *The Book of Common Prayer According to the Use of the Church of Ireland* (Dublin: Hodges, Foster & Co, 1871).
Reid, J.S., *Seven Letters to the Reverend C.R. Elrington Occasioned by Animadversions in His Life of Ussher* (Glasgow: Ogle & Son, 1849).
———, *The History of the Presbyterian Church in Ireland* (3 vols, Belfast: W. Mullan, 1867).
Russell, C., *The Causes of the English Civil War* (Oxford: Clarendon, 1990).
———, *The Fall of the British Monarchies, 1637–1642* (Oxford: Clarendon, 1991).
Sawyer, J.F.A., *A Modern Introduction to Biblical Hebrew* (London: Oriel Press, 1976).
Schillebeeckx, E., *The Eucharist* (London: Sheed & Ward, 1977).
———, *Christ the Sacrament of the Encounter with God* (London: Sheed & Ward, 1977).
Searle, A. (ed.), *Barrington Family Letters, 1628–32* (London: Royal Historical Society, 1983).
Seymour, S.D., *The Puritans in Ireland* (Oxford: Clarendon, 1969).
Sharp, A., *Political Ideas of the English Civil War, 1641–1644* (London: Longmans, 1983).
Sharpe, K., *The Personal Rule of Charles I* (New Haven: Yale University Press, 1992).
Shuckburgh, E.S., *Two Biographies of William Bedell* (Cambridge: Cambridge University Press, 1902).
Skinner, Q., *The Foundations of Modern Political Thought* (2 vols, Cambridge: Cambridge University Press, 1978).
Smith, D.L., *Constitutional Royalism and the Search for Settlement, c1640–1649* (Cambridge: Cambridge University Press, 1994).
Smith, T., *Vitae quorundam eruditissimorum et illustrium virorum* (London: Apud Davidem Mortier, 1707).
Sommerville, J.P., *Politics and Ideology in England, 1603–1640* (London: Longman: 1986).
Southern, R.W., *Scholastic Humanism and the Unification of Europe* (Oxford: Blackwell, 1995).
Sparrow-Simpson, W.J., *Archbishop Bramhall* (London: SPCK, 1927).
Spurr, J., *The Restoration Church* (Newhaven: Yale University Press, 1991).

Stuart, J., *Historical Memoirs of the City of Armagh* (Newry: Longman, 1819).
Sykes, N., *The Church of England and Non–Episcopal Churches in the Sixteenth and Seventeenth–Centuries* (London: SPCK, 1948).
———, *Old Priest and New Presbyter* (Cambridge: Cambridge University Press, 1956).
Todd, M. (ed.), *Reformation to Revolution* (London: Routledge, 1995).
Townshend, D., *The Life and Letters of the Great Earl of Cork* (London: Duckworth, 1904).
Treadwell, V., *Buckingham and Ireland* (Dublin: Four Courts Press, 1998).
Treasure, G., *The Making of Modern Europe, 1648–1780* (London: Methuen, 1985).
Trevor-Roper, H., *Archbishop Laud* (London: Macmillan, 1962).
———, *Catholics, Anglicans and Puritans* (London: Fontana, 1987).
———, *From Counter-Reformation to Glorious Revolution* (London: Secker & Warburg, 1992).
Tuck, R., *Philosophy and Government, 1572–1651* (Cambridge: Cambridge University Press, 1993).
Tyacke, N., *Anti-Calvinists: The Rise of English Arminianism, c.1590–1640* (Oxford: Clarendon, 1990).
———, *England's Long Reformation, 1500–1800* (London: Taylor & Francis, 1998).
———, *Aspects of English Protestantism, c.1530–1700* (Manchester: Manchester University Press, 2001).
Ullmann, W., *A History of Political Thought: The Middle Ages* (Baltimore, 1970).
Ussher, R.G., *The Reconstruction of the English Church* (2 vols, New York: Appleton, & Co, 1910).
———, *The Rise and Fall of the High Commission* (Oxford: Clarendon, 1913).
Von Rad, G., *The Message of the Prophets* (London: SCM, 1968).
Wallace, D.D., *Puritans and Predestination: in English Protestant Theology, 1525–1695* (Chapel Hill: University of North Carolina Press, 1982).
Walsham, A., *Providence in Early Modern England* (Oxford: Oxford University Press, 1999).
Ware, J., *Whole works concerning Ireland* (2 vols, Dublin: 1739–1746).
Wedgewood, C.V., *Strafford, 1593–1641* (London: Jonathan Cape, 1935).
———, *Wentworth, A Revaluation* (London: Jonathan Cape, 1961).
White, P., *Predestination, Policy and Polemic* (Cambridge: Cambridge University Press, 1992).
Williams, P., *The Tudor Regime* (Oxford: Clarendon, 1979).
Wills, J., *The Lives of Illustrious and Distinguished Irishmen* (4 vols, Dublin: MacGregor, Polson, 1842).
Woodhouse, H.F., *The Doctrine of the Church in Anglican Theology* (London: SPCK, 1954).
Wright, W.B., *The Ussher Memoirs* (Dublin: Sealy, Bryers & Co, 1889).
———, *A Great Yorkshire Divine of the Seventeenth Century* (York: John Sampson, 1899).
Wylie, J.A., *The History of Protestantism* (3 vols, London: Cassell, 1879).
Zagorin, P., *A History of Political Thought in the English Revolution* (London: Routledge & Paul, 1954).

2 Articles and essays

Abbott, W.M., 'James Ussher and "Ussherian" episcopacy, 1640–1656: the Primate and his Reduction manuscript', *Albion*, XXII (1990): 237–59.

Albertz, R., 'Religion in pre–exilic Israel', in J. Barton (ed.) *The Biblical World* (2 vols, London: Routledge, 2002).

Barnard, T.C., 'Crises of identity among Irish Protestants, 1641–1685', *Past & Present*, CXXVII (1990): 39–83.

———, 'The Protestant interest, 1641–1660', in J. Ohlmeyer (ed.), *Ireland from Independence to Occupation, 1641–1660* (Cambridge: Cambridge University Press, 1995).

Barnett, S.J., 'Where was your church before Luther? Claims for the antiquity of Protestantism examined', *Church History* (March, 1999): 14–41.

Barr, J., 'Why the world was created in 4004 BC Archbishop Ussher and biblical chronology', *Bulletin of the John Rylands University*, vol. 87, no. 2 (1985): 573–608.

Barry, A., 'Ussher', *New Ireland Review*, vol. V (April 1896): 71–80.

Bernard, G.W., 'The Church of England, c.1529–c.1642', *History*, 75, 224 (June 1990).

Bolton, F.R., 'Archbishop Ussher's scheme of church government', *Theology* (January 1947): 9–16.

Boran, E., 'An early friendship network of James Ussher, archbishop of Armagh, 1626–1656', in H. Robinson-Hammerstein (ed.), *European Universities in the Age of Reformation and Counter-Reformation* (Dublin: Four Courts Press, 1998): 116–34.

———, 'The libraries of Luke Challoner and James Ussher, 1595–1608', in H. Robinson-Hammerstein (ed.), *European Universities in the Age of Reformation and Counter-Reformation* (Dublin: Four Courts Press, 1998).

———, 'Reading theology within the community of believers: James Ussher's "Directions"', in B. Cunningham and M. Kennedy (eds), *The Experience of Reading: Irish Historical Perspectives* (Dublin: E.S.H.S.I., 1999).

———, 'Propagating religion and endeavouring the reformation of the whole world: Irish bishops and the Hartlib circle in the mid-seventeenth century', in V.P. Carey and U. Lotz-Heuman (eds), *Taking Sides? Colonial Mentalities in Early Modern Ireland* (Dublin: Four Courts Press, 2002).

Bossy, J., 'The Counter-Reformation and the people of Catholic Ireland, 1596–1641', *Historical Studies*, VII (1971): 155–69.

Bottigheimer, K.S., 'The failure of the Reformation in Ireland: une question bien posée', *Journal of Ecclesiastical History*, XXXVI (1985): 197–207.

———, 'Revisionism and the Irish Reformation', *Journal of Ecclesiastical History*, vol. 51, no. 3 (July 2000): 581–91.

Bottigheimer, K.S. and Lotz-Heumann, U., 'Ireland and the European Reformation', *History Ireland*, vol. 6, no. 4 (Winter 1998): 13–17.

Bradshaw, B.I., 'The Edwardian Reformation in Ireland', *Archivium Hibernicum*, XXVI (1976–77): 83–99.

―――, 'Sword, word and strategy in the Reformation in Ireland', *Historical Journal*, XXI (1978): 475–502.

―――, 'Revisionism and the Irish Reformation: a rejoinder', *Journal of Ecclesiastical History*, vol. 51, no. 3 (July 2000): 587–91.

Bradshaw, C., 'David or Josiah? Old Testament kings as exemplars in Edwardian Religious polemic', in B. Gordon (ed.), *Protestant History and Identity in Sixteenth Century Europe* (2 vols, Aldershot: Ashgate, 1996).

Brice, W.R., 'Bishop Ussher, John Lightfoot and the age of creation', *Journal of Geological Education*, vol. 30 (1982): 18–26.

Burns, J.H., 'The idea of absolutism', in J. Miller (ed.), *Absolutism in Seventeenth –Century Europe* (London: Macmillan, 1990).

Canny, N.P., 'Why the Reformation failed in Ireland: Une question mal posée', *Journal of Ecclesiastical History*, XXX (1979): 435–50.

―――, 'Protestant, planter and apartheid in early modern Ireland', *Irish Historical Studies*, vol. xxv, no. 98 (Nov. 1986): 105–15.

―――, 'The foundation of the Irish mind: religion, politics and Gaelic Irish literature, 1580–1750', in C.H.E. Philpin (ed.), *Nationalism and Popular Protest in Ireland* (Cambridge: Cambridge University Press, 1987).

―――, 'The attempted Anglicization of Ireland in the seventeenth century: an exemplar of British history', in J.F. Merrit (ed.), *The Political World of Thomas Wentworth, Earl of Strafford, 1621–41* (Cambridge: Cambridge university Press, 1996).

Capern A., 'The Caroline church: James Ussher and the Irish dimension', *Historical Journal*, XXXIX (1996): 57–85.

Christianson, P., 'Reformers and the Church of England under Elizabeth I and the Early Stuarts', *Journal of Ecclesiastical History*, XXXI (1980): 463–82.

Clarke, A., 'The government of Wentworth, 1632–40', in T.W. Moody, F.X. Martin and F. Byrne (eds), *A New History of Ireland* (Oxford: Clarendon, 1976).

―――, 'Varieties of uniformity: the first century of the Church of Ireland', *Studies in Church History*, XXV (1989): 105–22.

―――, 'A woeful sinner: John Atherton', in V.P. Carey and U. Lotz-Heumann (eds), *Taking Sides? Colonial and Confessional Mentalities in Early Modern Ireland* (Dublin: Four Courts Press, 2003).

Collinson, P., 'Protestant culture and the cultural revolution', in M.Todd (ed.), *Reformation to Revolution* (London: Routledge, 1995).

Cunningham, B., 'Seventeenth-century interpretations of the past: the case of Geoffrey Keating', *Irish Historical Studies*, xxv, no. 98 (Nov. 1986): 116–28.

Curtis, M.H., 'The alienated intellectuals of early Stuart England', *Past & Present*, XXIII (1962): 25–43.

Daly, J.W., 'John Bramhall and the theoretical problems of royalist moderation', *Journal of British Studies*, XI (1971): 26–44.

De Quehen, H., 'Politics and scholarship in the Ignatian controversy', *The Seventeenth- Century*, vol. XIII, no. 1 (Spring 1998): 69–84.

Eliot, T.S., 'John Bramhall', *Selected Essays* (London: Faber & Faber, 1951).

Fincham, K., 'Episcopal government, 1603–1640', in K. Fincham (ed.), *The Early Stuart Church 1603–1642* (London: Macmillan, 1993).

Fincham, K. and Lake, P.G., 'The ecclesiastical policy of James I', *Journal of British Studies*, XXIV, 2 (1985): 169–207.

———, 'The ecclesiastical policy of James I and Charles I', in K. Fincham (ed.), *The Early Stuart Church* (London: Macmillan, 1993).

Ford, A., 'The Protestant Reformation in Ireland', in C. Brady and R. Gillespie (eds), *Natives and Newcomers: Essays on the Making of Irish Colonial Society, 1534–1641* (Dublin: Irish Academic, 1986).

———, 'Correspondence between Archbishop Ussher and Laud', *Archivium Hibernicum*, XLVI (1991–92): 5–21.

———, 'Dependent or independent: the Church of Ireland and its colonial context, 1536–1647', *The Seventeenth-Century*, X (1995): 163–87.

———, 'The Church of Ireland: a critical bibliography, 1603–41', *Irish Historical Studies*, XXVIII, 112 (1993): 345–59.

———, '"Standing one's ground": religion, polemic and Irish history since the Reformation', in A. Ford, J.I. McGuire and K. Milne (eds), *As by Law Established* (Dublin: Lilliput Press, 1995).

———, 'The Church of Ireland 1558–1641: a puritan church?', in A. Ford, J.I. McGuire and K.L. Milne, *As by Law Established* (Dublin: Lilliput Press, 1995).

———, 'The origins of Irish dissent', K. Herlihy (ed.), *The Religion of Irish Dissent, 1650– 1800* (Dublin: Four Courts Press, 1996).

———, 'James Ussher and the creation of an Irish protestant identity', in B. Bradshaw and P. Roberts (eds), *British Consciousness and Identity: The Making of Britain, 1533– 1707* (Cambridge: Cambridge University Press, 1998).

———, 'James Ussher and the godly prince in early seventeenth-century Ireland', in H. Morgan (ed.), *Political Ideology in Ireland, 1541–1641* (Dublin: Four Courts Press, Dublin, 2000).

Gaffney, D., 'The practise of religious controversy in Dublin, 1600–1641', in W.J. Sheils and D. Wood (eds), *The Churches, Ireland and the Irish* (Oxford: Blackwell, 1989).

Giblin, C., 'Vatican Library Mss Barbarini Latini', *Archivium Hibernicum*, XVIII (1955): 395–405.

———, 'Aegidiuus Chaissy, OFM and James Ussher', *Irish Ecclesiastical Record* (June 1956): 393–405.

Gillespie, R., 'The religion of Irish Protestants: a view from the laity', in A. Ford, J.I. McGuire and K. Milne (eds), *As by Law Established* (Dublin: Liliput Press, 1995).

Gordon, B., 'The changing face of Protestant history in sixteenth-century Europe', in B. Gordon (ed.), *Protestant History and Identity in Sixteenth Century Europe* (Aldershot: Ashgate, 1996).

Green, I., 'Anglicanism in Stuart and Hanoverian England', in S. Gilly and W.J. Sheils (eds), *A History of Religion in Britain* (Oxford: Blackwell, 1994).

———, '"The necessary knowledge of the principles of religion": catechisms and catechizing in Ireland, *c*.1560–1800', in A. Ford, J.I. McGuire and K. Milne (eds), *As by Law Established* (Dublin: Lilliput Press, 1995).

Gribben, C., 'Rhetoric, fiction and theology: James Ussher and the death of Jesus Christ', *Seventeenth Century*, XX (2005): 53–75.

Hadfield, A., 'English colonialism and national identity in early modern Ireland', *Eire–Ireland*, vol. 28, no 1 (Spring, 1993): 69–149.

Hirst, D., 'The king redeemed: a revisionist account of the reign of Charles I', *Times Literary Supplement* (15 January 1993).

Hunt, A., 'The Lord's supper in early modern England', *Past & Present*, CLXI (1998): 39–83.

Jourdan, G.V., 'The rule of Charles I', in W.A. Philips (ed.), *The History of the Church of Ireland from the Earliest Times to the Present Day* (3 vols, Oxford: Oxford University Press, 1933).

Kilroy, P., 'Sermon and pamphlet literature in the Irish reformed Church, 1613–1634', *Archivium Hibernicum*, XXXIII (1975): 110–21.

———, 'Bishops and ministers in Ulster during the Primacy of Ussher', *Seanchas Ardmhacha* VIII (1977): 284–98.

———, 'Protestantism in Ulster, 1610–41', in B. MacCuarta (ed.), *Ulster 1641* (Belfast: Queens University Belfast, 1993).

———, 'Radical religion in Ireland, 1641–1660', in J. Ohlmeyer (ed.), *Ireland from Independence to Occupation* (Cambridge: Cambridge University Press, 1995).

King, P., 'The episcopate during the civil wars, 1642–49', *English Historical Review*, LXXXIII (1968), 523–34.

Knox, R. B, 'Archbishop Ussher and Richard Baxter', *The Ecumenical Review*, XII (October 1959): 50–63.

———, 'James Ussher and the Church of Ireland', *Church Quarterly Review* (April–June, 1960): 148–62.

———, 'The English civil-war: Archbishop Ussher and his circle', *London Quarterly and Holborn Review* (January 1962): 60–66.

———, 'A Caroline trio: Ussher, Laud and Williams', *Church Quarterly Review* (October–December 1963): 442–57.

Lake, P.G., 'The significance of the Elizabethan identification of the Pope as antichrist', *Journal of Ecclesiastical History*, XXXI (1980): 161–78.

———, 'Calvinism and the English church, 1570–1635', *Past & Present*, CXIV (February, 1987): 32–76.

———, 'Anti–Popery: the structure of a prejudice', R. Cust and A. Hughes (eds), *Conflict in Early Stuart England: Studies in Religion and Politics, 1603–42* (London: Longman, 1989).

———, 'Protestants, Puritans and Laudians', *Journal of Ecclesiastical History*, XLII (1991): 618–28.

———, 'The Laudian style: order, uniformity and the pursuit of beauty of holiness in the 1630s', in K. Fincham (ed.), *The Early Stuart Church, 1603–1642* (London: Macmillan, 1993).

———, 'Predestinarian propositions', *Journal of Ecclesiastical History*, XXXXVI (1995): 110–123.

———, 'Retrospective: Wentworth's political world in revisionist and post-revisionist perspective', in J.F. Merrit (ed.), *The Political World of Thomas Wentworth Earl of Strafford* (Cambridge: Cambridge University Press, 1996).

Lawlor, H.J., 'Primate Ussher's library before 1641', *Royal Irish Academy proceedings*, 3rd Series 6 (1900–02): 216–64.

Leerson, J., 'Archbishop Ussher and Gaelic culture', *Studia Hibernica*, XXII–XXIII (1982–83): 50–58.

Lotz Heumann, U., 'The Protestant interpretation of history in Ireland: the case of James Ussher', in B. Gordon (ed.), *Protestant History and Identity in Sixteenth- Century Europe* (2 vols, Aldershot: Ashgate, 1996).

McCafferty, J., 'John Bramhall and the Church of Ireland in the 1630s', in A. Ford, J.I. McGuire and K. Milne (eds), *As by Law Established* (Dublin: Lilliput Press, 1995).

———, '"God bless your free Church of Ireland": Wentworth, Laud, Bramhall and the Irish convocation of 1634', in J.F. Merritt (ed.), *The Political World of Thomas Wentworth, Earl of Strafford, 1621–1641* (Cambridge: Cambridge University Press, 1996).

———, 'St Patrick for the Church of Ireland: James Ussher's discourse', *Bullan*, vol. 3, no. 2 (Winter 1997/Spring 1998): 87–161.

McGuire, J.I., 'The Dublin convention, the Protestant community and the emergence of an ecclesiastical settlement', in A. Cosgrove and J.I. McGuire (eds), *Parliament and Community* (Belfast: Appletree Press, 1983).

McKim, D.K., 'The foundations of Ramism in William Perkin's theology', *The Sixteenth Century Journal*, vol. XVI, no. 4 (1985): 503–17.

Marshall, P., 'Fear, purgatory and polemic in Reformation England', in W.G. Naphy and P. Roberts (eds), *Fear in Early Modern Society* (Manchester: Manchester University Press, 1997).

Miller, J., 'Britain', in J. Miller (ed.), *Absolutism in the Seventeenth-Century Europe* (London: Macmillan, 1990).

Millett, B., 'James Ussher, Francis Barnaby and blessed Conor O'Devany', *Collectanea Hibernica*, no. 38 (1996): 40–51.

Milton, A., 'A qualified intolerance: the limits and ambiguities of early Stuart anti-Catholicism', in A.F. Marotti (ed.), *Catholicism and Anti-Catholicism in Early Modern English Text* (London: Macmillan, 1999).

Morgan, H., 'Writing up early modern Ireland', *Historical Journal* (1988): 701–12.

Morrill, J., 'A very British patriarchy? Ecclesiastical imperialism under the early Stuarts', in A. Fletcher and P. Roberts (eds), *Religion, Culture and Society in Early Modern Britain* (Cambridge: Cambridge University Press, 1994).

———, 'The three kingdoms and one commonwealth? The enigma of mid-seventeenth-century Britain and Ireland', in A. Grant and K.J. Stringer (eds), *Uniting the Kingdom: The Making of British History* (London: Routledge, 1995).

Murphy, N., 'Archbishop Ussher', *Irish Ecclesiastical Record*, 4th Series, Volume 1 (February 1897).

Naphy, W.G., '"No history can satisfy everyone:" Geneva's chroniclers and emerging religious identities', in B. Gordon, *Protestant History and Identity in Sixteenth- Century Europe*, (2 vols, Aldershot: Ashgate, 1996).

Nye, C., 'John Bramhall', *Church Quarterly Review*, CXVII (1934): 267–91.

Oakley, F., '"Anxieties of influence": Skinner, Figgis, conciliarism and early modern constitutionalism', *Past and Present*, CLI (May 1996): 60–110.

———, 'The absolute and ordained power of God and the king in the sixteenth and seventeenth-centuries: philosophy, science, politics and law', *Journal of the History of Ideas,* (1998): 669–89.

———, ' The absolute and ordained power of God in Sixteenth and Seventeenth-Century Theology', *Journal of the History of Ideas*, vol. 59, No. 3 (1998): 437–61.

O'Bauchalla, B., 'James our true king: the ideology of Irish royalism in the seventeenth-century', in D.G. Boyce, R. Eccleshall and V. Geoghegan (eds), *Political Thought in Ireland Since the Seventeenth-Century* (London: Routledge, 1993).

Ohlmeyer, J., 'A failed revolution?', in J.H. Ohlmeyer (ed.), *Ireland from Independence to Occupation, 1641–1660* (Cambridge: Cambridge University Press, 1995).

O'Sullivan, W., 'Ussher as a collector of manuscripts', *Hermathena*, LXXXVIII (1956): 34–54.

———, 'Review of R. Buick Knox, James Ussher, Archbishop of Armagh', *Irish Historical Studies*, no. 12 (September 1968): 215–19.

———, 'Correspondence of David Rothe and James Ussher, 1619–23', *Collectanea Hibernica*, XXXVI–XXXVII (1994–95): 7–49.

Oulton, J.L., 'The study of divinity in Trinity College, Dublin since the foundation', *Hermathena*, LVIII (1941): 3–29.

———, 'Ussher's work as a patristic scholar and church historian', *Hermathena*, LXXXVIII (1956): 3–11.

Overhoff, J., 'The theology of Thomas Hobbes's Leviathan', *Journal of Ecclesiastical History*, vol. 51, no. 3 (July, 2000): 527–55.

Pocock, J.G.A., 'A discourse of sovereignty: observations on the work in progress', in N. Philipson and Q. Skinner (eds), *Political Discourse in Early Modern Britain* (Cambridge: Cambridge University Press, 1993).

Pogson, F., 'Making and maintaining political alliances during the personal rule of Charles I: Wentworth's associations with Laud and Cottington', *History*, vol. 84, no. 273 (January, 1999): 52–73.

Perceval-Maxwell, M., 'Strafford, the Ulster Scots and the Covenanters', *Irish Historical Studies*, XVIII, 72 (1973): 525–551.

———, 'Ireland and the monarchy in the early Stuart multiple kingdom', *Historical Journal*, XXXIV (1991): 279–95.

Ranger, T., 'Strafford in Ireland', *Past & Present*, XIX (1961): 27–45.

Russell, C., 'The British background to the Irish rebellion of 1641', *Historical Research*, LXI (1988).

Sanderson, J., 'Serpent-salve, 1643: the royalism of John Bramhall', *Journal of Ecclesiastical History*, XXV (1974): 1–14.

Sharpe, K., 'The king's writ: royal authors and the royal authority in early modern England', in P.G. Lake and K. Sharpe (eds), *Culture and Politics in Early Stuart England* (London: Macmillan, 1994).

———, 'Archbishop Laud', in M. Todd (ed.), *Reformation to Revolution* (London: Routledge, 1995).

Sheils, W.J., 'Reformed religion in England, 1520–1640', in S. Gilley and W.J. Sheils (eds), *A History of Religion in Britain* (Oxford: Blackwell, 1994).

Smith, R.B., 'James Ussher: biblical chronicler', *Anglican Theological Review*, XLI (1959): 84–91.

Sommerville, J.P., 'The royal supremacy and episcopacy iure divino', *Journal of Ecclesiastical History*, XXXIV (1983): 548–58.

———, 'Absolutism and royalism', in J.H. Burns (ed.), *Cambridge Companion to the History of Thought*, 1450–1700 (Cambridge: Cambridge University Press, 1990).

———, 'The English and European political ideas in early the seventeenth-century: revisionism and the case of absolutism', *The Journal of British Studies*, XXXV no. 2, (April 1996): 168–94.

Styles, P., 'James Ussher and his times', *Hermathena*, LXXXVIII (1956): 12–33.

Sykes, N., 'James Ussher as churchman', *Hermathena*, LXXXVIII (1956): 59–80.

Tighe, W.J., 'William Laud and the reunion of the churches, some evidence from 1637 and 1638', *Historical Journal*, XXX (1987): 717–27.

Tyacke, N., 'Puritanism, Arminianism and counter revolution', in M. Todd (ed.), *Reformation to Revolution* (London: Routledge, 1995).

———, 'Archbishop Laud', in K. Fincham (ed.), *The Early Stuart Church* (London: Macmillan, 1993).

Tyacke, N. and White, P. 'The rise of Arminianism reconsidered', *Past & Present*, CXV (1987).

Walsham, A., 'The parochial roots of Laudianism revisited: anti-Calvinists and "parish Anglicans" in early Stuart England', *Journal of Ecclesiastical History*, vol. 49, no. 4 (October 1998): 620–51.

Watson, W.E., 'James Ussher', in W.E. Collins, *Typical English Churchmen*, (London, SPCK, 1902).

White, P., 'The rise of Arminianism reconsidered', *Past & Present*, CI (1983): 34–54.

———, 'The via media in the early Stuart church', in K. Fincham (ed.), *The Early Stuart Church* (London: Macmillan, 1993).

Wriedt, M., 'Luther's theology', in D.K. Mckim (ed.), *The Cambridge Companion to Luther* (Cambridge: Cambridge University Press, 2003).

3 Unpublished theses

Capern, A., '"Slipperye times and dangerous dayes" James Ussher and the Calvinist Reformation of Britain, 1560–1660', University of New South Wales, Ph.D. Thesis, 1991.

Cooper, E.E., 'Hobbes and God', University of Ulster, M.A. Thesis, 1991.

Hadfield, A., 'The English view of Ireland *c.*1540–1600', New University of Ulster, D. Phil. Thesis, 1988.

McCafferty, J., 'John Bramhall and the reconstruction of the Church of Ireland, 1633–1641', University of Cambridge Ph.D. Thesis, 1997.

Tollefson, R.J., 'A study of the church in the life and thought of Archbishop James Ussher', Iowa University, Ph.D. Thesis, 1963.

4 Works of reference

Attwater, D., *The Penguin Dictionary of Saints* (London: Penguin, 1965).

Burtchaeli, G.D. and Sadler, T.U. (eds), *Alumni Dublinenses* (Dublin: A. Thom & Co, 1935).

Butterick, G.A. (ed.), *The Interpreter's Dictionary of the Bible* (Nashville: Abingdon, 1962).

Cohn-Sherbok, D., *A Dictionary of Judaism and Christianity* (London: SPCK, 1991).

Cross, F.L. and Livingstone, E.A. (eds), *Oxford Dictionary of the Christian Church* (Oxford: Oxford University Press, 2005).

Donovan, B.C., and Edwards, D. (eds), *British Sources for Irish History, 1485–1641* (Dublin: Irish Manuscripts Commission, 1997).

Eager, A., *A Guide to Irish Bibliographical Material* (London: Library Association, 1980).

Edwards, P. (ed.), *The Encylclopedia of Philosophy* (8 vols, New York: Macmillan, 1967).

Edwards, R.D. and O'Dowd, M. (eds), *Sources for Early Modern Irish History* (Cambridge: Cambridge University Press, 1985).

Friar, S., *A Companion to the English Parish Church* (Gloucestershire: Allan Sutton, 1996).

Gillow, J., *Bibliographical Dictionary of English Catholics,* (London: Burns & Oates, 1885).

Hastings, J., *Encylopaedia of Religion and Ethics* (24 vols, Edinburgh: 1964).

Hillerbrand, H.J. (ed.), *The Oxford Encyclopedia of the Reformation* (4 vols, Oxford: Oxford University Press, 1996).

Jacobs, L., *The Jewish Religion: A Companion* (Oxford: Oxford University Press, 1995).

Matthew, H.C.G. and Harrison, B. (eds), *The Dictionary of National Biography* (60 vols, Oxford: Oxford University Press, 2004).

Metzger, B.M. and Coogan, M.D., *The Oxford Companion to the Bible* (Oxford: Oxford University Press, 1993).

Stephen, L. and Lee, S. (eds), *The Dictionary of National Biography* (22 vols, Oxford: Oxford University Press, 1968).

Venn, J.A. and Venn, J. (eds), *Alumni Cantabrigienses* (Cambridge: Cambridge University Press, 1922–27).

Walsh, M. (ed.), Dictionary of Christian Biography (London: Continuum, 2001).

Wood, A.A., Athenae Oxonienses (4 vols, London: Rivington, 1820).

Zwi-Werblowsky, R.J. and Wigoder, G. (eds), The Oxford Dictionary of Jewish Religion (Oxford: Oxford University Press, 1997).

Index

Abbot, George, Archbishop 9n, 155
Abbot, W.M. 146–7
Adair, Archibald, Bishop 197–8
Albigensians 90–91, 98–100
Allen, John 124
Altars x, 15–16, 63, 65, 72–3, 76, 116, 164, 178, 184, 187
Ambrose, St 121, 125
Anabaptists 34, 192
Andrews, George 31, 173, 186, 191, 209
Andrews, Lancelot 95, 167, 216
Antichrist 90–91, 98–9, 105, 125, 148, 158–9, 162–3
Antinomianism 46
Aquinas, St Thomas 51, 73, 86
Ark of the Covenant 62, 64, 88
Arminius, Jacobus viii, 48
Arminianism vii–ix, xiv, 18, 24, 31, 48, 76, 111, 158, 161, 170, 172n, 173, 181, 194–5
Assurance 52, 58
Atherton, John 30, 222
Augustine, St 2, 47, 49, 106, 160
Augsburg, Confession of 150

Baille, Robert 166
Ball-Wright, W. 1, 6, 23, 26, 174, 220
Baptism 11, 24, 50–51, 69–71, 82
Baronius, Caesar 85
Barrington, Thomas 171, 212
Baxter, Richard 19–20, 25–6, 35n, 37, 67, 75, 94, 149–50, 158, 224, 165, 167, 201, 210
Bedell, William 170n, 172, 188, 196–7
Bellarmine, Robert, Cardinal 6, 89, 95
Bernard, Nicholas vii, 2–3, 5, 7, 8n, 21n, 22, 38, 147, 149, 180, 191n

Beza, Theodore 91
Biblical motifs x–xv, 42–3, 45, 48–52, 55, 57 60–64, 67, 70, 72–3, 79–83, 86, 88, 90–91, 94, 99, 104, 109, 145, 164, 168, 169, 176, 201–3
Black Oath 32, 198
Blair, Robert 173–4, 192
Bodin, Jean 131, 140
Book of Common Prayer 16, 67, 80, 187
Book of Sports 14
Borromeo, Carlo 203
Boyle, Richard 164, 179, 206, 214
Bramhall, John
  Answer to Captain Steward 82
  Answer to de la Milletiere 36
  Answer to Mr Hobbes 35n
  Answer to S.N. 66, 74
  Archdeaconry of Meath 29
  Catching of the Leviathan 35n, 118–19
  Chaplain to Lord Deputy 28
  Bishop of Derry 29
  Death of 39–40
  Debate with Hobbes 35, 44–9, 118–19
  Edward VI Grammar School 23
  Exile vii, 7–9, 35–6, 97, 111, 115, 118, 151, 159
  Fair warning 118
  Journey to Spain 36
  Just Vindication of Church of England 36, 105–6, 165
  Northallerton debate 25–6, 157–8, 206
  Ordained 26
  Persons dying without Baptism 50

Primate of Ireland 38–9
Right way to safety 83
Schism Guarded 37–105
Serpent salve 34, 111, 115–9, 128, 130–43
Star Chamber 192
Vindication from the Presbyterian charge 37
Vindication of true liberty 35n
Brereton, William 14–15, 210
Brueggemann, Walter 62, 87–8, 91, 107n
Bucer, Martin 50, 74, 203
Burghclere, Lady 37, 174n, 188, 195, 214
Butterick, G.A. ix–x, 61–2

Cajetan, Cardinal 203
Calvin, John 120, 125, 150, 160, 164, 203, 207
  Institutes of the Christian Religion xi, 47, 50–52, 54, 66, 70, 80, 120, 125, 211
Camden, William 8, 100
Cameron, Eaun 64, 70, 73, 214
Canons, Irish, 163–4, 152, 175, 180–89, 191–2, 196–7, 209
Canny, N.P. 171n, 214, 222
Capern, Amanda 11n, 177, 188–9, 222, 227
Carte, Thomas 72n, 183, 185n, 211
Casaubon, Isaac 9, 107n
Challoner, Luke 8–9, 181
Chappel, William 30, 194–6
Charles I xii, 11, 13, 14, 17–20, 33–8, 41, 97, 102, 112, 114, 117, 120, 126, 129, 135, 140–41, 146, 154–5, 171, 175, 183, 187–8, 195
Charles II 36–8, 79, 164
Chichester, Sir Arthur 12
Christ's Church Cathedral, Dublin 24n, 43, 178
Chrysostom, John 49

Clarendon, Edward Hyde 17, 37–8
Coke, Sir John 14, 188
Collins, W.E. 26–7
Collinson, Patrick xii, 4, 24, 55, 105, 214, 222
Conciliarism 95, 108, 129, 139, 152
Convocation, Irish, 1615 11–12, 184, 200
Convocation, Irish, 1634 vii, 15, 30–31, 102, 169, 180–91, 194, 200, 209
Cosin, John 167
Cotton, Robert 8, 206
Crewe, John 19
Cromwell, Oliver 16–17, 19n, 20–24, 35, 37, 149, 174, 198, 207, 210, 213, 218

Daly, J.W. 117, 119, 132–222
Daniel, book of 10
De Vaux, Roland 61–3, 215
De Vic, Henry 35
Deuteronomy, book of 62
Devereux, Robert 5, 115
Digges, Dudley 116–17
Donne, John 89
Dort, Synod of 24, 69, 170
Downham, George 17, 30, 172, 207

Echlin, Robert, Bishop 30, 174
Edward VI 85, 145
Eirenicon *see* Ussher, *Reduction Manuscript*
Elizabeth I 24, 93, 114
Elrington, C.R. 2n, 7n, 8n, 13n, 16, 27, 147, 169n, 174, 195, 209, 215, 219
Emmanuel College, Cambridge 4–5, 69n
Episcopacy 15, 22, 30, 93–104, 113, 115, 146–53, 170, 198–202
Eucharist 51, 71–80, 83, 97, 202
Evelyn, John 211
Ezekiel, prophet 7, 43

Ferne, Henry 117

Index

Figgis, J.N. 119–23, 129, 131–4, 140, 215, 225
Filmer, Robert 114, 117, 139, 141, 143, 217
Fitzsimonds, Henry 6
Ford, Alan xvii, 4n, 9, 154, 156, 158, 175, 182, 216, 223
Foxe, John 89–91, 93, 162, 210
Fullerton, James 3–4

Gaffney, Declan 8, 223
Gardiner, S.R. 146–7, 165, 211, 216
Genesis, book of 71, 120
George, C.H. and K. xiv, 43, 57, 71, 83
Goodman, Christopher 8
Gordon, Alexander 23
Green, Ian 7n, 52, 94, 99, 223
Grenville, Richard 37
Grotius, Hugo 131, 138, 150

Haddon, Arthur W. 23, 26, 29n, 33, 115, 210
Hall, Joseph, bishop 19, 147, 156n
Hamilton, James 3–4, 9, 192
Hammond, Henry 53, 94, 96, 98, 107, 149, 211
Hampton, Christopher 8, 13, 100, 170
Hanson, Paul 87–8, 216
Henry VIII 101, 167n
Hermandszoon *see* Arminius
Heylin, Peter 11, 76, 184, 191, 200
High Commission 190–92, 197, 205
Hirst, Derek 41, 138, 158, 216, 224
Hobbes, Thomas 35, 44–9, 117–19, 211, 214, 226–7
Hooker, Richard 163

Ignatian letters 98, 148–9, 209, 167, 222
Illyricus, Matthias Flaccius 85, 148
Irish Articles 1615 11–12, 16, 52, 180–81, 184, 200
Irish language 69n, 187
Isaiah, prophet 6, 62, 64, 91

Israel ix–xii, 34, 39, 43, 62–4, 71, 86–8, 90–91, 120, 202–3

James I 9, 11n, 93, 127–8, 140, 154, 160, 167, 169–70, 175, 209
Jeremiah, prophet x, xiii, 22, 91
Jerome, St 20, 122
Jewel, John 81, 90, 125, 210
Jurie divino 111, 115, 128, 139–44, 200
Justification, doctrine of 49–50, 58, 99, 101, 115, 123, 129–30, 181

Kadosh x–xi, xiv–xv, 61, 92, 164, 168, 177
Killen, William 7n
Knox, R.B. 7n, 11, 13n, 16, 21n, 98, 114, 123, 169, 217, 224

Lake, Peter vii, 55, 63–4, 83, 223–4, 226
Lambeth Articles 11n
Latimer, Hugh 81
Laud, William, Archbishop vii, 14, 17, 18n, 23–32, 41, 52, 63–4, 71, 94–6, 99–111, 113–14, 119, 145, 164, 167, 170n, 171–80, 183, 200
Laudianism viii n, 24, 43, 48, 50, 60, 65, 72, 82, 93, 99, 102, 146, 158–9, 180–81, 184
Leland, Thomas 12, 217
Leslie, Henry, Bishop 30, 173, 192
Leviticus, book of 61
Lincoln's Inn 20
Livingston, John 173
Loftus, Adam, Archbishop 8
Lombard, Peter 68, 78
Lotz-Heumann, Ute 101
Ludlow, Edward 17
Luther, Martin xi–xii, xiv, 47–52, 57, 63, 70, 73, 79–81, 85, 89, 96, 107, 125, 164, 199, 211

McAdoo, H.R. 86

McCafferty, J. xvii, 28n, 29, 100n, 102, 105, 186–7, 189, 225, 227
Malone, William 13, 47, 50, 65, 77, 81, 160, 162, 211, 212
Mant, Richard 23n, 30, 218
Matthew, Tobias, Archbishop 26–7, 159
Maxwell, John, bishop 30, 117, 174
Milton, Anthony 80, 92, 167, 176, 218, 225
Milton, John 35, 146n
Molina 45
Montgomery, William, Bishop 12–13
Morrill, John 97, 173, 175, 180, 218, 225
Mountjoy, Lord Lieutenant 7–8
Mysterium tremendum x, 60, 83

Neile, Richard, Bishop 28n, 178
Negative Oath 20n
Newcastle, William Cavendish 34–5, 115, 211
Numbers, book of 67

Oakley, Francis 120n, 138–9, 218, 225
Otto, Rudolf x, 60, 218

Parr, Richard 3, 5, 7n, 11, 13, 20–21, 209, 211
Patrick, St 53, 102
Pelagius 47, 52, 103
Penance 80–85, 42, 70
Perceval-Maxwell, Michael 33, 219, 226
Perkins, William 2, 73, 138
Predestination 11, 14, 17, 44, 51–7, 69, 101–2, 172, 174
Presbyterianism ix, 11, 25, 27, 31, 37, 39, 53, 67, 146, 149–50, 158, 166, 188, 192, 197
Perseverance 57–61, 69, 77
Prynne, William 16–18, 114, 172n, 181, 211, 217
Purgatory 13, 225
Pym, John 16n

Quarles, John 22, 85, 212

Ramee, Pierre de la 4
Ramist 3, 10, 42, 122, 195
Reid, J.S. 27–31, 172, 174, 188, 192, 195n, 215, 219
Relics 49, 72
Revelations, book of vii n, 7, 10, 98, 153–4
Richelieu, Cardinal 36n
Rothe, David 13n, 226
Russell, Conrad viii, 15, 43, 141–2, 146–7, 170, 175, 219, 226

Sacraments xi, xiv, 43, 59, 61–85, 94, 162, 178, 182n, 201
St Patrick's cathedral, Dublin 8–9, 56, 66, 164
St Paul's Cathedral 178
Sanderson, John 116, 119, 132–3, 226
Schillebeeckx, Edward 78–9, 219
Scotland 3, 15, 29, 41, 152, 178, 198–200
Scudamore, Viscount 97
Selden, John 8–9, 17n, 21
Sergeant, John 106–7, 165
Sharpe, Kevin viii, 41, 65, 83–4, 112, 114, 219, 226
Sheils, William 59, 223, 226
Sibthorp, Christopher 100, 212
Sleidan 4, 25, 90
Solemn League and Covenant 32
Sommerville, Johann 130–32, 139–40, 142–3, 219, 227
Spain 25, 36, 151, 155, 158
Sparrow-Simpson, William 93–4, 137, 181, 219
Spelman, John 117, 132
Spenser, Edmund 101
Spurr, Jonathan 46, 98, 146, 219
Stanihurst, Richard 2, 10, 100
Stapleton, Thomas 6, 164
Star Chamber 192
Stephens, Archibald 184, 191n, 212

Sykes, N. 11n, 35n, 220, 227
Strafford *see* Wentworth
Suarez 45

Taylor, Jeremy 24, 27, 32, 39, 94, 107n, 147, 179, 181, 212
Temple, William 4
Thomas, Keith xi, 44, 80
Thirty-nine Articles 52
Transubstantiation 25, 78–80, 157
Trent, Council of 57, 68, 74–5, 79, 85
Trinity College, Dublin 3–5, 10, 23–4, 69n, 194–5, 208
Tyacke, N.R.N. viii, 63, 220, 227

Ussher, Arland 1, 5
Ussher, James
  Annales 5, 89
  Answer to a challenge made by Jesuit 13
  Antiquities of the British Churches 43, 57, 89, 170, 208–9
  Bishop of Meath 13, 169
  Chronologica Sacra 89
  Directions concerning liturgy 67, 11, 210
  Discourse of Religion anciently professed 13, 52, 88, 100, 151, 207
  Funeral 22
  Gravissimae Quaestionis de Christianarum 9, 88–92, 98, 100
  Historia Dogmatica 89
  History of Gotteschalk 14, 54
  Lincoln's Inn 20
  Ordained 7
  Original of bishops 97, 147
  Power communicated to Prince 111, 113–15, 117, 133, 135–6, 139, 142
  Principles of Christian religion 53
  Reduction Manuscript 146–9
  Tractatus de Controversiis 89
  Vice-Chancellor, Trinity 10, 195–6

Via media vii, 24
Von Rad, Gerhard 86, 220
Vossius, Gerhard 14n

Waldensians 90–92, 97, 101, 150, 214
Walker, George 23n, 25, 36n, 179
Wandesforde, Christopher 26–7, 205
Ward, Samuel 24, 69, 171, 190
Watson, E.W. 3, 10, 53, 92, 104, 198n, 227
Wedgwood, C.V. 33, 177, 220
Wentworth, Thomas 14, 27–33, 41, 112, 146, 175–89, 192–8
White, Peter viii, 48, 203
Whitelocke, Bulstrode 17n, 21, 212
Wyclif, John 100

Zwingli, Ulrich 63, 211
Zwinglian 76, 150